READINGS IN
MARRIAGE
and the FAMILY

PRENTICE-HALL SOCIOLOGY SERIES

Herbert Blumer, Editor

READINGS *in*

MARRIAGE

and the FAMILY

EDITED BY

JUDSON T. LANDIS
UNIVERSITY OF CALIFORNIA, BERKELEY

MARY G. LANDIS

NEW YORK   PRENTICE-HALL, INC.

First Printing..........October, 1952
Second Printing.......February, 1953

Preface

STUDENTS of marriage and the family are becoming more and more interested in reading and interpreting for themselves the basic information that is available on courtship, marriage, and family life. This book includes articles reporting on as many as possible of the research studies that have contributed significantly to basic knowledge of marriage and the family. We have included also some selections that do not deal with research findings directly, but that enlarge upon research findings or contribute to an understanding of marriage and the family through their presentation of thought provoking ideas and concepts.

In some areas research is not conclusive, and on some subjects thoughtful students of marriage and the family disagree in interpreting available knowledge. Where there are such differences in viewpoint we have sought to include the various opposing viewpoints. A reading of the conflicting conclusions reached by some of those who have long studied marriage and family interaction may help the reader to maintain an open mind and to avoid dogmatism in his concepts of family interaction.

All writers of textbooks, at least in part, are subject to the tendency to draw upon and quote research findings that support the particular viewpoint or philosophy to which they subscribe. Therefore, it is to the advantage of the student to seek objectivity and a better perspective by reading the reports of research as offered by the researchers themselves, and to read the various views and philosophies concerning marriage and the family as presented by the proponents of the different points of view.

Therefore, this book is designed for use either as a reference source for outside reading, to accompany a textbook in courses in marriage or the family, or as the text or the basic reading for a course, supplemented by lectures and class discussions.

All credit for the good qualities of this book go to the authors of the selections included in it. They have taken time from busy schedules to examine knowledge about marriage and the family, to reflect upon meanings underlying such knowledge, to discriminate between fact and folklore, and to conduct research in efforts to discover truth and to test ideas. They and their publishers have been very gracious in giving permission for the use of their work in this book.

JUDSON T. LANDIS

MARY G. LANDIS

v

Table of Contents

I · THE CONTEMPORARY AMERICAN FAMILY

One · The Contemporary American Family
as an Anthropologist Sees It

MARGARET MEAD
Anthropologist, American Museum
of Natural History

What is the American family like? How would it ap-
pear to one from another culture? How does the family you grew
up in compare with the "norm" of American family life as appraised
here by an anthropologist? *

AN anthropologist looks at the American family as
one of the many forms which the family has taken throughout human history since human beings first invented ways in which adult
males could become more or less permanently responsible for the
care of females and their children. With a few exceptions which
are so curious and contrived that they only emphasize the ubiq-
uitousness of the institution of the family, all human societies have
patterned the relationship between sexually paired adults and dependent young. The tie between the father and child may not be
recognized as biological. It may be conceived as fostering only or
as a spiritual contribution only in which the father gives spirit, the
mother body. The children of other men may be accepted readily;
children of several brothers may be regarded as having equivalent
claims on the care of one of the brothers; brothers may be treated
interchangeably in their access to each other's wives; or sisters may
be regarded as potential wives of the same man. The primary fostering tie between parent and child may be extended to include a
three-generation family with many collateral lines or shrunk to the
tiny biological family of the modern three-room apartment dwellers
who have no kin within a thousand miles. The authority of the
father may last until death, or all social relations between father
and son, even speech, may end at puberty. Women may become
completely absorbed into the kin group of their husbands, taking
their names and their burial places, or they may even retain control over their own dowries. The life of the next generation may be
minutely described in terms of family relationships or family
choices made by the parents, or each generation may construct its

* Reprinted from *The American Journal of Sociology*, 1948, 53: 453–459,
by permission of the author and of the University of Chicago Press.

1

family life for itself. Marriages may be for life between one man and one woman, or serially monogamous, or between one man and several women, or, less usually, between one woman and two or more men.

But nowhere are these crucial relationships, within which women are protected and cared for during childbearing and little children nurtured and reared, left unpatterned and unregulated. During periods of very rapid social change, of migration, of war and epidemic, the carefully devised and delicate patterns, which rely far more for their preservation on the habituated bodies and vivid expectations of those who were reared within them than upon any external sanctions, may break down. Then, for a period, the primary unit tends to become what it is among the primates, females and young, with the males exercising a nonspecific dominative and protective function in regard to the whole group. During such periods or in certain sections of a population almost the whole support of the children may fall on the mother, as in certain lower economic groups in large cities, or among ethnic groups at the moment of cultural breakdown. Old forms of legal marriage may become so expensive and cumbersome that a large part of a population may be said, at some period, to be living out of wedlock, but the new, altered, or simplified form will in time again become the recognized form of the family for that group.

Traditionally, societies have depended upon reproducing their orderly forms of family life by rearing children within families, who will regard that form of family life within which they were reared as normal, natural, and desirable. Children absorb during infancy and early childhood the whole pattern of family interrelationships which they then will be able to repeat, subject to the distortions introduced by hiatuses in their own experience, or idiosyncrasies of their own constitution and personality. Even in a society which changes as rapidly as our own, a large proportion of our patterns of family life are attempts—often faulty attempts because circumstances are so changed or the other partner has learned such different patterns—to reproduce the family behavior learned in childhood. A large part of the disorganization of family life today, the frequency of divorce, the incidence of neurosis and disease, may be laid to the discrepancies and contradictions between the expectations learned in childhood and the actualities of the present time.

The American family pattern is an urban middle-class pattern, although upper-class patterns occur, and lower-class practice deviates sharply from middle-class standards, and rural family life still retains the stamp of an earlier historical period. Films, comic strips, radio, and magazines presuppose a middle-class family. This family is typically formed at marriage, when young people finally cease to speak of "my family" as referring to the parental family and begin to look toward a family of their own. It is expected t consist exclusively of husband, wife, and minor children, with the presence of in-laws to be prevented if possible and almost universally to be deplored, particularly by the unrelated spouse. Support from parents to married children is not expected, and, where married children have to give support to their parents, this is regarded as a handicap, a burden on the young marriage. Nor are married children expected to plan their lives on the expectation of ultimately inheriting from either set of parents-in-law; such inheritances when they come along are windfalls, good luck rather than something which may be properly looked forward to. While married children will acknowledge some responsibility for the support of aging parents, especially when widowed, almost no responsibility is taken for brothers and sisters and their children, except in cases of extreme emergency or disaster. Unmarried adult women are expected to support themselves and are often also expected to assume a larger share of the support of a parent than that which is shouldered by married sons and daughters.

The orientation of the new family is forward, and the young couple are normally expected to provide their own establishment. The parents may provide for a wedding or give them a house or a car, but these are works of supererogation, not expected parental behavior, such as is expected in countries in which the parents have to set the young couple up with full household equipment. The assumption is that the parents have given their children of both sexes a "good education" which equips them to choose a mate, earn a living, and manage their lives for themselves with a minimum of help, advice, or interference.

The new family is expected to be formed entirely on the choice of the young people, with the young man taking the formal initiative in making the actual proposal. In selecting a mate, the primary considerations are personal attractiveness in the girl and attractiveness and ability as a breadwinner in the boy; all other considerations, even health, are regarded as subsidiary to them. Common background is very often subsumed under personal attractiveness and congeniality, and the skills which may be necessary to homemaking and mating are regarded as appropriately learned after marriage by practicing them on and with the chosen partner. Here a convention of premarital chastity for the girl and a preference for minimal premarital experience for the boy combine with an equal expectation that the girl will know nothing about running a house or a man about budgeting his income and that during the early years of marriage romantic ardor must balance ignorance and lack of skill. Young people may, without criticism, marry without any accumulation of property of any sort, without any certainty of where they are going to live, and, provided they have a little cash in hand and the man has proved earning power, without his having a job at the moment. Very few human societies have encouraged

young people to start a new family with such very small backing
from parents and the wider kin group. Actually a great deal of
help, both formal and informal, is given to new marriages, but it
is not only not something which may be legitimately expected but
is actually something about which young people may feel considerable hesitation if not a real sense of inadequacy in accepting.

The American wife is expected to be educated, as well educated
although not as highly trained as the husband, for there is more
expectation that he will have a special money-bringing skill than
that she will. Differences in education between men and women
vary from couple to couple, and the only consistencies are a generally accepted delegation of earning to the husband and management of consumption to the wife. Which spouse prefers driving the
car, listening to the radio, keeping up with the news, or participating in the community is a matter of individual adjustment subject
to the rules of local groups or cliques but not a matter which is
patterned by role for husband and wife. Until marriage the girl has
been almost as free as her brother; if she has had a job, she has
spent her money as she wished, giving her family something for her
board where circumstances dictate such a course, and in recent
years often leaving home to work and live in another city, with
steadily decreasing protests from parents. For an unmarried son to
leave home is still regarded as more usual than for an unmarried
daughter. Until her decision to marry she is expected to be guided
by the same considerations in the choice of a job which influence
her brother—chance for advancement or security, interest, or money,
or any combination of these. Once engaged, however, her life-
orientation is expected to undergo a sharp change—ambition to
shift from job to home.

The new home, so unsupported by parents or kin, is designed
and planned by the young couple, very often an ill-assorted compromise between home memories and the new standards of contemporaries, of the department stores, and of women's magazines.
Even the simplest middle-class home in the United States is a sort
of stage set, constructed with thought, on which the family are going to enact their parts, against which the wife sees herself and the
rest of the family. If the furniture is not new, it is at least newly
bought second hand, and refurnished and rearranged with care.
Within this home, the wife is expected to occupy herself, using it
also as a platform from which she goes out into community life, of
which, however, she has very little during the early years of her
marriage. Where marriages have not taken place inside an existing
youthful clique, it is expected that former friends of either spouse
will prove trying and uncongenial and that new social groups will
be formed based on neighborhood and community ties cultivated
by the wife and on business ties cultivated by the husband. The
claims of the wife for the local ties grow stronger when there are

children and when their neighborhood companionships have to be considered. Husband and wife are expected to rely exclusively on each other as far as cross sex relationships are concerned and never to go out in mixed company without the other partner. On the whole, where men continue social relations with men after marriage, they are either labeled rather dubiously as "business" or frankly regarded as periods of relaxation,—fishing, card-playing, yarning,—antithetical to the more regulated home life. Women's relations with women outside the home are patterned either as parts of a local prestige game or as earnest endeavors to "do something worth while," and the grounds upon which men and women resent their spouses' outside interests tend to be very different.

A small family, with at least one child of each sex, for whom the parents can make adequate, educational allowance, is regarded as more commendable than a larger family of children in which the children have to forego an education. A large family, however, all of whom receive good educations through a combination of parental help and their own energies is a great credit to everyone. It is regarded as unfortunate when children are born within the first two years after marriage, as this ties the young couple down too soon. Parenthood is a responsible anxious matter, in which the mother must keep herself continually up to date with changing standards of child care. Having children, for a woman, is pretty close in feeling to having a job, for a man—a necessary proof of adequacy and wholeness as a human being, something which one does not so much enjoy but something which one would be unwilling not to have done. Unemployed married women without children are under some compulsion to explain their lack of occupation to themselves or to their neighbors; until recently women who had successfully reared even one child felt that they had made an appropriate and dignified social contribution for which they deserved recognition and support for the rest of their lives. When the children marry and leave the home, the American woman is faced with the same type of readjustment as that facing her husband perhaps two decades later when he retires. The discrepancy in the timing of the husband and wife's retirement periods presents one of the problems of American marriage, as it is motherhood rather than housewifeliness which is the source of pride and self-sacrifice in the urban married woman. The period between the children's leaving home and old age is the main source of voluntary civic and social activity in the United States, as the married woman, trained to years of responsible social behavior in the care of family, finds her task cut in half while her strength is still unimpaired.

Marriage is for life, and all breaks in marriage are treated as failures, and failures which involve some degree of moral turpitude —either sexual or economic irresponsibility. At the same time, the extremely wide prevalence of divorce means that the possibility of divorce, defined as failure and as a disaster, is included in the picture of marriage. Women learn that they must keep their husbands, not merely from casual adventures or time spent wastefully elsewhere, but as husbands; and men learn that it is their wives' duty to keep them and that the world is filled with other women, married or unmarried, who, having failed or decided not to keep their own husbands, will try to attract them away from their present wives. This question of a wife's maintaining her attractiveness, in the face of the domestic routines, the sick baby, the broken drain, the unwashed coffee cups after last night's party, is felt to be a test of her adequacy and her sense of responsibility. A wife is not expected to try to keep her husband's love simply because love is a warm and pleasant thing or simply because she loves him and wants him to love her. Rather she must be continually on the alert to be a successful wife who is making a good job of her marriage. The moral alternatives are whether a woman is regarded as selfish because she "is just interested in keeping her husband" or is "unselfishly working to make a success of her marriage," which includes a sense of responsibility to her husband and children. With this burden of making the marriage relationship a continuous articulately happy experience in which each partner would choose the other over again each day—which puts a premium on never being unshaven or in curlers—there goes an explicit recognition that it is wrong to insist on the trappings of success where one has failed. The husband or wife who holds an unwilling partner—whatever the reason for the unwillingness—to a marriage from which he or she is trying to escape is regarded as behaving in an unsportsman-like manner. It is the wife's duty to make her husband want to stay and to shy away from taking too great risks with other women's efforts to impress him with their superior attractiveness. Similarly it is the husband's duty to provide for his wife and children so that she will want to stay with him. But, except within orthodox religious groups who still regard marriage as a sacrament, it is neither husband nor wife's duty to stay, once they are sure they want to leave, and, indeed, they may be regarded as doing harm to the other spouse and the children by bringing them up in a "home without love." The average American male's job insecurity, the fear that his security, which is based on his ability to earn his own living and provide completely for his family, may be taken from him by personal failure or by a depression, is matched by the average American wife's fear that she may fail at her job of homemaking and end up without a husband and perhaps with children to support.

Within this family, children are given an extraordinary amount of attention when judged by the standards of most other societies. Their needs, their wishes, and their performances are regarded as central and worthy of adult attention. The mother is the principal disciplining and character-molding parent and must both give love, comfort, and care and stimulate and goad the child to achievement and outside contacts. Her inevitable oscillation between demanding achievement as a proof of the child's love and threatening to withhold her love if the child does not achieve produces some of the typical conflicts in American character which were especially apparent in young draftees in World War II. The mother also has to train the male child in assertiveness, bidding him at the same time to be peaceful and co-operative and to stand up for himself, which training is responsible for some of the characteristic American uncertainties about their own strength. The father's role is to provide at one time a more horizontal fraternal relationship, supporting the growing child, especially the son, in conflicts with his mother when her demands are excessive or she is too unwilling to let the child grow up, and occasionally introducing a sharp unpredictable bit of violent disapproval in reinforcement of the mother's discipline. While the relationship to the mother introduces into the American child's character the principal strains and conflicts in regard to ethical behavior and giving and receiving of love, the relationship to the father provides a fairly steady, although not very aggressive, support of the child's individuality and pressure toward maturity. Both parents offer the child an appreciative audience for his growing independence, achievement, and autonomy and thus establish firmly his habit of acting, while young, weak, and inexperienced, with the overemphasis which is not regarded as inappropriate because the child is so small that it is all right to show off.

In the training of the young child there is a strong emphasis upon habit training, his learning to eat and eliminate and to sleep at the right times, and an enormous interweaving of beliefs about health and hygiene with morality. Next in importance is the attainment of some degree of motor autonomy. Training of the emotions is a matter more of teaching a child that it should not feel disapproved emotions, like jealousy, hate, or envy, than of any great attending to manners or minutiae of interpersonal relationships, and an ethical insisting that the other person's feelings, rights, etc., must be taken into account. Children are expected to develop consciences modeled upon the admonitions and supported by the rewards and punishments administered by parents. Each child is given its own property; a room to itself is the ideal, and toys and books and tools are personal possessions, respect for which is enforced among brothers and sisters. The custom of paying children for small jobs in the home, and encouraging them to undertake small money-earning jobs outside the home as good for their characters, is widespread. Children are permitted to exert considerable pressure upon the family's choice of food, magazines, and radio programs, and American advertisers regularly exploit this willingness to take consumption cues from children. Weaning is a gradual matter, punctuated by new privileges granted on birthdays and culminating in the period when either son or daughter becomes self-supporting. Self-support is defined not as actual ability to support one's self outside the home but as having a full-time paid job, all of which may actually go into clothes and pleasure, while the parents continue to provide most or all of the board. The tendency to overestimate and overstate an earning child's own money—so sharply contrasted with urban working-class practice in many European countries—has a later reflection in the tendency to treat a married woman's earnings as in some peculiar sense her own and not simply the resource of the whole family—which is the view held of the husband's earnings. The expectation is that children will press toward maturity and that parents will provide an admiring audience, practical help, and a certain check on their impetuosity, which, however, should actually serve as a further stimulus to make them take on more responsibilities.

The relationship between the character formation of the child and the life-history of its own immediate family, its financial ups and downs, accidents, illnesses, etc., is extraordinarily close, because of the isolation of each small family. Events which would be blurred or reinterpreted by the behavior of neighbors and relatives here become crucial in forming the personalities of the children. This extreme importance of the small, intimate family is to some degree compensated for by the great importance of the age group and by the extent to which group standards supersede family standards at adolescence.

Two major readjustments are taking place in the American family pattern today. The first is the new ways of life which are becoming necessary as the isolated biological family becomes more and more usual, at a period when the demands made on the housewife as a result of new knowledge of nutrition, pediatrics, psychology, and home management in general have also greatly increased. Society is expecting more of the wife and mother at the very period when she, through isolation and lack of help and resources, is less able to meet these demands. Community services of all sorts—all-year-round school facilities, housekeeping services, twenty-four-hour boarding for children during illness in the home, prepared foods, expert advisory services to supplement the homemaker's traditional behavior, which is no longer adequate—are the results.

These innovations find cultural support in our American focus on the welfare of children and in the major contribution to future success which is given by careful education in childhood. Resistance to these changes and a continued insistence that, because families managed in the past to meet every emergency of illness, unemployment, insanity, accident, death, without formalized outside help, they should continue to do so now are rooted in the American cultural belief in the importance of autonomy, independence, and responsibility. Only by a widespread recognition that the family of today is being asked to do a much more difficult task of child-rearing, with much fewer resources than were available to the farm and small-town family, nested among relatives and neighbors and informed by a trusted tradition, can this resistance be shifted.

The second great readjustment which is occurring in the family pattern is the terminability of American marriage. As the old religious sanctions which enjoined fidelity until death, regardless of such ephemeral considerations as congeniality or "happiness," have faded for large sections of the population and have been powerless to save many more marriages from dissolution, new ways of holding marriages together are developing. The life of a family is coming to be seen as a ship which may be wrecked by any turn of the tide unless every member of the family, but especially the two parents, are actively and co-operatively engaged in sailing the boat, vigilantly tacking, trimming their sails, resetting their course, bailing in storms—all to save something which is worth their continuous care. This new ideal, in which all the members of a family work together to keep alive an ever changing relationship, may in time provide us with the necessary new ethical sanction within which to give our changing family dignity and safety.

Two · Culture Configurations in the American Family

JOHN SIRJAMAKI
Sociologist, Yale University

In the reading that follows * an attempt is made to identify and interpret the approved rules or sentiments which motivate American family behavior. With the preceding anthropological description of the family this reading will serve as a basis for discussion.

MOST sociological studies of the family deal with it either as a social system or as a social institution. An important supplement to these approaches is the cultural analysis of the family in terms of its dominant configurations. When these can be specified for the family, it is possible to interpret the basic moral ideas which give the family its distinctive and identifying characteristics.

* Reprinted from *The American Journal of Sociology*, 1948, 53: 464–470, by permission of the author and the University of Chicago Press.

Culture configurations are the moral principles which comprise the social philosophy of a society. They are patterns of covert behavior; as such, they are the culturally approved rules or sentiments which motivate overt behavior and which integrate it into consistent patterns; and they can be deduced only from behavior. Such configurations exist on the level of the culture and arise in the context of everyday living. Members of a society comprehend the meaning of such precepts in the process of socialization, even when they are expressed tenuously or obscurely; and, indeed, configurations are difficult to state abstractly inasmuch as they generally operate below the level of awareness. Taken together, the configurations delineate the ethos of a culture.

Configurations are thus the basic units of the value system of a society. They differ from the absolute ethics of religious or philosophical systems in that they are mundane, practical, this-worldly; having developed within the culture, they express the dominant values which are thought to be necessary for the continued functioning of the society.

The concept of the configurations of the culture, and a knowledge of the manner in which these are expressed within an institution, illuminates the study of the family. Configurations reach into the most intimate areas of individual and family behavior; they furnish the meanings and determine right and wrong behavior in courting, in husband-wife and parent-child relationships, in heterosexual social activity, and in ideas about sex. Thus they supply the moral sentiments by which family members are influenced and make explicable the vagaries of their behavior.

At least four qualifications may be raised concerning the validity of applying culture configurations to the study of the American family. First, since such configurations are inferred by the investigator from the overt behavior of people, he must have available a considerable amount of observational data which, however, is currently lacking. Second, the use of such configurations should await an analysis of the total culture, and this has been attempted thus far in the most tentative manner. The analysis of parts of the culture, however, will assist in the determination of the total culture ethos. Third, generalizations about American culture must be stated in the most broad terms and can attempt only to strike an average, since regional and ethnic subcultures obviously differ from the main pattern. To whom, it may be asked, do configurations apply? The answer is that configurations are generally valid, or will tend to become so, for the entire American society, in the sense that they represent the moral standards by which all behavior is evaluated, and which exert a social pressure to secure some degree of conformance. Families of ethnic minorities thus quite apparently have patterns dissimilar to those of native-born families, but in time the American culture configurations come to influence the actions of at least the immigrant children and to bring their behavior into conformity with the general requirements of society. Finally, configurations are not easily amenable to quantification; they may seem to be accurately stated, but they are difficult to measure. There is no real answer to this objection other than to predicate the statement of configurations upon as careful objective analysis as is possible. A value system patently exists in every culture, and its appraisal should be sought by the social scientist.

The following configurations, among others, appear in the American family:

1. *Marriage is a dominating life-goal, for men as well as for women.* It is felt that married life is the normal, desired condition for all adults, that it brings the greatest personal happiness and fulfilment, and that it permits the proper exercise of sex for the procreation of children and for individual satisfaction. The single adult life by contrast, according to this attitude, is empty and barren. That there is a considerable societal concern that women marry is generally recognized, but the greater courting and sexual initiative assumed by men has obscured the comparable pressure on them to marry, and adult men who postpone marriage into their thirties become objects of distress and conspiracy among friends and relatives. Most Americans marry in their twenties, and, for a considerable share of them, marriage at that age means a happy union of individual volition and social pressure.

Long ago Professor E. A. Ross pointed out that Americans are the most marrying nation in Western Christendom. United States census figures have shown that since 1890 they have married in steadily increasing proportions and at earlier ages. About 92 per cent of adults will have been married at some time in their lives by the age of sixty-five, and this is a sufficiently high number to suggest that nearly all persons marry who are physically and mentally capable of contracting marriage.

2. *The giving and taking in marriage should be based on personal affection and choice.* Marriage is thought to be pre-eminently the linking of the lives of two young people drawn to each other by personal attraction. Arranged marriages, or those based on fraud or calculation, receive considerable disapprobation.

Dating is thought by many sociologists to precede serious courting and to be an educational process leading to it. Waller first analyzed it in terms of its distinctive cultural patterns. In dating, the young woman undoubtedly receives the greatest cultural estimation of her personal qualities: merely to be a young, nubile female of attractive phenotype means that she is the object of considerable masculine attention and chivalry. But, despite this high evaluation of young women, most men grow up in American society with the assumption, culturally derived, that the decision to marry rests with them; they expect in the fulness of time to lead some dear girl to the altar. Women, on the other hand, regardless of their personal qualities, can never be completely sure that they will receive a marriage proposal which they can consider seriously, or, more to the point, be asked to marry by the man upon whom they have fastened their desire. The culture does not permit them to undertake active courting by themselves; to be a man-chaser is to suffer an ostracism which is enforced by the women themselves. Women are obviously not completely helpless in these sentimental matters, but they must use guile and finesse to bring the male to their side.

Since the biological fact of bisexuality predisposes women for the having and rearing of children, and therefore for the maintenance of a home, they are compelled to drive as good a bargain in the marriage market as they can. This they can manage only by a careful exploitation of the rules which specify correct maidenly deportment. Men, on the other hand, have greater volition in their marriage choices and are much more disposed as a result to manage their marital ventures in the bathos of culturally approved romance.

3. *The criterion of successful marriage is the personal happiness of husband and wife.* Mutual compatibility is made the basis of marriage, and marital bliss becomes dependent upon the emotional sentiments, fluctuating and volatile as they may be, with which a couple regard their relationship. Ultimately their fullest felicity is believed to be achieved by having children, whose arrival and subsequent nurture are viewed as bringing satisfaction to basic biological and social needs. Childless couples are sometimes regarded as possessed of a selfishness which blights their union. Happiness in marriage is thus predicated upon a personal equation, the individual satisfaction and the opportunity for development of the couple.

The cultural accent upon happiness in marriage is of relatively recent origin. Marriages are ordinarily contracted and their success gauged by their contribution in the struggles of life. These may be the partnership co-operation of man and wife, the production of children, the social recognition of adult status, or the stability of marital status. Many such marriages may be buttressed by institutional supports, the most important of which is generally the exchange of property. The spouses may be selected for each other by the parents or other adults, after a careful scrutiny of their relative merits and upon some property agreement, in the belief that normal young people, once married, can fashion for themselves a successful marital life.

A corollary of the American patterns of courtship and marriage which is not always recognized is the logical necessity of a relatively easy system of divorce. From a cultural viewpoint, if marriages are made on the basis of personal and inevitably shifting emotions, without the added support of other institutional devices, then they should be equally easy to dissolve. Persons marry to find happiness and, finding it not, turn to divorce as a way out. The present high divorce rate, therefore, is in this sense made explicable and partially condoned by the cultural rules of marriage.

4. *The best years of life are those of youth, and its qualities are the most desirable.* A high evaluation is placed upon youth and early middle age in American society, while the old are sometimes treated with indifference and even callousness. Youth is regarded as a period of innocence, energy, and enthusiasm; it is inventive and pragmatic when faced with new experiences and is glad of change—qualities fondly believed to be typical of Americans in general.

Among the young, the unmarried girl, aged perhaps twenty, attractive of face and limb, is the center of attraction in thought and deed. In other societies young men, or old men, or mothers are variously regarded as ideal symbols; in the United States it is the young, pretty girl. She therefore receives at this age the greatest gratification of her ego drives which will probably ever come to her. With men the ideal age is somewhere in the thirties; they need time in which to win occupational and social placement and need not depend so much upon chronological age for their acceptance.

From this high esteem on youth there derive important social consequences. Wherever the young are involved, whether it be in the conduct of schools, or juvenile delinquency, or maltreatment of children, or provision for their play opportunities, there is likely to be at least a quick emotional response to their needs.

Such sentiments as these do not, of course, arise in a social vacuum. They exist, rather, and become understandable in terms of American social history. Youth has received a high evaluation, precisely because its resourcefulness and resilience were valued qualities in the exploitation and development of the American continent. There have been, in addition, as compared to the age groups in European societies, relatively high proportions in the younger age categories in the American population; Americans have in this sense been a young people and correspondingly eager to admire the virtues of youth. The aged, on the other hand, have emerged as a significant social group only recently, and they are not yet favorably regarded.

Related to this cultural theme of youth is the existence of a considerable rift, not to say antagonism, between the generations. The conflict between the old and the young is common enough in human groups; what is significant is its intensity in American society. This is due, in large part, to the rapidity of social change in the United States and to the differing rates with which the generations have adjusted to those changes. Keller speaks somewhat nostalgically of the aged in primitive society as revered "repositories of wisdom"; in American society they are unlikely to be regarded as possessors of a truth that has any relationship to their age.

5. *Children should be reared in a child's world and shielded from too early participation in adult woes and tribulations.* This configuration is obviously closely related to the high cultural esteem of youth. It is modified by social class: the sentiment is held most strongly by the upper levels of society, much less so by the lower, but even among the poor the social conditions of the American community prevent a too considerable precocity among the children.

The cultural ideal is that children shall mature slowly in terms of their nature and age-sex grades in a prolonged child's world, which is characterized by a segregated class of children's activities. In this juvenile social world they are allowed to grow, develop their abilities, indulge in play, and occasionally to perform such small and often artificial tasks as may be assigned them. Generally they are protected from the responsibilities of adults, and laws and custom prevent their too early gainful employment. In many American homes, particularly in the cities, there is actually not much useful work that children can perform even if they wish. Especially in middle-class families is the configuration most completely observed. The child is accepted as an individual, and his relationships with parents are often warm and affectionate.

Folsom has contrasted this pattern with that which prevails in certain western European families, in which the child is incorporated into the family of adults and in which he lives in their world rather than in a segregated youth society. Moreover, unlike the American middle-class child who may become somewhat exhibitionist in his behavior because of the attention shown him, the European youth is often hastened along in the process of maturation and trained to deference and respect toward parents and elders in general.

Such training as the American child receives may start him off with a psychologically secure character structure, but in other respects it prepares him inadequately for later life. Sometimes he has not broken the emotional ties with his parents or developed definite heterosexual interests; hence his fondness for "Mom." During World War II the British thought the American soldier adolescent. James Graham Leyburn has pointed out that the American family is itself often at fault because of its inadequate integration with the larger community. It may be unable, as a result, to prepare and to place its members into job, school, clique and class, association, and other social relationships in the society. Thus it delays the processes of maturation.

6. *The exercise of sex should be contained within wedlock.* Prior to marriage premarital intercourse is strongly condemned, and sex knowledge is kept hidden from children lest it be damaging to their moral character. After marriage, adultery is similarly proscribed.

Sex may thus be legitimately expressed only within marriage, and the speaking of marriage vows makes highly moral sexual behavior which before then had been grossly immoral. The couple, previously prohibited from intercourse, may now embark upon an active, and socially approved, sex life. Sex, to speak figuratively, explodes upon marriage.

About sex there is considerable tension, preoccupation, frustration, shame, and deceit in American society. Judeo-Christian influences, and more immediately Puritanism, have given a sinful cast to sex and have condoned its expression in marriage only because of the grossly physical method of human reproduction. The tradition has particularly valued virginity, more especially in women, before marriage. But the strong interdictions upon sex have tended to heighten rather than to lessen the fascination with sex which exists among Americans. The furtiveness with which it is often approached and the numerous colloquialisms which refer to it indicate the uneasiness with which it is treated. Kinsey's exploration of the sex histories of American males has documented their actual performances. These data indicate that the sex configuration is held with varying intensity at the several levels of society, apparently least so in the lower class. Even here, however, the materials reemphasize the manner in which restrictive cultural attitudes condition and limit sexual outlets.

7. *Family roles of husband and wife should be based on a sexual division of labor, but with the male status being superior.* According to this configuration, the husband is head of his family, its main economic support, and its representative in the larger community. Women, consigned to domesticity, are mothers and homemakers. These roles, biologically and culturally conditioned, provide for the structuring of all types of heterosexual relationships, in which the presumption of dominance generally rests with the males. Men are trained to develop the qualities necessary to fulfil their roles in economic, social, sexual, and other activities and to view themselves with self-respect when they have secured a competence in their performances. Women, too, are trained to their respective feminine roles, and these generally involve some degree of catering to men, somewhat as a complement to the expectation of greater male initiative. Terman's analysis of the desired pattern of sex typing in husband and in wife indicated how the cultural conception of the manly man and the womanly woman fall into the cultural mold.

Women's behavior is governed by a double standard of morality which expects greater masculine enterprise not only in the sexual spheres but in many other areas of life. Women live, in male estimation, under a blanket of oppressive mores which restrains their ordinary, everyday movements. Where men have a relative freedom of action, women must cater to a public opinion of what is womanly behavior. In social life women are under greater disapproval than men when they smoke or indulge in narcotics. On the job they may encounter much male prejudice which affects their pay and possibilities of promotion. They are more protected by social legislation which governs their hours and conditions of employment.

These cultural attitudes persist despite the social and economic events of modern times which have released women from the control of husbands and fathers. Before the law women have achieved a near-equality with men; they may seek gainful employment and retain their earnings; they have equal rights with men to education; they have all the freedoms necessary to live their own lives as they wish. Democratic sentiments further foster the desire that women develop as persons to enjoy the manifold blessings of American life and to have many of the privileges given men.

Women are thus caught in a process of social change, in which the cultural configuration restrains them to traditional roles, while new ones are proffered by economic and social forces. There is much confusion among them as a result. The young college girl, for example, may have difficulty in knowing to which force to respond: should she be content with the domestic role and look to the main chance of marriage, or should she seek outlets which include both marriage and other roles? Apparently some urban upper-level women find the puzzle extremely hard to resolve and respond to it neurotically.

Men, too, it must be pointed out, suffer in the realignment of roles, since they as much as women are conditioned to the status quo and may find it hard to accommodate themselves to change.

8. *Individual, not familial, values are to be sought in family living.* The family is obviously affected by the considerable cultural affirmation of individualism, and the lack of a tradition of familism in American culture has further aided in the development of a configuration in which the family exists for the benefit of its members. The emphasis has been upon the individualization of all members of the family, the children as well as the parents, the wife as much as the husband. Obviously, the husband's prerogatives, nurtured in the bosom of the patriarchal family, have had to be parceled out to the other members.

There are many important social consequences from the stress on individualism in the family. On the one hand, its promise is for the richer, fuller development of personality. On the other hand, it weakens the unity of the family. The stresses of American life, including industrialization, urbanization, internal migration, and social class, press hard against the frail shell of the family, attenuated as it is by the thinning of larger kin groups and often limited to its own resources in times of crisis. Further, since the family is not primarily important in placing its members into positions in the larger community, its members feel the strain of loyalties divided between the family and the outside affiliations.

If some of the configurations of the American family have been correctly stated, they indicate a social philosophy in which the values of individualism are paramount, or, more specifically, those which support the development of individual personality in the context of family and community relationships. A primary stress is placed on the family as a social group rather than on the functions which it performs for society. The family exists for its members rather than the members for the family. In this respect the family is in relatively close adjustment to the total culture, in which the democratic realization of the potentialities of all its members is an ideal.

But the family is pre-eminently an association based on antagonistic co-operation, and in times of hardship the antagonisms may predominate. The straining of family members for individualistic goals may blunt their sense of obligation to each other and to the larger society. When achievement of the desired values for which they grope seems far off and difficult, individualism may decay into gross egotism and selfishness. The family based on the chimera of personal values seems then faced with a dolorous future.

The American family, however, is not without resources. Contributing to its strength is the immense popularity of marriage, and through marriage the possibility of parenthood, both of them regarded as major life-goals. Staying power is also given the family by the affection and compatibility which draws two people into marriage, the warmth of relationships between parents and children, and the individualization of all members of the family. The structure of the family is such as to permit the desired nurturing of stable and democratic personalities.

In view of the ethos of the culture the direction of evolutionary change in the family, and of desirable efforts at rational adjustments, is in the continued emphasis upon the social relationships within the family and upon the family as a social system through which fundamental life-purposes can be achieved.

Three · The Changing Functions of the Family

WILLIAM F. OGBURN
Sociologist, University of Chicago

*Conceptions of the functions of the family are chang-
ing in our society. The next reading * explains some of the factors
that underlie our changing conceptions.*

THE best way to understand what is happening to
the family is to think of it as doing two things. One of these is to
provide certain economic and social services such as cooking, sewing, laundering, making soap, affording protection to women and
children, furnishing recreation, and the rest. These may be thought
of as economic and social functions performed by the family as a
social institution.

The other thing the family does is to perform certain psychological functions in contrast to the economic and social functions.
These psychological functions are chiefly ones that influence and
affect the personalities of those who comprise the family. Thus the
family affords opportunity for the expression of affection between
husband and wife, between parents and children, and between
children themselves. It is also influential in shaping the personality
of the young.

These two classes of activities of the family, the economic and
social on the one hand and the psychological on the other, are not
mutually exclusive. But they constitute a classification which will
show clearly what is happening to the family and enable us to see
what the family of the future is likely to be.

THE ECONOMIC FUNCTIONS

These economic services have been decreasing. The family no
longer spins, weaves, makes shoes, tailors men's suits, makes soap,
butchers hogs, cures leather, or makes furniture to any large extent. The change is an old story where a complete transfer of work
has taken place such as is the case with weaving. But there is still
a great deal of economic production in the family that has not been
transferred to outside agencies. This is true of baking, of canning,
of washing, of ironing, of making women's dresses and children's

---

* Reprinted from *Journal of Home Economics,* 1933, 25: 660–664, by permission of the author and publisher.

clothes, and of sewing in general. But recent investigation shows that the home continues to lose these activities. However, their degree of departure varies. Baking is done outside the home to a much greater extent than laundering. Making of men's shirts began leaving the home much earlier than did the making of women's dresses.

Another class of economic services is still done very largely in the home, as for instance, cooking, house cleaning, and care of children. The indications of these functions departing from the home is only slight. However, there are restaurants and stores that sell cooked food, and these have been growing in number about three or four times as fast as have the number of urban families.

It is a mistake to think of these forces as affecting all families alike. There are families, for instance, where the cooking stove, the broom, and the cradle have followed the spinning wheel, the loom, and the soap vat to agencies outside the home. These are the families who live in apartment hotels, without children or with children in nursery schools. Next are the families living in apartment houses where some cooking and housework are done. If these families have young children their care requires more time than in farm families. There is still less transfer of functions from the family living in a single dwelling in a smaller city, and still less for the village families. The rural family has not changed as much as the city family; yet profound changes have occurred in it. Indeed, nothing less than a revolution is taking place in rural life, due to the adaptation of power applicable to small units. Electricity and gasoline are mechanizing the farm and bringing the industrial revolution in full to agriculture. The trends in the rural family are expected to follow somewhat the pace being set by the city family. This is particularly true in regard to the birth rate, for instance. Here again, there is no longer just one type of farmer. The dairy men, the fruit growers, the cotton planters all have somewhat different social life, and their home industries are also different.

THE SOCIAL FUNCTIONS

These economic changes, springing from mechanical invention, bring many correlated social changes in the family. For instance, they affect the age of marriage, the training of girls, the activities of women, vocational guidance, the authority of parents, family security, the labor of children, and other conditions. These correlated or near-correlated social functions may be thought of as five in number: the protective, the recreational, the educational, the religious, and that family function which gives status to the individual. These five functions have all been weakening, as has the economic function, and are being transferred to outside agencies such as the state or industries.

Thus protection is furnished now by police, insurance companies, safety legislation, and so on.

Recreation is not so much a family matter now. The individual members find play outside the home in parks and playgrounds furnished by the state, or in moving pictures, dance halls, along the highways or at athletic contests furnished by private industry.

Education is not much longer in the home except for the earlier years of the child, and even at these tender ages the teacher is becoming a competitor of the parent. The school teacher, usually unmarried, has taken over many of the duties of the parent.

In regard to religion, family prayers or Bible readings, blessing rituals at meal time, all seem to be waning. Difference in the religions of bride and groom is less a bar to matrimony.

And, finally, in the determination of status a person is no longer known chiefly as a member of a particular family so much as an individual. When young persons marry, their union is one of individual rather than of family arrangement.

It thus appears that the social functions of the family are declining as truly as the economic functions. In many cases they decline because the economic functions have changed. For example, economic change has brought varied industry in comparison with farming. Hence, education cannot be furnished by farm life, but there must be vocational education in schools outside the home. What is happening to the family can be seen in large part by tracing the course of these economic and social functions.

THE PSYCHOLOGICAL FUNCTIONS

There is, however, one other function that the family performs, that of furnishing media for the expression of affection between mates and between parents and children. It is not so obvious that family affection has been declining along with the other functions. Divorce is usually cited as evidence. But it is argued that the increase in divorce is no more evidence of decline of affection than an increase in the number of hospitals is evidence of decline of health. Also, along with the increase in divorce has gone an increase in the percentage of the population that is married. It is true that the members of the family spend less time at home and more in clubs, offices, factories, on the roads, than formerly. So much so, indeed, that the home has been referred to as merely a parking place. Hence, more friendly relationships appear to be formed outside the home. So it may be that there has also been a slight transfer of affectional expression from within the home to the outside. But in the main there appears to have been no such diminution as in the case of the economic and social functions.

This difference in transfer is leading to a somewhat different conception of the family than that which exists in many other countries and that existed here in Colonial times. The family is thought of as less of an economic and social institution and more as an agency for personality relationships. The individual personality has become more of an end and the social institution less so. Thus we say the family has become individualized. It is easy to exaggerate this trend, of course. The total number of families are the greatest group of consumers, and the economic power wielded by their purchasing capacity is great. Also quite a few economic functions are still performed by families. Nevertheless, and relatively speaking, the personality functions are coming to be considered more and more important. These include not only the affectional function just discussed but also in part the educational function previously listed under social and economic functions. The object of education is largely that of shaping the personalities of the young. For these families that have children this personality function continues to be one of its most important functions, and of course a majority of families will have children.

Divorce or the instability of the family is due to the fact that these seven functions or bonds are weakening, and the members of the family thus fall apart. The trend indicates that the stability of the family will rest more and more on the personality functions, since the others are tending to weaken, though by no means to cease to exist—a weakening due in part to electricity, in part to economy, and in part to sentiment.

Four · The Family in a Changing Society

ERNEST W. BURGESS
Sociologist, University of Chicago

Ernest Burgess explains below * *some of the implications of the great diversity in family life and of the changing emphasis in family functions.*

NEVER before in human history has any society been composed of so many divergent types of families. Families differ by sections of the country, by communities within the city, by ethnic and religious groups, by economic and social classes, and by vocations. They are different according to the family life-cycle and by number and role of family members. They vary by the locus of

* Reprinted from *The American Journal of Sociology*, 1948, 53: 417–421, by permission of the author and the University of Chicago Press.

ERNEST W. BURGESS

authority within the family and by widely different styles of life. There are the families of the Hopi Indian (primitive maternal), of the old Amish of Pennsylvania (patriarchal), of the Ozark mountaineers (kinship control), of the Italian immigrant (semipatriarchal), the rooming-house (emancipated), the lower middle class (patricentric), the apartment house (equalitarian), and the suburban (matricentric).

UNITY IN DIVERSITY

With due recognition of all the diversity in American families, it is still possible and desirable to posit the concept of *the* American family. In a sense it is an ideal construction in that it attempts to concentrate attention upon what is distinctive of families in the United States in comparison with those of other countries. These differential characteristics are largely in terms of process rather than of structure and represent relative, rather than absolute, differences from families in other cultures. Chief among these distinctive trends are the following:

1. *Modifiability and adaptability* in response to conditions of rapid social change
2. *Urbanization*, not merely in the sense that the proportion of families living in cities is increasing but that rural, as well as urban, families are adopting the urban way of life
3. *Secularization*, with the declining control of religion and with the increasing role of material comforts, labor-saving devices, and other mechanical contrivances like the automobile, the radio, and television
4. *Instability*, as evidenced by the continuing increase in divorce, reaching in 1945 the proportion of one for every three marriages
5. *Specialization*, on the functions of the giving and receiving of affection, bearing and rearing of children, and personality development, which followed the loss of extrinsic functions, such as economic production, education, religious training, and protection
6. The *trend to companionship*, with emphasis upon consensus, common interests, democratic relations, and personal happiness of family members

THE FAMILY AND SOCIETY

With all the variations in American families, it is apparent that they are all in greater or less degree in a process of change toward an emerging type of family that is perhaps most aptly described as the "companionship" form. This term emphasizes the point that the essential bonds in the family are now found more and more in the interpersonal relationship of its members, as compared with those of law, custom, public opinion, and duty in the older institutional forms of the family.

The point is not that companionship, affection, and happiness are absent from the institutional family. They exist there in greater or less degree, but they are not its primary aims. The central objectives of the institutional family are children, status, and the fulfilment of its social and economic function in society.

The distinctive characteristics of the American family, as of the family in any society, are a resultant of (1) survivals from earlier forms of the family, developing under prior or different economic and social conditions; (2) the existing social and economic situation; and (3) the prevailing and evolving ideology of the society.

1. *Survivals.* The American family has had a rich and varied historical heritage, with strands going back to all European countries and to the religious ideologies of the Catholic, Jewish, and Protestant faiths. What is distinctive in the American family, however, has resulted from its role, first, in the early rural situation of the pioneer period, and, second, in the modern urban environment.

The growth of democracy in the family proceeded in interaction with the development of democracy in society. Pioneer conditions promoted the emancipation both of women and of youth from subordination to the family and to the community. Arrangements for marriage passed from the supervision of parents into the control of young people.

The rural family of the United States before World War I, however, had progressed toward, but had not achieved, democratic relations among its members. Control was centered in the father and husband as the head of the farm economy, with strict discipline and with familistic objectives still tending to be dominant over its members. Children were appraised in terms of their value for farm activities, and land tenure and farm operations were closely interrelated with family organization and objectives.

2. *The Evolving Urban Environment.* The modern city, growing up around the factory and serving as a trade center for a wide area, provided the necessary conditions for the development of the distinctive characteristics of the American family. It still further promoted the equality of family members and their democratic interrelationships, initiated and fostered to a certain degree by the rural pioneer environment. In the urban community the family lost the extrinsic functions which it had possessed from time immemorial and which continued, although in steadily diminishing degrees, in the rural family. The urban family ceased to be, to any appreciable extent, a unity of economic production. This change made possible a relaxation of authority and regimentation by the family head. Then, too, the actual or potential employment of wife and children outside the home signified their economic independence and created a new basis for family relations. In the city the members of the family tended to engage in recreational activities sepa-

rately, in their appropriate sex and age groups. Each generation witnessed a decline of parental control over children.

This increased freedom and individualization of family members and their release from the strict supervision of the rural neighborhood was naturally reflected in the instability of the family. The divorce rate has averaged a 3 per cent increase each year since the Civil War.

Urbanization involves much more than the concentration and growth of population. It includes commercialization of activities, particularly recreational; specialization of vocations and interests; the development of new devices of communication: telephone, telegraph, motion picture, radio, the daily newspaper, and magazines of mass circulation. All these still further promote the urbanization and secularization of families residing not only in cities but even in remote rural settlements.

3. *The Ideology of American Society.* Democracy, freedom, and opportunity for self-expression are central concepts in the American ideology. The frontier situation favored their expression in the social, economic, and political life of the people. As they found articulation in the American creed, they reinforced existing tendencies toward democracy and companionship within the family.

Urban life in its economic aspects provided less opportunity than did the rural environment for the exemplification of the American ideology. For example, the development of big business and enormous industries decreased the opportunities for the husband and father to run his own business. But the city greatly increased the economic freedom and independence of the wife and children by providing employment outside the home. The social conditions of the modern city led to the emancipation of family members from the institutional controls of the rural family. The urban family tended to become an affectional and cultural group, united by the interpersonal relations of its members.

THE FAMILY IN PROCESS

The paradox between the unity and the diversity of the American family can be understood in large part by the conception of the family in process. This means, first of all, that it is in transition from earlier and existing divergent forms to an emergent generic type and, second, that it is in experimentation and is developing a variety of patterns corresponding to the subcultures in American society.

1. *The Family in Transition.* Much of what is termed the "instability" of the American family arises from the shift to the democratic companionship type from the old-time rural family of this country and the transplanted old-world family forms of immigrant groups.

Many of the current problems within the family are to be explained by the resulting conflicting conceptions in expectations and roles of husbands and wives and of parents and children. The husband may expect his wife to be a devoted household slave like his mother, while she aspires to a career or to social or civic activities outside the home. Immigrant parents attempt to enforce old-world standards of behavior upon their children, who are determined to be American in appearance, behavior, and ideas.

2. *The Family in Experimentation.* The changes taking place in the family have constituted a vast experiment in democracy. Hundreds of thousands of husbands and wives, parents and children, have participated in it. Couples have refused to follow the pattern of the marriages of their parents and are engaged in working out new designs of family living more or less of their own devising. This behavior has been fully in accord with the ideals and practices of democracy and has exemplified the American ideology of individual initiative and opportunity for self-expression.

This experiment in family formation, while apparently proceeding by individual couples, has been essentially collectivistic rather than pluralistic behavior. Each couple has naturally cherished the illusion that it was acting on its own. To be sure, individual initiative and risk-taking were involved. Many individual ventures have ended in disaster. But actually it has been a collective experiment in the sense that the couples were acting under the stimulus of current criticisms of family life and were attempting to realize in their marriage the new conceptions of family living disseminated by the current literature, presented by the marriages of friends, or developed in discussion by groups of young people.

ADAPTABILITY VERSUS STABILITY

In the past, stability has been the great value exemplified by the family and expected of it by society. This was true because the family was the basic institution in a static society. American society, however, is not static but dynamic. The virtue of its institutions do not inhere in their rigid stability but in their adaptability to a rapid tempo of social change.

The findings of recent studies underscore the significance of adaptability for the American family. Angell began his study of the family in the depression with the hypothesis that its degree of integration would determine its success or failure in adjustment to this crisis. He found, however, that he needed to introduce the concept of adaptability to explain why certain families, highly integrated and stable before the depression, failed, and why some moderately integrated families succeeded, in adjusting to the crisis. A restudy of these cases indicated that adaptability was more significant than integration in enabling families to adjust to the depression.

Adaptability as a personal characteristic has three components. One is psychogenic and represents the degree of flexibility in the emotional reaction of a person to a shift from an accustomed to a different situation. The second component is the tendency of the person as culturally or educationally determined to act in an appropriate way when entering a new situation. The third component of adaptability is the possession of knowledge and skills which make for successful adjustments to a new condition.

Successful marriage in modern society with its divergent personalities, diversity of cultural backgrounds, and changing conditions depends more and more upon the adaptability of husbands and wives and parents and children. The crucial matter, then, becomes the question of the adaptability of the family as a group, which may be something different from the adaptability of its members.

The growing adaptability of the companionship family makes for its stability in the long run. But it is a stability of a different kind from that of family organization in the past, which was in large part due to the external social pressures of public opinion, the mores, and law. The stability of the companionship family arises from the strength of the interpersonal relations of its members, as manifested in affection, rapport, common interests and objectives.

Flexibility of personality is not sufficient to insure adaptability of the family to a changing society. Its members should also be culturally and educationally oriented to the necessity for making adjustments. For example, the prospects of successful marriage would be greatly improved if husbands on entering wedded life were as predisposed in attitudes as are wives to be adjustable in the marital relation. Finally, adaptability in marriage and family living demands knowledge and skills on the part of family members. These are no longer transmitted adequately by tradition in the family. They can be acquired, of course, the hard way by experience. They can best be obtained through education and counseling based upon the findings of social science research.

Five · The Changing Family

PAUL H. LANDIS
Sociologist, The State College
of Washington

*The reading below * describes some of the contrasts
between family life of yesterday and today, and explains certain
problems and gains which arise with the changes in family life.*

THE American family of yesterday was male-domi-
nated, duty-bound, parent-centered, and fertile. It was made sturdy
by the rigorous demands of an unrelenting work world, where a
man's status was measured no less by his time of rising in the morning and his industry than by his tangible possessions. It was unified
in the mutual struggle for economic necessities. It gave little place
to such values as happiness, personal expression, self-development,
and individual rights. Life was family-centered, not individual-
centered.

That family was a part of the rural world in which it had its
setting. To find it in its ideal form today, one must go to the mountain sections, where the traditions and vocabulary of Daniel Boone's
time hold sway; to agricultural areas where ox-cart and hoe methods of survival are yet current. But attitudes characteristic of this
family form still survive in all rural America and are deeply buried
in the residual beliefs of the urban family.

There are current in the United States today, as a consequence,
two family philosophies—the one rooted in the historic tradition
which strongly emphasizes the *dutiful* or *institutional* aspects of
family life; the other arises from contemporary individualism, which
emphasizes the *romantic* and *companionship* aspects of marriage
and family. The two systems of values are in conflict.

Honor and obedience are the key attitudes of the parent-child
relation in the institutional family. It is expected that the wife will
be subservient to the husband, and that the family will struggle
together for the ownership of tangible property. The welfare of the
individual is subservient to the common good.

Discipline is assumed to be good for the child and necessary to
the preservation of the father's authority. The security of the parent
is assured by teaching the virtues of work and responsibility to his

* Reprinted from *Current History*, 1950, 19: 151–153, by permission of the
author and *Current History*.

children. If the code of work and duty is well instilled, they will look after him in old age and respect his hoary crown to the end.

Seeing this system of family attitudes in operation, a writer in the *Kansas City Times* recently observed, "One of the first things a man notices in a backward country is that the children are still obeying their parents."

In a very real sense, the traditional family as an economic unit is work-centered and production-minded. Men are measured by their work accomplishments. As a biological unit, the success of the family is appraised by the number of children born to the union. To be barren is a curse, and to have one's quiver full of arrows a blessing.

Marriage is a conclusive arrangement—for life—and genealogies and family heirlooms bind the generations together. The pressures of neighborhood and community are ever present policemen to guard the traditional obligations and vows of wedlock.

The above values are the old ways for which many critics of modern marriage cry. But inherent in this family system are values less praiseworthy. There is little equality. There is much brutality. Adolescents face the choice of continual submission to work demands and physical punishment, or an open break with family authority. The cost of the latter is often being driven from home by an irate and tyrannical father.

The old revival song, "Oh, where is my wandering boy tonight?" is the voice of a mother's troubled longing for a son, too often in the institutional family driven away by the father because there is no natural place where the patriarchal hand can, in recognition of growing maturity, relax its rule.

THE NEW FAMILY

In direct contrast to the attitudes of the traditional family described are the emerging cultural values of the new family system which places romantic considerations above all else. Love of mates for each other is the first consideration. If this is absent, the sense of obligation is weak indeed; in fact, unless the demands of romantic love are met, the marriage has no meaning. Sex, in its broadest sense, becomes the aim and goal of striving for both men and women. The individualistic marriage clearly places pleasure above responsibility and duty. It aims at the satisfaction of the individual rather than the perpetuation of the race or economic productivity. The institution exists for man, and not man for the institution.

In parent-child relations, the duty of parents to children, rather than of children to parents, is stressed. Guidance and cooperation rather than discipline and authority are the keynote of the democratic pattern. The parent has no authority to protect, and no concept of duty to instill. It is expected that the child will be trained to become a self-sufficient and independent member of society at as early a time as possible. As quickly as he grows in maturity and experience the parental hand is relaxed in recognition of approaching adulthood. The youth is thus prepared to move out into an urban society, free of most of the claims and obligations of the family. Social security in its many forms has replaced the claim of parents on their children.

And the family has become consumption rather than production minded. The measure of a man is no longer, in an industrial, union-organized economy, *production*. It is *consumption*. The goods one is able to use, the leisure he can command, bring status. In the old order the first man up in the morning was most respected by his neighbors. The clock is now reversed. A man's prestige and power in the world are measured by the lateness of his hour of rising.

No longer does the family work as a unit. The individual, rather than the family, is *all*. He may love and marry when he chooses, without regard to parental preference. He may move where he will and free himself from the ties of real property and from the social pressures of gossipy neighbors and kinfolk.

Most families today, especially in the middle class, have a mixture of the attitudes of the institutional family and the romantic family types. Against ideas of duty, loyalty, and faithfulness are projected the newer cultural standards of affection, supreme love, mutual physical and psychological satisfaction of spouses.

One cannot understand modern marriage and the modern family without understanding the conflict between these two systems of cultural values which are represented in the attitudes of the average American. In the parental family young people are taught the traditional loyalties which their own parents have had toward each other, but on the screen, in fiction, and in the conversations and dreams of youth the romantic conception of marriage is accepted.

Youth therefore tend to seek a love that will surpass all other experience. They expect a marriage that will produce supreme happiness—a happiness that will override all the practical considerations that face every man. After marriage their expectations continue to be unrealistically high. As a consequence, the stark realities of the daily adjustment of married life—facing troubles and sickness, economic hardships, and other trials that marriage brings —often prove more than young people can endure in the light of their previous expectations.

It is in part the conflict between the two systems of values, especially as they are realized in marriage, that provides the background of attitudes which makes divorce in the modern companionship family such a commonplace affair.

That happiness has become the aim of the romantic marriage toward which we are moving is in itself significant. Is it an unrealistic goal? Have there been tangible gains to mankind as this goal has become more prominent in human striving?

Never has the child been so highly valued, so well provided for, and so well trained to realize his full capabilities, as when the ideals of the democratic family, cooperative in spirit and respectful of the rights of even the weakest member, have been realized.

Failure of this marriage system is of course tragic for the child. He often becomes a pawn in the conflict of parental dissension in the struggle for his affections and loyalties at the expense of the mate. And when the break comes and custody is awarded, he has his loyalty allocated to one parent. The cost of failure of the companionship marriage is often very great to spouses also, because the expectations of participants were so high.

The most obvious gains have been to the freedom and happiness of women. Throughout history, woman has been more nearly a slave of man than his equal. She is so today throughout much of the world where the ideals of the companionship marriage are unknown.

Never have couples realized so much in each other in marriage as they do today, where the ideals of the romantic marriage are even approximated. Such unity of personality was not conceived as possible in the old patriarchal family, where the obligations of wife to husband were stressed rather than their mutual realizations in each other. Democracy, as it has gradually spread throughout the family, admits woman to share in the educational and occupational privileges of the male. She has, if not equal rights, in courtship, at least rather absolute freedom of choice as to whom she will court and whom she will marry, and whether she will marry at all.

Growing economic independence of women gives them a chance to actually exercise their freedom as no generation of women has been able to do. There are other alternatives to marriage.

She may participate in sex with the same abandon and pleasure as the male, thanks to contraception and the new morality which sanctions its use, thus realizing the full physical and psychological release from sex tensions.

Students of the contemporary family hold that one reason marriage fails so often is that the demands made upon it are so great as to be difficult of attainment. Once man depended on many ties of his primary group—the large family and neighborhood group—for intimacy. The world of localities in the pre-automobile age was a relatively stable one, in which the person had many roots. Or to change the simile for point of emphasis, he had many props to his emotional life and sense of personal worth.

The highly mobile urban society of our time is essentially a lonesome one in that men are dissociated from intimate primary groups, where strong and all inclusive ties bind one to his fellows. In the anonymity and strangeness that comes with mobility, the individual

tends to seek in a mate all of the qualities of intimacy and friendship and security that earlier societies gave him through the large
family and neighborhood groups. For this reason the individual in
a mobile society makes much greater demands on marriage and the
marriage partner than have ever been made before. Man longs for
love, intimacy, and emotional security and finds only the single
outlet of marriage for it. If his marriage fails to give him this warm
intimacy it is bankrupt.

II · PERSPECTIVE ON MARRYING AND THE FAMILY CYCLE

One · The Family Cycle

PAUL C. GLICK
Chief, Social Statistics Division
Bureau of the Census

In the following article * Paul Glick, a statistician, points out that families, like individuals, go through a regular cycle, and that this cycle is changing.

FROM its formation until its dissolution, a family passes through a series of stages that are subject to demographic analysis. Typically, a family comes into being when a couple is married. The family gains in size with the birth of each child. From the time when the last child is born until the first child leaves home, the family remains stable in size. As the children leave home for employment or marriage, the size of the family shrinks gradually back to the original two persons. Eventually one and then the other of the parents dies and the family cycle has come to an end.

During the life of the typical family, important changes occur not only in the composition but also in many other measurable characteristics of the group. The family is likely to move to one or more new locations in the process of adjusting to new housing requirements or of improving employment opportunities. A home may be purchased; the rental value of the living quarters may change. The probability of employment of the husband and of his wife will differ from one phase of the family cycle to another. Occupational shifts and corresponding variations in earnings are usually experienced during the lives of the average family's breadwinners.

In this paper the analysis of family composition and characteristics will be limited, where possible, to families of the "husband and wife" type in which both members of a married couple are living together in their own private living quarters. About three-fourths of all households contain a family of this type. Groups not included in this analysis are married couples who are living with an established family, persons living alone, broken families, and households maintained by single (unmarried) persons. Likewise

* Reprinted from the *American Sociological Review*, 1947, 12: 164–169, by permission of the author and *American Sociological Review*.

excluded are the residents of institutions, transient hotels, and of large lodging houses.

TABLE 1. MEDIAN AGE OF HUSBAND AND WIFE AT EACH STAGE OF THE FAMILY CYCLE, FOR THE UNITED STATES. 1940 AND 1890

Staging of the Family Cycle	Median Age of Husband		Median Age of Wife	
	1940	1890	1940	1890
A. First marriage	24.3	26.1	21.6	22.0
B. Birth of first child	25.3	27.1	22.6	23.0
C. Birth of last child	29.9	36.0	27.2	31.9
D. Marriage of first child	48.3	51.1	45.6	47.0
E. Marriage of last child	52.8	59.4	50.1	55.3
F. Death of husband or wife	63.6	57.4	60.9	53.3
G. { Death of husband, if last	69.7	66.4	—	—
{ Death of wife, if last	—	—	73.5	67.7

The Bureau of the Census has collected and published statistics on several characteristics of families during World War II and since the end of hostilities, but these data are available in insufficient detail for our present purposes. Figures for this unsettled period would be less appropriate, even if available, than statistics for the more stable prewar period. Family behavior within another year or two from now is likely to resemble more closely that of families in 1940 than that of families in 1945. Accordingly, the main findings reported in this paper are based on tabulations of the decennial census returns of 1940 or on birth and death statistics for prewar years.

STAGES OF THE FAMILY CYCLE

Marriage. Half of the men in this country who marry for the first time do so before their 25th birthday and half of the women before their 22nd birthday, according to data from the 1940 Census. More specifically, as shown in Table 1, the median age at first marriage for men was 24.3 years and for women 21.6 years. The average couple marrying 50 years ago was a little older than the average couple in current times. Results derived from the 1890 Census showed that the median age at first marriage was 26.1 years for men and 22.0 years for women at that time. Thus, the average married man of 1940 was his wife's senior by about three years, whereas his grandfather was likely to have been senior by four years.

Men on farms tend to marry at relatively older ages than those not on farms. The decline since 1890 of nearly two years in the median age of men at first marriage may be attributed in part, therefore, to the decline in the proportion of farm people in the United States. Another factor may be the more widespread knowledge today of means of family limitation. In the earlier period postponement of marriage was probably more often relied upon as a means of limiting family size.

It should be recognized, of course, that not all couples establish a separate home when they marry. In ordinary times, approximately one couple out of every five moves in with relatives or lives in rented rooms as lodgers for a while after marriage. The proportion of couples living in this manner declines sharply until middle age and reaches a low point of about 3 per cent for couples in their 50's.

Over a considerable period of time there has been a growing tendency for married couples to make their homes with an established family. There is evidence in unpublished data from the Censuses of 1930 and 1910 that smaller proportions of couples at these earlier dates than in 1940 were failing to maintain their own households. A survey made in June, 1946, showed an increase of only 9 per cent since 1940 in the number of private households as compared with an increase of 40 per cent in the number of couples living doubled up in private households. The latter increase developed, no doubt, as a consequence of the lack of housing facilities to accommodate the great numbers marrying during, or since the end of, the war.

Child bearing. Following marriage, about a year elapses before the average mother bears a child. This interval has not varied greatly since 1917, when the Bureau of the Census first published national figures on children by order of birth. The median age of mothers bearing their first child in 1940 was 22.6 years. In 1890 it probably was about 23.0 years. Between 1940 and 1942 it remained practically unchanged in spite of a rather large increase in the proportion of first births among all births.

For women who had married and had reached the end of their reproductive period (45 to 49 years old) by 1940, the average number of children born per woman was approximately 3.1. Statistics on children by order of birth indicate that these 3.1 children were born about two years apart, hence a period of only about four and one-half years elapsed between the birth of the first and the last child, as a rule. The typical mother had, therefore, borne her final child at the (median) age of 27.2 years.

Because families were so large two generations ago, the average woman at that time had twice as long an interval between the birth of her first and last child as does the woman of today. She had borne 5.4 children with an estimated interval of 9 years between the first and the last. Not until the age of about 32 years had she given birth to the last child.

At this point it is appropriate to mention in passing, at least, those women who have never borne any children. Among women who had married and completed their period of fertility (45 to 49 years old) by 1940, 15.4 per cent had had no children. For 1890 the corresponding figure was only half as large, 7.9 per cent.

Children leaving home. From the time the last child is born until the first child leaves home, the size of the family usually remains stable. Probably a majority of children depart from the parental home for a new permanent place of residence within less than a year from the time they marry.

Let us assume as a reasonable approximation, therefore, that the average (ever-married) woman of completed fertility (45 to 49 years old) in 1940 had had three children who grew to maturity, married, and left home at the same age that their parents married. The decline in the number of children living at home would accordingly have taken place when the mother was between the ages of 45 and 50 years. By way of comparison, the average woman of her grandmother's era would have been 47 to 55 years old, if she had lived as long as that, when her five surviving children were leaving home.

Dissolution of the family. This brings us to the final stage of the family cycle, when first one then the other of the parents is expected to die. For the average couple who married in 1940, the chances are 50-50 that, under mortality rates observed at that time, they will survive jointly for about 39 years. At the end of that period the wife would be 61 years old and the husband 64. They would have lived together for 11 years since the last of their three children married. By comparison, the typical couple of two generations ago could have expected to survive together for only 31 years after marriage, that is, until the wife would have attained age 53 and the husband 57. This is two years short of the time when their fifth child would have been expected to marry.

Thus, the decline in size of family and the improved survival prospects of the population since 1890 not only have assured the average parents of our day that they will live to see their children married but also have made it probable that they will have one-fourth of their married life still to come when their last child leaves the parental home. This represents a remarkable change since 1890. It is one of the most dramatic, and at the same time one of the most significant changes from the viewpoint of the life experiences of the parents, of all changes in the family cycle in the last 50 years. It has a multitude of social and economic implications.

The wife would ordinarily be expected to survive longer than her husband, partly because she is usually younger and partly because mortality rates are more favorable for women than for men, age for age. In the typical situation, therefore, the period of joint survival of husband and wife is terminated with the death of the husband. In this case, the average wife would be expected, under present conditions of mortality, to live on after her husband's death for about 13 years, to age 74; 50 years ago, she would have looked forward to living until age 68. In the less common situation, the period of joint survival is broken by the death of the wife. In that case, the average husband, under mortality conditions of today, would be expected to live on for 6 years, to age 70, whereas 50 years ago he would have been likely to live until age 66.

With the dissolution of the family by the death of both spouses, the end of the last stage in the usual family cycle has been reached.

CHANGES IN FAMILY COMPOSITION

Family size. As the family passes through its life cycle, it expands in size and then contracts, not only because of the changing number of children in the home, but also because of the varying number of adult relatives in the household who have not formed separate families or have moved in with the family after a period of living elsewhere.

At all stages of the family cycle, except perhaps for brief periods at the beginning and the end, the majority of the husband and wife families have one or more persons in the household who are relatives of the couple. During the period which includes middle age (35 to 54 years old) about four out of every five couples had relatives in the home. The modal or most frequently occurring family size during this phase was 5 or more related persons, including the husband and wife; nearly 40 per cent of the families comprised this number of persons. While the family head was in his 50's, the size of family dropped off rapidly. Half of the couples at ages 65 and over were once again living alone.

Two · Statistical Perspective on Marriage

KINGSLEY DAVIS
Sociologist, Columbia University

The percentage who marry and the age at marriage varies from one time to another and from one country to another. This reading * calls attention to some of the interesting variations.

IN the Western world, family behavior has become increasingly subject to short-run fluctuations. These fluctuations,

* Reprinted from *The Annals* of the American Academy of Political and Social Sciences, 1950, 272: 9–15, by permission of the author and the editor.

recently gaining in speed and amplitude, are integrally related to the economic and political fluctuations which characterize our highly interdependent type of society. Individuals increasingly make their marital and reproductive decisions deliberately, taking into account their personal situation of the moment as they see it. Since the personal outlook of masses of individuals is affected in a similar way by the general economic and political conditions of the moment, the result is that whole populations tend to make the same kind of decision at the same time. Finding conditions bad, they postpone marriage or childbearing. Later, finding conditions good, they decide to marry or, if already married, to have children, thus driving up the marriage and birth rates in some cases by 100 per cent. Superficially, it appears that family behavior has fallen into the zone of what we call fashion; and there is doubtless an element of fashion in the fluctuations, but the causes are deeper than the term implies.

In addition, certain long-run trends have occurred which cut through the fluctuations. One of these is the decline in completed family size (the total number of children that couples have during their lives). Another is the tendency to stop reproduction early in life, thus bunching one's children in a limited period. Added to this is a slight decline during the last few decades in the age at marriage, which enables the mother all the more easily to complete her fertility before age 30. With the extension of the average length of life in modern society (to approximately 70 years for females), couples have a much longer period remaining after their children are born and after the children have left home. The reduced burden of child care and the longer period of life after the burden is over mean that women can enter the labor force in greater abundance. This in turn makes marriage less of a financial commitment for the husband, strengthens the tendency to marry earlier, and gives marriage more of a personal or companionate character. The redefinition of marriage in these terms means, finally, that the breaking of marriage is taken more lightly—so that there has been a rising rate of family dissolution, especially by legal divorce. In fact, death has been displaced as the chief home breaker, its place being taken by divorce and separation.

These changes, some of which are documented in the present paper, have amounted to a revolution in the family institution. They have, however, hardly appeared in most of the world, because most of the world is still in the peasant-agricultural stage of cultural evolution. As the urban-industrial stage continues to diffuse, the new family organization will doubtless diffuse with it.

FLUCTUATIONS IN THE MARRIAGE RATE

The degree to which modern populations compress their weddings into particular periods is truly remarkable. In the United

States, for example, the number of marriages per 1,000 population reached an all-time high in 1946, when it was 16.4. This was double the all-time low of 1932, which was 7.9. Later, in 1949, it was already down to 10.7, a drop of 35 per cent from the 1946 peak. In England and Wales the highest recorded rate was reached in 1940, when there were 11.2 marriages per 1,000 population, which was almost 50 per cent higher than the 1932 figure of 7.6 eight years earlier.

The main causes of short-run fluctuations in the marriage rate are the business cycle and war. When these causes are operating jointly in favor of marriage, the highest rates occur. During the four deep depression years, 1930–33, approximately 800,000 marriages did not occur in the United States which normally would have occurred. After that, conditions began slowly to improve, and the marriage rate gradually climbed. But, except for 1937, when the marriage rate was 116,000 above normal, the depression was not really over until rearmament got under way in 1940. The great improvement of business conditions, with the threat and execution of the draft coming *at the same time,* not only led many of the postponed marriages to be consummated but also induced many to marry earlier than they would otherwise have done. The result was the most gigantic wave of marriages the country had ever seen. During the ten years 1940–49, there were approximately 3,670,000 more marriages than would have been normally expected. We may naturally expect a marriage rate below normal in the 1950's even if economic conditions are good, because a large portion of the marriageable population has been, so to speak, used up in the matrimonial marathon of the 1940's.

THE CONSTANT PROPENSITY TO MARRY

Although the moment of history when people choose to marry now fluctuates markedly, the decision ultimately to marry has remained notably stable. In other words, people may postpone or advance the date of their marriage in accordance with current conditions, but they do not put off marrying forever. In Great Britain, the United States, and New Zealand, for example, where there have been gyrations in the annual marriage rate, the percentage of persons aged 45–54 who are or who have been married has remained remarkably constant. The only trend observable is a consistent downward trend among females in both Britain and New Zealand, due mainly to an increasingly feminine sex ratio in the relevant ages.

The stability of the proportion who ever marry shows that the changes in the marriage *rate* from one year to another do not represent lifetime decisions to enter or stay permanently out of wedlock, but rather decisions as to the particular time of marriage. This is the real meaning of "postponement" or "borrowing on the future." It follows that a period of low marriage rates is almost sure to be followed by a period of high rates, and a period of high rates by one of low rates.

Although the fluctuations in current rates do not affect the proportion who ultimately marry, they do affect the age at marriage. In addition, the age at marriage is also affected by other factors, some of a long-run character. As between one country and another, a high age at marriage is generally connected with a low proportion who ever marry. Thus in India, where a high percentage of females 15–19 are married, the proportion who ever marry is extremely high; whereas in Ireland, where almost no females are married at young ages, the proportion who ever marry is extremely low.

The lowest ages at marriage are generally found in peasant-agricultural countries, such as India and China. During the rapid growth phase of urban-industrial nations, the average age at marriage apparently rises; but later the age at marriage once more turns downward, though not rapidly. In the United States the median age at first marriage has declined steadily since 1890, as Table 1 shows.

The postponement of marriage during the depression decade tended to keep the median age stationary among men and to advance it a third of a year among women, but the high marriage rates of the 1940's accelerated the downward trend. Similar phenomena have been noted in Australia, Canada, and Great Britain.

In so far as there has been a trend in advanced countries toward earlier marriage, it can perhaps be attributed to the fact that fertility has been controlled by other means than late marriage, that

TABLE 1. MEDIAN AGE AT FIRST
MARRIAGE, U. S. A.

Year	Male	Female
1890	26.1	22.0
1900	25.9	21.9
1910	25.1	21.6
1920	24.6	21.2
1930	24.3	21.3
1940	24.3	21.6
1947	23.7	20.5

divorce has generally become easier to procure, that the size of the household has diminished, that more married women are in the labor force, and that the state has taken an increased share in child support.

Since our own country most exemplifies the changes inducing a low age at marriage, it is no accident that "the chances of marrying at an early age are much greater in the United States than in any

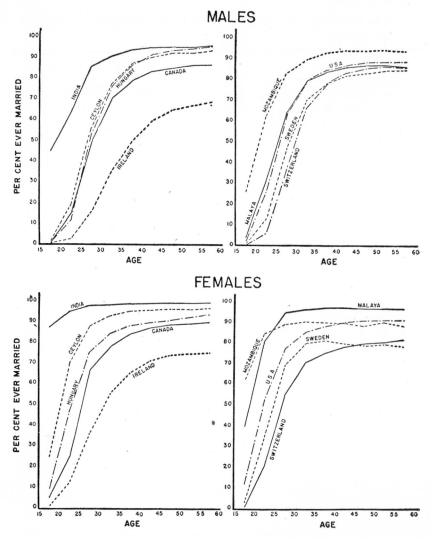

FIG. 1. *Percentage Ever Married, by Age and Sex, Selected Countries.*
(Source: Bureau of Applied Social Research, Columbia University.)

other country of the Western World." This is shown by Figure 1,
which gives for selected countries the proportion ever married at
different ages. Indeed, males in the United States marry younger
than do males in Ceylon, and both males and females marry
younger than do those in Hungary. In 1940 more than a fourth of
our young men aged 20–24 were already married, whereas in Ireland only 3 per cent and in Switzerland only 6 per cent of them
were. The proportion who ever marry by an advanced age is also

high in the United States, although not quite so high as in Ceylon or Hungary.

The United States thus stands in marked contrast to such countries as Sweden, Switzerland, and Ireland, where both the age at marriage and the proportion who remain permanently single are high. In 1941 Ireland was still the least-married country in the world. Only 36 per cent of its women had ever been married prior to age 30, and over a fourth of the women remained unmarried throughout the reproductive span. It is primarily through the postponement of marriage that Ireland has reduced its birth rate, whereas in the United States the birth rate has been brought down by the use of contraception in wedlock.

At the other end of the scale stands India, where almost nine out of every ten girls are married by age 20, and where 98 out of every 100 are married by age 30.* Other peasant-agricultural countries, such as Malaya and Mozambique, are in much the same situation. Malaya, because of heavy Chinese and Indian immigration, has a surplus of males; consequently its males marry late, but its women marry earlier than do those in any western country, and the proportion of women who eventually marry is noticeably higher than the proportion of men who do so. Ceylon, which also has a large immigrant population, manifests a late age at marriage for males as compared with other Asiatic areas.

Three · *Mate Selection*

PAUL POPENOE
Director, American Institute
of Family Relations

The reading below ** *considers the differential marriage rate and examines some factors which might affect the marriage rate of college women.*

MEN and women tend to select their mates on the basis of general resemblance in such traits as age and socio-economic background, and propinquity. The correlations of assortative

---

* An Indian custom increasing the percentage ever married is the taboo on the remarriage of widows. If a man cannot take a widow to wife when he himself is widowed, he must choose a woman who is not yet married—and in a country where mortality is high, this means that every available woman is taken.

** Reprinted from the *American Sociological Review,* 1937, 2: 735–743, by permission of the author and the *American Sociological Review.*

mating for IQ and educational level are fairly high (.60 to .70) and most other desirable qualities are correlated with these, even beauty in women being correlated with intelligence to the extent of about .40.

Since 90% of the population that reaches middle life is or has been married, there is evidently no general quantitative problem in failure to mate. No one can doubt that at least 10% of the population ought not to marry. Indeed, if one adds together such groups as the insane, the feeble-minded, the alcoholic, the homosexual, the epileptic, and those with various physical diseases and disabilities, it is likely to produce a pessimistic state of mind: one may conclude that too many people are marrying already.

The most practical approach to the problem of mate selection is therefore to analyze it in more detail, asking how some undesirable partners can be eliminated, how some desirable partners can be aided to mate, and generally how people who do marry can be helped to select more satisfactory partners.

Two problems—how some desirable partners may be aided to mate, who otherwise would remain unmated, and how all persons who mate may be helped to choose more wisely,—may conveniently be considered together, since the issues they involve are not easily separable. The greatest problem is offered by educated women, whose marriage rate is still unduly low in spite of some improvement during recent decades. Their difficulties result from a number of factors, some relating to personal qualifications or "inherent marriageability," others to the opportunities for meeting suitable partners. Among these difficulties are the following:

1. Leaving obvious physical defects out of account, an important part in marriageability seems to be played by sexual normality. This whole field of sexual development is one of the most obscure areas of human biology; the Terman-Miles scale for the measurement of masculinity and femininity should lead to progress in its exploration. Preliminary results do not reveal any marked tendency to mate selection on the basis of degree of femininity (which may be a very different thing from the physiological normality mentioned above), though they do indicate that the happiest marriages are those of women with the most pronounced femininity.

Many other persons of both sexes are unmarriageable because of emotional immaturity and infantile fixations. With girls these difficulties are likely to take the form of a fear of sex. With boys, the Institute's observations bear out the popular opinion that a mother-fixation is responsible for the celibacy of many old bachelors who otherwise might have been superior husbands. Growing up in a broken home probably handicaps one in mate selection as well as in marital happiness.

An excessive paranoid component of the personality is a serious handicap, the etiology of which is obscure. Since it is associated with the introvert temperament and the asthenic body-build, it may have a constitutional basis. It has been explained psychoanalytically as resulting from latent homosexuality, but there is no evidence that this is generally true. In the light of the Institute's observations, it deserves more attention than it has received.

Another handicap (as to which statistical evidence is lacking, however, as in most other aspects of the whole problem of mate selection) is the erroneous idea of many educated women that their diplomas should make them especially attractive to desirable husbands, who, they suppose, are particularly yearning for intellectual comradeship in a wife.

In a study of 250 highly successful and also highly educated married couples, inquiry was particularly directed to the question why the partners found each other so satisfactory. What was it in the individual that made the spouse think him or her so superlative? Most of the women stressed companionability. Not so the men. The qualification that the man particularly admired in his wife was "her ability to handle the job,"—to be equal to the many responsibilities that marriage placed on her.

In addition, though they did not emphasize it, one may be sure that the wife was valued for her feminine attractiveness, her emotionally satisfying qualities and her ability to enhance the husband's ego.

Now if a college girl lacks these two qualities,—domestic competence and emotional attractiveness,—that a man really wants, she will not go far by putting forward as her only asset something that he does not particularly want, namely, an assumed capacity to satisfy him intellectually.

2. Supposing one to have an adequate and not unmarriageable personality, the technique of mate-attraction may be decisive. It is closely associated with some of the factors that have just been mentioned. Educated women often stand in their own light because of erroneous ideas of sex psychology that have been circulated as dogmas of feminist faith during the past generation. Such a woman, failing to interest a possible husband, sometimes rationalizes her own inadequacy by condemning the mores which discourage women from taking the initiative. If custom allowed her to seek out a man and propose to him, she hints, she would long since have had a home of her own.

The Terman-Miles identification of aggressiveness as perhaps the chief factor in masculinity illuminates this question of "bi-sexual initiative" in mating. The tendency for the male to take the initiative in sexual affairs,—the role of the female being seductive and alluring rather than aggressive,—goes back in evolution not only far beyond the human, but even far beyond the mammalian, stage. It appears to be one of the fundamental reactions of the organism, and it is very unlikely that any woman can disregard it safely at the present time. Certainly one of the common complaints of un-happy husbands is that their wives are too aggressive, of unhappy wives that their husbands are not aggressive enough.

The demand that woman be allowed to become the aggressor in mate selection is sometimes merely a reflection of the "masculine protest" which Alfred Adler has described so fully. No law now pre-vents a woman from proposing, but common observation shows that it is, as a rule, not worth while for her to do so. The woman who is not clever enough to maneuver a man into a position where he will propose might not be clever enough to hold a man after she got one.

Discussion of the technique of "getting your man,"—or woman, as the case may be,—is beyond the scope of this paper. An out-standing difficulty of some men in winning a suitable mate is their own egocentricity and their failure to offer that companionability which almost every educated woman seeks. An outstanding diffi-culty of some women is their tendency, already mentioned, to try to behave in too many respects like second-class men instead of like first-class women. A realistic study of the psychology of sex, begin-ning not later than the high school, is urgently needed to improve mate selection.

3. Age is one of the factors that tells most heavily against the educated woman. She will probably not graduate from college be-fore 22; at that age one-half the native white women of the United States are already married. Each year of delay thereafter impairs her chances doubly: the available men are not only diminishing in number by marriage to other girls, but also by the operation of the age differential. This means that the average disparity between the ages of husband and wife increases steadily. In Philadelphia the average man of 25 married a girl of 22.2, a difference of 2.8 years between them. The average man of 35 married a girl not of 32 but of 28.5, the difference of 6.5 years being nearly two and one-half times as great as for the earlier marriage. This means that as the girl grows older, the number of eligible men diminishes not pro-portionately but very much more rapidly. There are relatively few bachelors at 35, still fewer at 40, who are in every respect good prospects as husbands.

If the college girl takes a job, then, for a few years after gradua-tion, the delay in mating means that her statistical chances of matrimony approach the vanishing point.

4. The "mating gradient" is another of the college girl's most serious handicaps. This is the widespread (and praiseworthy) tend-ency of women to seek to marry above their own level; and of men to want to marry below. In one California study, the average IQ of the husband was found to be 8 points above that of his wife; in a second, two-thirds of the men were found to have married women with lower IQ's than their own; in a third, 43% of the men

married women with fewer years of formal education, only 24%
women with more schooling than their own.

The college girl sometimes has standards that are fantastic and
unattainable. In the absence of help from the curriculum, she has
had to get her education on marriage from the other great educational agencies of the present day; the movies, the radio crooners,
the billboards, the newspaper headlines, and the wood-pulps. It is
not surprising that the standards built up from these sources sometimes do not go beyond the level of romantic infantilism.

But even if she would be content with a man no better than herself, she is still handicapped, for the men of her own level, who are
rare enough to start with, are marrying girls slightly below her
level. There are too few men, above her level, to go around.

Instead of lowering her own standard year by year to conform
to reality, she raises it as she becomes more independent economically and culturally. Taken in connection with her own increasing
age, her complaint that she meets no marriageable men is therefore all too true.

5. Occupational segregation increases her difficulties. Meetings
occurring through business or professional contacts form one of the
main opportunities for marriage selection. Philadelphians were
found to marry those in their own occupations nearly three times
as frequently as chance would allow. But a large part of the educated women go into occupations where there is a shortage of men,
such as school teaching, library work, nursing, religious, charity
and welfare work.

In selecting a career to follow after graduation, girls might do
well to consider its matrimonial opportunities more carefully.

6. The irregular geographical distribution of marriageable men
further complicates the picture. As I have pointed out elsewhere,
some of the northwestern states have two or three times as many
such men per 100 women, as do some of the southeastern states.
Cities are likely to have an excess of unmarried women, farming
areas of unmarried men. In some instances, one seeking a mate
would do well to move to a more favorable location.

7. Even where, in a given area, there are many young men and
young women well adapted to each other, they may suffer from the
lack of social machinery to bring them together.

"Pick-ups" and casual encounters at places of commercial amusement play an important part in the lives of youth of the lower
socio-economic strata, but not with the educated class. The educational system itself is the most important matrimonial agency for
the latter; but if they have not found partners in high school or
college, if their occupations do not throw them with possible mates,
and if they lack an assured social position based on the contacts
of their families in a settled population, they may receive very little

help in making those acquaintances which are as necessary to their mental hygiene as to their matrimonial prospects.

The various dormitories (Y.W.C.A., business girls' clubs, and the like) in which these girls congregate usually make little effective effort to provide a normal social life, and by remaining in them the girl becomes more and more adjusted to a world of one sex, and less and less able to make the heterosexual friendships she craves. Men's dormitories are even worse. Church young people's societies are often too small and cliquish to be helpful. "Get-acquainted societies" and similar *ad hoc* organizations exist in most cities but usually attract an elderly clientele and have nothing to offer to educated young people.

Too often a girl thus gets into a rut which she never leaves. She forms the habit of going about with some other girl in like case, thus baffling any man who might like to strike up an acquaintance with her. To escape from this wilderness, she must travel alone and study the map.

She must, in the first place, go where men are; but these must, in the second place, be the right kind of men; and in the third place, conditions must favor acquaintance. It is no use for her to go to a motion picture theatre, merely because there are men in the audience. Going to a cut-in dance may be almost as useless; the experience of exchanging commonplaces with a dozen men for three or four minutes each is not likely to lead to a permanent friendship.

The higher one's standards of the desired mate, the wider must be the range of acquaintance if the standards are to be met. With the educated young woman, and often the educated young man as well, in a large city, conditions are reversed. The higher the standards, the fewer the people of any kind,—good, bad, or indifferent,— who are met. No wonder celibacy ensues!

For profitable acquaintance, the best opportunities are offered by groups in which young people share some common interest. In every city there are almost countless organizations devoted to sport, religion, recreation, philosophy, art, music, literature, science,— everything under the sun. One who wants to make acquaintances should canvass systematically all such groups in whose objects he has, or could acquire, an interest. He (or she) can visit them one at a time, drop them at once if no "worth-while" young people are found, cultivate them further if they promise to be worth cultivating. Such groups are usually anxious to get new members who share their enthusiasms, and the newcomer who goes alone and endeavors to be appreciative will find a warm reception, whether it be from a club of amateur astronomers or a choral society, a group of hikers or an organization to promote more fluent conversation in French.

Taking two a week, a young person in a large city could visit a hundred such groups in a year. It would be surprising if at least one of them did not prove to be repaying!

At the same time, development of one's own personality is essential. Some girls can dramatize themselves so successfully as to be mysterious and interesting at first sight; others try to do so but merely make themselves ridiculous; others always look and act just as flat failures as they feel.

Here again the colleges are partly to blame: many of them make little effective attempt to socialize their student bodies or to develop the personality and emotional maturity of their students. It is possible for a girl to go through a coeducational college for four years and in all that time never have a "date." If she goes to a "mixer," she is allowed to be a wallflower and returns to her room more convinced than ever that she is a failure in life and that no one will ever care for her. An over-privileged few of both sexes may have more social life in college than is good for them; the majority probably have nothing like enough. Special-interest groups and extra-curricular activities should be used more widely and intelligently.

The girl alone in a large city may be one of these whose four college years have done her more harm than good, so far as the development of her personality is concerned. She would profit by systematic psychological counselling, if it were available; but much can also be done through some of the excellent books on the art of being popular, of making friends, and of achieving happiness, of which at least a dozen have been published during the last few years. She may be able to find an evening class in adult education, which will help to supply this need,—and these evening classes also owe some of their popularity, no doubt, merely to the fact that they give people a chance to make acquaintances. Some of the standard tests of temperament, personality, emotional qualities, and attitudes should be taken; though they do not pretend to micrometric accuracy, they help to give one a more objective knowledge of his own assets and liabilities. He can play his cards better if he knows what sort of a hand he holds.

Perhaps the young man has become just as self-centered as his sister; just as afraid of himself and of other people so that he can not bring himself to make acquaintances or to interest those who make his acquaintance. Inadequate personality is in one way a greater obstacle to successful mating for men than for women, because the man does not have to overcome some of the other obstacles that confront his sister, such as the age differential and the mating gradient. He has to face less competition from his own colleagues, and if he has a good character and personality he will be sought out and introduced around.

The shortage of bachelors to furnish husbands for the educated and unmarried women is partly offset by the widowers and divorcees who, if they remarry, usually prefer to wed a maiden rather than an older woman of their own status. Unfortunately the divorcees, who are the most plentiful, are to some extent biological inferiors and discards who do not offer good matrimonial prospects. Those who do remarry probably represent the more desirable of the whole group, and their success in a second marriage is not very much less than that of the rest of the population in a first-and-only marriage. Divorcees should be examined critically, therefore, but not necessarily rejected, although widowers probably average somewhat higher in quality.

Hundreds of unpublished case histories collected by my students at the University of Southern California bear out the plain inferences to be drawn from the Census and vital statistics. They show that the failure of educated men to marry is most frequently due to physical or emotional disabilities of such a nature that if they did marry, they would not be desirable husbands or fathers.

The failure of many educated women to marry, on the other hand, is more frequently due to circumstances such as age differences and the mating gradient, which are not to their discredit.

The problem of the educated woman who meets no marriageable men is a difficult one, because there is an actual shortage of such men for her; but she can do much to meet the difficulty by studying the psychology of sex, improving her own personality, getting out of a rut, and devoting at least as much time and thought to marriage as she does to a career.

III · DATING AND COURTSHIP— THEORY AND PRACTICE

One · Courtship Practices and Contemporary Social Change in America

NILES CARPENTER
Sociologist, University of Buffalo

This selection * *presents an examination of the func-tions of courtship in America and an analysis of the effects of social change upon courtship behavior.*

FOUR functions are fulfilled by courtship in contem-porary Western society.

First, it is an adjunct to the process of sexual selection. The prospective partners, through the medium of their tentative ap-proaches, one to the other, are enabled to appraise each other as to attractiveness, health, social position, economic status, and the like, and on the basis of such an appraisal either to carry their associa-tion on to marriage or to withdraw from it. From this point of view, courtship is significant in respect to the matings that it forestalls as well as those that it promotes.

Second, it is an apprenticeship in mutual accommodation. As in-timacy develops, the prospective mates find themselves under the necessity either of adjusting to each other, or else of severing their relationship. The closer and less restricted the comradeship of courtship, the greater opportunity does it afford the couple con-cerned to discover themselves to each other and to find out the elements in each other's personality that make for incompatibility or congeniality, and to begin the process of mutual accommodation that will—if their union is to be successful—be continued through-out their marriage.

Third, courtship is a stimulus to maturation. As it progresses, the young man and woman concerned begin to look towards and to plan concerning the obligations involved in marriage, and thereby prospectively to undergo the sobering and maturing influences that accompany such responsibilities. Moreover, courtship—particularly when it reaches the stage of a tacit or avowed engagement to marry—carries with it a definite status, which is recognized by the

* Reprinted from *The Annals* of the American Academy of Political and Social Sciences, 1932, 160: 38–44, by permission of the author and the editor.

associates and relatives of the prospective mates no less than by themselves. This status, implying as it does a stage on the way to marriage, carries with it the assumption that the couple concerned is approaching full adulthood. To the extent that this recognition of approaching adulthood takes place in courtship, the sociological and psychological development of the prospective mates is hastened.

Maturation is also promoted by the education in mutual adjustment described above, and by the sexual component in courtship discussed below.

Fourth, courtship is an essential link in the chain of allure and pursuit by means of which the prospective mates are ultimately carried on towards biological union. The degree to which the sexual component in courtship proceeds varies with the individuals concerned and with the cultural milieu in which they are placed.

SOCIAL CHANGE

As has just been suggested, the specific pattern assumed by courtship practices varies from culture area to culture area, and from time to time. Particularly is it affected by that intricate complex of technological and socio-psychological innovations that go by the name of social change. Of outstanding significance to courtship practices in contemporary America are those phases of social change which may be denominated as: (1) urbanization and "rurbanization"; * (2) the increased speed of transportation, particularly through the motor vehicle; and (3) the changed status of women, particularly as regards relaxation of inhibitory conventions, widened choice of occupation, and coeducational higher education.

URBANIZATION AS AFFECTING COURTSHIP

Recently the writer was transplanted suddenly from a city of 600,000 to a self-contained rural community whose largest town numbers less than 1,000, and whose nearest "city," with a bare 5,000 population, is 60 miles away. The contrast between the two types of communities is startling. In many respects it is more striking than that observed in journeying from the United States to Europe. Such an experience as this serves to throw into high relief the nature and the extent of the change that is being wrought in American society by the growth of city life. Of the four major functions of courtship which have been enumerated, one seems to be most definitely colored by the urban trend—namely, sexual selection.

In this connection, attention should be directed first to the sex

---

* This word has been coined by Galpin, to describe the interpenetration of urban and rural life, particularly the penetration of the countryside by influences emanating from the city.

structure of the average city. There is to be found there a relative preponderance of females. In Europe, their preponderance is absolute. In the United States—largely because of the presence of large numbers of immigrant males—there is a slight excess of males over females, but it is very much smaller than is the case in the rural community. Such a situation naturally widens the range of choice of the prospective husband, but correspondingly limits that of the prospective wife. Stated another way, it means that the young man who contemplates marriage is able to make a more leisurely and discriminating choice than the young woman—with the result that, in so far as a marriage is the consummation of a deliberate selective process, *that selection is more likely to be made by the male than by the female.*

Both prospective mates, however, enjoy a wider range of choice in the city than they would if they lived in the country. Not only are there actually more people per square mile in the former than in the latter; there are also more *young* people, there being a relative dearth of very young and very old individuals in urban populations. More than this, city populations are infinitely more varied as to physical and racial type, occupational and social status, and personality development than are rural populations.

One special phase of this urban-rural contrast in regard to sexual selection requires particular mention. It has to do with the consanguineous mating. The relative immobility of rural populations, coupled with their high fertility, makes it much more likely that individuals who are blood relatives in some degree of consanguinity will be thrown together and drift into marriage in the country than in the city. The eugenical connotations of this fact are obvious.

OTHER URBAN CHARACTERISTICS—"RURBANIZATION"

Offsetting to some degree these differential factors between city and country in this matter of sexual selection are, first, the relative isolation of city life, and, second, the process of "rurbanization." The feebleness of neighborhood life, the insignificant rôle of the primary group, the high degree of anonymity and mobility—such characteristics of urbanism as these bring it about that young men and women are cut off from their fellows to a much greater extent within the city than outside of it. In so far as this is so, the range of choice of prospective mates in the city is considerably reduced.

The process of "rurbanization" serves in some measure to introduce into the countryside those influences making for relatively greater latitude in the scope of sexual selection which are chiefly associated with city life, and thus to narrow the differential between city and country in this respect. Of particular moment is the greater mobility imparted to the countryside by the interpenetration of the urban and rural worlds. The urban visitor to the rural com-

munity adds to the number of potential mates from whom the rural
dweller can make a marital selection. Likewise, the young men and
women residing in the city come within the periphery of the rural
dweller's choices whenever the latter travel thither.

MATURATION AND COURTSHIP IN THE CITY

The third function of courtship practices, namely, maturation, is
probably somewhat retarded by the contemporary trend towards
city life. The mobility of the city, as well as its hostility to the
maintenance of traditional culture norms, lends an atmosphere of
casualness and fluidity to sex contacts of all sorts—courtship included—which is quite different from the quasi-formalized status
imparted to courtship in the rural community. To these influences
must be added that of the anonymity of city life and the nebulous-
ness of the neighborhood and of primary groups generally in the
city.

Thus it is that, whereas in the country the fact that a couple is
"going around together" becomes promptly known throughout a
wide circle of acquaintances and—excepting perhaps for the opposition of a rival—is given tacit recognition and ratification, nothing
of the sort normally occurs in the city. A courtship may indeed
proceed through its several stages up to the very eve of marriage
without attracting more than passing attention on the part of the
couple's circle of acquaintances.

More than this, each of the prospective mates may drift into and
out of two or three courtships before entering into the one which
forms the prelude to their union. As a result, during the greater
part of this final courtship, the attitude both of themselves and of
their intimates is likely to be much the same as that which was
exhibited towards their earlier, abortive experiences.

For such reasons as these, any given courtship is likely to hold
less significance in the eyes both of the principals and their associates in the city than in the country. As a consequence, the young
people concerned will probably experience less of a sense of having
moved along the road towards the status and the responsibility of
adulthood, and to that extent will lose some measure of the maturing influences that would otherwise accompany their association.

TRANSPORTATION—THE MOTOR VEHICLE

Increased speed and range of transportation is associated with
the development of mechanized instrumentalities of movement and
carriage. The most conspicuous instance at present is the motor vehicle. Like other phases of American culture, courtship has been
affected by this group of material culture innovations. The most
significant form of influence exercised upon courtship practices by
these developments is so obvious that it needs little elucidation. It
is the promotion of the second major function of courtship, namely,

the mutual accommodation following upon relatively unconstrained intimacy.

American folkways have never made it very difficult for prospective mates to enter into close-knit and natural comradeships of a sort that greatly facilitates the mutual unfolding and adjustment of their personalities. This process of apprenticeship in the difficult art of getting on together is greatly aided by the developments in rapid transportation which the past thirty years have witnessed. A means has been provided by which a couple may escape not only direct chaperonage, but also the restraint and embarrassment of being accompanied by, or under the eyes of, relatives and friends. In the space of an hour or less, the prospective mates are able to get away from their intimates and "be alone together." Inevitably, the facilitation of intimate companionship arising in this way carries with it opportunity for the mutual unfolding and accommodation of personality.

The writer has the impression—unverified by more than casual observation—that the long drawn-out honeymoon is rapidly dropping out of American marriage habits. If this is so, it may possibly be in part a consequence of the fact that a considerable part of the function of initiation into companionship that has traditionally been associated with the honeymoon is now being preëmpted by the courtship period.

INTIMACY VERSUS PRIVACY

Whether the increased intimacy that results from the rapidity of transportation and the ease of avoidance of relatives and friends consequent upon it, also conduces to a greater emphasis on the sexual component in the courtship relation, is problematical. It probably does so to the extent that it permits escape from the prospective mates' own social milieu into the enveloping cloak of anonymity, and also to the extent that it promotes recourse to isolated and remote sections of the open country.

On the other hand, the distinction between privacy and intimacy must be noted in this connection. A couple may gain complete *intimacy,* in the sense of being free from interruption or from the observation of relatives and acquaintances, by taking a motor ride, by boarding an excursion steamer, or by going "down town" to a theater or a dance-hall; and yet may secure no *privacy* whatsoever.

Moreover, the isolation and remoteness of the countryside have been greatly lessened by the very means which has made access to it easy—to wit, the motor vehicle. Such is the case particularly where the twin processes of urbanization and "rurbanization" have proceeded very far. For illustration, note the rapid increase in blackmailing, robbery, and even murder of the occupants of motor vehicles parked in the open country.

Earlier in this discussion, mention was made of the bearing upon courtship of the anonymity of city life. Attention was directed to the fact that, by being able to avoid the oversight of relatives and friends and neighbors, the prospective mates were likely to lose somewhat the sense of having achieved a definite social status, and, accordingly, the sobering and maturing experience involved in such a status. At this point it may be observed that the anonymity implied in the ability to escape, by means of rapid transportation, from their relatives and other intimates probably tends towards a similar result.

A third consequence of the development of rapid transportation has been implied in the preceding section. The process of sexual selection is greatly aided, in that the young man, or woman—in common with the entire population—travels more frequently and more widely than has been the case in any other era; is given an opportunity for meeting a greater number of prospective mates; and, by the same token, is given a larger number of alternative choices from which to pick his, or her, mate.

THE CHANGED STATUS OF WOMEN

As stated above, there are three phases of the alteration in the position of women that are of moment to this discussion. They are: the relaxation of conventional inhibitions on freedom of action; widened choice of occupation; and coeducational higher education.

All three of these forms of social change operate to promote both the widening of the range of sexual selection, and apprenticeship in mutual accommodation, through intimacy.

SEXUAL SELECTION

Sexual selection is facilitated by the lightening of the burden of restraint upon the conduct of women in that men and women are able to meet more frequently, under a greater variety of circumstances, and on a nearer approach to a plane of equality than formerly. The average young man or woman in search of a mate is, in other words, likely not only to encounter a greater number of individuals of the opposite sex, but—what is more significant—to see them under conditions that permit a much more accurate appraisal of personality than was possible under the artificial and limited contacts of an earlier period.

To take one example among many—the freedom with which young men and women participate together in such sports as tennis, golf, skating, and the like enables each to secure a far better idea of the other's physical coördination and stamina, energy, persistence, sportsmanship, reaction to success or adversity, and so on than would have been possible in a generation when any activity on the part of a woman more strenuous than croquet or a sedate canter on the back of a gentle horse was considered to be "unmaidenly."

The widening of the occupational choices open to women increases the range of sexual selection in much the same way as does the relaxation of the restrictions upon their conduct. The opportunities for young men and women to meet each other are multiplied, and they are enabled to observe and appraise each other under circumstances calculated greatly to deepen their knowledge of each other. One has only to contrast for a moment the relationship between the young man and woman who see each other only in the evenings, over the week-end, and on occasional holidays, and that of those who work together in the same division of an office or department store, eight hours a day, six days a week, through the welter of all the ups and downs, the trials and temptations of the daily round of the job, to realize that sexual selection under the second set of conditions is likely to proceed from a far more substantial and realistic basis of choice than under the first.

The same is the case with the higher education of women, particularly through coeducation (or through the approximation to coeducation resulting from the close proximity of "separate" colleges). Here again, encounters between young men and women are multiplied, and the prospective mates are able to secure a fully rounded knowledge of each other.

The college campus might indeed be considered as an almost ideal setting for the operation of the function of sexual selection. Its formal courses in hygiene, its health services, and its program of intercollegiate and intramural sport place a strong emphasis upon physical fitness. Its seemingly endless round of social functions gives ample scope for the display of social abilities—or the lack of them. The classroom and the laboratory provide a means for the appraisal not only of intellectual caliber but also of the virtues and the shortcomings in temperament and character which serve to facilitate positive achievement or to block it.

Finally, the whole gamut of campus life, with its intricate and shifting social groupings, its fraternity and "political" intrigues, its keen and unremitting competitiveness—above all, its intensity and unrestraint—brings into play every side of the young man's or woman's personality, and thereby permits each to obtain a fully rounded and penetrating understanding of the other.

APPRENTICESHIP IN MUTUAL ACCOMMODATION
THROUGH INTIMACY

The manner in which intimacy and mutual accommodation are promoted by the three aspects of the changed status of women discussed above is self-evident. The loosening of conventional restraints upon the behavior of women is an agency superlatively well suited to the bringing about of such a result. The growing *camaraderie* of young men and women looms large in the present-day panorama of social change.

Similarly, the entrance of women into occupations hitherto closed to them has made possible the development of a new sort of friendship between prospective mates, to wit, the fellowship of the job. As a consequence, this present period is witnessing an increasing number of courtships where the function of training in mutual accommodation is reënforced by the salutary experience of working together.

The intensity of the intimacies developed in college life is proverbial. Not only are young men and young women thrown together at an age of high emotional sensitivity, not only are they provided with a far larger share of leisure than is vouchsafed to their fellows in field, factory, and office, but they are also impelled to seek each other's companionship because of the artificial makeup of the communities in which they are placed.

THE CAMPUS COMMUNITY

The significance to the relations of young men and women of this unbalanced make-up of the average college community is very great. The young men and women in it are, to begin with, removed by scores and hundreds of miles from their own homes, and thus from the full force of their emotional attachments to parents and to brothers and sisters. They are, in the second place, set in the midst of a community that consists of an overwhelming proportion of post-adolescents, and—by the same token—a relatively insignificant proportion of infants and children on the one hand, and of adults and elderly people on the other. They are thus led, by default, to seek virtually all of their comradeship at their own age level, and that age level is the one most closely associated with courtship. This observation applies with lessened weight to the nonresidential urban university. Nevertheless, the forces described above may be found in an attenuated form there, since the students of such an institution constitute a quasi-independent community through their classroom contacts, social gatherings, extracurricular activities, and the like.

Whether there is a higher sexual potential in the courtship relations of college communities than in other groups is uncertain. If there is, it is likely that the lack of emotional insulation described above is of significant importance. Attention also should be directed to the fact that the absence of the average college student from his family and from his own community greatly weakens the effectiveness of the primary-group enforcement of customary standards, in this as well as other aspects of human relations. Witness the penchant of college students for mob violence and destruction of property.

That the loosening of customary restraints upon women, discussed above, operates towards a franker exploitation of the overtly physical element in courtship, seems obvious.

Two · *Changing Courtship Customs*

JOHN F. CUBER
Sociologist, Ohio State University

The selection below * *discusses courtship and dating behavior norms, and considers some problems arising during a period of changing norms and standards of conduct.*

IT is difficult to be entirely accurate when one embraces a group so inclusive as the American nation with its various social classes, regional differences, and rural-urban cleavages, although it is becoming increasingly possible to treat all these subcultures as a unit because of the gradual disappearance of many of the previous uniquenesses among them. It is, however, not to be assumed because a given trend is reported, that that trend is equally evident in the courtship patterns of an Iowa farming community, Brooklyn, and New Orleans, but rather that all three may manifest varying degrees or rates of change in the direction indicated, or possibly even some countertendencies. Moreover, most of the trends discussed in this paper are trends in the urban courtship pattern, being more apparent among groups having free access to the urban culture.

GREATER APPROVAL OF CASUAL MAN-WOMAN RELATIONSHIPS

The heritage of premarital exclusiveness in association, and the concept of courtship as that period during which one seeks to discover and adjust to a suitable life mate, are becoming increasingly archaic ideologies. The nonexclusive man-woman relationship—however much or little in the way of physical intimacy may be attendant—is now apparent as a behavior norm. The great demand is for men and women as dating partners who want "no strings attached," and partners to whom the relationship per se "is its own excuse for being" are sought rather than those who desire the more stereotyped relationship in which marriage is either the expressed or implied objective.

Just prior to the outbreak of World War II a sample of over three hundred young men and women, about half of whom were university students, were asked to indicate why they dated. Their

* Reprinted from *The Annals* of the American Academy of Political and Social Sciences, 1943, 229, 31–34, by permission of the author and the editor.

replies were anonymous. First and most prominently mentioned, although variously worded, was that they enjoyed the activity as an end in itself and as a means to nothing at all. Second in order was the view that these persons received status among their associates on the basis of the quality and the number of dates which they could attract. Third in order was the idea that the recreational patterns which were desired were inaccessible or inconvenient except in a pair relationship. And lastly, dating was considered "practical" as a means of finding a life mate or of testing the desirability of a contemplated marriage. The average age of the group was twenty-four years. The objection may be raised that man-woman interaction not oriented to marriage is outside the scope of courtship, but failure to observe and interpret such behavior leaves one very naïve indeed relative to the total sequence of man-woman interaction which may culminate at some future time in engagement and marriage. To be realistic in our day, one must study formal courtship and pre-courtship as one continuous process.

It may appear that this trend would be hard to establish in view of the recent high marriage rate. The point, however, is not that persons do not ultimately marry, but that before they marry or until marriage appears imminent, preference seems to be for the "no-strings-attached" type of relationship. The implications of this widespread experience with the opposite sex for the personality of men and women and for successful marriage may be more significant than is now generally realized.

NORMS OF PHYSICAL INTIMACY

Concerning the question of norms of physical intimacy, relatively too much thought and research may have gone into the question—variously formulated—as to what degree of physical intimacy is generally permitted by women of various ages and social types and desired by men of various ages and social types. According to the conclusion of the writer and also implied in the data of some other researchers, the appropriate inquiry would be not so much *what* do they do, but *with whom* do they do it. Most careful researches have reasonably established the fact that former taboos against physical intimacies in courtship are materially weakened and to many persons practically nonexistent. The data usually consist of statistics on the proportion of a given sample of women and men who were, for example, virginal at marriage or who had participated in one or another defined kind of erotic intimacy. The more significant change, however, appears to have occurred not so much in the *type* of erotic experience of the unmarried person, but in (a) the casual nature of the man-woman relationship in course of which the act was performed, (b) the frequency with which the act is being performed, and (c) the degree of moral compunction on the point. In these last three considerations seems to lie the essence of the "moral revolution" if there may be said to have been one.

It would be a mistake, however, to assume that these changes were caused by the war. At most, the war may be said to have accelerated the trend already established, by greater mobility of the people, particularly where large numbers of unmarried men and women move out of their accustomed orbits of association with most thought of normal erotic life through marriage precluded for an indefinite time to come.

AN EMERGING SINGLE STANDARD

There seems likewise to be a rather consistent trend in the direction of a more nearly single standard of courtship behavior. More than a vestige of the double standard remains, of course, but it is less and less evident as time goes on. Careful observation indicates the following patterns widely practiced: (1) women taking the initiative in arranging dates (formerly only a man's prerogative); (2) the "Dutch treat," or sharing of expenses more or less equally by the man and the woman; (3) the woman paying the expenses of the recreation and in general planning the program; (4) women taking the initiative in suggesting the form which a date shall take, not just accepting or rejecting the proposal which the male initiated in the traditional pattern; and (5) less evidence of a double standard of morality.

EMOTIONAL TENSION

Although difficult to establish statistically, there appears to be considerable justification for the generalization that man-woman relationships, like many other relationships in this day, are fraught with great emotional tensions within the person and between the partners. Case studies reveal largely what one would expect to find on purely a priori grounds. During a period of rapidly changing norms and standards of conduct, different persons change in varying degrees and with varying rates. Consequently many pairs find themselves "unequally yoked together," without as a rule being able to understand the forces responsible for their recurrent frustrations.

Moreover, many persons find it hard to be consistent within themselves; they are moderately schizoid in their beliefs, their overt behavior, or both. The young woman, for example, who "rationally" believes that sex freedom is right but after yielding her virginity finds it difficult to retain her self-respect, and the girl who retains her self-respect and then regrets what she had to forego in order to keep it, are obvious cases in point.

It appears not improbable that a majority of currently dating men and women do not have any pronounced and clearly defined beliefs one way or another on most moral questions involved in man-woman relations. They follow a vacillating path, yielding now to this pressure and then to that, verbally espousing one set of standards and overtly living according to an entirely different one, insisting upon absolute celibacy for two or three fortnights, living hedonistically for two or three, and then going back to celibacy.

The characteristic mobility of the times has served to complicate the problem further. Whether in industry or in the armed services, the unmarried man (or woman) finds himself associated with persons of different standards of conduct. So long as these other persons are not dated, differences remain largely academic; but once the relationship becomes other than platonic, the differences in standards cease to be theoretic. There is little doubt that many persons, not always women, have awakened to find themselves participating in or already habituated to patterns of behavior which intellectually or emotionally they were unable to condone. Mental ill health in some degree is the almost inevitable result of such incongruity.

Three · Some Changes in Courtship Behavior in Three Generations of Ohio Women

MARVIN R. KOLLER
Sociologist, Kent State University

*The preceding two readings have stressed changes in courtship practices. Following is a report * on research which attempted to find how much change has taken place during three generations.*

THIS study was confined to young married college-trained women, their mothers, and their maternal grandmothers. The study was focused on the first courtship terminating in marriage since some of the mothers and grandmothers had been married more than once.

After developing and pre-testing, a total of 1,575 questionnaires was distributed during the period from February, 1949, through August, 1949, mostly at the Ohio State University in Columbus, Ohio. The return of 665 questionnaires constituted 43 per cent of all questionnaires released. The round figure of two hundred cases

* Reprinted from the *American Sociological Review*, 1951, 16: 366–370, by permission of the author and the *American Sociological Review*.

at each generation level was chosen for the sample because this was the approximate distribution of the returns and, further, there was the added advantage of maintaining an equal number for each generation.

A summary of the chief background characteristics of the group of women indicates the following: The third-generation respondents consisted of young, college trained, native born, white, urban, Protestant Ohioans who had experienced ever-widening economic opportunities compared with their maternal grandmothers. The second generation were middle aged, high school educated, native born, white, half rural, half urban, Protestant Ohioans who were somewhat deprived of the privileges later enjoyed by their daughters. The first-generation women were elderly, elementary school educated, native born, white, rural, Protestant Ohioans in their rearing.

The differences between the three generations of women appear to be age, school level, rural-urban rearing, and opportunities to be employed beyond the parental home. These might be expected to influence differentially the courtship behavior engaged in by the three generations.

While dating is not necessarily a part of courtship, it does constitute the first activity in the process of leaving the parental home. Accordingly, the women of each generation were asked whether their parents approved of the boys whom they dated.

The pattern that appears is one of increasing frequency of disapproval of boys being dated, with the third generation experiencing the greatest degree of parental disapproval.

There are a number of possible interpretations of this pattern. One would be that it reflects, in part, the preference of each generation for behavior more akin to that of its girlhood. Another might be that the third generation has greater opportunity for dating boys concerning whom the mothers (second generation) might have objections. Still another interpretation might be that the greater controls placed upon the behavior of a young woman in rural areas of years ago, as well as the limited roles she could play, could account for the women of the first generation having the most parental approval of the men they dated. Some support for this interpretation is obtained by the returns on the matter of how the women behaved in each generation when they did experience parental disapproval.

Twenty-three per cent of the women of the first generation yielded to their parents' wishes rather than attemping to change the minds of their elders. Only 9.5 per cent of the women of the third generation yielded to their parents' wishes when they differed about dating certain men. By contrast, 49.5 per cent of the women of the third generation used argument and persuasion to change their parents' attitudes, whereas only 13 per cent of the women of the first generation resorted to such devices to secure parental approval.

Control by the local community during the girlhood of the maternal grandmothers and the restructuring of such controls in the girlhood of the granddaughters were evident in the returns in the various generations on the place of meeting their mates. Forty-three per cent of the maternal grandmothers named the general community or the immediate neighborhood around the parental home as the place where they met their mates. Only 15 per cent of the granddaughters had the same experience two generations later. Contacts made in church services and in the home accounted for the additional marriages in the first generation, while the third-generation women tended to disregard these avenues and relied more heavily upon school and secondary-group situations to find their mates. A multiplicity of places served as meeting points for the third generation while the range of possibilities for the maternal grandmothers was quite limited.

With the first generation quite limited in the range of personal associations and the second and third generations experiencing a greater range, one would expect most women of the later generations to give serious consideration to several possible mates before making a choice. The findings of the study do not support this assumption.

Most of the women in each generation claim to have considered seriously only one man, the one they finally married.

Another point of similarity in the courtship patterns of the three generations is the age of entrance into the courtship which led to the first marriage. The mean age at first date with the man who eventually became her husband was 19.37 for the grandmothers. The mean age at first date for the second and the third generation was 18.90 and 19.19, respectively. No significant difference appears when critical ratios are computed.

A third point of similarity appears to be the paying of costs incident to dating. In ninety per cent of the cases, the man financed the dating activities in all generations.

Notes appended to the questionnaires by the grandmothers aid in interpreting this finding. Many of the grandmothers noted that there was little need to spend money in rural areas in their time. Hence, the financing of the dates by the men of the first generation was comparatively meager in terms of present-day standards. Some grandmothers replied that the pattern of "home-dating" or "parlor dates" gave them an opportunity to display their culinary and home-making abilities before their potential mates, a practice denied the third generation due to the great amount of time spent outside their homes. Ostensibly, it was a "man's world" and the men "naturally paid" for all the dates. Subtly, however, the women of the first generation took care of the "financing" of the dates, and the conclusion that men *always* paid in each generation is not quite correct.

Differences appear when the degree of chaperonage experienced by each generation is examined. Fifty-two per cent of the first-generation respondents reported that they were *never* chaperoned. This compared with 36 per cent of the second generation and 40 per cent of the third generation who reported no chaperonage. A factor influencing this finding is possibly a change in the definition of chaperonage itself. Chaperonage may be formal or informal, consciously practiced or unconsciously practiced. Since many of the first generation reported that their dates centered about the church, home, and community, they felt they were not chaperoned in the formal sense of the word. They were, however, under informal surveillance when in the company of young men whether they were aware of it or not. Those who were aware of chaperonage in the first generation did report a high degree of chaperonage compared with their granddaughters who experienced formal chaperonage only occasionally.

When modal averages are employed, the first generation had one or more dates per week before engagement, the second generation about two dates per week, and the third generation four or more dates per week. The first generation median for dating frequency was one date per week, the second generation two per week, and the third generation three per week. A direct relationship between frequency of dates per week and the generation concerned is, thus, uncovered. The younger the generation, the higher the frequency of dates per week.

Gift exchanges between men and women in each generation during their courtship give some measure of male-female role differentials. The returns uncovered over two hundred different types of gifts of which the women received the greater share in all generations. This finding suggests the strength of the belief over the past sixty years that the woman is the one whose favor is to be won. Several grandmothers appended a note to the effect that they resented any notion that they courted men. "On the contrary," wrote one grandmother, "men court women, *not* vice versa."

Close examination of the gift exchange lists reveals, nevertheless, an increasing number of gifts given to the men by the women during their courtship. The grandmothers gave gifts to their men rarely. The second generation women, however, began to give gifts to their men more frequently and, by the third generation, the young women were in many cases giving more gifts to the men than they received in turn.

The women in all the generations made a point of visiting the homes of both sets of parents as part of their courtship experience. A frequency of one to two visits per week to the homes of both their parents and their future husbands' parents was recorded by all the generations during their courtships. No significant difference appears between the generations when critical ratios are computed.

Inquiry was made in the questionnaire about items discussed by the respondents and their fiancés concerning their future marriage.

Approximately one-fourth of the first generation did not discuss a single problem area concerning the future marriage. This follows the earlier pattern that one does not prepare for marriage, one simply encounters marital problems and "works them out" as "common sense" dictates. Forty-nine per cent of the third generation, on the other hand, discussed every item suggested in the questionnaire. This corresponds to the 4.5 per cent of the first generation who also discussed every item suggested in the questionnaire. Only 1.5 per cent of the third generation failed to discuss any items suggested as possible problem areas in the future marriage. These were, no doubt, serious discussions, since 85 per cent of each generation experienced only one engagement, the one that led to their first marriage.

When medians are compared, there appears to be a steady decline in the length of engagement as one approaches the younger generations. The first-generation women were engaged approximately 11 months, the second generation 8 or 9 months, and the third generation 6 months. The means for the length of engagement in months for the first, second, and third generations were 8.99, 8.45, and 7.18 respectively. In other words, the first generation spent considerable time in engagements but did not discuss problem areas relating to their happiness in marriage, whereas the younger generations spent less time in engagements but probed into troublesome matters which could jeopardize the marriage.

It is suggested that perhaps the first-generation women did not need to try to understand their potential mates as they were well acquainted with them. The data, indeed, show that the women of the first generation tended to know their men over longer periods of time than did those of the later generations. Many grandmothers stated that they had known their men for a lifetime. Such a phenomenon was a rarity among the third generation. For example, 19 per cent of the women of the first generation knew their mates one year or less prior to marriage. This compared with 22 per cent of the second-generation women and 29 per cent of the third-generation women. While 23.5 per cent of the women of the first generation knew their men seven or more years prior to marriage, 11.5 per cent of the second-generation women and 12 per cent of the third-generation women knew their men for that length of time. Further, the stability of marital roles did not necessitate much study on the part of the first generation. The variety of possible roles in marriage in the present, however, does necessitate this preliminary discussion on the part of the third generation.

The study found a tendency towards minimizing the age differences between the mates through the three generations. The median age difference for the first generation was four years, for the second generation two years, and for the third generation one and a half years. The mean age difference for the first generation was 4.45, for the second generation 3.78, and for the third generation 2.74 years.

The data on the total length of time involved in the courtships through the three generations revealed a median of one to one-and-a-half years for all the generations. There have been statements by the elder generations that the younger generations have short and hasty courtships. The study indicates that this condition was fairly common even in grandmother's day. No one generation appears to have spent more time on their courtship than another.

In interpreting the findings, it should be quite clear that the methodology and techniques were conditioning factors. There was always the factor of memory losses and distortions on the part of the first generation when required to recall details of relationships of many years ago. The high selectivity of the group with which this study dealt also played a part in the returns. This group of women were not "just any" group of young married women with any group of mothers and any group of grandmothers. They were a select group of college-trained women, their mothers, and their mothers' mothers. They were women who were rising in social status as measured by several indices. They may have reported "favorable" data and colored the unfavorable aspects of their respective courtships. Over fifty per cent of the questionnaires distributed were not returned by women who promised to do so. Thus, those who had the disagreeable, the unconventional, the unusual, the disapproved, the unhappy relationships in courtship might conceivably have neglected to return their questionnaires. Finally, the aspects of courtship selected for study might possibly be the very ones that would not display much change through the generations. All aspects of courtship behavior were not investigated, and the omission of sexual and other types of behavior which possibly would have manifested some changes through the years might account for the stability of some of the returns.

It appears to be true that as a whole the social controls of the past remain strong and unshaken. They are changing only at specific points such as we have enumerated. These changes began at least sixty years ago and their full import is not yet manifest. It is becoming increasingly evident that the older view that marriage really required no preparation is being challenged by the younger generations who believe in giving their courtships much forethought and attention.

Four · The Rating and Dating Complex

WILLARD WALLER
Sociologist

Have dating practices changed since the late Willard Waller analyzed the dating practices of college students as described below? * Does the description fit the dating pattern on college campuses known to the reader?

COURTSHIP may be defined as the set of processes of association among the unmarried from which, in time, permanent matings usually emerge. This definition excludes those associations which cannot normally eventuate in marriage—as between Negro and white—but allows for a period of dalliance and experimentation. In the present paper we propose to discuss the customs of courtship which prevail among college students.

The mores of courtship in our society are a strange composite of social heritages from diverse groups and of new usages called into existence by the needs of the time. There is a formal code of courtship which is still nominally in force, although departures from it are very numerous; the younger generation seems to find the superficial usages connected with the code highly amusing, but it is likely that it takes the central ideas quite seriously. The formal code appears to be derived chiefly from the usages of the English middle classes of a generation or so ago, although there are, of course, many other elements in it.

The usual or intended mode of operation of the formal mores of courtship—in a sense their "function"—is to induct young persons into marriage by a series of progressive commitments. In the solidary peasant community, in the frontier community, among the English middle classes of a few decades back, and in many isolated small communities in present-day America, every step in the courtship process has a customary meaning and constitutes a powerful pressure toward taking the next step—is in fact a sort of implied commitment to take the next step. The mores formerly operated to produce a high rate of marriage at the proper age and at the same time protected most individuals from many of the possible traumatic experiences of the courtship period.

* Reprinted from the *American Sociological Review*, 1937, 2: 727–734, by permission.

The decay of this moral structure has made possible the emergence of thrill-seeking and exploitative relationships. A thrill is merely a physiological stimulation and release of tension, and it seems curious that most of us are inclined to regard thrill-seeking with disapproval. The disapproving attitude toward thrill-seeking becomes intelligible when we recall the purpose of such emotional stirrings in the conventional mores of courtship. Whether we approve or not, courtship practices today allow for a great deal of pure thrill-seeking. Dancing, petting, necking, the automobile, the amusement park, and a whole range of institutions and practices permit or facilitate thrill-seeking behavior. These practices, which are connected with a great range of the institutions of commercialized recreation, make of courtship an amusement and a release of organic tensions. The value judgment which many lay persons and even some trained sociologists pass upon thrill-seeking arises from the organizational mores of the family—from the fact that energy is dissipated in thrills which is supposed to do the work of the world, i.e., to get people safely married.

The emergence of thrill-seeking furthers the development of exploitative relationships. As long as an association is founded on a frank and admitted barter in thrills, nothing that can be called exploitative arises. But the old mores of progressive commitment exist, along with the new customs, and peculiar relationships arise from this confusion of moralities. According to the old morality a kiss means something, a declaration of love means something, a number of Sunday evening dates in succession means something, and these meanings are enforced by the customary law, while under the new morality such things may mean nothing at all—that is, they may imply no commitment of the total personality whatsoever. So it comes about that one of the persons may exploit the other for thrills on the pretense of emotional involvement and its implied commitment. When a woman exploits, it is usually for the sake of presents and expensive amusements—the common pattern of "gold-digging." The male exploiter usually seeks thrills from the body of the woman. The fact that thrills cost money, usually the man's money, often operates to introduce strong elements of suspicion and antagonism into the relationship.

With this general background in mind, let us turn to the courtship practices of college students. A very important characteristic of the college student is his bourgeois pattern of life. For most persons, the dominant motive of college attendance is the desire to rise to a higher social class; behind this we should see the ideology of American life and the projection of parents' ambitions upon children. The attainment of this life goal necessitates the postponement of marriage, since it is understood that a new household must be economically independent; additional complications sometimes arise from the practice of borrowing money for college expenses.

And yet persons in this group feel very strongly the cultural imperative to fall in love and marry and live happily in marriage.

For the average college student, and especially for the man, a love affair which led to immediate marriage would be tragic because of the havoc it would create in his scheme of life. Nevertheless, college students feel strongly the attractions of sex and the thrills of sex, and the sexes associate with one another in a peculiar relationship known as "dating." Dating is not true courtship, since it is supposed not to eventuate in marriage; it is a sort of dalliance relationship. In spite of the strength of the old morality among college students, dating is largely dominated by the quest of the thrill and is regarded as an amusement. The fact that college attendance usually removes the individual from normal courtship association in his home community should be mentioned as a further determinant of the psychological character of dating.

In many colleges, dating takes place under conditions determined by a culture complex which we may call the "rating and dating complex." The following description of this complex on one campus is probably typical of schools of the sort:

> Dating at X College consists of going to college or fraternity dances, the movies, college entertainments, and to fraternity houses for victrola dances and "necking"; coeds are permitted in the fraternity parlors, if more than one is present. The high points of the social season are two house parties and certain formal dances. An atypical feature of this campus is the unbalanced sex ratio, for there are about six boys to every girl; this makes necessary the large use of so-called "imports" for the more important occasions, and brings it about that many boys do not date at all or confine their activities to prowling about in small industrial communities nearby; it also gives every coed a relatively high position in the scale of desirability; it would be difficult to say whether it discourages or encourages the formation of permanent attachments. Dating is almost exclusively the privilege of fraternity men, the use of the fraternity parlor and the prestige of fraternity membership being very important.
>
> Within the universe which we have described, competition for dates among both men and women is extremely keen.
>
> Young men are desirable dates according to their rating on the scale of campus values. In order to have Class A rating they must belong to one of the better fraternities, be prominent in activities, have a copious supply of spending money, be well-dressed, "smooth" in manners and appearance, have a "good line," dance well, and have access to an automobile. Members of leading fraternities are especially desirable dates; those who belong to fraternities with less prestige are correspondingly less desirable.
>
> The factors which appear to be important for girls are good clothes, a smooth line, ability to dance well, and popularity as

a date. The most important of these factors is the last, for the girl's prestige depends upon dating more than anything else; here as nowhere else nothing succeeds like success. Therefore the clever coed contrives to give the impression of being much sought after even if she is not. It has been reported by many observers that a girl who is called to the telephone in the dormitories will often allow herself to be called several times, in order to give all the other girls ample opportunity to hear her paged. Coeds who wish campus prestige must never be available for last minute dates; they must avoid being seen too often with the same boy, in order that others may not be frightened away or discouraged; they must be seen when they go out, and therefore must go to the popular (and expensive) meeting places; they must have many partners at the dances. If they violate the conventions at all, they must do so with great secrecy and discretion; they do not drink in groups or frequent the beer-parlors. Above all, the coed who wishes to retain Class A standing must consistently date Class A men.

Many of the girls insist that after two years of competitive dating they have tired of it and are interested in more permanent associations.

The rating and dating complex varies enormously from one school to another. In one small, coeducational school, the older coeds instruct the younger that it is all right for them to shop around early in the year, but by November they should settle down and date someone steadily. As a result, a boy who dates a girl once is said to "have a fence around her," and the competition which we have described is considerably hampered in its operation. In other schools, where the sex ratio is about equal, and particularly in the smaller institutions, "going steady" is probably a great deal more common than on the campus described. It should be pointed out that the frustrations and traumas imposed upon unsuccessful candidates by the practice of "going steady" (monopolistic competition) are a great deal easier to bear than those which arise from pure competition. In one school the girls are uniformly of a higher class origin than the boys, so that there is relatively little association between them; the girls go with older men not in college, the boys with high school girls and other "townies." In the school which is not coeducational, the dating customs are vastly different, although, for the women at least, dating is still probably a determinant of prestige.

True courtship sometimes emerges from the dating process, in spite of all the forces which are opposed to it. The analysis of the interaction process involved seems to be quite revealing. We may suppose that in our collegiate culture one begins to fall in love with a certain unwillingness, at least with an ambivalent sort of willingness. Both persons become emotionally involved as a result of a summatory process in which each step powerfully influences the next step and the whole process displays a directional trend toward the culmination of marriage; the mores of dating break down and the behavior of the individuals is governed by the older mores of progressive commitment. In the fairly typical case, we may suppose the interaction to be about as follows: The affair begins with the lightest sort of involvement, each individual being interested in the other but assuming no obligations as to the continuation of the affair. There are some tentatives of exploitation at the beginning; "the line" is a conventionalized attempt on the part of the young man to convince the young woman that he has already at this early stage fallen seriously in love with her—a sort of exaggeration, sometimes a burlesque, of coquetry—it may be that each person, by a pretence of great involvement, invites the other to rapid sentiment-formation—each encourages the other to fall in love by pretending that he has already done so. If either rises to the bait, a special type of interaction ensues; it may be that the relation becomes exploitative in some degree and it is likely that the relationship becomes one in which control follows the principle of least interest, i.e., that person controls who is less interested in the continuation of the affair. Or it may be that the complete involvement of the one person constellates the other in the same pattern, but this is less likely to happen in college than in the normal community processes of courtship.

If both persons stand firm at this early juncture, there may ensue a series of periodic crises which successively redefine the relationship on deeper levels of involvement. One form which the interaction process may assume is that of "lover's quarrels," with which the novelists have familiarized us. A and B begin an affair on the level of light involvement. A becomes somewhat involved, but believes that B has not experienced a corresponding growth of feeling, and hides his involvement from B, who is, however, in exactly the same situation. The conventionalized "line" facilitates this sort of "pluralistic ignorance," because it renders meaningless the very words by means of which this state of mind could be disclosed. Tension grows between A and B, and is resolved by a crisis, such as a quarrel, in which the true feelings of the two are revealed. The affair, perhaps, proceeds through a number of such crises until it reaches the culmination of marriage. Naturally, there are other kinds of crises which usher in the new definition of the situation.

Such affairs, in contrast to "dating," have a marked directional trend; they may be arrested on any level, or they may be broken off at any point, but they may not ordinarily be turned back to a lesser degree of involvement; in this sense they are irreversible. As this interaction process goes on, the process of idealization is reenforced by the interaction of personalities. A idealizes B, and presents to her that side of his personality which is consistent with his idealized conception of her; B idealizes A, and governs her behavior toward him in accordance with her false notions of his nature; the process of idealization is mutually re-enforced in such a way that it must necessarily lead to an increasing divorce from reality. As serious sentimental involvement develops, the individual comes to be increasingly occupied, on the conscious level at least, with the positive aspects of the relationship; increasingly he loses his ability to think objectively about the other person, to safeguard himself or to deal with the relationship in a rational way; we may say, indeed, that one falls in love when he reaches the point where sentiment-formation overcomes objectivity.

The love relationship in its crescendo phase attracts an ever larger proportion of the conative trends of the personality; for a time it may seem to absorb all of the will of the individual and to dominate his imagination completely; the individual seems to become a machine specially designed for just one purpose; in consequence, the persons are almost wholly absorbed in themselves and their affair; they have an *egoisme à deux* which verges upon *folie à deux*. All of these processes within the pair-relationship are accentuated by the changes in the attitude of others, who tend to treat the pair as a social unity, so far as their association is recognized and approved.

Five · Dating Theories and Student Responses

SAMUEL HARMAN LOWRIE
Sociologist, Bowling Green
State University

*Samuel Lowrie discusses the different theories of dating and then compares current high school and college student practices in dating with these theories.**

IN the broad social sense Waller finds no useful function that dating serves, nothing that contributes to more successful marriage or greater social well-being. Certain effects on participants from the dating process would undoubtedly be regarded as advantageous by the individuals involved; Waller looks upon many of them as dubious, some as positively injurious. First among these gains to participants is prestige. "Competition for dates . . . de-

* Reprinted from the *American Sociological Review*, 1951, 16: 335–340, by permission of the author and the *American Sociological Review*.

termines a distributive order," and individuals are "extremely conscious of these social distinctions and of their own position in the social hierarchy." Second, dating determines status in one's own sex group. Highest rating comes from dating, and if possible exploiting, those who are near the top in social rank without falling in love. Third, dating is fun. To play the game, to parry blows without becoming emotionally involved, to win over others, is a primary source of satisfaction and enjoyment to those who succeed. Fourth, dating provides thrills. On "the pretense of emotional involvement and its implied commitments" one gains the emotional thrills of love making and courtship, but "the pursuit of the thrill violates the organizational mores of society. . . . Thrill is akin to vice." Fifth, dating is educational. However, "courtship educates for courtship more than marriage," the attitudes formed will not always "be helpful in either sexual or personal adjustments of marriage." Sixth, the exploitative element in dating is definitely harmful. Injustice arises when meanings are not the same for the two individuals or "when one person deceives the other." Finally, many are injured and thereby hindered from forming the successful marriages they might otherwise have formed. ". . . the capacity to love is permanently injured in many . . . they suffer . . . traumas which permanently interfere with the development of favorable love attitudes and their expression."

This theory of dating has been taken over, seemingly without reference to its origin, by the anthropologists, Margaret Mead and Geoffrey Gorer. They associate it with a supposed American idiosyncratic desire for association and a masculine fear of being considered sissy. Gorer is surprised that dating "is admitted and abetted by parents and teachers who, many of them, hold the puritan attitudes toward sex and the pleasures of the body." Also Mead finds that dating is a barrier to happiness in marriage in that "the more successfully young adolescents deal with the difficult problems of freedom and demanded dating, the less prepared they are" to make successful sex adjustments in marriage.

Much more moderate is Burgess and Locke's conception of dating. They define the term as "a social engagement between two young people with no commitment beyond the expectation that it will be a pleasurable event for both." In comparison with traditional courtship they look upon dating as "a widely different view of the association between the sexes. It involves six points: (1) an end in itself, signifying no further necessary involvement; (2) the opportunity of having friendly associations not with just one or two, but with a large number of the opposite sex; (3) an increased range of contacts; (4) a multiplication of the occasions for social engagements; (5) the selection of companions in the hands of youth with the absence or a minimum of parental influence; and

(6) rating or the predominance of the standards of the age group in personal selection."

From their treatment of the subject Burgess and Locke seem to regard dating as a distinctive yet preliminary phase of courtship. Even in their discussion of rating they give no emphasis to the insincerity and pretense that occupy such a large place in Waller's analysis. To them rating is not the major end of the process, though for many students "dating becomes a game, an end in itself, the object being to date as many high-ranking persons of the opposite sex as possible." Clearly they consider that dating ends when it comes to involve the same pairing repeatedly. In their words, dating "under certain circumstances is the prelude to keeping company and going steady." However, they somewhat ambiguously refer to this change as a transformation of dating *many* into dating *one*.

The positive nature of the Burgess and Locke conception of dating stands out in the functions they ascribe to it. They do not deny the occasional exploitative nature of the process. They recognize that gaining prestige and enhancing one's social status are frequent motives for individuals to date. At the same time they list four additional and definitely constructive functions of the process. First, dating provides opportunity for friendly association with a large number of the opposite sex. Second, it permits a wide range and increased number of social contacts and engagements. Third, it gives opportunity for persons to determine compatibility and community of interests before becoming involved emotionally. Last, it broadens an individual's choice of a mate.

An extension of the Burgess-Locke view gives a third and more extreme conception of dating. According to this theory, dating is a gradual, almost unconscious development from the customs of courtship whereby young people obtain the training and experience needed for sensible selection of mates. In other words, it is an educational process by which the young enlarge the probability of a full and rich experience in marriage built upon companionship and affection between equal mates. The need for such training has arisen from the gradual relaxation of parental control and influence in the selection of mates and from increase in freedom whereby individuals make their own choices. The social need for individual selection of mates is augmented by the development of a new form of marriage in which mates are held together as much by affection and community of interest as by social pressure to maintain a traditional institution. As might be expected, dating relationships have not yet been effectively selected to meet adequately the social ends which gave rise to their development. Instead these relationships are, through social inertia, overlaid with the patterns of courtship from which they come, customs which in many respects hinder the social and educational ends of dating.

Contrary to Waller, this view does not regard dating as a time-

filler during a period of waiting brought into being by postponement of marriage. Rather it recognizes that the age of marriage has
been going down for at least sixty years, the period in which dating
has arisen. It looks upon dating as a development due, first, to
greater freedom of association between the sexes and, second, to
the extension of coeducation.

According to this conception a considerable number of functions
of dating can be listed. Outstanding among the gains a developing
individual gets from dating are broader experience, enriched personality, greater poise and balance, more and more varied opportunities to mix socially, increased ability to adjust to others under
diverse circumstances, reduced emotional excitement on meeting or
associating with those of the opposite sex, greater ability to judge
individuals of the opposite sex objectively and sensibly, added
prestige among those his own age, wider acquaintance, and broader
and thereby a sounder choice of a mate.

The definition of dating, according to this educational theory, is
different from that of Waller or of Burgess and Locke. Since the
word comes from popular usage, its colloquial significance is taken
as a primary point of departure. To participants of the present
time, dating is the process of paired association between members
of the opposite sex before marriage. A first appointment between
two teen-age children or the last prearranged meeting of an engaged couple before marriage are both dates. In contrast, Waller's
restriction of the term to those who feed each other an insincere
"line" while they wait to get old enough to court and marry, has no
support in every-day speech. Burgess and Locke's definition of dating as a social engagement between two young persons without
further commitment is accurate, particularly for early dating. Indeed there is support for recognizing that *one* meaning of the word
is the initial phase of paired sex association, though the distinction
is probably found more often in textbooks than in popular usage.
Certainly to exclude paired relationships involving love from the
term dating is a travesty upon common practice.

Actually the rise of the custom and its designation as dating
seems to have been a response to a need to characterize, on the one
hand, a new relationship and, on the other, to reject an old one.
Paired sex association without further obligation or commitment
was something new and without name. Rejection of the term, courtship, failure to extend it to the new relationship, particularly to the
late phases of sex association where it might logically apply, points
to the central distinction between courtship and dating, to the reason for the enlargement of the American vocabulary.

By long practice courtship is a social term involving obligation,
a kind of chain process which, once initiated, one is under social
pressure to carry through to completion in marriage. In Colonial
times when a boy asked for permission to call on a man's daughter,

he in effect asked for permission to marry her if she would consent. Much more recently a first call by a man on a young woman was a public indication of interest in marriage, and repeated calling was the near equivalent of announcement of an engagement and forthcoming marriage. From its initiation to its end courtship is a public avowal of intent to marry. Back of that avowal, there has long been in America social pressure upon the individual to carry out his commitment.

In contrast, dating is a relationship expressing freedom, lack of commitment or public obligation for any sort of future action. In truth, up to the time of announcement of engagement dating participants have a minimum of accepted responsibility to continue the relationship. Continuation is largely a matter between the two concerned. That is to say, the rise of the term dating is a reflection of the freedom of the young to associate in pairs without others—parents or the community—assuming or insisting that merely because they are dating they have further responsibility to each other or to the community. Such freedom is what distinguishes dating from courtship.

Research concerning these theories of dating is meager. In a study of university students Kirkpatrick and Caplow sought, among other things, to check specific phases of Waller's theory. The evidence they secured bears more on relative sex roles and changing standards than on Waller's ideas.

As a part of a larger inquiry, the writer asked high school and college students to select anonymously from a list of eight the three reasons for dating which they considered most important. The high school respondents, 782 boys and 813 girls, represented a more than ninety per cent return from the two upper classes of three high schools from cities of eight, twenty, and three-hundred thousand inhabitants. The college group, 203 boys and 181 girls, were those under twenty-two years of age from the three lower classes of a small denominational institution. With slight allowance for variation in small samples, the responses from each of the high schools and from the college were much alike in the reasons selected and the relative emphasis given to them. Probably responses vary somewhat by age, but the number of cases in the sample is too small to demonstrate the fact clearly.

In Table 1 the reasons for dating are distributed according to the sex of the respondents. All responses are included, though a small proportion of individuals indicated only one or two, instead of three, reasons for dating. In forming the table the reasons given for dating were rearranged from the haphazard order used in the questionnaires into related groups. Into the first were placed the two reasons that reflect association pointed toward marriage, affection and selection of a mate. These are the reasons most clearly associated with courtship as traditionally conceived. A second group includes those reasons which in statement are frankly educational, "to learn to get along with others" and "to gain poise or ease." The third group includes all the reasons, the remaining four, which in any way reflect the Waller theory of dating as a competitive game, dating "just for fun," "to get to social affairs," for

TABLE 1. STUDENT REASONS FOR DATING, ACCORDING TO SEX

Reasons for Dating	Boys		Girls		Total	
	No. of Responses	Per Cent	No. of Responses	Per Cent	No. of Responses	Per Cent
Group I						
Affection	582	27.2	585	24.8	1167	25.9
Select Mate	298	13.9	370	15.7	668	14.9
Subtotal	880	41.1	955	40.4	1835	40.8
Group II						
Learn to Adjust	181	8.5	314	13.2	495	11.0
Gain Poise or Ease	434	20.3	599	25.4	1033	23.0
Subtotal	615	28.8	913	38.7	1528	34.0
Group III						
Fun	174	8.1	188	8.0	362	8.0
Get to Social Affairs	275	12.9	261	11.1	536	11.9
Prestige	67	3.1	33	1.3	100	2.2
Neck	128	6.0	11	0.5	139	3.1
Subtotal	644	30.1	493	20.9	1137	25.2
Grand Total	2139	100.0	2361	100.0	4500	100.0
No. of Students Responding *	782	....	813	....	1595	....

* Responses from older students were excluded, only those from individuals 16 to 21 years old are shown.

"prestige—to be popular," and "to neck or pet." The purpose of such an arrangement is to get some idea of the relative emphasis students, at least in their verbal responses, place upon mate selection, education and competition or prestige. In the nature of the case this procedure does not give a measure, only a rough indication, of the place any reason for dating occupies in the reaction of students.

That primary place in such an analysis goes to love and mate selection is in line with common observation and American culture. Sociologists may with some accuracy say that individuals acting upon such motives are courting. On the other hand, the young people involved call what they are doing dating. The result is to bring to the fore the opposing conceptions of dating. The persons involved do not recognize, do not use or think in terms corresponding to, the Waller or Burgess-Locke distinction. To the participants they are dating, whether the primary reasons are mate selection, educational development, or prestige.

The unexpected result of the inquiry is the large emphasis placed on learning processes in dating. To find more than one-third of all the reasons given specifically educational is astounding. In reality such a proportion is an understatement. Some of the reasons in the third group, particularly getting to social affairs, have a learning or developmental aspect. Further, though inadequate, the data suggest that this educational motive is stronger in the early years of dating and decreases with age and experience. For instance, in comparison with the total the 366 respondents sixteen years old put educational reasons even above the affectional, 38 per cent of their reasons falling in the educational class.

In contrast to this large place given to consciously developmental dating, is the small emphasis on reasons which are, in any interpretation, of the competitive-prestige type. Only one-fourth of all the responses fall in this category. However, not all this proportion can be accurately attributed to prestige motivation. The most important reasons in the group, to get to social affairs, accounting for twelve of the twenty-five per cent, was mentioned above as certainly involving in some part an element of learning through participation. The specific prestige reason represents only 2.2 per cent of the responses.

The two sexes differ in the percentage of responses emphasizing education in contrast to prestige. Girls put larger stress on educational reasons, 38.7 per cent in comparison with 28.8 per cent by the boys. On the other hand, boys emphasize the items of Group III more, 30.1 per cent in contrast to 20.9 by the girls. Over half the difference comes from the greater interest of the boys in necking and petting. The most that can be made of these differences between the sexes is that boys give more nearly equal place than girls to educational and prestige reasons for dating. If allowance is made for educational elements in the reasons in the third group, boys place as much, possibly more, emphasis on education than on prestige.

The method of inquiry is not necessarily perfect; indeed, how theories of an activity are to be checked is highly debatable. Reasons students give for action are certainly not the real reasons without modification or limitation. The specific set of reasons from which they chose was necessarily to some degree suggestive, and limited responses. Still with all its shortcomings the method gives an indication of student reactions and is of value in pointing toward the truth until a more accurate procedure is devised.

Insofar as the evidence in hand may be accepted, the limitations Waller and Burgess and Locke put on definitions of dating are artificial and contrary to the conceptions of participants. Further, Waller has centered his theory around a relatively small part of the dating process, to the neglect of much more significant elements. True, he chose to focus attention on, and draw evidence from, fraternity-conscious college groups; but he stated that such groups reflect the phenomenon most clearly. Mead and Gorer follow Waller in conceiving dating as an exploitative, competitive game. The responses of the students surveyed in this study suggest that such exploitative relationships are a minor phase of the dating process. Indeed, one may question whether a desire for prestige and an element of competition may not at times be socializing in their effects rather than always insidiously exploitative.

The Burgess-Locke description of dating is more in line with student behavior. However, in describing courtship as an existing American practice, both they and Waller seem out of touch with the usage of young people. The distinction these theorists make between dating and courtship apparently comes from confusing former with present practices and assuming that the difference between the two centers about love and marriage. Certainly students of dating age make no such distinction. Instead, the term courtship is, insofar as their own behavior is concerned, not a part of their vocabulary. As previously suggested, if courtship and dating must be distinguished, the separating quality lies not in love and marriage but in the intent the public may accurately assume about paired association between the sexes. In courtship the community properly assumes that marriage is the end in view. In dating only the individuals involved necessarily know the purpose of the association; from the mere fact of association the public can correctly assume nothing.

The educational theory of dating recognizes the element of freedom as a primary reason for the rise of dating. At the same time it sees the large emphasis on love and mate selection as a logical carry-over from courtship. In truth, dating is a process by which mates are chosen and must therefore be expected to include love, though romantic emphasis is, because of the cultural setting, probably unduly large at present, especially in early dating. Like any objective view of dating, this theory sees the exploitative nature of some dating and regards it as one among many problems of current practices. In a new development not yet clearly defined and in great measure lacking in supporting and reenforcing social standards, dubious departures and aberrations are to be expected. In time the meaning of dating and its functions are likely to be defined and become known generally in the community, to adults as well as to participants. In that case more uniformity may be expected and pressure may be applied to reduce, if not eliminate, practices admitted to be contrary to individual and public well-being.

Such a view of dating has sufficient breadth to see the vital importance, the social and individual gains, of dating. At the same time it regards the problems associated with the phenomenon as largely the consequence of cultural lags and of random attempts to adapt to new situations. From these in time the community is likely to select the more advantageous modes of behavior and to reduce, if not weed out, the socially disadvantageous deviations.

Six · Courtship in a Group of Minnesota Students

CLIFFORD KIRKPATRICK
Sociologist, Indiana University

THEODORE CAPLOW
Sociologist, University of Minnesota

*Sociologists have been interested in testing Waller's hypotheses on dating. Clifford Kirkpatrick and Theodore Caplow report on a study * which takes Waller's theories into consideration and seeks to shed new light upon the courtship experience of university students.*

THIS article reports an investigation made among students at the University of Minnesota inquiring into (1) courtship difficulties, (2) growth patterns in courtship experience, (3) conflict and confusion in student love affairs, and (4) the breaking of love affairs as a bereavement experience.

Our sample, like those utilized by most investigators in the study of the family, is by no means representative. The individuals, investigated in 1940, were not necessarily typical students, being drawn exclusively from sociology courses on the elementary or intermediate level. Co-operation on the part of the subjects was excellent; only three students refused to fill out a questionnaire in whole or in part. The study is based upon 399 questionnaires, reporting 896 serious love affairs. There were 141 questionnaires filled out by men reporting 314 affairs. There were 258 questionnaires filled out by women reporting 582 affairs. Of the serious affairs reported by men, 73.0 per cent had been broken up; and, of those reported by women, 71.0 per cent.

The mean age of the men was 22.0 years and that of the women 21.9 years. Both men and women had completed an average of 2.8 years of college work.

* Excerpts reprinted from *The American Journal of Sociology* 1945, 51: 114–125, by permission of the authors and the University of Chicago Press.

COURTSHIP DIFFICULTIES

Sociologists are increasingly interested in the conception of family life as a continuous ongoing pattern of social interaction, with causative factors operating from generation to generation. The family group provides both incentives and obstacles to its own self-perpetuation through courtship, marriage, and reproduction. More specifically, two hypotheses may be presented to which our data are relevant: (1) There is reason to think that complex and ambivalent emotional patterns within the family both facilitate and hamper the difficult transition from intrafamily interaction to the more mature interaction involved in courtship. (2) Many adolescents feel inadequate and isolated in venturing into the courtship market. The difficulties may be due to the mere fact of adolescence, to ties and complexes acquired in the family group, to personal defects, or to external difficulties in the larger impersonal environment.

Certain of the findings bear upon the first hypothesis. The response of students to a question concerning their father's attitude toward first dating is indicated in Table 1. There is a bare suggestion in these figures that fathers, as the Freudian theory maintains, are more inclined to resist the threatened emotional loss of their daughters than of their sons. The corresponding responses in regard to mothers' attitudes are indicated in Table 2.

The most significant finding is between the proportions of girls and boys who were encouraged by their mothers in initial courtship experience. There is a suggestion here—in accordance with Freudian theory—of a willingness on the part of mothers to eliminate potential rivals from the family group. But since mothers were more inclined than fathers to encourage the dating of sons as well, a Freudian hypothesis must be qualified by the recognition that mothers may simply be more interested than fathers in the mating process; they perhaps acquire vicarious experience through identification.

As to the second hypothesis—that of inadequacy and isolation in early courtship experience—two types of evidence might be cited, the first having to do with reported overt behavior, the second with evaluations. Only 5.7 per cent of the 141 men replying reported no dating. The corresponding percentage for 251 girls is 2.7. The mean number of individuals dated more than once by men was 10.3. In the case of girls, only 3 reported no repeated dating, but a rather suspicious number—56—left the question unanswered. For the 202 girls replying, the mean of individuals dated more than once was reported as 11.7.

Obviously, dating relationships vary tremendously in intimacy and significance. Out of the male sample, 135 reported at least one important love affair, as defined in terms of "going steady, long duration, closeness to marriage, and emotional attachment." Of the female sample, 251 reported at least one important love affair. The average number of important affairs reported for men is 2.23. The average number of important affairs reported for women is 2.26. It can only be speculated as to whether a given affair is really important or merely seems important to the student against a background of limited experience.

TABLE 1. ATTITUDES OF FATHER TOWARD FIRST DATING

ATTITUDE OF FATHER AS REPORTED BY STUDENTS	MALE		FEMALE	
	No.	Per Cent	No.	Per Cent
Prohibited or disapproved .	.....	8.5	.....	18.0
Indifferent ...	.....	70.7	.....	62.3
Encouraged ..	.....	20.8	.....	19.7
Replying	130	......	239	......
Blank	11	......	19	......
Total	141	100.0	258	100.0

TABLE 2. ATTITUDES OF MOTHER TOWARD FIRST DATING

ATTITUDE OF MOTHER AS REPORTED BY STUDENTS	MALE		FEMALE	
	No.	Per Cent	No.	Per Cent
Prohibited or disapproved.	.....	7.3	.....	9.5
Indifferent ..	.....	57.6	.....	39.6
Encouraged ..	.....	35.1	.....	50.9
Replying	137	......	240	......
Blank	4	......	18	......
Total	141	100.0	258	100.0

Indirect objective evidence concerning the adequacy of courtship opportunity may be obtained from "endogamous" courtship behavior of members of various religious groups. It might be expected that members of minority religious groups would have to accept "exogamous" affairs, that is to say, affairs with members of different religious groups.

TABLE 3. AFFAIRS "ENDOGAMOUS" BY RELIGIOUS AFFILIATION (FIRST THREE AFFAIRS)

RELIGIOUS AFFILIATION	MALES		FEMALES	
	No.	Per Cent "Endogamous"	No.	Per Cent "Endogamous"
Protestant	176	79.5	391	80.8
Catholic	53	58.5	71	38.0
Jewish	29	72.4	52	84.9
No preference or incomplete..	38	...	38	...
Total	296	...	552	...

A comparison of the religious groups in the first three affairs combined are found in Table 3.

These rather surprising findings might conceivably be due to a greater tolerance by Catholics of premarital courtship relationships. More probably Catholics, particularly Catholic girls, are handicapped as a minority group in the courtship market and, rather than be left out, seek or accept relationships with persons of another religion. It might be argued that this latter hypothesis is refuted by the endogamy of the Jewish group. In this case, however, a stronger endogamous tradition with reference to Jew and Gentile may prevail over the willingness of a numerically smaller religious group to seek courtship partners outside their own religious circle.

Taking up the student's own evaluation of the adequacy of his courtship experience, it would seem that over a third of the college students in the sample did feel that they had difficulty in initial participation in the courtship market.

This evidence that a surprising proportion of students in even a coeducational college lack opportunity to meet persons of the opposite sex is borne out by an extensive survey made at the University of Minnesota in 1934.

Student reactions to their present opportunities to meet members of the opposite sex indicate that, from one cause or another, at least a third of the sample of Minnesota students find their opportunities to meet members of the opposite sex inadequate.

Does such a situation described above imply frustrated romantic longing or is there a practical eagerness to find realistic adjustments? Subjects were asked whether they would patronize a dating bureau established by a respectable agency. To this "yes-or-no" question, of the 136 men replying, 79.4 per cent said "No"; of the 250 girls answering, 84.4 per cent replied in the negative. Perhaps it is not just dates that students want but also success in competition for dates.

GROWTH PATTERNS IN COURTSHIP

Quite aside from a possible trend toward increasing likeness in status, there is the possibility of growth trends, that is, that some developments are due to either biological or social maturation. They may imply progressively *either* greater or lesser similarity between the sexes. A number of hypotheses present themselves, none of which, to our knowledge, has ever been adequately tested.

1. It would be plausible to set forth the hypothesis that exclusiveness as an index of affair significance would increase with later affairs. The schedule called for an estimate as to what proportion of the relationship involved "going steady" (exclusively) with the affair partner. The exclusiveness continuum involved the following categories: "All the time; Three-fourths of the time; One-half of the time; One-fourth of the time; Less than one-fourth of the time; Not at all." There were altogether 296 first, second, and third affairs re-

ported by men. For 295 of these, information was given concerning exclusiveness. There is evidence of only a slight trend toward exclusiveness in later affairs reported by males. In the case of 541 of the 552 first three female affairs reported, information was given concerning exclusiveness. In the case of female students there is only an insignificant trend toward greater exclusiveness in later love affairs.

2. A closely related hypothesis is that later relationships would be regarded as relatively more important. Response categories to the question, "Did you feel that the relationship was the most important thing in your life?" were "Often," "Occasionally," and "Never." By this criterion, there is some slight evidence of increasing significance of later affairs for males.

Another question in the schedule consisted of a check list of twenty-five emotional states. The proportion of men checking the item "Love" was: first affair, 56.3; second affair, 69.5; and third affair, 78.6. In the case of girls there is likewise a tendency toward increasing expression of "love" from affair to affair. The percentages are: first affair, 46.6; second affair, 63.1; and third affair, 70.8.

3. A final hypothesis concerning possible growth patterns in courtship might posit a progressive sex differentiation. In other words, beyond a certain point, unfolding courtship experience might follow one path in the case of men and another with women. Thus Professor Waller assumes that a basic factor in biosocial sex differentiation in courtship would be differential maturity with reference to matrimony. Waller implies that men go through a period of dalliance in which there is an exploiting attitude toward women and an avoidance of entanglements which might lead to premature marriage.* In our culture, women tend to marry at a somewhat earlier age than men and are as yet less burdened with the problem of financial adequacy for marriage. The outstanding problem for girls is to find a mate. Men have to find both the mate and the means.

A more specific version of the hypothesis would then be that there is increasing conflict, sex frustration, and unhappiness for males as economic forces separate young men from girls in their own age group. Obviously, this aspect of the courtship drama will depend much upon sex ratios, relative economic status, and range of social participation.

That the alleged "period of dalliance" is not altogether associated with superficial emotion on the part of men is suggested by our data concerning love. It will be recalled that the proportion of men reporting love increased with later affairs. The percentages tend to

* Willard Waller, *The Family* (New York: Dryden Press, 1938), esp. pp. 223–25.

be higher than the corresponding percentages for girls, combining all schedules.

Again, we find by combining affairs that the proportion of men's schedules reporting melancholy is 19.4; the corresponding proportion of women's schedules is 8.9. The difference has a critical ratio of 4.2.

More conclusive evidence of increasing difficulty of adjustment for men struggling with a double problem of mate-finding and mate-supporting is found in the reports concerning emotions experienced in the affairs. For purposes of condensation, the twenty-five emotional states in the check list were arbitrarily classified as "Pleasant," "Unpleasant," and "Ambiguous."

There is some evidence that men undergo increasing relative maladjustment because of their double burden of mate-finding and mate-supporting. On the other hand, there is little evidence in these data that young men protect themselves during social and economic immaturity by a casual attitude toward love relationships.

CONFLICT AND CONFUSION

The so-called "older generation" has only a very hazy idea about the amount of conflict and confusion involved in the courtship of college students. All students of the family must seriously consider the brilliant analysis of ego-rivalries in courtship as made by Waller. His principle of least interest is a challenging one. Unfortunately, our own data do not bear too directly upon this principle. The students were asked, "Did you worry about being more deeply involved than he or she?" Since there was no pronounced trend, the four affair categories have been combined. The results are given in Table 4.

TABLE 4. WORRY ABOUT INVOLVEMENT

RESPONSE	MALE		FEMALE	
	No.	Per Cent	No.	Per Cent
Often		10.5		10.0
Occasionally ..		35.5		26.7
Never		54.0		63.3
Replying	313		577	
Blank	1		5	
Total	314	100.0	582	100.0

TABLE 5. PERCENTAGES OF VARIOUS ITEMS CHECKED ON COMBINED SCHEDULES

CONFLICT ITEM	MALES (N = 314)	FEMALES (N = 582)
Jealousy	28.0	23.2
Possessiveness	22.0	23.7
Criticism	21.0	17.9
Irritability arising from emotional tension..	19.4	15.3
Dislike of friends ...	19.1	13.4
Accusations of loss of interest	15.3	14.1
Disagreement about the future	13.1	17.3
Dominance	9.6	8.9
Dependence	3.2	4.3
Exploitation	1.4	3.5

There is a slight tendency, perhaps over-compensatory, on the part of the girls to insist that they did not worry about depth of involvement. Whether in these percentages evidence is found of a clash between love and pride depends merely upon the amount of conflict of this kind which is expected. The figures tell nothing, of course, about the actual dominance and subordination in the relationships.

The schedule used in this study included a check list of possible causes of conflict in the relationship. The percentages of the combined schedules on which various items were checked are indicated in Table 5.

There is the implication in Waller's discussion of "Rating and Dating" that under certain conditions, particularly when males are scarce, girls are forced to compromise in matters of sex morality in order to avoid the breaking of relationships by dominant males who are making the most of their period of dalliance. In view of our policy of avoiding questions concerned with sex, which might reduce student co-operation, we do not have data which bear specifically upon this hypothesis. The students were asked concerning their affairs, "Did you give in on important theoretical or moral issues for fear of losing him or her?" The replies are indicated in Table 6 which shows that there is a striking tendency for women to deny giving in.

It is unfortunate that definite general conclusions cannot be drawn. There is evidence of ego clash, which may or may not exceed expectations. The Ross-Waller principle of least interest is not verified by the present data—but neither is it refuted.

Pending the advent of a social engineer who can guide young people directly to their ideal mates, a more or less painful process of selection and rejection—of making and breaking courtships— must take place. Within certain limits, a willingness to look further implies the finding of straighter sticks. There is some danger that an individual may lag in his search through inertia, lack of confidence, guilt feelings, or excessive sympathy. Sometimes there is the feeling that too much has been invested in even an unsatisfactory relationship to justify its rupture. One gambles, as it were, on the possibility of success in the old relationship because of one's share in the "jackpot." To test the general hypothesis of inertia, subjects were asked, "Did you have a feeling of being trapped in the relationship?" All affair schedules are combined in Table 7.

This evidence corroborates the prior statement of sex differentiation in courtship patterns and may reflect the vague perception by the men of the double burden of finding and supporting a mate.

As a question bearing more specifically upon the question of inertia, the subjects were asked, "Did you continue the relationship after it had ceased to be satisfactory?"

In the difference between the proportions of men and women responding "Yes" there is a bare suggestion that males may be more

inclined to feel caught in relationships which they can neither readily break nor carry through to marriage.

TABLE 6. "GIVING IN"

RESPONSE	MALE		FEMALE	
	No.	Per Cent	No.	Per Cent
Often	......	4.5	......	3.0
Occasionally .	......	28.7	......	16.3
Never	......	66.8	......	80.7
Replying	310	....	569	....
Blank	4	....	13	....
Total	314	100.0	582	100.0

TABLE 7. "FEELING TRAPPED"

RESPONSE	MALE		FEMALE	
	No.	Per Cent	No.	Per Cent
Often	......	7.1	......	5.4
Occasionally .	......	23.1	......	15.2
Never	......	69.8	......	79.4
Replying	312	....	574	......
Blank	2	....	8	......
Total	314	....	582	......

A rich source of conflict and confusion in the courtship of young
people might well be the vagueness which apparently now exists in
the definition of courtship roles. Subjects were asked, "Did the men
pay all the expenses incurred in common?" and were presented
with various exclusive categories to be checked.

The significant finding here is the tendency of females to insist
that all expenses were paid by their courtship partners, while males
are more inclined to substitute "Most" for "All." Many men, however, failed to reply. There is nothing necessarily illogical or men-
dacious in this discrepancy, since the girls responding were not
necessarily the courtship partners of the boys responding. One is
impelled, however, to suspect that women strain a little to report
themselves in a traditional feminine courtship role.

TABLE 8. INITIATIVE-IN-DATING

RESPONSES	MALE		FEMALE	
	No.	Per Cent	No.	Per Cent
Never	....	29.4	....	56.5
Occasionally	....	54.8	....	39.5
Often	....	11.3	....	3.6
Very often	....	4.5	....	0.4
Always	....	0.0	....	0.0
Replying	313	....	564	....
Blank	1	....	18	....
Total	314	100.0	582	100.0

Another item diagnostic of confusion in roles was the question,
"Did the girl take the initiative in telephoning, visiting, and so
forth?" The findings are given in Table 8.

All the sex differences appear to be statistically significant. There is, again, no absolute proof of confusion of roles in view of the fact that the girls in the sample were not necessarily courtship partners of the boys questioned. One does, however, conclude that there is no longer close conformity to standardized courtship roles and that there is probably a sex difference in the interpretation of whatever actually does take place in the initiating and financing of courtship activities. This second conclusion is, of course, less well founded than the first. In view of prior evidence concerning worry about involvement, initiative in courtship, and moral issues, one feels that the women in the sample like to present themselves in a conventional, respectable, and sought-after role.

THE BREAKING OF LOVE AFFAIRS

Courtship selection as it now operates involves the making and breaking of love affairs. Much trouble might be spared the human race if first love were the right love, but such is not yet the case. From the evidence concerning the status of affairs at the time of filling in the schedules it seemed best to estimate the true number of broken affairs for men as 230 and for women as 414.

We gain some insight into the actual or pretended roles played by women as compared with men when causes responsible for the breakup are considered. The students were asked, "Who or what was responsible for the breakup?" Since more than one category or response could be checked, it is most meaningful to consider the percentages of total checking responses directed toward particular causes. A total of 192 specific responses were checked by men and 326 responses specifying causes of breakup were checked by women. Presumably these were all from students having broken affairs. More than one response could be checked. The relative emphasis on specific causes included in the check list is indicated in Table 9. In 73 male schedules and 121 female schedules the vague category "Other" causes was checked. Such responses are not included in the process of establishing a base for percentages given in Table 9.

TABLE 9. CAUSE OF BREAKUP CHECKED BY MALES

Cause for Breakup	Male (N = 230)	Female (N = 414)
Parents	5.2	8.6
Friends	3.1	5.8
Subject's interest in another person	15.1	32.2
Partner's interest in another person	29.7	15.3
Mutual loss of interest	46.9	38.1
Total	100.0	100.0

It is clear from the figures that the happy circumstance of mutual loss of interest is the one most commonly mentioned, yet differential loss of interest—the chief source of heartache—is implied in nearly half of the responses. It is interesting to note the frequency with which men as subjects admit loss of interest, as compared with women. The difference between the percentages (32.2 − 15.1) has a critical ratio of 4.7. The same implication is found in the critical ratio of 3.7 between the percentages of male and female responses (29.7 − 15.3) accusing their partners of loss of interest. Again we find evidence that the girl student in our sample either enjoys the role of being sought after or wishfully identifies herself with the role.

SHOCK AND READJUSTMENT

The preceding discussion makes pertinent a more specific inquiry into the emotional consequences and adjustive mechanisms associated with the breakup of love affairs. The students were asked concerning their affairs, "How did you feel about the way it ended?" Their responses by category are again expressed in Table 10 as percentages of the *total number of responses,* since an individual might indicate more than one emotional state.

TABLE 10. EMOTIONAL STATE

Reaction	Male (N = 230)	Female (N = 414)
Bitter	5.9	4.4
Hurt	10.0	14.3
Angry	3.3	3.5
Remorseful	6.6	6.7
Crushed	1.8	5.0
Indifferent	19.4	16.2
Relieved	15.2	16.8
Satisfied	11.5	8.5
Happy	4.4	3.5
Mixed regret and relief	21.9	21.1
Total	100.0	100.0

By way of check upon bitterness, rationalization, and overcompensation, the subjects were asked the question, "Do you feel that you were more honest and straightforward than he or she?" The results are presented in Table 11. The more striking implication of the evidence is a general tendency to moral self-justification regardless of sex or affair. The only way to avoid this interpretation is to assume that both the men and the women have courtship partners morally inferior to those included in the sample, although not inferior in social status, intelligence, income, or education. College students, like other mortals, perhaps need ability to see themselves as others see them.

While relatively few of our sample verbally admit serious emotional complications in the breakup, one should remember the evidence of overcompensation found by Waller in his study of divorced persons. We have just noted evidence of moral self-justification; another question brings evidence suggestive of repression and frustration. There were 488 responses made by men to a check list of adjustive reactions, and 977 responses made by women. The percentages *of responses* falling in various categories are indicated in Table 12.

TABLE 11.* JUDGMENTS OF RELATIVE HONESTY

JUDGMENT	PER CENT REPLYING		
	First Affair	Second Affair	Third Affair
Males (N = 230)			
More	25.5	29.3	37.2
Equally	62.0	58.5	43.1
Less	12.5	12.2	19.7
Total	100.0	100.0	100.0
Females (N = 414)			
More	26.9	33.3	36.7
Equally	59.6	59.5	46.6
Less	13.5	7.2	16.7
Total	100.0	100.0	100.0

* Only completed schedules for first three affairs included. Very few broken affairs were fourth affairs.

It is interesting to note that between a fifth and a third of the responses indicate either nocturnal dreaming or daydreaming about the former courtship partner. It is also interesting to note the incidence of the wishful illusion of recognizing the former partner. This phenomenon has been noted in the case of divorced persons by Waller. Waller likewise has noted, in his analysis of the alienation process, that a definite break tends to set up a certain glorification of a severed relationship. Our data show a greater tendency to remember pleasant than unpleasant things.

TABLE 12. ADJUSTIVE REACTIONS

BEHAVIOR	Male (N = 230)	Female (N = 414)
Frequenting places with common associations...	11.3	10.0
Avoiding places with common associations......	2.9	3.4
Avoiding meetings	4.7	5.1
Attempting meetings	5.9	4.3
Remembering only unpleasant things	2.3	3.9
Remembering only pleasant things	15.6	15.8
Dreaming about partner	15.5	11.2
Daydreaming	14.3	11.4
Imagining recognition	6.4	7.9
Liking or disliking people because of resemblance	5.5	5.4
Imitating mannerisms	1.8	2.1
Preserving keepsakes	7.0	10.8
Reading over old letters	6.8	8.7
Total	100.0	100.0

Perhaps the most direct evidence concerning actual severity of a possible trauma following breakup is found in the length of time required for readjustment. The subjects were asked, "How long was the period of readjustment after the breakup?" The results are reported in Table 13.

TABLE 13. ADJUSTMENT DURATION

ESTIMATE	PER CENT REPLYING	
	Males (N = 230)	Females (N = 414)
None	51.4	49.4
Several weeks	33.6	19.5
Several months	7.7	19.5
A year ...., ..	5.0	6.3
Several years	2.3	5.3
Total	100.0	100.0

The data based upon combined affairs leave unaltered the implication that about one-half the students have no readjustment problem. Again, it may be noted that any evaluation of the findings depends in part upon preconceptions about heartbreak.

IV · HOW MATES ARE SORTED

One · Cultural Factors
in Mate Selection

AUGUST B. HOLLINGSHEAD
Sociologist, Yale University

Americans like to think that in our culture the individual is entirely free in his choice of a mate. The reading below * *shows that there are many limiting factors which tend to control mate choice.*

THE question of who marries whom is of perennial interest, but only during the last half-century has it become the subject of scientific research. Throughout American history there has always been a romantic theory of mate selection, supported by poets, dramatists, and the public at large. Social scientists, however —a group of jaundiced realists, by and large—have little faith in this pleasant myth as an explanation for the selection of marriage mates. Their theories can be divided between (1) the homogamous and (2) the heterogamous. The theory of homogamy postulates that "like attracts like"; the theory of heterogamy holds that "opposites attract each other."

Viewed in the broadest theoretical perspective of democratic theory, the choice of marriage mates in our society might be conceived of as a process in which each unattached biologically mature adult has an equal opportunity to marry every other unattached biologically mature adult of the opposite sex. Viewed from the narrowest perspective of cultural determinism, biologically mature, single males or females have only limited opportunity to select a marital partner. The first proposition assumes complete freedom of individual choice to select a mate; the second assumes that mates are selected for individuals by controls imposed on them by their culture. If the first assumption is valid we should expect to find a strong association between one or several cultural factors and who marries whom. The second proposition, however, allows for individual choice within limits of cultural determinism; for example a Jew is expected to marry a Jew by the rules of his religion; moreover, he is more or less coerced by his culture to marry a Jewess of

* Reprinted from the *American Sociological Review*, 1950, 15: 619–627, by permission of the author and the *American Sociological Review*.

the same or similar social status, but he has a choice as to the exact individual.

In the remainder of this paper I shall test five factors—race, age, religion, ethnic origin, and class—within the limits of the theories of homogamy and heterogamy and the abstract model I have outlined. The data utilized to measure the influence of these factors on the selection of marriage mates were assembled in New Haven, Connecticut, by a research team, during the last year, through the cooperation of the Departments of Vital Statistics of the State of Connecticut and the City of New Haven.

RACE

Our data show that the racial mores place the strongest, most implicit, and most precise limits on an individual as to whom he may or may not marry. Although inter-racial marriages are legal in Connecticut, they are extremely rare; none occurred in New Haven in 1948. Kennedy's analysis of New Haven marriages from 1870 through 1940 substantiates the rule that Negroes and whites marry very infrequently. Thus, we may conclude that a man's or woman's marital choice is effectively limited to his or her own race by the moral values ascribed to race in this culture. Race, thus, divides the community into two parts so far as marriage is concerned. Because there were no interracial marriages in 1948, and because of the small percentage of Negroes in New Haven, we will confine the rest of our discussion to whites.

AGE

Age, like race, is a socio-biological factor that has a definite influence on marital choice. While there is a very strong association between the age of the husband and the age of the wife at all age levels, it is strongest when both partners are under 20 years of age. Men above 20 years of age tend to select wives who are in the same five year age group as they are, or a younger one. After age 20 the percentage of men who marry women younger than themselves increases until age 50. After 50 the marital partners tend to be nearer one another in age. Thus, controls relative to age rather effectively limit a man's choice to women of his age or younger, but the woman cannot be too much younger or counter controls begin to operate. Evidence accumulated in the interviews shows it is widely believed that a young woman should not marry "an old man." The effects of this belief and practice are reflected in our data. Only 4 men above 45 years of age, out of a total of 144, married women under 30 years of age. The age-sanctions that impinge on a woman with reference to the age of a potential husband narrow her opportunities to men her age, or to slightly older men. In short, differences in the customs relative to age and marital partners place greater restrictions on a woman's marital opportunities than a man's. Nevertheless, it is clear that the values ascribed to age restrict an individual's marital opportunities within narrow limits.

RELIGION

The effects of religious rules on an individual's marital choices were very clear. Next to race, religion is the most decisive factor in the segregation of males and females into categories that are approved or disapproved with respect to nuptiality. Ninety-one per cent of the marriages in this study involved partners from the same religious group. In the case of Jews, this percentage was 97.1, among Catholics it was 93.8 per cent; it fell to 74.4 per cent for Protestants. The differences in percentages, we believe, are a reflection of the relative intensity of in-group sanctions on the individual in the three religious groups. A striking point that emerged from our data is that the effect of religion on marital choice has not changed between the parental and present generations. The number of mixed marriages was about the same in both generations. We would remark that there is no consistent bias between sex and mixed Catholic-Protestant marriages; either partner is likely to be a Catholic or a Protestant. On the other hand, in Jewish-Gentile marriages it has been the Jewish male who has married a Gentile female.

ETHNIC ORIGIN

Today, New Haven is composed mainly of three large religious groups, and seven European-derived ethnic stocks: British, Irish, German, Scandinavian, Italian, Polish and Polish Jewish. We cannot discuss how ethnicity is related to the selection of a marriage mate apart from religion, because religion and ethnic origin are so closely related. Ethnicity within a religious group has been a very potent factor in influencing the mate selection process in both the parental and present generation, but it was stronger a generation ago than it is now. Although ethnic lines are crossed within the Catholic and the Protestant faith more frequently in the present than in the parent generation, this is not true for the Jews. Furthermore, ethnic lines in both generations were crossed, for the most part, within religious groups. This means that the Catholics are becoming a mixture of Irish, Polish and Italian as a result of intermarriage between these groups, but there is still a large block of unmixed Italian stock in New Haven, and smaller blocks of Irish and Polish. The Protestants, on the other hand, select marriage partners mainly from the British segment of the city's population: a minority choose a partner from the Northwestern European group, and in some cases both partners will be of German or Scandinavian descent.

CLASS

The analysis of 1,008 marriages where the husband, the wife, and their families were residents of New Haven revealed that the class of residential area in which a man's or a woman's family home is located has a very marked influence on his or her marital opportunities. In 587 of these 1,008 marriages, or 58.2 per cent, both partners came from the same class of residential area. When those that involved a partner from an adjacent class area were added to the first group the figure was raised to 82.8 per cent of all marriages.

While the modal, as well as the majority, of marriages at all levels united class equals, when class lines were crossed the man selected a woman from a lower class far more frequently than was true of women. In general the data regarding marriage across class lines reveal that the man has a much wider range of choice than has the woman. From whatever way we view it, it is evident that the class position of a family is a factor that exerts a very important influence on the marriage choice of its children.

Education operates in the same way as residence to sort potential marriage mates into horizontal status groups within the confines of religion. Within each religious group men with a particular amount of education married women with a comparable amount of education in significant numbers. This tendency was strongest in the Jewish and weakest in the Catholic groups.

The data presented demonstrate that American culture, as it is reflected in the behavior of newly married couples in New Haven, places very definite restrictions on whom an individual may or may not marry. The racial mores were found to be the most explicit on this point. They divided the community into two pools of marriage mates and an individual fished for a mate only in his own racial pool. Religion divided the white race into three smaller pools. Age further subdivided the potential pool of marriage mates into rather definite age grades, but the limits here were not so precise in the case of a man as of a woman. The ethnic origin of a person's family placed further restrictions on his marital choice. In addition, class position and education stratified the three religious pools into areas where an individual was most likely to find a mate. When all of these factors are combined they place narrow limits on an individual's choice of a marital partner.

Two · *Homogamy in Social Characteristics*

ERNEST W. BURGESS
Sociologist, University of Chicago

PAUL WALLIN
Sociologist, Stanford University

Burgess and Wallin have studied homogamy in such characteristics as social participation, courtship behavior, and conceptions of marriage. Their data, summarized below,* were obtained from 1000 engaged couples.

SOCIAL PARTICIPATION

Under social participation are presented data upon the extent and type of social activities participated in by the engaged couples. These data on (*a*) their friendships with persons of the same and opposite sex, (*b*) their participation in organizations, (*c*) their leisure-time activities, and (*d*) their drinking and smoking habits were analyzed for evidences of assortative mating.

The findings indicate that to a degree somewhat greater than chance the "lone wolf" mates with the solitary person; the gregarious with his kind; that those who have no, few, or many friends of the opposite sex select a life-partner with similar experience; and that those who are and who are not considered indifferent to the opposite sex tend to gravitate toward others like themselves.

Participation in social organizations shows a small degree of like attracting like. The highest association here is by number of organizations which both regularly attend, followed by number of offices held in organizations to which they belonged in the past.

In leisure-time preferences both the "stay-at-homes" and those wanting to be "on the go" are disposed to become engaged with their own kind. On the average, those who like to see plays keep company with other theatergoers, while dance enthusiasts seek each other's company.

There is a marked tendency for persons to select marriage partners with drinking and smoking habits similar to their own, with the extent of homogamy being considerably greater for the former. Since drinking and smoking habits are, at least in part, associated with religious training, the finding of homogamy here may be a

---

* Reprinted from *The American Journal of Sociology*, 1943, 49: 117–124, by permission of the authors and the University of Chicago Press.

reflection of assortative mating by religious affiliation and behavior. In part, too, the finding may be an indication of the influence of propinquity. Persons who neither drink nor smoke are likely to mingle socially with groups where such abstention is common, and the members of the opposite sex with whom they associate are therefore likely to have habits similar to their own. The same would be true of persons who did drink and smoke.

COURTSHIP BEHAVIOR

The data on courtship behavior offer further support for the hypothesis of homogamy. By far the highest correlation here is the correspondence in age at which members of the couples started keeping company with each other. This finding, of course, reflects similarity in age of engaged persons.

Among the items on courtship behavior the next highest association is the mating of those with like experiences in having gone steady with none, one or two, or three or more other persons previous to keeping company with the person to whom they are now engaged. But also, interestingly, the engagement of those who have or have not been previously engaged conforms to the principle of homogamy. There is also a tendency for persons who report having discussed their engagement with others to mate with one another. This tendency is indicated, too, for those who have not discussed their engagement. This association may, however, be due in part to the fact that there is a problem in the engagement which leads both members of the couple to seek advice. This patterning of association by frequency of "going steady," of previous engagements, and of discussing the engagement with others may perhaps be an index of the presence or absence of sophistication. If such an interpretation is valid, the findings on courtship behavior would indicate that persons who are more sophisticated and experienced in their relations with the opposite sex tend to select as partners persons resembling themselves in this respect, and similarly with the less sophisticated.

CONCEPTIONS OF MARRIAGE

Young people before and during engagement are imbued with certain attitudes, ideas, and ideals about marriage. It is interesting to know to what extent the members of engaged couples cherish the same or different conceptions about marriage, about children, about divorce, and about the role of the wife in modern marriage.

The answers to seventeen questions indicative of the conceptions of modern young people about various aspects of marriage indicate that, in this sample, widely divergent as are their notions, in every case there is a tendency greater than chance for engagements to take place among persons with the same conceptions. This is true both of attitudes toward loveless or romantic marriages and of opinions about the justifiability of divorce and separation. Interestingly, there is a higher tendency to form unions according to negative than according to positive conceptions of marriage, although the association is in either case low.

There is a rather marked tendency for engaged young people to entertain the same ideas about the advisability of dating with others during engagement. There is much more accord on this than on the question of the husband's or the wife's going out with the opposite sex after marriage. In both instances, however, these attitudes may be influenced more by association in engagement and accordingly be consequences of the engagement rather than evidence of homogamy.

Four questions deal directly or indirectly with conceptions of the role of woman in marriage, and all show a more or less marked association of the like-minded. Couples tend to agree on the pros and cons of the husband's being the head of the family, of the wife's keeping her maiden name, of the wife's working, and of living in a house or an apartment. The most marked association is on the question of a woman's working after marriage, where the responses were grouped under three categories: (1) no; (2) yes, desirable for economic independence of wife, wife better companion when occupied with a career or occupation, and woman desires career or occupation; and (3) yes, if necessary (husband's income not sufficient for purposes of establishing home on firm economic basis and to aid husband to complete schooling).

The two questions in this series on wholesomeness of first sex information and adequacy of present knowledge of sex showed the same tendency to selective grouping, although somewhat greater for the latter than for the former.

Outstanding as a selective factor is similarity of attitude toward having children and agreement on number desired. Correspondence of desire for a given number of children appears to be slightly more discriminating an item than strength of desire for children. There is, of course, no doubt that the extent of homogamy indicated by these findings is spuriously high in so far as discussion between couples has influenced their attitude both as to desire for children and as to the number they should have.

It is evident that in all the questions upon conceptions of marriage, with the exception of the wholesomeness of first sex information, the association of the couple may be, and undoubtedly is, in part, a contributing factor in the extent of resemblance. It is also reasonable to assume that, in part, those with similar conceptions tend to meet and fall in love with each other. From the existing data there is no way of separating the effect of these two factors. Therefore, similarity of conceptions of marriage secured from engaged couples cannot be considered unqualified evidence of homogamy.

SUMMARY AND CONCLUSIONS

1. The data presented in this report demonstrate that assortative mating takes place by social factors such as religious affiliation and behavior, family background, courtship behavior, conceptions of marriage, social participation, and family relationships.

2. The influence of homogamy upon engagement is indicated by the fact that all the characteristics considered in this study show a higher actual than expected proportion of assortative unions. In all but 6 of the 51 items studied the differences between the actual and the expected association of responses of the members of the couples are statistically significant.

3. The degree of like mating with like varies by our groups of items, being highest for religious affiliation and behavior, next for family cultural background, and lowest for family relationships.

4. By taking responses of engaged rather than of married couples as the basis for a study of homogamy the effect of marital association and of common experience is eliminated. Correlations found in previous studies on attitudes and values may be spuriously high due to influences effective after marriages.

5. The point should be made that the engagement, although much shorter than the marriage period, may operate to make for similarity in the behavior and attitudes of engaged couples because of the mutual responsiveness during the courtship relationship. A careful scrutiny indicates that this may be true for several items: number of persons with whom discussed engagement as indicative of the presence of a problem as well as of a tendency to seek advice; church attendance and possibly church membership as in part affected by engagement; attitude toward having children and number of children desired; perhaps, to a limited extent, drinking and smoking habits; all the questions under conceptions of marriage except wholesomeness of first sex information.

6. Any group of engaged couples will contain a considerable proportion who do not marry. If broken engagements occur more frequently among couples who are unlike than like, then the findings based upon engaged couples may minimize somewhat the actual influence of assortative mating.

7. Finally, the reader should be cautioned against assuming that the findings reported here can be generalized beyond the universe sampled in this study. They are, however, consistent with the findings of other studies of assortative mating and therefore strengthen the case for the theory of homogamy. Further research is necessary to determine differences in degree of homogamy in various social

characteristics for the country as a whole and for its component regions, urban and rural areas, communities and social classes.

Three · The Influence of Parent-Images upon Marital Choice

ANSELM STRAUSS
Sociologist, Indiana University

It has been believed that people tend to marry mother and father substitutes. We present conclusions * *from a research project designed to test the importance of parent-images upon mate selection.*

PARENT-IMAGES are viewed, by various social psychologists, as playing a crucial role in the process of choosing a marriage partner. This view is based upon a certain conception of how human personality develops.

The child, it is held, is profoundly shaped by the character of his early affectional relationships. He learns to love, hate, desire, envy, avoid, and so forth, through personal contact with people during the earliest years of his life. The way his parents and other members of his family treat him, and their personalities, determine to a great extent the development of his own traits, emotions, feelings and reactions. The images which the child develops of the chief persons in this environment—namely, his parents—are derived largely from specific experiences he has had in this environment. These parent-images have associated with them powerful emotions; this is because it is in interaction with his parents that the child first learns to experience emotions and feelings. Adult feelings and reactions toward persons are held to be largely a reliving of the early childhood relationships.

Consequently the kind of individual whom the adult will love or hate, embrace or avoid, is determined largely by the kind of people he learned to love or hate as a child. The individual whom one chooses as a mate will resemble or be different from one's parents in just those important physical or personality traits the person liked or disliked in his parents when he was a child.

The present paper is the outcome of an attempt to check, through

* Reprinted from the *American Sociological Review*, 1946, 11: 554–559, by permission of the author and the *American Sociological Review*.

both interview and statistical data, this general theory of the influence of parent-images upon marital choice.

Fifty engaged or recently-married persons were interviewed; all were women, because of the difficulty of contacting men for interviewing during wartime. Interviews averaged about three hours in duration. The interviewer did not adhere to a strict detailed outline; his procedure consisted rather of covering the same general topics with each individual, taking his cues for many specific questions from what information had been elicited already. General topics included: the individual's family life, her parents, her early childhood relationships with family members, her marriage partner, the narrative of how she "chose" him, her other boy friends. The interviews were conducted in a relatively informal and conversational manner. Usually they occurred in the interviewer's office; occasionally they took place at the woman's home.

On the basis of about half these interviews, a questionnaire was designed. A group of 373 engaged, informally engaged, or recently-married persons (200 women, 173 men) filled out this detailed questionnaire.

The people studied through both interview and questionnaire were, roughly, in their twenties; of college level; white; American; with at least one of the couple residing or having resided in the Chicago metropolitan area. The findings to be reported in this paper have application, perhaps, only to this kind of population.

FREQUENCY OF RESEMBLANCE BETWEEN MATE AND ONE OR BOTH THE PERSON'S PARENTS

Various psychologists believe a mate is chosen who resembles one or the other of the person's parents. Analysis of questionnaire-returns yielded data bearing upon this question of whether there are such mate-parent resemblances.

Physical resemblances between mate and either parent were not very marked. Even those individuals who were designated as "the person liked next best to the preferred mate" resembled parents physically about as closely as did the actual mate. Where resemblances do exist between mate and either parent, however, the mate chosen tends to be physically like the opposite-sex parent.

With regard to whether people choose a mate who resembles parents in opinions and beliefs: as in the instance of physical similarities, resemblances in opinion-beliefs are not very marked. These resemblances are, however, greater than could be attributed to chance.

Concerning whether people select marriage partners who resemble parents in personality and temperament: the data revealed resemblances which were, as in the instance of both physical and opinion resemblances, not particularly startling but which were greater than could be attributed to chance alone. A significant difference in personality-temperament appeared between resemblance of men's mate and mother and women's mate and mother: men's wives tend to resemble men's mothers more closely than women's husbands resembled women's fathers.

In order to get some further measure of temperamental-personality resemblances existing between mate and each parent, our population was asked to do the following.

> Compare on the scale which follows the personality traits of *your parents,* and *your fiancé(e).* Write *F* for father, *M* for mother, *S* for fiancé. If either of your parents is dead, rate as remembered.

Very much so	*Consid-erably*	*Some-what*	*A little*	*Not at all*

Takes responsibility willingly
Dominating
Irritable
Easily influenced by others
Moody
Angers easily
Gets over it quickly
Jealous
Aggressive
Easygoing
Selfish
Stubborn
Sense of duty
Sense of humor
Easily hurt
Makes friends easily
Cares what people say and think
Likes belonging to organizations
Acts impulsively
Easily depressed
Easily excited
Understanding and insight into people
Easy to confide in
Feelings of inferiority
Self-confident.

Each person's questionnaire answer was then scored in the following manner. The distance between adjoining boxes was rated as a difference of one point. For example, the distance between "very much so" and "considerably" would be a difference of one point. But the distance between "very much so" and "somewhat" would be a distance of two boxes, therefore two points difference. The distance between "very much so" and "not at all" would be a distance of four boxes, or four points difference.

With this scale of ratings, it was possible to score the point-difference between mate and each parent for each temperamental trait. Thus if the mate were rated for "aggressiveness" as "very much so" and the father was rated as "not at all," the point difference between father and mate would be four points for "aggressiveness."

After each trait had been so scored it was possible to determine scores of total point differences in temperament between father-mate and between mother-mate. This was done for each questionnaire return by adding up the point differences for each temperamental trait and then summing up the total point differences at the bottom of the page.

A similar operation was performed in order to get a comparable score of resemblances existing between just any random marriageable person of opposite sex and the person's own parents. To do this, we substituted for the person's own mate's temperamental ratings the ratings given for someone else's mate on another questionnaire. So that, for example, if a person rated both his mate and his father "considerably" aggressive, but the substituted random person had a rating of "not at all" aggressive; then there would be a difference of three points between the father and the random marriageable individual. In this way total point difference scores could be obtained for each person's parents as over against some random potential marriageable individual.

The results of this scoring procedure show that, for both sexes, there is a normal curve distribution of random-father and random-mother scores. This normal curve distribution is definitely not characteristic for mate-parent point scores. In the latter scores a much larger per cent bulk in the low point-difference score range. It seems justifiable, therefore, to conclude that both mother-mate and father-mate temperamental resemblances exist in considerably greater number than random expectation would lead one to anticipate.

A further breakdown of mate-parent temperamental resemblances was carried out. An attempt was made to determine which temperamental traits were most significant with regard to such mate-parent resemblances. A tabulation of coefficients of contingency was made, thus giving some measure of which specific temperamental traits might be considered most important with regard to mate-parent similarities.

Three temperamental traits had coefficients averaging over .55 for both sexes (mate-both parents): (1) gets over anger easily, (2) self-confident, and (3) sense of duty. Three temperamental traits had coefficients averaging under .40 for both sexes (mate-parents):

(1) takes responsibility willingly, (2) understanding and insight into people, and (3) easy to confide in.

This section dealing with statistical evidence for parent-mate resemblances can be summarized by stating that there appear to be resemblances between mate and parents that are significant—they would not be expected on the basis of chance alone. That is to say, it would seem that mate-parent resemblances in physique, opinions, and personality-temperament are sometimes associated with the choice of a mate. It would appear also that physical resemblances are less associated with that choice than are resemblances in opinion and personality-temperament. Furthermore, certain specific temperamental similarities between mate and parent are more evident than are certain other temperamental similarities.

These findings tie in with the general theory that states that parent-images influence one's marital choice. They do not support, however, the specific hypotheses that state that one's mate is like or unlike the opposite-sex parent. Generally speaking, strong sex differences did not appear in the data; so that except for some confirmation with regard to physical resemblances between mate and opposite-sex parent, the data do not tend to support this specific aspect of the general theory. The sex of the parent in relation to ideational and personality traits seemed not to be important in the selection.

TYPES OF PARENT-IMAGE INFLUENCE

Similarly, analysis of interview data, while it supports the general theory that parent-images influence marital choice, does not support the specific hypothesis that the image of the opposite-sex parent necessarily strongly influences marital choice. Instead of speaking merely of an opposite-sex-parent image which influences choice, it seems possible to speak of kinds of parent-image influence. While the number of cases analyzed was too small to yield a satisfactory classification of types, certain kinds of parent-image influence were brought out by inspection of and judgment on each of the fifty documents. These included the following: *

Choice of mate resembling father.
Choice of mate influenced by satisfactory relationships with brother and father.
Choice of mate resembling father in all except temperament, in which he resembles mother.
Choice of mate influenced by a combined parent-substitute and mate-image.
Choice of mate influenced by ambivalent feelings toward mother and friendly feelings toward father.
Choice of mate influenced by unsatisfactory relationships with father.

* Documents secured from women only.

Choice of mate influenced by violent reaction against father and friendly feelings toward mother.

Choice of mate influenced by unsatisfactory relationships with mother and indifferent relationships with father.

Choice of mate influenced by satisfying relationships with mother and unsatisfying relationships with father.

Choice of mate influenced by satisfactory relationships with both parents.

Choice of mate influenced by reaction against both parents.

Choice of mate influenced in complicated fashion by mother, father, and nursemaid images.

It is very probable that there are many more kinds of parent-image influence playing upon marital choice. The above instances suggest merely the great wealth of concrete human contexts within which it can be said that parent-images affect selection of a marriage partner.

Interview documents, then, brought out the great diversity of processes by which the influencing of choice of parent-images occurs; they suggested how in childhood different persons experience quite different affectional relationships with their parents, so that they build quite different kinds of images of their parents. Consequently the concrete fashion that these emotionally loaded parent-images enter into selection of a mate will differ greatly.

Brief synopses of several cases illustrating types of parent-image influence will be presented, since it is not feasible in a short paper to present the lengthy documents themselves. These synopses, in some instances, should illustrate not only types of parent-image influence but should give some insight into *how* parent-images enter into the process of choosing a mate.

Choice of a mate resembling the father. This woman's satisfying affectional relationships with her father in childhood and in adolescence, and her corresponding conception of him, seem to have been associated with her choice of a man who resembled markedly her father physically and psychically. She identified definitely and strongly the two men as being similar, and attached a meaningful significance to this fact. The document suggests strongly that satisfying relationships with the father played some role in the woman's selection of a mate who resembled the father.

Choice of a mate influenced by unsatisfying relationships with the father. The person's experiences with a parent may be unsatisfying in some very important respect; and this unsatisfactory state of affairs may play a significant part in the person's choice of a mate. One woman complained that she had never been able to find companionship in her father. She had never been able to confide in him, confer with him about her affairs, especially emotional ones. What she admired most in her marriage partner was the very thing her father lacked: considerateness and understanding. As she said:

"he takes the place of my father." The father failed conspicuously to play a certain role in the woman's life—namely someone who would listen understandingly and sympathetically to her problems, and discuss them with her. The mate selected was one who could fill this parental lack.

Choice of a mate influenced by violent reaction against the father and friendly feeling toward the mother. This woman reacted violently against her father's treatment of her; and her choice of mate seemed to be in part an expression of that reaction. Involved also in the choice was some influence deriving from affectional relationships with the mother; particularly the relationship wherein the mother supported the girl in her conflicts with the father. There was a history of continuous strife between father and daughter. The mother played a role of mediator in father-daughter battles, and lent the daughter emotional and advisory support. The mother's qualities were brought home to the girl by their contrast with the father's distressing qualities. These qualities found helpful, supporting, and likeable in the mother—and which were markedly lacking in the father—were precisely those which the woman brought out in her description of her marriage partner.

Resemblance between mate and mother linked with satisfying mother-image and unsatisfying father-image. The woman may choose a mate resembling her mother rather than her father. One woman described how her mother had always made her the center of a great deal of "fuss" and attention; whereas as a child she had conceived of her father as a tyrant—someone who was always punishing her. In contrast to the mother his temper was bad, he was not understanding, he did not admire her nor make a great fuss over her. The marriage partner selected by this woman strongly resembled the mother in temperament. Furthermore it was very evident that the relationship existing between the woman and her marriage partner in some measure repeated the childhood relationship between the girl and her mother. Like the mother he made a great fuss over her, making her the center of a great deal of attention. Markedly contrasting with this was the woman's account of differences between husband and father: in temperament they were quite unlike each other; and whereas the husband was helpful, understanding, sympathetic, adoring, the father had never treated her in such fashion.

Reaction against both parents influencing choice. Antagonism and emotional reaction against both parents may be a factor influencing marital choice. One woman's husband appeared to be virtually a symbol of the woman's revolt against her parents. Although the girl's early childhood relationships with her parents seemed not to have been markedly unsatisfying, when she grew up she felt her relationships with them to be very unsatisfying. Her description of both parents was replete with signs of dissatisfaction, antagonism, revolt, and bitterness. They are pictured as having restricted and confined her. The things she wanted as she grew to adulthood were "reactions against what I've been brought up with." Her husband was clearly symbolic of adult standards of values and aims, and those values and aims were strictly at variance with those represented by her parents. She herself made articulate the linkage between parent-images and mate-images: "I think the kind of person he is is sort of a symbol of everything that's just opposite to them." He represented to the woman release from the world of her parents.

The above brief synopses of types of parent-image influence should serve to give some indication of the great wealth of concrete human contexts within which it can be said that parent-images affect selection of a marriage partner. They suggest, too, how childhood affectional experiences with parents are linked with adult love choices.

Four · Cupid Is My Business

CLARA LANE
Director, Friendship Centers

A contrasting approach to the subject of mate selection follows. The director of a marriage introduction service has reached conclusions through her business experience that agree with research findings of family sociologists.*

I HAVE been told that I have one of America's strangest large business enterprises. Sometimes I'm called a "marriage broker," though I don't like the expression. What I do is introduce people who are interested in making enduring friendships that lead to marriage.

I must confess that I still view my business as a fantastic phenomenon. As I see it, I'm simply filling a void created by the fact that America has drifted away from the kind of community life enjoyed when I was a farm girl living near Davenport, Iowa. Then, I knew every boy in the county. Today, millions of American girls don't even know the boy next door.

Our bulging cities today are teeming with lonely, rootless people.

* Reprinted from *The American Magazine*, 1949, 30–31, 140–141, by permission of the author and *The American Magazine*.

And hundreds of our smaller towns are filled with transients, commuters, and migrant newcomers. We have become a nation of strangers.

Where can eligible men and girls, including our millions of divorcees and widows, meet their future mates, if they live in places where there is little community spirit? The extroverts can meet in taverns and ballrooms. But what about the quiet, reserved ones? Until our society faces up to this critical new problem many will have to remain lonely, or muster their courage and come to someone like me. Last spring I introduced a man and a girl who, it developed, lived only three doors away from each other in Fairview, New Jersey. . . .

People try to appraise themselves in the best possible light. They crave to be known as "nice" people. Consider some of the appraisals women make of themselves: "I am considered a fine-looking woman." Or "They tell me I am not bad to look at."

And of course no woman likes to feel that she *looks* as old as she is. Here are three comments from this week's mail: "I am 56 years old—but don't show my age." "I am 48 years *young*." Or from a girl who admitted to 38 years, "I am taken for about 30 years of age, or at most 33."

At the Center we have learned to refer to every feminine member under 60 as "a young lady." When we take a woman's vital statistics during an interview we mark down the age she gives us, and then in a great many cases circle the figure. The circle means: Probably 5 to 10 years older.

Men don't lie so much about their age, but still they are anxious not to be underestimated. One veteran made a point of telling me, "My character was rated Excellent by the Army." And another man informed me, "I haven't any money but I have character."

In pairing up people, whether they come in person or correspond, we try to apply the same principles of compatibility that leading marriage counselors endorse. We regard as nonsense the saying that "opposites attract," and we don't encourage Cinderella notions among our members. A congenial marriage can be made only with basically congenial people. The closer they are alike in intelligence, cultural and economic backgrounds, outlook on life, recreational enthusiasms, and religious beliefs the more likely it is that their union can endure.

One of our headaches in pairing is that people think they know exactly what they want, but actually don't. A girl told us she wanted a tall, lean man greying at the temples, but she passed up three who matched that description and married a short, bald-headed man who was thoughtful, cheerful, and who enjoyed going to concerts with her. She had forgotten to mention her passion for music, and music lovers are the toughest to match.

Frankly, I agree with the marriage authorities that romantic love has been badly overrated in America. Nonsense about sentimental romance has tended to make us lose sight of the real, basic pillars required in building a happy marriage.

What are these pillars? First, I believe the two people must feel a deep *need* for each other. Second, they must *respect* each other as persons. Third, they must have congenial tastes so that they can achieve a lasting *companionship*. Finally, they must be *determined* to make their marriage work. If they have these four pillars to build on, then love is almost bound to flourish.

Five · The Family and Romantic Love

ANDREW G. TRUXAL
Sociologist, Hood College

FRANCIS E. MERRILL
Sociologist, Dartmouth College

For some years sociologists have been critical of the emphasis upon romantic love as a basis for stable marriage in America. The following selection * is representative of those who take this point of view.

ROMANTIC love has been defined as "that complex of attitudes and sentiments which regards the marriage relation as one exclusively of response. This romantic attitude pictures the marriage relationship in terms of love—sexual attraction in large part—and sets up a standard according to which marriage is measured by the satisfaction of a highly idealized desire for response." Rich and poor, young and old, boys and girls from all walks of life are exposed to this cluster of beliefs from the time they are able to walk. Their hope of an exciting and romantic marriage is one of the few bright spots in a life bordered by the kitchen, the factory, the office, and the grave. They enter the delightful period of courtship and the long and serious business of marriage with their eyes covered by the rose-colored glasses of romance.

The group of expectations making up romantic love has been further characterized by Folsom in terms of the following beliefs: "(1) that in marriage will be found the only true happiness, (2) that affinities are ideal love relations, (3) that each may find an

* Reprinted from *The Family in American Culture,* by Andrew G. Truxal and Francis E. Merrill. New York: Prentice-Hall, Inc., 1947, pp. 121–130, by permission of the publisher.

ideal mate, (4) that there is only one, and (5) this one will be immediately recognized when met . . ." This culture complex has been further defined in broader terms as comprising: "(1) individual freedom and social irresponsibility in choice of partner . . . ; (2) exclusive devotion to the one love partner; (3) the man's preparedness to seize and take the woman . . . ; (4) the honoring of love . . . ; (5) idealization, aesthetic appreciation, and worship . . . of woman by man; (6) adventure and braving of dangers in the process of courtship; (7) aesthetic and dramatic settings for courtship."

Romantic love may be further defined in stark functional terms. Romantic love is what it does. It is recognized as the "only valid basis for marriage." In Middletown, and everywhere else in the United States, young people discover their partners in marriage by the informal process of "falling in love." "Middletown adults," remark the Lynds, "appear to regard romance in marriage as something which, like their religion, must be believed in to hold society together. Girls are assured by their elders that 'love' is an unanalyzable mystery that 'just happens.' 'You'll know when the right one comes along,' they are told with a knowing smile." This acceptance of the inevitability and necessity of falling in love before marriage is the essence of romantic love. The very fact that it is not questioned places romance in the category of the mores. Men and women do not question the eternal verities of their social order.

Marriage and romantic love are considered as inextricably intermingled. The success or failure of a marriage is measured by the presence and continuance of this form of attachment. The fallacy that clings to this conception rests in the belief that the romantic relationship of lover and sweetheart can continue unchanged after marriage. As a noted psychiatrist remarks, "Romance lasting for many years is only imaginable in Utopia. . . . No person can remain in the grip of a strange fascination for a long time. . . . Romance is a nine-day wonder." The difficulty often arises from the failure to understand and allow for the inevitability of this change and the accompanying belief that the cooling of romance signals the failure of marriage. Under the spell of romantic love, men and women fail to realize that happiness in marriage is not a fortuitous and delightful event but a long and gradual process, involving many complex readjustments of two persons to each other.

Romantic love in the American family is the result of a long and complicated social development. Philosophy, literature, economic relationships, religion, morality, and popular belief have all played their part in the development of the group expectations comprising the romantic pattern. When we examine these component parts and realize their long cultural development, it becomes clear that John Jones and Mary Smith would never fall romantically in love if they were, since birth, the sole inhabitants of a desert island. When

Mary sighs that her greatest ambition is to meet and to marry the man of her dreams, she is acting in terms of a long social tradition, whether she realizes it or not. Her conceptions of romance, marriage, and family relationships are a logical outgrowth of this tradition.

Personal satisfaction in the family is an important element in any culture. It is naturally not a matter of complete indifference to the French peasant or the Chinese merchant whom he shall marry, but it is seldom of such all-consuming importance as it is with us. In the majority of societies, primitive and civilized alike, the family is so closely linked with the other institutions that it continues intact even if the husband and wife are not romantically in love with each other. In America, on the other hand, love is not a luxury but a necessity. Without love, the marriage is seriously weakened. As Jessie Bernard points out, "We have to be concerned about love because we depend upon it to a large extent for marriage and family stability; it is all part of the emphasis upon individuality that is one of the most characteristic traits of our culture." Viewed in this light, it is true that we cannot get along without love. We need it in our family business.

The preservation of the human species squarely depends upon the sex urge. In the analysis of romantic behavior, this biological fact is taken for granted. It is grist for our mill.

But when we have admitted the presence of these biological factors, we have not answered the question of romantic love. Actually, we have only begun it. We have not explained why John Smith and Mary Jones fall in love at first sight and vow to marry and live happily ever after, why they believe there is no other possible mate for them, why they save theater stubs and dance programs as symbols of their courtship days, why they disregard the advice of their parents and marry someone of another religion, nationality group, or social class—why they do these and a hundred other things. The instinctive explanation is completely insufficient to explain such behavior. Some other explanation must be advanced, one based upon culture and human nature. "We love," says Waller in this connection, ". . . in accordance with the culture in which we have formed our sentiments." Romantic love is clearly not instinctive. The instinctive basis of the sex urge has become so overlaid with culture accumulations by the time the individual has reached adolescence that the one cannot be distinguished from the other.

The social relationships between the sexes which form the basis of romantic love are the result of thousands of years of refinement, during which many of the contemporary expectations slowly evolved. Romantic lovers believe that men and women who are sexually attracted to one another are "naturally" kind and solicitous, anxious to devote their best efforts to their mutual welfare, and have no other purpose than the safety and comfort of the children brought into the world through their sexual collaboration. Sexual lovers are thought to be selfless toward one another, uniting in their passion all the generosity and affection which are accepted as the traditional roles of husband and wife in our culture.

This assumption is scientifically unfounded. The "natural" manifestations of the sex drive in human beings, stripped to their most elemental terms, are anything but tender, loving, and solicitous. Sex is selfish. The individual who uses another purely as a sexual vehicle is interested only in the release of his own tensions, rarely in the happiness of the other. In conduct determined largely by the sexual impulse, the sex object is considered a means to an end, rather than an end in itself. The personal feelings of the mistress whose appeal is primarily sexual are not considered as important as those of a romantic sweetheart. The presence of the sexual object is welcome only at the time of desire, neither before nor after. Sexual desire is as self-centered as hunger or thirst.

ROMANCE AND REALITY

The average man or woman in America does not lead a particularly exciting life. Neither does the average man or woman in any other place. The daily routine of existence in any society, from the mountain Arapesh of New Guinea to the upland villager in Brooklyn Heights, has comparatively few high points. In an effort, deliberate or not, to compensate for the boredom of daily life, different peoples have evolved different means of relaxation and mass euphoria. The Australian primitive has his corroboree, the Roman citizen his Saturnalia, and the little man of the Third Reich had his party festivals. We have romantic love. The escape from reality on the part of other cultures has, for the most part, been an institutionalized affair, with prescribed rituals and ceremonies that give the individual something to look forward to, to relieve him temporarily of the routine of living .These people, "primitive" or "civilized," go periodically crazy together, as it were, augmenting their individual excitement by contact with other similarly excited persons under socially prescribed conditions. Festivals, games, dances, orgies, carnivals, and the like provide necessary release from the humdrum activities of daily living.

In characteristic fashion, Americans leave this release largely up to the individual to carry out as he sees fit, to find what personal satisfaction he can from the search for a romantic love affair. Aided and abetted though he is by the motion picture and other mechanisms of mass release, the individual must seek and find his salvation as an individual, rather than a member of a functioning group. Romance is a highly acceptable method of finding this release, in contrast to other methods that are not sanctioned by the mores. All of the conditions under which the individual falls in love and marries are socially prescribed, although the application is primarily individual. We seek our romance and establish our families as individuals, a procedure with both the faults and the virtues of our society.

In the normal peacetime routine, the possibility of a romantic love affair, to be followed by an equally romantic marriage, is the most exciting prospect on the proximate or ultimate horizon of the individual. He may actually experience such a romantic courtship and marriage, in which event he considers that life has treated him handsomely, as indeed it has. But if he does not actually have such an experience, he can have it vicariously, not once but any number of times. He can read a book or a magazine, hear a popular song on the radio, or go to a movie. Each time he has any of these experiences, he receives a certain romantic excitement, brought about by partially identifying himself with the hero of the novel, story, song, or motion picture. These substitute satisfactions for romantic marriage may not be the real thing, but they will do until the real thing comes along. For many people, these surrogates are the nearest to the real thing they ever get. Such persons may go through life lamenting that they have been deprived of the greatest satisfaction life can give them—a romantic marriage. They have been taught to hope for more than they can reasonably expect.

An observer of the American folkways, David L. Cohn, made this statement concerning our tendency to engage in romantic flights from reality: "A cardinal characteristic of immaturity is dread of reality; the fear or the inability to look facts in the face. It is this dread, on the one hand, and a false romanticism, on the other, which has caused us to surround marriage with a mawkish sentimentality." The belief that happy marriages are made in heaven, that each boy and girl has a preordained affinity, and that the discovery of this affinity will automatically result in perfect marital happiness is unreal in the sense that it ignores such prosaic factors as sheer physical propinquity in romantic love, not to mention other equally fortuitous and prosaic factors. If John and Mary did not happen to go to the same high school, work in the same store, office, or factory, or live on the same street, they would probably never meet and marry. Romance would never come to either of them, unless it is admitted that it could equally well have come with another person. Such a realistic admission, however, denies a fundamental of the romantic faith—namely, that there is only one ideal husband or wife for everyone and that if an individual does not find such a person the first time, he is in romantic duty bound to try again.

"The point is of course," continues our observer, "that compatibility is not the result of preordination, accident, or mysterious gift, but of design; and this is to conclude that the romantic concept of marriage is false and dangerous." It is false and dangerous, he believes, not in suggesting that an individual may be extremely happy with the husband or wife of his choice but rather in thinking that, if this happiness does not measure up to what we have been taught to expect, something is wrong with the marriage. The quiet pleasures of conjugal happiness are thus in a sense a denial of the romantic faith, which tells us that we should continue to burn with the same pure, gemlike flame for the rest of our lives as during the early weeks of marriage. Taking the other for granted in tranquil matrimony is, strictly speaking, against the romantic rules.

One · Marriage Adjustment and Engagement Adjustment

ERNEST W. BURGESS
Sociologist, University of Chicago

PAUL WALLIN
Sociologist, Stanford University

*Burgess and Wallin's study reported here * makes a significant contribution to attempts to establish methods of scientific prediction of marital adjustment. This study assumes that marriage is a continuation of an interpersonal relationship begun earlier and not radically altered by marriage. If the assumption is correct, adjustment during engagement is predictive of adjustment after marriage.*

THE subjects of this study of the relation between adjustment in engagement and marriage are 505 couples who participated in the research during their engagement and then again approximately three years after marriage. They are part of an original sample of a thousand engaged couples selected for a larger study of engagement and marriage.

While engaged, the couples filled out eight-page schedules which included a series of questions intended to evaluate their satisfaction with their engagement relationship. Separate schedules were used for each member of a couple, thus providing a separate measure of the engagement satisfaction of the man and the woman.

The schedules were distributed largely through sociology and psychology classes of colleges and universities in metropolitan Chicago. Students were asked to place the schedules with engaged persons of their acquaintance, an engaged person being defined as one who had a formal or informal understanding with a member of the opposite sex that they would marry at some future date.

To the best of our knowledge, the large majority of the schedules were answered independently by the members of the couples as requested and then mailed directly to the research project. Assurance was given of the confidential treatment of all information. Moreover, subjects had the option of answering schedules anon-

* Reprinted from *The American Journal of Sociology*, 1944, 49: 324–330 by permission of the authors and the University of Chicago Press.

ymously or signing their names (*a*) to indicate willingness to be interviewed or (*b*) to facilitate reaching them after marriage. Thirty-five per cent of the men and 39 per cent of the women chose to remain anonymous.

At the time of filling out the schedules, the members of the couples on the average had known each other 45.0 months, had been keeping company 31.5 months, and had been engaged 13.2 months. They were living in the Chicago metropolitan region and were almost entirely in the age range from twenty to thirty. Three-fourths of the young men and not quite two-thirds of their fiancées were at the college level of education, and the remainder were nearly all high-school graduates. Forty-nine per cent of the men were Protestants, 14 per cent were Catholic, 18 per cent were Jewish, and 13 per cent reported no religious affiliation. The corresponding percentages of the women were 54, 13, 18, and 8. They were all of the white race, approximately 60 per cent being the offspring of parents both of whom were native-born. The large majority of the subjects were from lower-middle-class and upper-middle-class families, and their fathers were primarily in business or the professions.

Two methods were employed for keeping in touch with the couples to obtain their co-operation in the follow-up marriage phase of the study. The majority gave their names and addresses through which they could be reached some years after marriage. But for these couples as well as for the others who wished to remain anonymous, a second method of maintaining contact was used. All persons who distributed schedules to couples were asked to fill out forms containing (1) their own names and addresses through which they could be reached in the future, (2) the code number listed on each schedule they distributed, and (3) some identifying sign (nicknames, initials, etc.) for each couple to whom schedules were given—a sign which would enable the distributors to remember to whom they had given the schedules. At the time of the follow-up marriage study, letters were sent to the schedule distributors, requesting them to ask the consent of the anonymous couples to having their names given to the research project for the follow-up study. Permission to do this was secured from almost all the anonymous couples.

The marriage schedules were filled out under supervision. This was considered essential, first, to eliminate the possibility of collaboration between husbands and wives and, second, to encourage frankness in the subjects, since the conditions under which they filled out the schedules protected them from the contingency of being asked to show their spouses what they had written. In most instances couples worked on their schedules as members of groups, the husbands and wives being in separate rooms. When completed, the schedules were given directly to the supervisor. When couples were not in groups, they answered the schedules either at home or in the project office but always in the presence of a supervisor to whom the schedules were given on completion.

The marriage schedules were eighteen pages in length and, like those used in the engagement period, included a series of questions the answers to which provided a measure of each subject's satisfaction with his or her marital relationship. The schedules were filled out by the couples after approximately three or four years of marriage. The data presented below consequently constitute a study of the relation between adjustment in engagement and adjustment after three years of marriage.

ADJUSTMENT IN ENGAGEMENT

The questions used for appraising adjustment in engagement and the scores assigned to various possible responses to the questions were as follows:

1. In leisure time do you prefer to: be "on the go" all or most of the time (M 3, W 3),[1] stay at home all or most of the time (M 10, W 10); fifty-fifty reply or equivalent (M 5, W 5); emphasis on stay at home (M 7, W 7); man and woman differ (M 4, W 4).

2. Do you and your fiancé(e) engage in interests and activities together? All of them (M 10, W 10); most of them (M 6, W 6); some of them (M 2, W 3); few or none (M 0, W 0).

3. Do you confide in your fiancé(e)? About everything (M 5, W 5); about most things (M 2, W 4); about some things M 0, W 2); all other replies (M 0, W 0).

4. Does your fiancé(e) confide in you? About everything (M 5, W 5); about most things (M 3, W 3); about some things (M 0, W 2); all other replies (M 0, W 0).

5. Frequency of demonstration of affection shown fiancé(e). Practically all the time (M 10, W 10); very frequent (M 8, W 8); occasionally (M 2, W 3); all other replies (M 0, W 0).

6. Are you satisfied with the amount of demonstration of affection? Responses of a couple were here scored as a combination. Both satisfied (7); one satisfied, other desires more (3); one satisfied, other desires less (2); both desire more (4); one desires less, other more (1); both desire less (0).

7. Extent of agreement between couple on money matters, matters of recreation, religious matters, demonstrations of affection, friends, table manners, matters of conventionality, philosophy of life, ways of dealing with their families, arrangement for their marriage, dates with each other. Extent of agreement on each of these eleven issues was indicated by a check on a scale ranging from "always agree" to "always dis-

---

[1] The figures in parentheses are the scores for the various responses. The "M" score is that of the man, the "W" score is that of the woman.

agree." The scale points and their values for each item are: always agree (6); [2] almost always agree (4); occasionally disagree (3); frequently disagree (2); almost always disagree (1); always disagree (0). The total points on the above items were multiplied by 1.65 to give a total agreement score.

8. Do you ever wish you had not become engaged? Never (10); once (5); occasionally (1); frequently (0).

9. Have you ever contemplated breaking your engagement? Never (10); once (5); occasionally (1); frequently (0).

10. What things annoy you about your engagement? If "none" or its equivalent (10); one thing mentioned (7); two things (1); three or more (0); if "its length" only is mentioned as annoyance (9); if "being separated" is cited (8); "length" and "separation" (7); "length" and one other annoyance (6); "separation" and one other annoyance (5); two or more annoyances and "length" and/or "separation" (1); "length" and "separation" and one annoyance (3); question left unanswered (4).

11. What thing does your fiancé(e) do that you do not like? "None" written in (7); one thing mentioned (5); two (1); three or more (0); question left blank (4).

12. Has your steady relationship with your fiancé(e) ever been broken off temporarily? Never (10); once (5); twice (2); three or more times (0).

13. If you could, what things would you change in your fiancé(e)? (*a*) in physical condition or appearance; (*b*) in mental or temperamental or personality characteristics; (*c*) in ideas; (*d*) in personal habits; (*e*) in any other way.

14. If you could, what things would you change in yourself?

Questions 13 and 14 were treated as a unit in the scoring. If "no change" desired in self and fiancé(e), score given is 10; otherwise 2 points are deducted from 10 for each desired change mentioned, five or more changes getting a 0 score. If both questions are left unanswered, the score is 5; if either is left blank, 2 points are deducted from a total of 7 for each change mentioned.

These questions and the scores given the various possible responses are roughly similar to those of the Burgess-Cottrell marriage adjustment scale, from which they were adapted. The questions making up the latter were used because they appeared equally relevant for measuring adjustment in engagement. The corresponding scores were employed as a matter of convenience, since arbitrary or more rigorously derived weights would in all likelihood have yielded similar results.

Having formulated the questions for the engagement adjustment inventory and having determined upon the scores, it was possible to examine the responses of the couples, to score and total them,

---

[2] On this and all following questions men and women were scored identically.

and thus to obtain a numerical measure of the adjustment of each of the men and women. The adjustment scores of the 505 couples of this study and the 1,000 couples of the more inclusive study referred to above are quite similar and in both there is little divergence between the score distribution of the men and women. In all four distributions there is an evident skewness in the direction of the higher adjustment scores indicative of good adjustment. In some part, this probably can be attributed to the fact that good adjustment was a selective factor making for participation in the study. Another factor which may contribute to the skewness is the reluctance of certain persons to admit explicitly—even to themselves —that they have become implicated in an unpleasant or unsatisfactory engagement relationship.

An interesting question may be raised as to the degree of correspondence between the adjustment of the men and women of the couples in the engagement period. This was determined by correlating the adjustment scores of the men and women. The association found for the 1,000 and the 505 couples was, respectively, .57 ± .02 and .53 ± .03. This association is less marked than might have been expected. It indicates that the satisfaction with the engagement of one member of a couple does not insure the satisfaction of the other; that one may be satisfied and regard the relationship favorably while the other is dissatisfied.

Two important questions in regard to the measures of engagement adjustment are: (1) How valid are they, that is, do they discriminate between the well and poorly adjusted engaged couples? and (2) How reliable are they, that is, do persons repeating the test after a lapse of time tend to get approximately the same scores? The data available in this study indicate affirmative answers to both questions.

The validity of the measures was investigated by comparing the scores obtained by 123 couples who severed their engagements with those of 877 couples who continued to marriage. It was anticipated that if the engagement adjustment scale possesses any validity, persons who broke their engagement would generally have lower adjustment scores than those who did not. This expectation was borne out.

In the case of both the men and the women, a larger proportion of those from broken engagements fall in the low adjustment score groupings and a smaller proportion are found in the high groupings. Of the men who broke their engagements, 14.6 per cent have scores of 119 or under, as compared with 5.7 of those whose engagement was unbroken. The corresponding percentages for the women are 17.1 and 5.8. On the other hand, only 28.5 per cent of the men and 21.9 per cent of the women from broken engagements have scores of 160 or over in contrast to 38.3 and 39.7 per cent of the men and women who were members of unsevered relationships.

Finally, the mean adjustment scores of men from broken and non-broken engagements were 146.4 and 153.1, respectively. The means for the women were 144.2 and 153.2. These findings on the difference in adjustment scores of the two types of engaged persons indicate that the measure of adjustment differentiates with appreciable accuracy between the extremes of adjustment in engagement. In future studies, however, it would be desirable to make a more refined test of its validity.

The reliability of the engagement adjustment scale was studied by having 81 couples fill out an abbreviated schedule containing the adjustment questions some time after they had answered the original schedule.[3] Adjustment scores calculated from the former were correlated with those of the latter, yielding a coefficient of .75 ± .05 for the men and .71 ± .06 for the women. This indicates a satisfactory degree of reliability for the adjustment scale.

ADJUSTMENT IN MARRIAGE

The marriage adjustment of the subjects was measured by the questions comprising the Burgess-Cottrell scale. Since the questions and their weights are reported in full elsewhere, they will not be given here. Discussion of the validity and reliability of the marriage adjustment measures is also omitted because they are considered in detail elsewhere. Suffice it to say that the marital adjustment scale was found reliable and valid enough to warrant its being used in studies of marriage adjustment.

The subjects of this report answered the marriage schedule after approximately three years of marriage. Their replies to the adjustment questions were scored, and their total scores are shown in Table 1. These scores, like the engagement scores, are skewed in the direction of good adjustment. Such a positively skewed distribution has been found in other studies of marital adjustment. Four possible explanations of this phenomenon are: (1) there may be a selection in marriage studies of the more happily married or better-adjusted couples; (2) a large proportion of the more poorly adjusted couples do not proceed to marriage; (3) couples who are separated or divorced may not be included in this study; and (4) admission of failure in marriage in our society is difficult because of the cultural emphasis on success, and hence persons may consciously or unconsciously judge their marriages as more successful than they are.

The marriage adjustment scores further parallel the engagement scores in that they, too, reveal a marked degree of independence between the adjustment of the members of couples. The correlation between the marital success scores of the husbands and wives is

[3] The mean interval between the time of the first and second schedules was 7.5 months for the men and 6.8 months for the women.

.41 ± .04. This is somewhat lower than the correlation of .59 ascertained by Terman for his 792 couples.

TABLE 1. MARRIAGE ADJUSTMENT SCORES OF 505 COUPLES

ADJUSTMENT SCORE	MEN		WOMEN	
	No.	Per Cent	No.	Per Cent
180–189	90	17.8	92	18.2
170–179	101	20.0	128	25.3
160–169	101	20.0	107	21.2
150–159	71	14.1	70	13.9
140–149	61	12.1	45	8.9
130–139	38	7.5	32	6.3
120–129	24	4.7	15	3.0
110–119	10	2.0	10	2.0
100–109	5	1.0	2	0.4
90– 99	4	0.8	4	0.8
Total	505	100.0	505	100.0

RELATION OF ADJUSTMENT IN ENGAGEMENT
TO ADJUSTMENT IN MARRIAGE

Having secured a measure of the adjustment of the subjects in engagement and marriage, it was possible to test the hypothesis that the former is positively associated with the latter and that, therefore, it can serve for purposes of predicting marital success or failure. The engagement and marriage scores were correlated and yielded correlations of .43 ± .04 and .41 ± .04 for the men and women, respectively. These correlations are consistent with the hypothesis being tested and indicate the utility of measures of adjustment in engagement for forecasting adjustment in marriage. Although the correlations with marital adjustment are not high, they compare favorably with those for background and personality factors obtained in the Burgess-Cottrell and Terman studies. It seems probable that efficiency in prediction may be increased by the combined use of engagement adjustment scores with background and personality scores in the prediction of marital success.

Two · Personality and Marriage Adjustment

ROBERT F. WINCH
Sociologist, Northwestern University

The following article * provides partial evidence to support the view that personality factors determine aptitude for marriage.

IN 1938 Professor Terman and his associates, of Stanford University, published a report of their research on marriage, which showed a highly significant association between responses of a "neurotic" order to various personality tests and low rating on their index of "marital happiness." [1] The personality tests used were the Benreuter Personality Inventory, the Strong Interest Test, and a test of opinions regarding the ideal marriage. Terman's scale of

* Reprinted from *The American Journal of Sociology*, 1941, 46: 686–693, by permission of the author and the University of Chicago Press.

[1] Lewis M. Terman *et al.*, *Psychological Factors in Marital Happiness* (New York: McGraw-Hill Book Co., Inc., 1938), p. 360. Correlations of marital happiness with personality scales were as follows:

Variables	Husbands (N = 200)	Wives (N = 200)
Bernreuter (Bn.)	.38	.42
Strong items (St.)	.36	.35
Opinion items (O.)	.22	.22
Personality total (multiple of Bn. + St. + O.)	• .47	.46

"The Bernreuter inventory yields scores for neurotic tendency, self-sufficiency, introversion, and dominance. These four measures really reduce to three, since it has been found that the traits designated as neurotic tendency and introversion are practically identical. The Strong Interest Test can be scored so as to differentiate the interest patterns characteristic of people in some thirty-five different occupations. Many of these patterns, however, are very similar; and in this study we scored the test for only seven occupations, each selected as best representing a particular constellation of interests. In addition, the Strong test yields a measure of interest maturity and another of masculinity-femininity of interests" (Terman *et al.*, *op. cit.*, p. 17).

Thirty-four items "call for expressions of opinion about the ideal marriage. Each of these deals with a separate aspect of marriage and requires the respondent to give a rated judgment as to the desirability or undesirability of the factor indicated" (*ibid.*, p. 36).

marital happiness [2] was practically the same as that used by Professors Burgess and Cottrell; and, although Terman did not use any other criterion of validity than internal consistency, Burgess and Cottrell validated their procedures in samples of their total number of cases by obtaining ratings on the happiness of marriages from outsiders acquainted with the subjects and by having judges rate the happiness of marriages after reading the case materials.

The Terman study did not include two or more temporally separated observations on the same subjects which would have provided some evidence regarding the relative temporal sequence of personality factors and marital adjustment. Despite the absence of this type of evidence Terman proceeded on the basis of his findings to impute primary causal significance to the personality factors and to interpret marital happiness as resultant. Terman and his associates have been severely criticized for this rashness by H. L. Hollingworth, who asserts that, because of the tendency for well-adjusted spouses to respond favorably on personality and other tests and for poorly adjusted to do the opposite (the "halo" effect of marriage), it is impossible to infer the direction of causation on the basis of Terman's evidence.

At this point in the development of marriage research it was of considerable interest to undertake a study which would supply some evidence to affirm or negate the opinion that personality factors are, roughly speaking, causes rather than effects of the type or degree of marital adjustment. Following the Burgess-Cottrell study, Professor Burgess and Paul Wallin undertook a study having a body of evidence on engaged couples to be followed up by further observations on the same couples after a period of three years of marital experience. The items in the marital-adjustment scale of the Burgess-Cottrell study were adapted so as to serve as an index of adjustment in engagement. Included in this study was an abridged personality test of the forty-two items from the Thurstone Schedule which were found by the Thurstones to differentiate most reliably neurotic from nonneurotic subjects. It was possible then to relate the "neurotic" scores of engaged individuals to their scores on the adjustment-in-engagement index.

This paper presents the results of the writer's attempt to relate the scores of engaged couples on personality questions to the men's scores on the adjustment-in-engagement index in the Burgess-

[2] This scale was based on questions relating to congeniality of tastes and interests; the spouses' ability to agree, their expressions of satisfaction with mate and marriage, general estimates of their marital happiness, and the enumeration of complaints and frictions. These items which were regarded by Terman on the basis of his judgment and experience as indicators of marital happiness were scored by him in a manner somewhat different from the procedure followed by Burgess and Cottrell. Cf. E. W. Burgess and L. S. Cottrell, Jr., *Predicting Success or Failure in Marriage* (New York: Prentice-Hall, Inc., 1939).

Wallin study. The purpose of the study was to introduce one of the missing links in the chain of evidence needed to ascertain whether or not we may impute causal significance to personality factors in relation to marital adjustment or "happiness." If approximately the same association should be found to exist between personality-test responses and adjustment in *engagement* as was found in Terman's study between personality items and *marital* adjustment, then it follows that marriage per se (the "halo" effect) is not responsible for the results of the personality tests. Obviously, however, this procedure would not rule out of consideration the possible influence of a "halo" effect of engagement upon the responses of the engaged couple.

Using the engagement data of the Burgess-Wallin research, the writer undertook an investigation to determine the relation between the adjustment-in-engagement scores of the men and the combined man-woman responses to the forty-two Thurstone items. The various permutations obviously are: man neurotic, woman nonneurotic; man nonneurotic, woman neurotic; both neurotic; and both nonneurotic. It should be borne in mind in discussing this study that the term "neurotic" is used to refer to one of two possible responses to a particular stimulus—in this case, a questionnaire item.

The procedure used may be briefly described as follows: The possible range of scores on the index of adjustment in engagement was from 0 to 194. After all schedules had been scored, the results of the various man-woman combinations on each neurotic question were compared with the resulting distributions of the men's mean adjustment scores. It was possible then to determine the significance of the difference between the mean adjustment scores within the various questions. The procedure used for obtaining a measure of the statistical significance of a difference between the mean adjustment scores was the familiar one of dividing the difference by the standard error of the difference. The limit of significance was arbitrarily selected as a critical ratio equal to or greater than 3.0. If any one of the six differences between the four means of any given question yielded a critical ratio of this magnitude, the question was regarded as "significant."

Using this criterion of significance it was found that twenty-eight of the forty-two questions yielded significant differences on the basis of the men's scores. The personality items found to be associated with poor adjustment were as follows. The poorly adjusted:

    1. Did not take responsibility for introducing people at parties
    2. Were troubled with shyness
    3. Did not make friends easily or quickly
    4. Did not feel that they were usually well dressed and made a good appearance
    5. Worried too long over humiliating experiences

   6. Worried over possible misfortunes
   7. Often felt lonesome even when with other people
   8. Often experienced periods of loneliness
   9. Lacked self-confidence
  10. Were troubled by feelings of inferiority
  11. Were troubled with ideas running through their heads
so that they had difficulty sleeping
  12. Daydreamed frequently
  13. Their interests changed quickly
  14. Their minds often wandered badly so that they lost
track of what they were doing
  15. Were bothered by a recurrence of useless thoughts
  16. Were hampered by an inability to arrive at decisions
  17. Considered themselves to be nervous
  18. Had spells of dizziness
  19. Were discouraged easily
  20. Were frequently burdened by a sense of remorse
  21. Were not usually in good spirits
  22. Had ups and downs in mood without apparent cause
  23. Their feelings were easily hurt
  24. Were not usually even tempered and happy in their outlook on life
  25. Could not stand criticism without feeling hurt
  26. Were touchy on various subjects
  27. Frequently felt grouchy
  28. Were not easily moved to tears

With respect to the last item above, the data indicate that a high
man's adjustment score is associated with that combination of responses in which the woman reports that she is *not* easily moved to
tears but the man reports that he *is* easily moved to tears—or, in
terms of our definition, the man-neurotic-woman-nonneurotic per-
mutation. Despite the fact that this question yielded a high critical
ratio, further study on the Burgess-Wallin investigation suggests
that this may have been a chance finding.

Another point of particular interest is that while the group in this
study showed a tendency for high adjustment in *engagement* to be
associated with a negative response to a question of worrying over
possible misfortunes, Professor Terman found in his study of *married* couples that the affirmative response to approximately the same
question was associated with high marital adjustment. One possible
interpretation of this difference is that the difference in the word-
ings of the question of the two studies might account for the variation in results. Terman's question was phrased "Are you the carefree
sort of person who doesn't worry over possible misfortunes before
they come?" while in this study it was "Do you worry over possible
misfortunes?" Professor Terman's interpretation of this seemingly
anomalous association was that the husbands who scored higher
in marital happiness were the husbands who were more concerned

over family fortunes, the husbands who assumed greater responsibility for the economic welfare of the family—those men, in short, who more closely approximated the cultural definition of the middle-class husband. Terman's finding may be reconciled with the evidence in this study as follows. Among the engaged men it was the better adjusted who stated that they did not worry over possible misfortunes. It may be inferred that the latter (engaged) group of men had not been subjected to situations in which they were forced to assume responsibilities, for obviously engagement does not involve responsibilities of the same type or magnitude that marriage does. A very small proportion of this group had been married previously, and consequently most of them had had only their own welfares to look out for as of the time they filled in the schedules.

More recently an analysis was made by Miss Frieda Brim, recently a research assistant to Professor Burgess, of approximately the same set of data. Miss Brim's data and procedure differed from those in my study in the following respects:

1. There was a small change in the total sample.
2. There was a change in the procedure for scoring neurotic and nonneurotic responses.
3. A modification was introduced in the basis of computation of the adjustment scores.
4. She used as the limit of significance a critical ratio of 2.5 rather than 3.0. (This more liberal criterion of significance increases the theoretical probability of chance variation from less than 3 out of 1,000 to a little more than 1 out of 100.)
5. Analysis was made of the responses to personality items with respect to the women's as well as to the men's adjustment scores.

Except for the last difference in procedure, which extends the scope of the study, these changes were of a very minor order; and in general her findings, with respect both to the men's and to the women's adjustment scores, were very similar to those in my study. That is, save for some exceptions to be noted below, the same personality items as reported above were found by her to be significantly associated with adjustment in engagement of both men and women subjects.

The following differences were revealed:

1. As noted before, the question "Is it difficult to move you to tears?" did not prove significant in her analysis either with respect to the men's or with respect to the women's adjustment scores.
2. Additional significant items found by her different procedure and lower limit of significance were as follows:

a) The more poorly adjusted men gave a significantly greater proportion of affirmative responses to the following items:
  (1) Being bothered by having people watch them at work
  (2) Being depressed over low marks in school
  (3) Frequently feeling states of excitement
  (4) Frequently feeling miserable
  (5) Feeling self-conscious in the presence of superiors

b) The more poorly adjusted women gave a significantly greater proportion of affirmative responses to the following items:
  (1) Frequently experiencing stage fright
  (2) Being troubled if watched at work
  (3) Frequently feeling miserable
  (4) Being self-conscious in the presence of superiors
  (5) Feeling a compulsion to do things over
  (6) Lacking self-confidence about their abilities

It must be noted that at this point we have still not actually demonstrated the causal function of personality factors in determining adjustment in engagement. Although it is still possible that the engagement itself may determine the response on personality items, common-sense judgment and evidence from case materials lend plausibility to the opinion that the personality factors are the pre-existing, and in that sense causal, factors.

We have shown, to be sure, that some personality responses of the type found by Terman to be associated with marital happiness are similarly associated with adjustment in engagement and hence are not the result of the marital situation. Upon the basis of this evidence it appears that Professor Terman was correct, if not logically justified, in imputing causal significance to the personality correlates of marital happiness. Before it can be shown rigorously that the responses of this type of personality test are associated with a personality organization which determines the degree of happiness and adjustment in engagement and in marriage, it will be necessary to institute a study composed of subjects before they have established with their future spouses deep attachments or the kind of relationships which are the equivalent of engagement. If, however, the interest is in predicting marital adjustment from personality factors as revealed in the engagement period, the question of causal analysis is immaterial, in view of the fact that the establishing of correlations is sufficient.

The general pattern revealed by the significant personality questions in these studies and in Terman's is one of association with marital unhappiness of a personality characterized by a sort of over-reactive touchiness and a sense of inferiority. From Professor Burgess' case materials it seems evident that through the medium of these crude personality tests it is possible to touch upon, or get a clue to, a much deeper psychological constitution. The manner of the genesis of this psychological constitution is still an open question. Professor Terman calls it "temperament," which he apparently regards as a personality organization which is fixed at birth. An equally plausible hypothesis is that this psychological constitution is a product, in part at least, of the early childhood situation and that the childhood situation, therefore, plays a very important part in the achievement of compatibility and happiness in engagement and in marriage.

Three • *A Study of 738 Elopements*

PAUL POPENOE
Director, American Institute
of Family Relations

*Why do people elope? What are the prospects for success in marriages that begin with an elopement? Seeking the answers to these questions, a marriage counselor studied the case histories of a large number of elopements, and reached the conclusions which follow.**

ELOPEMENT has received more attention in drama and fiction than in social science. To throw more light on the facts, I asked students in four classes on "The biology of family relations" at University College, University of Southern California, to collect data on elopements in the educated part of the white American population,—this restriction being intended to get at least a minimum of homogeneity. More than 100 students contributed these case histories; all of them were adults and most of them teachers or social workers.

At first sight the histories show such diverse motivation that one doubts how far a common classification as "elopements" is justified. Reference to the dictionaries, however, reveals that this diversity has always been recognized in the definition and that it is impossible to draw any definite lines between runaway marriages, secret marriages, sudden and impulsive weddings, and similar affairs. They have in common a lack of advance publicity, the purpose of which is usually to evade anticipated objections of one sort or another. Less than one-half of the marriages in this group are of the "classical" type in which the lover carries off the girl clandestinely

* Reprinted from the *American Sociological Review*, 1938, 3:1–4, by permission of the author and the *American Sociological Review*.

from the home of her parents, because the latter object to the marriage.

Further analysis of the histories showed that it was fairly easy to divide them into five groups, according to motivation.

PARENTAL OBJECTIONS

Even within this group there are many different types. In some instances the parents objected to the suitor in question, in others they objected to any marriage, being determined to keep the daughter unmarried, either from "sentimental" reasons or because they wanted her earnings. Sometimes the man might face the same difficulty. Miss A was a teacher, 30 years old, supporting her mother, married sister, and a niece. She had a number of brothers and sisters who could have shared this burden, but they were an enthusiastic unit in giving her the job and opposing any idea of marriage on her part. Her fiancé was in somewhat the same situation; whenever he spoke of marriage his mother would have a tantrum which kept her in bed for a week. They decided not to be living sacrifices any longer. An elopement was the obvious thing, and they have been happy ever since.

Perhaps the parents do not object to marriage "in principle," but feel that the girl should wait until she finishes college, or until she is older. When she marries without their consent, they may make a virtue of necessity with the traditional, "Bless you, my children"; but not always; in one instance they are still unreconciled after 25 years. A study of these histories does not throw the most favorable light on parents, even in the best educated strata of society. In a number of instances where a marriage failed, it is apparent that the parents caused its failure and that with a little co-operation from them it would have succeeded.

In a number of instances the parents were determined that their daughters go to college. The daughters, after finishing high school, preferred to wed; and in order to avoid a "scene" and conflict, presented the parents with an accomplished fact. Sometimes the situation is complicated by different sets of mores; the parents were born "in the old country" and take for granted their right to decide the children's matrimonial movements; the children are sufficiently Americanized to insist on deciding for themselves.

Frequently the trouble grows out of the parents' insistence that their daughter must have a "career." Perhaps they keep all young men away from the house; they do not want to risk having romance interfere with their determination. In this event the elopement may be largely an attempt to escape from parental domination, and may turn out badly, since the girl has had no chance to become acquainted with men and her own emotional nature; her range of acquaintance is extremely restricted; and her choice, based largely on desperation, may be an unwise one. In one such case the mother, taking no chances, went to college with her daughter and they were roommates for three years. During that time Julia's behavior was so exemplary that mama thought Julia could safely be left alone, her habits having been formed along correct lines. Mama had scarcely left town when Julia met a young man who persuaded her, on less than a week's acquaintance, to abandon music in his favor. He was as little prepared for marriage as she was, educationally, economically, and emotionally. The result was a tragedy.

A study of the marriages against parental opposition leaves, on the whole, a rather pessimistic picture of parental stubbornness, possessiveness, and selfishness,—in particular, of those traits in mothers. It lends support to the gloomy conclusions of Cottrell, that in case of difference of opinion between parents about the desirability of a marriage, young people will be safer in following the advice of father rather than that of mother; but that the happiest marriages are those in which all the parents on both sides are dead!

Of this group of marriages, a little less than half turned out to be definitely successful. It is hard to compare this with any norm, since conditions differ so widely. If they were all in Los Angeles county the showing would be good enough, for nearly half of all marriages in this county end in the divorce court. But they are not even confined to California (where one marriage out of every three is terminated by divorce); they are to a large extent representative of conditions throughout the United States. Perhaps the best available norm would be the findings in unselected marriages from the educated, white, American population, which were tabulated by other students in my classes for a different purpose, and which showed 58 percent to be happy. These were marriages, however, that had been in existence for at least five years, hence some unhappy ones had already disappeared from the group by divorce within five years from the date of marriage. The true figure would be considerably less and might justify the conclusion that the record of happiness in elopements of this group is not more than ten percent lower than the average.

AVOIDANCE OR ACQUISITION OF PUBLICITY

This group includes many school teachers who would have been discharged (in accordance with the traditions of medieval monasticism) if the fact of their marriage had become known. They wanted at least to finish the school year. Fortunately, a more intelligent attitude toward the marriage of women is slowly making its way among Boards of Education.

Somewhat similar was the motivation of two high school students, who knew that the rules made expulsion automatic on marriage. They married secretly in a neighboring state and did not

announce the fact until after the registrar had issued the grades in
June.

Occasionally the reason for avoiding publicity is that one of the
parties has been recently divorced, or the subject of some scandal,
and they prefer not to attract attention. Miss D, socially prominent,
was united to a man whom she really knew very slightly; the lavish
church wedding was the talk of the town's social circles for some
weeks. Within a few months, however, she discovered that her new
husband was insane and had the marriage annulled. She shortly
found another mate but shrank from the publicity attending another wedding and another set of invitations to innumerable friends
and acquaintances, another round of "showers" and teas, so soon
after the fiasco. They went off for a surprise marriage and after
nine years are very happy together.

Some elope to avoid publicity; others to acquire it! In the motion
picture circles of Hollywood, elopement to Yuma has almost become part of the mores. It makes a good publicity stunt,—sudden
departure of an airplane; arrival in Arizona; "I pronounce you man
and wife." The theory, probably correct because the local publicity
men know their business, is that the newspaper-reading public pays
more attention to such an event than to an ordinary wedding.

The fact that many of the elopers in this second group have
legitimate or even praiseworthy motive is reflected by the high percentage of success,—sixty percent.

ECONOMY

Many an elopement is due merely to a desire to avoid expense,
fuss, and the more or less infantile and asinine customs that so often
surround weddings. These, with sixty-three percent successful,
make the best showing of all.

In most instances the bride's parents are not in a position to provide an expensive wedding and the young people desire to save
them embarrassment or distress. Miss E's maiden aunt offered to
help out; she gave the girl a check for $500 and told her she could
keep everything above the actual cost of the wedding as a present.
The young people,—who, one suspects, were from Aberdeen,—conferred, and had a $5 elopement. Balance on hand, $495.

In the case of Miss F and her fiancé, on the other hand, the
scheme backfired. They had known each other for five years and
had been engaged for some time. The family planned an elaborate
and expensive ceremony. To avoid this, the young couple eloped.
When they returned and found how much this wedding meant to
the female relatives all around, they could not bring themselves to
break the news, so they went ahead and had a second ceremony,—
the main performance under the big tent, so to speak.

I have a number of histories in which the parents on both sides insisted on a big wedding but differed strongly as to how it should be held or who should be invited. The young people began to fear the life-long estrangement of the in-laws and cut the Gordian knot by eloping.

The "marriage of convenience" is a well-established institution; evidently there are also "elopements of convenience."

PREGNANCY

The forced marriage is also a well-known institution, and secrecy has the advantage of allowing the date to be misrepresented later. In this series, such marriages represent not merely the smallest group, but also the least successful.

In some instances, it was doubtless anticipated that the marriage would later be resolved by a divorce, the intention being primarily to protect the girl and her child from the stigma of illegitimacy. Under present social conditions, there are cases in which this solution of a difficult problem may be regarded as the least of evils.

There are several instances in which the bride-to-be became pregnant deliberately, as a means of trapping her man or perhaps taking him away from a competitor. So far as the record shows, there is in this group only one example of a type that is not rare,—that in which the girl merely pretends to be pregnant, in order to force a reluctant boy-friend into matrimony. In this case, when Mr. H. asked his friends to congratulate him on his surprise marriage they merely laughed at him, informing him that his bride had tried the same trick on half a dozen others, all of whom, however, were sophisticated or callous enough to refuse the bait. The couple divorced shortly; both later remarried unsuccessfully. A special study of "blackmail marriages" of this sort would be extremely interesting. Perhaps some of them turn out well, but all of which I have any knowledge have been failures, though some of them lasted for a lifetime.

MISCELLANEOUS

Most of the participants in this last group were either drunks, or thrill-seekers. One would not expect much from them, and the statistics show that they do not disappoint expectation. Several married on the impulse of the moment, merely to spite someone else. Fortunately, state laws requiring a few days' advance notice before a license is issued, are being more and more widely adopted and will largely do away with this particular type of matrimonial escapade.

Of the entire 738 marriages the happy ones had, at the time of report, lasted twice as long as the unhappy, the mean in the first case being 8.26 years and in the second 4.10 years. Among the happy marriages, 14 percent had occurred within 12 months prior to report. Undoubtedly some of these and other more recent marriages in the happy group may get into difficulties, thus reducing the percentage; but enough of the doubtfuls may eventually end in the happy group to offset, at least in part, this effect.

Of the unhappy marriages, 36 percent had lasted one year or less; most of these, however, were not recent marriages but marriages which had ended in divorce or annulment proceedings within a few weeks or months.

Great statistical accuracy cannot be expected of a study of this sort, in which each case is unique. It serves, however, to document the general knowledge that there are all sorts of reasons for eloping, some laudable and some despicable, and that the success of a marriage depends not so much on the nature of the ceremony as on the quality of the people who enter into it. On the whole, the success of the elopements, measured in terms of subsequent marital happiness, is greater than one might have anticipated.

VI · WEDDINGS

One · Of Weddings

FRANK HALLIDAY FERRIS
Clergyman, Mayville, New York

In America the wedding of any family member has come to be the most significant of family occasions. It serves as an opportunity for the two families involved to show themselves to the world most favorably. Methods used to achieve this end differ in different regions of the country and in different levels of society, but in almost all cases the aim, to put the family's best foot forward for the benefit of the public, is the same. Marriage announcements supplied for the newspapers by the family give information about the achievements of the bride, the groom, and the two families, whether the achievements are social, educational, or professional. If wealth is involved, that is also made known by such methods as the listing of residences, or the mention of exclusive schools attended, or the naming of wealthy or well-known relatives or ancestors. Many families of limited means feel it necessary to provide as splendid a wedding for their daughters as they can possibly finance, and at all levels of society there is a tendency at the time of the wedding toward making a display which is designed to fix in the minds of the world the impression that the bride's family at least is a family of solid worth and means. The number of attendants for the bride and the groom, the clothing worn, the number of guests invited, the size of the reception, and the place at which the reception is held, all are considered to be of greatest importance.

Though many of our wedding customs seem to have no sensible basis, the attachment of so much significance to the over-all combination of customs associated with weddings is based on the fact that society does have a stake in every wedding. The assumption is that each wedding is the permanent uniting of two family lines and the creation of a new family which will contribute successive generations to society. Theoretically, the wedding customs support monogamous marriage. Whether in fact the impressiveness of the wedding itself exerts any appreciable pressure toward the permanent stability of the marriage in present-day America is, of course, open to question.

133

*The selection below * is an illuminating evaluation of the wed-
ding as conducted in many parts of the United States.*

IN cynical moods I have sometimes felt that as officiat-
ing clergyman I was accomplice in—or, at least, accessory to—two
of the country's leading rackets: weddings and funerals. What
follows is based upon my observation during thirty years in the
Protestant ministry. With Roman Catholic and Jewish usage I am
less familiar.

Consider weddings. Consider how what is in essence a simple
ceremony can be built up into an elaborate, costly, and (to the
bride's mother, at least) nerve-racking ceremonial.

Preparations for a church wedding usually begin weeks and
months before the wedding day. If the bride is a church member,
she will usually want to be married in her own church. With her
mother, she interviews the minister or church secretary, who ac-
quaints her with the church's regulations concerning decorations,
the use of cameras, and the like, and reserves the use of the church
for her at the appointed time. If she is not affiliated with the
church, she frequently shops around. One of the experiences which
gives a minister a chance to develop the virtues of patience and
forbearance is to be visited by a mother and daughter who contemplate a wedding which will rate notice in the society columns and
are trying to find an appropriate site. He stands by while they discuss the pros and cons of what is to him a holy place where men
gather to engage in the highest act of which finite beings are capable—the attempt to link their lives with the infinite and eternal—
as a theater for staging a show. It seems to him a desecration. If
the decision goes against him and in favor of St. James'-across-the-
street with its wider center aisle and more spacious chancel, he is
able to conceal his disappointment.

Do not think me unsympathetic with family affection and family
pride. An indulgent father wants the daughter who is the apple of
his eye to have the handsomest wedding money can buy. The fond
mother wants her daughter to have the kind of wedding she would
like to have had, had her parents been up to it. Both look upon it
as an important and gala event in the family life, one to which they
want their daughter to be able to look back as a lovely memory.
But sometimes the wedding is also used as a symbol of worldly
success, an assertion of the fact that the family has arrived or an
attempt to climb a rung higher.

Of weddings from the standpoint of the couturier I cannot speak;
all I see is the splendid, eye-filling result as the wedding procession
moves slowly down the aisle. But an inkling of the couturier's point

* Reprinted from *Harper's Magazine*, 1945, 191, 496–499, by special permission of *Harper's* and the author.

of view came to me in a form letter which was mailed during the war to the ministers of my city by an association of the local bridal shops:

> To the Pastor:
> We are soliciting your co-operation in a matter that is of the utmost importance to our traditional marriages.
> Because of the rigid restriction, it has been very difficult to obtain Wedding Gowns and we know this condition will become more critical in the near future.
> About ninety per cent of the brides are marrying men in uniform and the servicemen and their brides express an intense desire for the ceremonial Wedding Gown and thereby express an attitude of religious reverence for the marriage ceremony. These feelings are stronger than in peace time.
> We feel that the disappearance of the white ceremonial Wedding Gown would detract from the dignity of religious wedding services and do injury to those who set great importance on its enduring associations in their memories.
> We would appreciate a letter from you expressing your opinion on the ceremonial Wedding Gown, so that we may present these letters from the Clergy to the proper authorities, who we feel will give great consideration to your judgment.
> Your co-operation will be greatly appreciated.

In certain cities, a new profession has arisen, that of wedding director. A wedding director is to a wedding what a funeral director is to a funeral. He takes all the details off the family's hands. He saves the harried and perhaps socially inexperienced mother from making mistakes. He places the order for the invitations and announcements and sees that the wording is in proper form. He "contacts" the society editors, providing them with photographs and data for publicity purposes. He arranges for the awning, the aisle cloth, policemen to keep the traffic moving, footmen to call the cars or park them. He engages the caterer for the reception, specifying the amount and kind of food and drink to be provided. He engages the florist and orders the decorations: the palms, the ferns, the altar piece, the bouquets for the bride and her attendants, the corsages for the mothers, the boutonnieres for the groom and best man. He engages the photographer and supervises the picture-taking. He places a microphone near the chancel to "pick up" the service for recording. He dispenses the proper gratuities to all who have lent a hand. He is a very useful factotum. It just isn't a man's job.

A big wedding is usually preceded by a series of parties, at which cocktails and champagne are in lavish profusion. The bride's home is full of friends who have gathered from near and far. The confusion and excitement are a bit wearing on the bride's mother, whose smile becomes glassy long before the last guest has departed.

The bride herself, instead of beginning her married life rested and composed, is tired and on edge, which is one reason why honeymoons are not always as blissful as they are supposed to be. (I am not making this up. I am reporting what has been told me in confidence.) Yet I must admit that the stamina of a twenty-year-old young woman fills a man of my age with envy; after a round of festivities which would land me in a sanitarium, she comes down the aisle with bright eyes (no longer, as of yore, demurely downcast) and a radiant smile.

Before the wedding comes the rehearsal. The wedding service itself is so simple as to require no rehearsal. The rehearsal is necessary to ensure proper timing and a symmetrical arrangement of the group after it reaches the chancel, and especially to impress the proper sequence upon the ushers: the seating of the guests, the seating of the mothers, the drawing of the ribbons, the removal of the upper layer of aisle cloth, the signal to the organist that all is ready for the trumpet notes which precede the sugary strains of the wedding march; then after the ceremony, the ushering out of the mothers, the removal of the ribbons, the dismissal of the congregation. Carefully instructed ushers are the key to a decorous and well-ordered wedding. If, as occasionally happens, the ushers come to the rehearsal a little high and inclined to regard the whole thing as a lark, almost anything can happen. At one large wedding, the ushers forgot to go for the mothers, who had to run down the side aisles and seat themselves after the wedding procession was under way.

The wedding is preceded by an organ recital and sometimes vocal music. Often the bride tells the organist what she wants played or sung. Usually these are compositions which have a sentimental association for her. The ones most frequently called for are Grieg's "Ich Liebe Dich," De Koven's "O Promise Me," "Cadman's "At Dawning," and Carrie Jacobs Bond's "I Love You Truly." These are romantic, not religious, music and when used as a prelude to an office of the church they violate the principle of unity of tone. Once our organist, an austere man, a devotee of Bach, came to me in great perturbation. The groom, it appeared, was a member of a certain learned society in tribute to which the bride requested that the organist play "The Sweetheart of Sigma Chi." "Do I have to play that?" he asked wrathfully. "No," I answered, "we've got to make a stand somewhere. It may as well be here."

It must be conceded that, as a bit of pageantry, a well executed church wedding is extremely effective. But it is difficult to avoid a Hollywood atmosphere. This can be heightened by playing with a rheostat so as to produce theatrical lighting effects and by the use of organ stops which produce what organists call "schmalz" and privately designate as "corny." Such a build-up is incongruous with the simple, deeply reverent character of the wedding ritual itself, as any sensitive person must perceive.

It is true that a wedding is not a personal matter only. Society has a stake in it. Its basic institution is the monogamous family. This is why it has thrown around marriage certain sanctions and taboos. In a day when divorce is increasing it is well that a wedding should be a serious if not a solemn occasion and that its social implications be made plain. But it is a fair question whether these ends are best accomplished by turning it into a spectacle. How can they be attained without the objections I have raised?

It is possible to have a church wedding without pomp and circumstance, even in the presence of a considerable gathering. During the war, I officiated at a number of weddings which were quickly arranged to coincide with a brief furlough or leave. Elaborate trappings could not be extemporized in days of man-power shortage; they were in questionable taste in wartime anyway. The decorations consisted of one bouquet of white flowers upon the altar. The wedding party consisted of the bride and a single attendant (often in street-length dresses), the bride's father, the groom, and the best man. Often, because the groom's contemporaries had a more pressing engagement with Uncle Sam, the groom's father served as best man, a pleasant and appreciated recognition of the one whose labors helped to rear the groom and fit him for the responsibilities of married life. Such weddings have been very moving and free from the artificiality which haunts weddings of the histrionic type.

Often these weddings have been "open church." It is impossible to have wedding invitations engraved when one does not know well in advance when the Army or Navy will grant leave. Hence, in lieu of invitations, announcement is made in the newspaper and the church bulletin that "Open church will be observed on Wednesday afternoon at four-thirty when Miss Mary Brown is married to Ensign John Paul Jones." This does away with invidious distinctions, the delicate decision as to who shall be invited. It means that whoever is sufficiently interested in the bride and groom to want to witness their marriage is welcome to do so. It also means that no one need feel obliged to send a gift. Sometimes a wedding invitation is interpreted as a refined solicitation. An ancient wedding jest concerns the card of admittance enclosed with the invitation reading, "Present at door"; the recipient was free to decide whether "present" was a verb or a noun.

Another type of wedding I like involves a reversal of the usual procedure. The usual procedure is to invite a large number to the church and enclose in some of the invitations a card to the reception. This conveys the impression that the wedding is a large, promiscuous affair, while the reception is reserved to the elect. In the type of which I speak, only the families and a few intimate friends come to the church. The wedding party meets in the vestry or minister's study and at the appointed hour proceeds without fanfare to the chancel, where in a quiet, intimate atmosphere, seen only by those who know and love them best, the bride and groom are married. Then they proceed to a reception to which more have been invited. The wedding is treated as a religious service; the reception as a social festivity. This I regard as an appropriate distinction.

Something is surely to be said for home weddings, at least where the bride's parents have a commodious home. Many churchmen will disagree with me. They believe that for all the offices of the church which signalize the successive steps or crises in the individual's life—baptism, confirmation, marriage, the burial office—the church is the proper place. Certainly this is true of confirmation, but for the other three the home is a fitting alternative. A true home is a holy place as surely as a church; and wherever the minister goes as the church's accredited representative, he carries the church with him. There is no more appropriate site for a wedding than before the fireplace in the living room, where the family life has centered through the years until it has rich and hallowing associations for the bride.

Ministers often feel they ought to have two wedding services and two burial services; one for professing Christians, a second for others. In the case of the burial service, it might sometimes be embarrassing for the minister to decide who was entitled to the first and who was not. He might feel as though he were usurping the prerogative of judge which belongs to God. In the case of the marriage service, no such embarrassment is necessary. He could ask any couple he did not know to read both services and decide which they preferred to have used. The point is that all the rituals presuppose that the bride and groom intend to live their lives on the Christian plane. It often happens that decent people come to a minister to be married, whom he has no scruples about marrying but who are not in communion with any church, nor professedly religious people. He does not want to advise them to go to a justice of the peace for a civil service. He is glad to invoke the blessing of God on their union. But it hardly seems candid to pledge them (by implication at least) to a manner of life they do not intend, simply because no alternative ritual is available.

Two · A Hindu Marriage in Bengal

D. N. MITRA

The following description * of a Hindu marriage is in-
cluded because it is in thought provoking contrast to contemporary
American marriage customs. It highlights some desirable and some
undesirable features of our modes of marrying.

NEGOTIATIONS

NEGOTIATIONS for marriages in a Bengali Hindu family start either directly or indirectly. In the former case a party of friends and relatives acting in behalf of a boy and one in behalf of a girl approach each other, usually through common friends and relatives; in the latter case, marriage-brokers or matchmakers—men and women—are engaged. The former are called *ghataks* and the latter *ghatkis* in Bengali. Both *ghataks* and *ghatkis* are usually illiterate and belong to the lower strata of society. There are, however, a few respectable and literate *ghataks*. These matchmakers supply information about a few boys to the guardian of a girl and about a few girls to the guardian of a boy; and, in most cases, they bring together both the parties. A few offices or organizations are also in existence for the negotiation of marriages; and, like the marriage-brokers, they put the guardians of the boys and girls in touch with each other. In all these cases, out-of-pocket expenses are to be paid; and, in the event of a successful negotiation, a certain fee or honorarium must also be paid. Matrimonial advertisements have been of late very much in vogue; and they are very interesting to read.

SEEING THE BOY AND THE GIRL

The next step is the "showing of girls and boys." A party of persons acting in behalf of a boy will go to see the girls and a party in behalf of a girl will, similarly, see the boys. Formerly, the final selection of a boy or a girl depended upon the men of the family. But, for some time past, it has become common for the women relatives, acting for the boys, to see the girls. The procedure is for the men to see the girls first and to select one or two or more; then the women will see the girls one by one, and they may either finally

* Reprinted from *The American Journal of Sociology,* 1946, 52: 255–258, by permission of the University of Chicago Press.

select one or reject them all. A girl has thus to appear for selection or rejection several times before the persons—male or female—representing a boy. But a boy has also to appear more than once before a girl's party because the male party in each case divides itself into groups—one group following the other. In some cases the boy, with his friends and relatives, goes to see the girl provisionally selected by the men and the women; and the final selection rests on him. But he is not allowed to talk freely with the girl, and sometimes he goes incognito. He should be satisfied with her appearance and with the words spoken by her in answer to the questions of others of the party.

A GIRL HAS TO FACE AN ORDEAL

It is an ordeal both for the boy and for the girl to appear before a party. But naturally it is a greater ordeal for the girl. She has to be dressed in her very best clothes, and she must put on jewelry to add beauty to her appearance; the jewels, in many cases, are bor-. rowed. She is repeatedly warned by her family to walk slowly, to bow down her head before the party, to sit properly, and to answer their questions very mildly. Any smartness on her part may be regarded as a disqualification. Questions may be put to her by the members of the party to test her knowledge in a variety of subjects. It reminds me here of the ordeal of a girl-graduate who had to appear before the male party of a boy. After she was asked her name (and this is generally the first question put to a girl), she was asked what the results were of each of her examinations. She replied with all courtesy and mildness. She was then asked to write a few lines in both English and Bengali on any subject she liked. She complied with the request (or order) with all possible humility. The next questions were whether she knew music, needlework, painting, cooking, etc., and in each case her reply was in the affirmative, and samples of her needlework and painting were immediately produced before the party by her guardians. She was then asked to play on an organ and to sing a song. This she did most gracefully. Then a youngster of the party asked her whether she knew dancing. This question was too much for her and exceeded the limits of her patience. She took an altogether different attitude and said very promptly in reply: "My mother has said, 'I have taught you everything except dancing, which your mother-in-law will teach you.'" With these words she left the room in disgust. The negotiations at once were discontinued.

DOWRIES AND PRESENTS

The final selection of a boy and a girl does not necessarily end in their marriage. The question of "dowries and presents" then comes in. Ordinarily it is the most important question and on its settlement the final marriage depends. The dowries and presents consist of cash, jewelry for the girl, presents such as dining-room, drawing-room, bedroom, and office furniture, silver, clothes, shoes, a car and a house, and what not! A valuable watch must be presented to the boy—no matter if he is a business man and possesses half-a-dozen watches. A list of dowries and presents is prepared. The items, of course, vary with parties according to their means, and the list is sometimes modified, omitting some items altogether. There are instances when the cash part of the dowry is demanded only to enable the boy's party to meet all the expenses of the marriage, and the rest is left to the discretion of the girl's party. In some cases no cash is demanded, but a demand for the rest is made. There are a few cases where no demand whatever is made and there is no talk about it between the parties. But generally these marriages take place in wealthy families and the boy's party knows very well that, without any demand, dowries and presents will flow in abundance. A girl of poor complexion and of inferior features may be selected through the strength of dowries and presents offered by her party. I knew of a highly educated and cultured man who used to say: "I have not married my wife but have married her wealth." I was told by a high official, in charge of the training of the newly recruited officers to the civil services, that he could negotiate marriages for them at a cost varying from 6,000 to 12,000 rupees (and these were pre-war prices), according to the different grades of service. And these prices were the minimum. I have two daughters to marry. Both of them are graduates, are good looking, and possess many accomplishments. I am, on principle, opposed to giving any dowries according to the prevailing market rates and demand. Nor can I afford it. I published two advertisements in the press. In the one I did not mention anything about the dowry and in the other I added: "No proposals with demand for dowry will be entertained." In response to the former I received a large number of letters and to the latter the number was only five—three of which were from widowers. This shows clearly in which direction the wind blows. Presents at the time of marriage are not the only ones that will be expected. They are to be given—though on a smaller scale—on the occasion of each festival in future years.

BRIDE AND GROOM

It will appear from the above that the boy and the girl to be wedded do not receive much consideration. Their wishes are seldom ascertained; they are thrust upon each other. They have no chance of knowing a bit of each other's nature, temperament, sentiments, feelings, or aspirations. But men and women of the older school are strongly in favor of this agelong custom. They say that marriages according to the old custom are much happier than those effected by the direct approach of boys and girls. They cite instances and quote statistics in support of their view. Their chief contention is that during the most plastic and emotional period of life a boy is not sound, sober, and well balanced enough to choose the right partner for his life; and the same thing is also said about a girl. They go on to say that a young man may be attracted by the beauty and appearance of one girl, by the high educational attainments of another, by other accomplishments of a third, etc. And ultimately he may choose the wrong one. The same remarks also apply to a girl. It is therefore safer and better to leave the matter to the saner judgment of the guardians of each. In this connection, horoscopes of the boy and of the girl are generally consulted to ascertain whether the match will be a happy and peaceful one. If the horoscopes do not agree, negotiations cease, in many cases, in spite of the desirability of the match. They will not take into consideration that, in spite of the agreement of the horoscopes, many marriages have been unhappy.

CEREMONIES

The *Pucca Dekha* (the final seeing of the girl and of the boy), the *Gaye Halud* (besmearing the bodies of the bride and bridegroom with a thick solution of turmeric), the marriage proper, and the *Ful Sajya* (the first night on which the husband and the wife are allowed to meet freely and to spend the night together) are the chief items. The first ceremony takes place a few days or even a month or two before the marriage. On this occasion the boy's party will come to the girl's home, will see the girl again and will give her a valuable present of jewelry. The priests will be there and they will bless the girl with *dhan* and *doorba* (grains of paddy and dub grass). Others who are present and senior to the girl will similarly bless her. Refreshments will then be served. The same procedure also takes place in the case of the boy. The next ceremony, i.e., the *Gaye Halud,* will take place in the boy's house: first a thick solution of tumeric is smeared on the body of the boy by the women and a little of it, taken from his body, is sent to the girl's home to be smeared on her body. With it presents—various articles of food (raw and cooked), clothes, etc.—are sent. A number of men carry the presents, and they are to be fed and paid *baksis,* or *pour boire.* The marriage usually takes place after sunset on a night very auspicious for the purpose. The bridegroom goes to the bride's home accompanied by the family priest, his father or guardian, relatives, friends, etc. He must fast the whole day. Similarly, the bride and her father or guardian also fast. At the time of the marriage the bridegroom must put on a special kind of *dhuti* made of silk, and he must have a bare body—even if it is a winter night. He will put on a *topor* (a helmet made of pith and mica). The girl will also put on special clothes of silk. The priests of both the parties will chant *mantras* before the deity and a fire. The fire should be fed with *ghee* and parched rice. The essence of the *mantras* is that before the deity and the fire the boy will promise to maintain the girl and the girl will promise to be loyal and faithful to the boy for life. But in nine out of ten cases they do not understand the true import of the *mantras,* as they are in Sanskrit. The girl's father also takes part in the proceedings. He gives away the girl. There is also a short comic ceremony in the course of which the girl squats, with her eyes closed, on a small plank of wood. She is lifted by four members of the family, and is carried around the boy seven times. At the last round she is raised high so that she can see the boy face to face as he stands. She is then asked to open her eyes in order to see the boy clearly, and the boy is asked to look at the girl. While they look at each other they are covered with a sheet of cloth so that nobody else can view their seeing each other. At this time garlands are exchanged. This ceremony is called the "Union of Four Eyes." After the marriage, the bride and the bridegroom are taken to a well-decorated room—called *Basar Ghar*—where they are given refreshments. Here the womenfolk rule. The whole night is spent in music and exchange of jokes. The next day, after more ceremonies, the bridegroom, escorted by some members of his family, goes with the bride to his home, taking with them their clothes tied in a piece of linen. After the arrival at his home they must attend more ceremonies, after which they are separated from each other and are not allowed to see each other until the next night.

On the next night the *Ful Sajya* ceremony is held. The husband and wife spend the night together on a bed decorated with flowers. The bride wears ornaments made of flowers, and the room must be well decorated. On this night presents, articles of food, etc., are sent by the girl's family. This is in exchange for the presents sent on the occasion of the *Gaye Halud* ceremony by the boy's family. Usually, on this night, the *Bow bhat* ceremony is also performed. The essence of the ceremony is that the *bow,* i.e., the bride, feeds the members of the family and other relations with *bhat* (cooked rice). The *bow* remains on a cushion in a decorated room, gorgeously dressed and wearing all her jewels. Those who are invited are taken to that room in groups and they give her presents. She is not allowed to speak to anyone but will accept the presents from each with a *namaskar* (bowing her head with her arms on her forehead). The menu of the *Bow bhat,* like the menu of the dinner given at the girl's place on the night of the marriage, is rich indeed, and it is an expensive affair.

There are instances—although very few compared with the magnitude of the evil—where young men are definitely opposed to the acceptance of dowry and have married without taking any dowry; in some cases they have married girls from very poor families. Similarly, young girls are rising to the occasion and have taken an attitude of opposition to marrying if dowry is demanded. Love marriages are also taking place, but, in most cases, these are intercaste marriages and not in accordance with the agelong Hindu custom.

Three · A Hindu Wife

D. N. MITRA

Though the article which follows * deals more with marriage adjustment than with the wedding it is included in this section because it has greater meaning when read with the preceding companion article.

In the following article I propose to give a true pen-picture of my deceased wife, who represented more or less a Hindu wife of a middle-class Bengali family of the present time.

I WAS married on August 4, 1914. (Mark the date please.) My wife was then about fifteen years of age and I was about twenty-five. She died on March 13, 1945. We, therefore, spent about thirty-one years of married life together. According to our custom I had no opportunity of meeting her before our marriage. My father and my two elder brothers selected her for me. A friend of mine, however, accompanied them and I got from him some idea about her appearance. And that was considered enough for me in those days. My mother was not alive then, and the opinion of the other women of the family was, therefore, not seriously sought in the negotiation.

We met each other for the first time on the night of our marriage but, strictly speaking, that was a meeting of the "four eyes" only. Though we spent the whole night in the *Basar Ghar* after the marriage there was no conversation between us. In the presence of the

* Reprinted from *The American Journal of Sociology*, 1946, 52: 259–262, by permission of the University of Chicago Press.

other women in the room (and that is the custom) she felt too shy to talk to me and I felt the same way. Our first meeting, therefore, took place in our house on the third night of the marriage, i.e., on the night of the *Ful Sajya.*

The bride stayed in our family on this occasion for about a week or so, as is the general custom. As a *bow* (bride) she had to be very cautious about her movements, her conversation with others, and even about her own comforts and conveniences. She was required to wear a veil almost all day. In every respect she was supposed to act according to the instructions of the elder women of the family. And she had not even the freedom to talk to her own people when they visited her, without the sanction of the authorities. She was escorted everywhere—even from one room to another. In a word, a *bow* has to undergo a "jail" life during this period. And she is considered an ideal *bow* if she looks up to the "jailer" and obeys her instructions in the minutest details. My wife adapted herself wonderfully, as other brides do, to the new environment and acted as the "most obedient servant" to all—old and young—in the family. And, naturally, she became a favorite with all, especially with my father who, having selected her, took a special pride in such a good-natured *bow.*

I had practically no opportunity of meeting her during the day because, according to the agelong custom, that would have been regarded as shameful behavior both on her part and on mine. I had to wait until about midnight, when she would stealthily come to my room, avoiding the eyes of all then awake. Similarly she had to leave the room very early in the morning, before anybody else was awake. The later a *bow* retires and the earlier she rises and comes out of her bedroom, the higher will be her reputation. Considering her age, she was a fully developed girl with plenty of common sense, humor, and zest. She knew Bengali well and possessed a fair knowledge of the world about her. She was familiar with all the household work of a Bengali Hindu family, and with music too. But music was not then regarded as an accomplishment for a girl. She, therefore, concealed this accomplishment from those who did not like it. Apparently she had obtained a good all-round training from her parents. I had, therefore, no grounds to regret my father's selection. As I have mentioned, we parted from each other after a week or so and with very great reluctance on both sides. But it could not be avoided; the custom had to be observed.

She went away with her parents to the upcountry station where her father was a judge. I went to her house during the *Pujahs* in October of the same year and stayed with her for another week. Although that was the second occasion on which we had met, we felt as if we were very well known to each other—the reason being that we had become very friendly through our letters, which were so numerous and so heavy in weight that it was the talk of all our relatives. Such a quick exchange of letters between a newly-wedded couple was not looked upon with favor in those days by most orthodox men and women; but we did not waver an inch from our correspondence and continued it with a vengeance until the last. She was not a *bow* in her father's house, thank God! She was, therefore, free to come and talk to me during the day, also, though with some hesitation lest anybody of the older school might make some uncharitable remark about her conduct. But fortunately, at the time, there were no others in the household except her parents, who were very liberal in this respect; and her mother used to ask her to give me her constant company. And I, being a stranger to the family and to the home, was completely in her hands. She was my friend, philosopher, and guide in the place. She had four more sisters—two elder and two younger—and an elder brother who was then in England being educated. That was practically our "honeymoon."

A year and a half rolled by before she came to live with me at my station in East Bengal with our first child—a handsome, healthy, and bonny girl. She realized from the moment of her arrival that she was not a *bow* there but was the mistress of the little house, and she was not at all slow to assume her position as such. She wore no veil there. She was quite free about her movements and conversation with me and others. She arranged the house according to her own plan without waiting for my consent. She was a responsible mother, too, and knew very well how to bring up a child. She looked after all the domestic work and did not consider it worth while to look to me for any instructions about work in the house. Though there was a cook, she always prepared one or two dishes herself; and I could not prevent her doing so, because cooking is symbolic to Hindu girls. She had a sewing machine and a harmonium too. She used to make most of the clothes for the child and for herself and did not feel shy about playing on the harmonium. Reading a daily paper in Bengali was almost a passion with her. And she discussed the important items of news with me every evening. She was not slow to make friends with all kinds of people, rich and poor, and she became one of the most prominent members of the *Mahila Samity* (Ladies' Association) there, of which the wife of the district magistrate was the president.

After her arrival I was not required to bother myself about any item of household work. And the house looked cleaner, things were kept in their proper places and were handy. Above all, the food was better. It is said that girls are more intelligent than boys and that they have a greater sense of responsibility than do boys of the same age; a Hindu wife may perhaps substantiate this view. It is strange how she plays her role with a husband about double her age, immediately after the wedding.

My wife was, unlike the majority of Hindu girls of her age, very bold and courageous and used to live alone with the child for the greater part of the month because I was then a touring officer and had to tour extensively. I remember that, in the course of a single year at that time, I spent 319 days on tour, and a member of the Indian Civil Service—then a subdivisional officer, now a judge of the Calcutta High Court—observed that it was not fair to my young wife. But I could not help it. I even had to leave her alone, to go to my work in the interior, when she was sick or when the child was sick. But she did not mind it and used to say that she was competent to look after herself and the child during my absence. In her opinion, even at that age, my work was the chief consideration.

She was required to stay with my people at home from time to time and her stay there used to last for months together; this, also, is a custom prevailing among us. And there she was again a *bow*—restrictions on her being, however, less than those which existed when she was newly wedded. These restrictions are being relaxed gradually with the age and time. They, however, vary according to the culture and rationality of the members of different families. But a *bow* is always aud everywhere a *bow* and she has to behave accordingly, complying with the restrictions of each family. She cannot be so free as she is while staying with her husband outside the family. The restrictions were not very rigid in our family— probably due to the absence of my mother. My wife was clever enough to please the members of my family by not committing such actions as were not liked by them. For example, she would not wear shoes in the presence of the elders, though she did not stir without them while staying with me. She used to bathe early in the morning and then enter the storeroom in the kitchen. She would not take any food before the elders had partaken of it. She would go to have a dip in the holy water of the Ganges with other women of the house, though she did not like an open-air bath. She would take the dust off the feet of the priests, though she did not believe in its efficacy. She used to blow the conch-shell in the evening and would place a burning *pradip* (a lamp made of earth) at the foot of a *tulshi* plant, which can be seen in almost all Hindu houses. She would not leave the house without a male escort.

A Hindu wife develops wonderfully a sense of responsibility, a culture, a rationality, and an outlook on life; and she gradually becomes the guiding spirit of the family. With advancing age she commands respect and confidence from all; and nothing important is done without her consent.

My wife developed these qualities remarkably well for the reason that she came of a very cultured family; and in my family too, as stated before, the agelong customs were not so strictly observed. There was also another reason: that was her stay with me in a station away from the family, where she could get proper scope to

develop her initiative, courage, rationality, and sense of responsibility. There were none of the older school to consult for instruction
and guidance; and one meets the challenge of circumstances.

She believed in God but not in the worship of the many deities
of the Hindus, an attitude which she had acquired from her father.
At the same time she would not show any disrespect to our deities.
On the other hand, she would attend the most important *Pujahs* and
would bow down her head before the deities. She could not, however, neglect the agelong customs of offering *Pujahs* and fasting on
certain auspicious days of the year which are observed for the good
of the husband and children.

She had not a bit of caste prejudice in her. She would eat food
prepared by other castes or communities, provided that it was clean
and that the cooks were clean too. But she would not keep a
Moslem cook in the family, because of the guests. Untouchability
was a word which was not to be found in her dictionary. But she
would not make a parade of all these things just to show that she
did not adhere to the agelong customs.

Strictly speaking, she did observe *Purdah,* but she would move
about freely, even in trams, buses, etc., with an escort, and used to
do the shopping herself. She entertained my friends, including the
Europeans that I introduced to her, even during my absence. She
would take food with them at the same table. She attended many
parties with me, and, unlike the average Hindu woman of her time,
she would not change her clothes and take a bath, on her return,
before entering her own rooms.

She was a wonderful nurse. It seemed as if she were born in the
atmosphere of nursing. She was a mother of ten children and,
though there were serious illnesses in the family, she nursed the
sick on each occasion unaided. It used to evoke the admiration of
medical men. She was a different person then, with a prayerful
mind always.

She was very brave and bold from her earlier days. She used to
travel alone with her children from East Bengal to the upcountry
and she knew very well how to handle the railway authorities, railway porters, and *gharry wallahs.* She was also very good at packing
for a railway journey. The proverbial storms and floods of Eastern
Bengal and even the air raids in Calcutta did not create any panic
or fear in her mind. She would take all possible measures for safety
and then say "God is over head." She was looked upon as a source
of courage to all of us. During the air raids a servant asked her one
day, "Mother, why are you looking so depressed today? If you look
like that how can we muster courage?" She smiled her usual smile,
and that was enough to comfort him.

She was of a very mild and genial temperament. She was never
harsh or hard to the children. She never rebuked them without a

smile. She was equally sweet to all, old and young, and she was, therefore, an attraction to them. And this is why there was a perpetual flow of visitors to her at all hours of the day. Even in illness she used to be dragged to a marriage or any other festival in the houses of her relatives, because without her there was no joy. It is most painful to think that her last illness was aggravated by a most unkind pressure by one of her relatives to attend a marriage in his family.

She had no university or so-called higher education, but she was educated enough to follow world politics and problems, and, until the last moment of her consciousness, she was anxious to know about the events and the course of the war. She was confident of victory but, alas, did not survive to see it. She taught all the children at home until they attained school age. She was a source of inspiration to me in all my work and she used to take an active interest in it. Due to pressure of work it was not always possible for me to give her the help and company I should have given, and my friends used to complain about it. When I wanted to know her feelings about it, she smiled and said, "A wife should be proud of her husband's work and not of his company at the sacrifice of his work."

She was very conscious of and sensitive about her self-respect and any harsh word used to tear her heart to pieces. But she would never utter a single word in protest. And we misunderstood her very greatly in this respect—I, especially, did.

She was not accustomed to worrying much about the future and was happy and content in the present. Her thought was: "We cannot change yesterday, that is clear. Nor begin tomorrow until it is here. So all that is left for you and for me, is to make today as sweet as can be." But ordinarily a Hindu wife is not of this nature and temperament. She thinks more of the future than of the present and is anxious to make provision for the former. It looked as if my wife was not attached to anything very seriously. She exhibited no display of love or affection toward her children or husband. Unlike ordinary Hindu wives she was not fond of jewelry or expensive clothes, but insisted on clean clothes.

She loved to be in the midst of her relatives and, even at the cost of her health, she loved to visit them. She loved the village life and the village folk and was fascinated by flowers and music. She used to behave like a child, particularly when she stayed with her parents; and they were very fond of her. She died like a child in her father's arms at his home, and she carried her forty-six years very lightly. Her mother had died about two years before.

We held divergent views on many matters, and sometimes she used to yield to mine with sweetness, but sometimes she did not. In certain matters, too, she was very obstinate and there was unpleasantness between us many a time. But that used to be temporary. With all my faults she loved me intensely and with all her faults I loved her deeply. This is what is called a "holy union," and this holy union is wonderfully brought about in a Hindu couple even though the parties had no chance of meeting each other before they were wedded.

VII · HUSBAND-WIFE INTERACTION

One · Psychological Factors in Marital Happiness

LEWIS M. TERMAN
Psychologist, Stanford University

Lewis M. Terman made one of the pioneer studies * *of the psychological factors associated with marital happiness. The basic information gained from his study is as applicable to marriage adjustment today as when the study was made, for husband-wife adjustments, like other human relationships, do not greatly change from generation to generation.*

AN examination of recent contributions to the literature on marriage reveals a great diversity of opinion about the factors most responsible for marital success or failure. On practically every aspect of the problem the pronouncements by leading authors are highly contradictory. The explanation of this situation lies partly in the bias of authors, partly in their willingness to generalize from inadequate data, and partly in the use of faulty techniques in the collection of information.

The fact that most of the earlier and many of the later investigations were made by members of the medical profession has led to excessive emphasis upon the importance of the sexual factors and to a corresponding neglect of psychological factors. The studies of Bernard, the Mowrers, Cottrell and Burgess, and other sociological workers have accomplished something toward the correction of this misplacement of emphasis, but ours is the first publication to report a major investigation of marital happiness from the more strictly psychological approach.

In a preliminary study of 341 married couples and 109 divorced couples, evidence was sought regarding the relationship between marital happiness and scores on 12 personality traits, including dominance, self-sufficiency, neurotic tendency, masculinity-femininity, interest maturity, and 7 types of interest constellations. The most important conclusion from this preliminary study was that the "traits" in question, as measured by the tests used (the Bernreuter

* Reprinted from *Psychological Factors in Marital Happiness*, by Lewis M. Terman. New York: McGraw-Hill Book Company, Inc., 1938, pp. 366–377, by permission of the author and publishers.

151

personality inventory and the Strong occupational interest test) are little correlated with marital happiness, but that the particularized attitudes expressed by subjects in response to many of the individual items in the two tests are significantly related to the happiness scores.

A second study was accordingly planned which would investigate for a larger number of subjects the relationship between happiness scores and a great variety of possible factors, including not only personality factors, but also background factors and factors having to do with sexual adjustments in the marriage. By the use of an improved technique for assuring anonymity of response, data were secured on these three sets of variables from 792 married couples who filled out the information schedules in the presence of a field assistant. The group studied represents a reasonably good sampling of the urban and semiurban married population of California at the middle and upper-middle cultural levels, though the sampling appears to be somewhat biased in the direction of superior marital happiness.

THE MEASURE OF HAPPINESS USED

The marital happiness score which was computed for each subject was based upon information regarding communality of interests, average amount of agreement or disagreement between spouses in 10 different fields, customary methods of settling disagreements, regret of marriage, choice of spouse if life were to be lived over, contemplation of separation or divorce, subjective estimates of happiness, direct admission of unhappiness, and a complaint score based upon domestic grievances checked in a long list presented. Graded weights were assigned the various possible responses to these items on the basis of intercorrelations, and the total happiness score of a given subject was the sum of the weights corresponding to his individual responses. The resulting numeral score is a serviceable index of the degree of satisfaction that a subject has found in his marriage even though it cannot be regarded as a precise quantitative measure of such satisfaction.

The happiness scores ranged from practically zero to a maximum of 87 points, with a mean of 68.40 for husbands and 69.25 for wives. The respective o's of the distributions were 17.35 and 18.75. The distributions for husbands and wives agreed closely throughout and were markedly skewed in the direction of high happiness. The scores of husbands and wives correlated to the extent of approximately .60, showing that the happiness of one spouse is to a surprising degree independent of the happiness of the other. This finding is new and perhaps rather significant. Its newness is probably explained by the fact that no previous investigation based upon a large group of subjects had secured its data by methods which prevented collaboration between husband and wife in filling out the information schedules. It is significant in the suggestion it carries that the degree of satisfaction which one finds in a marriage depends partly upon one's own characteristic attitudes and temperament and so need not closely parallel the happiness of one's marital partner.

PERSONALITY CORRELATES OF MARITAL HAPPINESS

The information schedule that was filled out by the subjects contained 233 personality test items dealing with interests, attitudes, likes and dislikes, habitual response patterns, and specific opinions as to what constitutes the ideal marriage. Of these, approximately 140 were found to show an appreciable degree of correlation with the happiness scores of either husbands or wives. The various possible responses to the valid items were then assigned score weights roughly in proportion to the extent to which they differentiated between subjects of high and low happiness scores. This made it possible to compute for each subject a "personality" score, which was merely the sum of the weights corresponding to the responses the subject had given. The personality score may be thought of as in some degree an index of the subject's temperamental predisposition to find happiness rather than unhappiness in the marital relationship. This index correlates approximately .46 with the marital happiness scores of each spouse. Evidently the attitudes and emotional response patterns tapped by the personality items are by no means negligible as determiners of marital happiness.

By noting and classifying the individual items that differentiate between subjects of high and low happiness, it has been possible to piece together descriptive composite pictures of the happy and unhappy temperaments. For example, it is especially characteristic of unhappy subjects to be touchy or grouchy; to lose their tempers easily; to fight to get their own way; to be critical of others; to be careless of others' feelings; to chafe under discipline or to rebel against orders; to show any dislike that they may happen to feel; to be easily affected by praise or blame; to lack self-confidence; to be dominating in their relations with the opposite sex; to be little interested in old people, children, teaching, charity, or uplift activities; to be unconventional in their attitudes toward religion, drinking, and sexual ethics; to be bothered by useless thoughts; to be often in a state of excitement; and to alternate between happiness and sadness without apparent cause.

The above characterizations hold for the unhappy of both sexes. In many respects, however, the differences between the happy and unhappy follow a different pattern for husbands and wives. For this reason it has been necessary to present four composite pictures, rather than two, in order to make clear the contrasting happy and unhappy temperaments as we find them in both men and women.

The qualities of personality that predispose a person to happiness or unhappiness in his relations with others are, of course, far from being the sole cause of success or failure in marriage. Their importance, however, is so obvious from our data that the problem calls for further investigation, preferably by a combination of the statistical and clinical approaches.

BACKGROUND CORRELATES OF HAPPINESS

Background factors which in these marriages were totally uncorrelated with happiness scores, or for which the correlation was so small as to have almost no practical significance, include family income, occupation, presence or absence of children, amount of religious training, birth order, number of opposite-sex siblings, adolescent popularity, and spouse differences in age and schooling. Nearly all of the factors in this list have been regarded by one writer or another as highly important, especially presence or absence of children in the home and differences between husband and wife in age and schooling.

It is doubtless true that the presence of children often prevents the breaking up of a marriage, but the evidence indicates that it has little effect on the general level of marital happiness. Childless women past middle age do show a slight tendency to be less happy than the average, but childless men of this age tend to have happiness scores above the average. If there are individual marriages that are made more happy by the presence of children, these appear to be offset by other marriages that are made less happy.

From the vantage point of our data it appears that much nonsense has been written about the risks entailed by marrying on inadequate income or by marrying out of one's age or educational class. The correlation of income with happiness scores is zero. The happiest wives in our group are those who are from 4 to 10 years older than their husbands; the happiest husbands are those who are 12 or more years older than their wives. Moreover, the spouses of these subjects rate as happy as the average for the entire population of subjects.

As for religious training, if this was ever a factor in marital happiness it appears no longer to exert such an influence.

It is encouraging to know that marital happiness as here measured shows little tendency to decrease with the passing of years. The scores are a trifle above average for the couples married less than 3 years, and there is a slight depression in the curves of mean happiness at 8 to 10 years after marriage and another at 15 to 17 years. It should be noted, however, that our study includes only marriages that had not been broken by separation or divorce.

We may designate as of slight importance the factors that show a barely significant relationship to the happiness of one or both of the spouses. This list includes age at marriage, absolute amount of schooling, rated adequacy of sex instruction, sources of sex information, age of learning the origin of babies, number of siblings, circumstances of first meeting between the spouses, length of premarital acquaintance, length of engagement, attractiveness of opposite-sex parent, resemblance of subject's spouse to subject's opposite-sex parent, amount of adolescent "petting," and wife's experience of sex shock or her age at first menstruation. No factor in this list is sufficiently related to marital happiness to warrant a prediction weight of more than one point for either husbands or wives. There has been a vast amount of exaggeration about the risks to marital happiness of early marriage, brief premarital acquaintance, inadequate sex instruction, adolescent "petting," and a history of sex shock on the part of the wife.

Expressed desire to be of the opposite sex tends to be associated with unhappiness in wives but not in husbands. A premarital attitude of disgust toward sex is unfavorable to happiness, and more so in men than in women. Frequent or severe punishment in childhood is reliably associated with unhappiness in both husbands and wives. The items mentioned in this paragraph carry a maximum prediction weight of two points for at least one of the spouses.

Next are five items carrying a maximum weight of three points for one spouse and two points for the other. They are: the relative mental ability of husband and wife, parental attitudes toward the subject's early sex curiosity, amount of conflict with father, and amount of attachment to both father and mother.

As to relative mental ability, the most favorable situation is equality or near equality. Marked mental superiority of husband makes for happiness in the wife but for unhappiness in the husband; marked inferiority of husband makes the wife unhappy but does not greatly affect the husband.

Subjects whose parents rebuffed or punished them because of their early sex curiosity are definitely less happy than the average, this effect being somewhat more marked in husbands than in wives.

Strong attachment to either parent is markedly favorable to happiness, especially in the case of husbands. Conflict with the father is unfavorable to happiness, especially in the case of wives.

We come now to the four most important of the background items: happiness of parents, childhood happiness, conflict with mother, and type of home discipline. All, of these carry a maximum weight of four or five points.

Happiness of parents rates highest, with a maximum weight of five points for husbands and four for wives. This item is more predictive of success or failure in marriage than a composite of half a dozen items such as income, age at marriage, religious training, amount of adolescent "petting," or spouse difference in age or schooling.

Hardly less important is the rated happiness of respondent's childhood, with a maximum weight of four points for each spouse. Carrying the same weights is absence of conflict with mother. It appears that a record of conflict with mother constitutes a significantly greater threat to marital happiness than a record of conflict with father.

Childhood discipline that is firm, not harsh, is much more favorable to happiness than discipline that is lax, irregular, or excessively strict.

The 10 background circumstances most predictive of marital happiness are:

1. Superior happiness of parents.
2. Childhood happiness.
3. Lack of conflict with mother.
4. Home discipline that was firm, not harsh.
5. Strong attachment to mother.
6. Strong attachment to father.
7. Lack of conflict with father.
8. Parental frankness about matters of sex.
9. Infrequency and mildness of childhood punishment.
10. Premarital attitude toward sex that was free from disgust or aversion.

The subject who "passes" on all 10 of these items is a distinctly better-than-average marital risk. Any one of the 10 appears from the data of this study to be more important than virginity at marriage.

SEX FACTORS IN MARITAL HAPPINESS

Our study shows clearly that certain of the sex factors contribute materially to marital happiness or unhappiness. It shows no less clearly that others which have long been emphasized by sexologists as important are practically uncorrelated with happiness scores. The data in fact indicate that all of the sex factors combined are far from being the one major determinant of success in marriage.

Among the items yielding little or no correlation with happiness are both reported and preferred frequency of intercourse, estimated duration of intercourse, husband's ability to control ejaculation, methods of contraception used, distrust of contraceptives, fear of pregnancy, degree of pain experienced by wife at the first intercourse, wife's history of sex shock, rhythm in wife's sexual desire, ability of wife to experience multiple orgasms, and failure of the husband to be as dominant as the wife would like him to be in initiating or demanding intercourse.

The sex techniques that many writers regard as the primary key to happy marriage may be worth cultivating for their immediate sensual returns, but they exert no appreciable effect upon happiness scores. Their absence or imperfection is evidently not a major source of conflict or a major cause of separation, divorce, or regret of marriage. What is even more surprising, it appears that such techniques have no very marked effect on the wife's ability to experience the orgasm.

On the other hand, the wife's happiness score (though not her husband's) is reliably correlated with the amount of pleasure that she experienced at her first intercourse, and the husband's happiness is reliably correlated (negatively) with the wife's tendency to prudishness or excessive modesty.

Five of the sex items that correlate quite markedly with the happiness scores are: number of sexual complaints checked, rated degree of satisfaction from intercourse with spouse, frequency with which intercourse is refused, reaction of the spouse who is refused, and frequency of desire for extramarital intercourse. The correlations, however, probably do not mean that the factors in question are to any great extent actual determiners of happiness or unhappiness. It is more likely that they are primarily symptoms. The discontented spouse rationalizes his (or her) unhappiness by finding fault with the sexual partner and at the same time develops longings for extramarital relationships.

Among the sex factors investigated are two that not only correlate markedly with happiness scores but are in all probability genuine determiners of them: *viz.*, the wife's orgasm adequacy and husband-wife difference in strength of sex drive.

Two measures were available on relative strength of sex drive. One of these was the ratio (computed for each subject) between actual and preferred number of copulations per month; the other was based on husband's and wife's ratings of their relative passionateness. The two measures agree in showing that equality or near equality in sex drive is an important factor in happiness. As the disparity in drive increases to the point where one spouse is in a more or less chronic state of sex hunger and the other in a state of satiety, the happiness scores of both drop off significantly. Even so, this factor is apparently less important than parental happiness, childhood happiness, or amount of conflict between child and mother.

First in importance among the sex factors is the wife's orgasm adequacy, which correlates about .30 both with her own and with her husband's happiness score. This is slightly higher than the correlation yielded by parental happiness. It is of special interest that orgasm inadequacy of the wife affects her husband's happiness almost as unfavorably as her own. Between wives of the "never" group and wives of the "always" group, there is a difference of 16.3 points in mean happiness, and a difference of 13.0 points in the mean happiness scores of their husbands. Nevertheless, one finds every grade of happiness both in the "never" group and the "always" group. Adequacy of the wife in this respect favors happiness but does not guarantee it, while on the other hand a considerable minority among the inadequates have happiness scores above the general average.

THE MYSTERY OF ORGASM INADEQUACY

Almost exactly a third of the wives fall in the inadequate group, attaining orgasm either "never" (8.3 per cent) or only "sometimes" (25.1 per cent). Adequates include the "usually" group (44.5 per cent) and the "always" group (22.1 per cent). These figures are in fairly close agreement with those reported by other investigators in Europe and America. Why is it that one woman out of three rarely or never succeeds in reaching the normal climax of sexual intercourse?

We have analyzed a large amount of data in the effort to throw some light on this mystery, but the resulting picture is far from clear. In this connection we investigated the relationship between wife's orgasm adequacy and both wife's and husband's responses to each of more than 300 items in the information schedule. Significant relationships were found for a large number of items. On the other hand, many factors that have been regarded as causative of orgasm inadequacy are uncorrelated with it in our data. These include attachment to father or to mother, conflict with father or with mother, amount of education, extent of religious training, sources of sex information, sex shock before the age of ten years, age at first menstruation, amount of childhood punishment, type of home discipline, happiness of childhood, premarital attitude of disgust toward matters of sex, admitted homosexual feelings, pain at first intercourse, methods of contraception used, fear of pregnancy, sleeping arrangements, date of birth, relative age of spouses, relative mental ability of spouses, length of marriage, and number of children.

Among the items most reliably associated with inadequacy are a goodly number of the Bernreuter and Strong type which appear to indicate neurasthenic tendencies, diminished responsiveness, and lack of zest, vigor, or colorfulness of personality. The picture is one that suggests the possible involvement of constitutional factors. In view of this picture and in view of our failure to find convincing evidence of the influence of emotional conditioning, we would raise the question whether the causes of orgasm inadequacy in women may not be biological rather than psychological, perhaps largely of genetic origin.

Whatever the causes may be, they are apparently deep seated, for our data show (1) that the tremendous cultural shift from the prudish sex attitudes of the 1890's to the liberal and frank attitudes of the 1930's has not appreciably reduced the proportion of inadequates among the younger wives of our group as compared with the proportion among the older; and (2) that if the orgasm is not established within the first year of marriage it is unlikely ever to be. In line with this is the opinion of Hamilton that the condition is rarely improved by a change of sexual partner.

THE RELATIVE IMPORTANCE OF SEXUAL AND PSYCHOLOGICAL COMPATIBILITY

Our data do not confirm the view so often heard that the key to happiness in marriage is nearly always to be found in sexual compatibility. They indicate, instead, that the influence of the sexual factors is at most no greater than that of the combined personality and background factors, and that it is probably less. The problem is complicated by the fact that the testimony of husband and wife regarding their sexual compatibility is influenced by their psychological compatibility. Couples who are psychologically well mated are likely to show a surprising tolerance for the things that are not satisfactory in their sexual relationships. The psychologically ill-mated show no such tolerance but instead are prone to exaggeration in their reports on sexual maladjustments. The two sexual factors of genuine importance are wife's orgasm adequacy and relative strength of sex drive in the two spouses.

THE EVIDENTIAL VALUE OF MARITAL COMPLAINTS

An important by-product of our investigation is the light thrown on marital complaints as evidence regarding the causes of domestic discord. The expression of numerous complaints is highly symptomatic of the presence of unhappiness, but the specific nature of the complaints made tells very little about the causes of unhappiness. It has been shown that some of the things most frequently complained of have little or no correlation with happiness scores. Inadequate income is the outstanding example. On the other hand, some of the things rarely complained of are usually quite serious when they are present. The clearest example of this is the wife's slovenliness in appearance.

Two · Separation and Marital Adjustment

MARGARET MEAD
Anthropologist, American Museum of
Natural History

The following discussion * *of the problems of marriage in wartime is pertinent because of the increasing mobility of
our population and the large number of men in military service—a
situation that will exist throughout the foreseeable future. The author's observations and conclusions concerning the effects of separation upon marital adjustment in general are applicable whether
the separation is due to war, occupation, or other causes.*

IS the family in danger, that institution within which
all the children of man have been nurtured to full individuality and
maturity? The family has survived polygamy and polyandry, it has
survived social codes under which a husband never saw his wife
except at breakfast, in which wives were all years younger than the
husbands who reared them, or years older than the husbands whom
they reared. The family itself is a very tough institution and has
survived a long time. Is it possible that the question isn't phrased
right, that those who talk about the family are being a little inhu-
man, worrying about an institution as if human beings were made
for institutions and not institutions for them? Isn't it possible that
the family is all right, undergoing some changes in form, perhaps,
adapting its code to wartime and migration and cramped quarters,
but still a very flourishing institution, more valued, more yearned
for, more patronized than usual?

But what about the people who live in families, who were reared
to expect one kind of condition within which to work out their relationships to each other and are now faced with another? Is it not
young husbands and wives, and husbands and wives not so young,
and their children, who are the real casualties, whose lives are
likely to be bruised and broken by their failure to cope with conditions for which nothing in their culture had prepared them? While
the family changes but survives, adjusted to a world of trailer
camps and pre-embarkation leaves, those who live in families may
find the going very hard. The serious consequences will be not a
body blow to our morals and mores (which will undoubtedly

* Reprinted from *Harper's Magazine*, 1945, 190: 393–399, by permission of
the author and the publisher.

stagger and recover, for society is resilient) but an enormous number of wrecked human lives.

For while the family can take an infinite number of forms, people in a given country at a given period, coming from a given stratum of their society, are usually prepared to live in only one form. In those societies where bride and groom are to meet as strangers, there are elaborate ceremonies which make that type of marriage bearable and stable. Young people in the United States, except in groups which retain their Old World customs, are brought up to expect to choose their own mates from within a very wide range of eligibility. They are cautioned against certain types of cross-religious marriages, and they are armored, without their knowledge, with a large number of delicate choice-making devices—sensitivity to clothing, to manners, to posture, to styles of funmaking and dating—which permit them, even in the incredibly wide group from which they nominally choose their mates, to make a workable choice. (The word *workable* is more appropriate than the terms from a previous age, such as suitable, or fitting, with their emphasis upon the parents' past rather than the bridal pair's future. A workable marriage means one in which the two partners have a chance, in American terms, to work out a relationship to each other which is satisfying enough to resist the temptation to change it for another one.) In a country where divorce is increasingly regarded as more reasonable than an unhappy marriage, the demands on the amount of satisfaction which a marriage gives of course go up correspondingly.

When it is not wartime and life is lived according to childhood expectations—so that children unconsciously assume their roles, following in the footsteps of parents and older brothers and sisters—a marriage based on personal choice is given a great deal of help by the community, by family, friends, business associates. However unsuitable the match, the bride and groom usually have friends in common who know about their marriage and treat them as if they were married for good, expect them to share a common residence, go out together, eat together, keep their clothes in the same place. Large, unwieldy wedding presents, investments in a house or overstuffed furniture, an insurance policy—all are present to give an air of permanence to the venture. If the young people are not to be labeled as too featherheaded even for their most youthful associates, they have to give it a try.

This means in practice that the growing pains of the new marriage are not allowed to disrupt it. The young husband may fling out of the house in anger in the morning, but he comes home at night because that, after all, is where his clothes are, where he sleeps. People would be surprised if he slept somewhere else; they would talk. Quarrels begun over the badly made coffee in the morning can be composed in the quietness of the night, over and over again. The common life can be renewed within the firm expectancy of other people that because two people are married they will spend most of their free time together under one roof. The often oddly matched pair get used to each other. Although originally they may have had nothing more in common than a dance step or two, they come to share a common life, made nostalgic by the times when eating an uncertainly cooked dish has preceded an evening of great tenderness.

Within this circle of habituation, children are born, and the young parents, following the course of their own parents, come to feel that they and the children belong together. Thus the majority of marriages succeed, at least in discharging their chief functions, providing affectionate companionship for people in pairs, and affording the only way we know to bring children up to be mature, responsible human beings.

The most serious thing that happens in wartime is that all this social support, this gentle, continuous, unremitting social pressure which keeps the two under one roof long enough for them to get used to each other, is withdrawn.

Honeymoons are begun and ended under the eye of strangers who probably suspect the newlyweds of not being married at all—an attitude which is very dampening to the formation of a new family. As the bride says farewell to her soldier husband, people mutter about the morals of soldiers if her kiss is long and fervent. She returns alone, to a world whose only recognition that she is married will be a negative one—disapproval if she has any fun. He goes back to camp to be kidded. There is no continuing common roof, no small bedroom in which their clothes hang side by side, no cheery "Why weren't you two at the movies last night?" no "Sorry you can't come, Bill. Too bad Mabel's sick"—with its firm expectation that the young husband wants to stay at home with his sick wife. Even when the young soldier's wife follows her husband, the uncertain and precarious conditions of camp-following provide only a slight frame for a developing marriage.

Then the babies are born with the fathers far away. Our literature is replete with tales of the young father walking the floor of the hospital waiting room, and taking the birth harder than his wife. But of such stuff fatherhood is built, and motherhood also, in our society. You can't withdraw this familiar scene, nor the much-heralded moment when the nurse announces the sex of the child, without taking something away from parenthood upon which both of the young new parents have been taught to depend. Desperately, the young carriers of our culture are struggling to evolve new patterns, as overseas fathers plead for infants of the right age and sex to hold in their arms. For the young father who has seen all of his buddies become fathers by V-mail, gradually this new long-distance form of parenthood may come to make sense; but it will not make the sense that following a pattern known from childhood would have made.

Then when he comes home there is the matter of getting acquainted with the baby. As getting acquainted with one's own child seems like such a bitter denial of all the usual values, neither father nor mother has any patterns for handling it. Both are nervous; and the baby, responsive to its mother's moods and the strange man's unpracticed clumsiness, screams. Years of comic strips have prepared the young father who stands in a hospital waiting room for his dismay when he sees a small and very uninviting red bundle in the nurse's arms. There hasn't been time for enough comic strips to prepare him for the circumstance that his year-old child may reject him at first. Often, before he has time to overcome the rejection, the furlough is over. And he finds that the father's role, on which he counted to keep his heart from wandering, isn't what it was cracked up to be.

Meanwhile the mother, who had lived a life of real relationship to her baby and of dream relationship to its father, has had to fit the two together and has found it difficult. Great numbers of young mothers withdraw from their husbands from time to time into a delighted communion with their babies. But in peacetime they are not permitted to stay withdrawn. There is dinner to be cooked, friends to be entertained; life, which includes the girl's husband, goes on. In wartime, when there is no continuous common life, when the husband's rivalry with the baby is compressed into a few dramatic days instead of being a familiar accompaniment of each early morning awakening, the whole situation is sharpened and dramatized. Tears and scenes are commoner than resigned griping and low-keyed reconciliations.

But the students of juvenile delinquency will be quick to insist that it is not only the new families which are suffering, but the marriages of those with half-grown or fully grown children. Families in which fathers after many years of successful fatherhood have gone off overseas or to distant wartime jobs; families in which mothers as well as fathers are working. Women whose husbands were not subject to draft but who insisted upon going anyway, men who are perfectly able to support their wives as they always have done and yet see their wives go to work, develop bitter resentments. Men far from home find they aren't so lonely after all. Women with high weekly wages in their pockets find their husbands' judgment less compelling.

It is not only that with new freedom, with unusual hours and opportunities, with long absences, both men and women find new sex partners. I am inclined to think that these temporary alliances, based on loneliness and war strain, are not the worst threat to the older relationship, but often a reaffirmation of its importance. The danger, in more mature marriages, lies not so much when the partners find a temporary new companion as when they find that the whole marriage scheme was restricting and unrewarding, and develop a preference for reading late in bed, alone. For just as in new, beginning marriages, young people are brought up to depend upon social pressures to give the marriage a chance, so for all the years that come after, American married couples, American parents, and American children have depended upon a social routine to keep them together.

It was the same sort of routine that gave the new, fumbling young lovers a chance to make their choice a permanent one—common residence, common meals, an expectation that they would spend many hours together, no place to go but home. Young people often found it boring, and some of my undergraduate students once insisted that the function of a room for each member of the family was to compensate for having to eat with the family. But the family dining room was still the place where you were sure of a meal, sure that you would be expected if not exuberantly welcomed; the place where you had a universally respected right to be. Husbands and wives got so used to sleeping in the same room that they were sleepless and restless apart from each other. This dependence, based on old affectionate habit, formed the basis of marriage. Husbands turned over their pay checks (or most of the money), children came home from school, wives swept and cooked and washed the window curtains, not because they especially liked these particular activities, but because it didn't occur to them—or to anyone —that there were any alternatives.

Sometimes commentators on the family talk about the disappearance of religious sanctions behind family life, as if bread were baked and lagging footsteps directed home from school, insurance premiums paid, and picnics taken in the family car, in imminent fear of the punishments of the Lord if any of these family rites were omitted. True, religious sanctions were more frequently invoked in the past against those who might have repudiated their marriages, and by those who half wished to repudiate them. But no family life, with its demands for a myriad of small unremembered acts of kindness and love, would hold together if threats of eternal punishment or promises of eternal reward had to be introduced every washday. Family life worked because that was the way family life was lived by people who had been reared to expect it would work that way.

It isn't that common meals or a common roof or twenty years without ever being a night apart are necessary conditions of family life. Regular Army and Navy wives, who tend to be chosen from Army and Navy daughters, expect long absences on the part of their husbands and become adjusted to them. The marriages of sailors and salesmen, missionaries, members of the American foreign service, construction gang men, actors—all have their special patterns within which human beings have found satisfying relationships and children have been reared—oftener than not to prefer the occupation of their seldom-seen parents. But the average American marriage had its pattern too—a wife who stayed home and put up with a lot (especially in the lower income groups), a husband who came home and put up with a lot, and children who expected to find Mother, jam, and admonitions when they came home from school.

From many millions of such families the war has torn away the protecting walls within which they lived. Most of the overt reasons which will be cited for divorce and delinquency and broken homes were there, to be sure: lack of background, unwise choice of mate, lack of preparation for parenthood, inexperience in adapting sex responses to a continuing human relationship, lack of experience in communicating emotions or articulating attitudes, lack of knowledge of homemaking on the part of both men and women, a restless desire for social mobility—all these were there. And schoolchildren preferred their age mates, were impatient with the parents who took no pains to understand them, were restive under home standards too unyielding and particular to stand the test of the way other people's families lived. But as long as the familiar peacetime conditions held, mother stayed at home and kept the house in reasonable order, and if her heart ached she was likely to blame it on her feet. Father sometimes felt he hadn't had all the breaks he might have had in life, but he came home night after night as fast as his car would carry him. The children growled and ate the jam and dreamed of the days when they would be old enough to have jobs and door keys and cars of their own. And the family, American style, 1940, held together.

Today, we know that the family, however sacred or secular we may personally feel it to be, changes its form, as house forms, methods of employment, methods of making war change through the centuries.

And we know one thing more: that although man cannot by taking thought add one cubit to his stature, he can, by taking thought, add a great deal of sense to his culture. The question is, how are young people—and older people—who have been reared to depend on one kind of family life going to maintain their human relationships without the forms it provided?

Just for example: The soldier who has been married and away for two years now acts as he learned, in his childhood and youth, that young men act who have been married for two years—and so does his wife. He doesn't court her any more. Nor does she bother about how her hair looks at home. Such gestures weren't necessary when two years of common living had bound them firmly together. But he has not been married—in the old sense—for two years. He has been married—in the old sense—perhaps two weeks, with an additional (and dangerous) period of mutual idealization thrown in—idealization which would never have survived badly fried eggs or inexpert shaving. If he can learn, from the stories he reads, from the comic strips he pores over, that his wife of two years is more like a girl who has just said "Yes!" but hasn't yet his ring on her finger—and also that she is a different girl by now from the girl who accepted him—he'll have a partial pattern ready-made for himself. Instead of presuming on two years that never were, he can start over, except to woo her again, and expect her to act as if she were just as anxious to keep his affection.

Older couples separated for months or years, and homes disrupted by the mother's working, will also need new patterns, to help the husband understand why his word doesn't seem quite so much like law, why his wife doesn't slip back into washing the window curtains regularly and like it. They will be more likely to be able to work out these patterns if they realize the nature of the adjustment that they face; and they will be more likely to realize it if the symbol-makers help them—if novels and movies, radio broadcasts, magazine stories and comic strips illuminate it, for them and for all of us.

In short, the ideal of the family still remains; in many of those who have lived weary years alone it is stronger than ever; but it will take a concerted effort, for those who must live in it and those who live by writing about it, to restyle it so that it is livable for these human beings who are caught between one family form and another.

Three · Separation and Adjustment — A Case

JOHN F. CUBER
Sociologist, Ohio State University

The following case * illustrates many factors that may be involved in a precipitous marriage. The problems are increased when separation is necessary (as in wartime), for separation early in marriage deprives the couple of the necessity for growing together at a time when the motivation for making adjustments is strongest.

THE war has added new insecurities to an already baffling array. Feelings of insecurity have profound effects on the

* Reprinted from *The Annals* of the American Academy of Political and Social Sciences, 1943, 229: 34–36, by permission of the author and the editor.

personality. This is reasonably well understood by most informed persons. One of the more profound sociological effects, however, is that a feeling of insecurity forces upon a person the necessity of making short-run adjustments to the problem of living. Long-run plans and adjustments are feasible only when some measure of security is felt. When a person's very existence is in jeopardy, when he is unable to make any reasonable plans for his professional or personal future, or, as in the case of women, when others upon whom one is emotionally dependent threaten to be taken away temporarily or permanently, persons are forced to live "for the day if not for the hour." There is no alternative which is practicable— or at least so it appears.

QUASI MARRIAGES

Since the war began there have occurred thousands of marriages which must be regarded as unique war marriages, not merely because they occurred in wartime, but in that their very essence is profoundly influenced by the war motif. The following excerpts from a fuller case study are not entirely typical, but certainly not completely atypical.

We were college "steadies" for six months with no mention of marriage ever made between us. We were not prudish in our erotic behavior though I did remain a virgin. . . . Then he was drafted. I promised to write him twice a week and he promised to write as often as he could. Gradually his letters became more and more ardent. And soon he proposed. Before I could collect my wits for a reply he was home for a furlough. We weren't alone for an hour before he was pressing the marriage issue with all the high pressure tactics I had heard of plus a few more. . . . I liked him very much. We did seem to have much in common. I doubted that I was in love but I couldn't prove it. We were both emotionally tense after months of separation. I don't know just how it happened but I suddenly realized that I was no longer virginal. The seven day furlough was almost over and the pressure to get married was now greater than ever. . . . We were married on the sixth day of the furlough. He then went back to camp. I didn't see him for three months. Then I received a letter from him stating that he had found a room for me near the camp and that he had made arrangements with his commanding officer to have his week ends free. I could surely find a job there. So over night I packed a few belongings and boarded a train for another part of America where I had never been before. And there I lived for three months a semi-prisoner. One and a half days each week were deliriously happy; five and a half were dismally lonely, like a prisoner in a foreign land. . . . Then he received orders to move and I went back to my home community because in his new situation it was impossible for him to live with his wife. At first I was lonely, but soon the exhilaration of being "among my own" again readjusted me. I moved in my old circle of friends. . . . One day someone suggested that I go on a "date"—a purely platonic date, of course, with a fraternity brother of my husband. And the date was platonic to the point of brutality. Both of us were so anxious that it remain platonic and that there be no infidelity that the whole affair was funny or tragic depending upon how you look at it. There being no harm on that date there was another and another and suddenly they weren't so platonic. Gradually I began to realize that I was falling in love with this man and he with me. And accordingly we broke off the relationship, abruptly. Soon thereafter I discovered that I was pregnant—by my husband, of course. (The other affair never having gone that far.) When I wrote the news to my husband he was very disturbed. Though solicitous of my welfare he couldn't help revealing the fact that the role of father was incomprehensible to him under the circumstances. I could understand him because I felt the same way. We had never really been truly married and both of us knew it. If we had had a normal home life we could perhaps have fallen into some kind of normal love relationship even after marriage. But the sum total of our married life was seven week ends in that not-too-pleasant room in a foreign culture. Meanwhile I was haunted by my recently discovered relationship with the second man. I cannot justify it ethically but I feel it emotionally. A week ago I learned that my husband has gone overseas. I shall not see him now for the duration, at least. The second man, like me, finds it difficult to call our relationship off, even though he knows that I am pregnant and I strongly wish to remain loyal to my marriage. . . . I haven't the slightest idea how it will all turn out but I must confess, being as rational as I can, that I can see many possible outcomes but none that is satisfactory.

This is the essential story of a war marriage between two persons, one 22 and one 24 years of age, both college graduates and both professionally trained. The case has been quoted at length because so many aspects of the war courtship and quasi marriage are revealed through it: ⟨1⟩ the hurried nature of many marriages between two persons not emotionally quite ready for marriage, or, stated otherwise, aborted courtship; (2) some of the effects of prolonged separation for married and unmarried pairs; (3) the problems of a quasi "home"; (4) the subtle and important influence of the ever potential third person in that kind of marriage; and (5) the wartime nuptial pregnancy.

For the future stability of many of these marriages the best prognosis was probably given by the woman: "I can see many possible outcomes but none that seems satisfactory" as a basis upon which to build a good family life for man, woman, and child.

Four · Time Required
to Achieve Marriage Adjustment

JUDSON T. LANDIS
Sociologist, University of California
at Berkeley

*The selection below * summarizes a study of marital
adjustment designed to determine the number of months or years it
takes couples to achieve working arrangements in the various areas
of living involved in marriage.*

OUR hypothesis was that not only does it take months
or years to arrive at adjustments in marriage but also that there is a
definite relationship between the time taken to adjust in the different areas and the happiness of the marriage.

We use the term adjustment in this study to refer to a working
arrangement which exists in marriage. This arrangement could be
one which is mutually satisfactory or one which is satisfactory to
one spouse but unsatisfactory to the other. The term adjustment is
used, then, to refer to the state of accommodation which is achieved
in different areas where conflict may exist in marriage.

Nine hundred freshman and sophomore students were asked to
send copies of a four-page questionnaire to their parents or to
friends with a request that the questionnaires be filled in and returned. It was made clear that the responses were to be anonymous.

Each spouse was asked to respond to the questionnaire independently of the other spouse. They were asked to check how long
it had taken them to work out an adjustment in each of the following six areas: spending the family income, relationships with in-
laws, sex relations, religious life in the home, choosing and
associating with mutual friends, and social activities and recreation.
They were also asked to state their present adjustment in each of
these areas and in one other area, the training and disciplining of
the children. In addition, they were asked to rate the happiness
of their marriage.

The study is, in the main, a study of successful marriages. The
sample represents a select group in the following respects: the
marriages have existed an average of twenty years; no divorced or
separated people were included in the sample; the respondents

* Reprinted from the *American Sociological Review*, 1946, 11: 666–677, by
permission of the *American Sociological Review*.

were largely the parents of college students; the incomes were above the average of the general population; and the number of years of education were above the average of the general population. The sample is probably representative of the parents of college students for whom courses in marriage and family relationships are being organized. Forty-eight per cent of those responding classified their marriages as very happy, 34.6 per cent happy, 16.4 per cent as average, and less than one per cent as unhappy or very unhappy. Thirty-four per cent received incomes from $1,000 to $2,999, 36 per cent from $3,000 to $4,999, 22 per cent from $5,000 to $9,999, and 8 per cent from $10,000 and over. Twenty-three per cent had had a grade school education, 43 per cent, a high school education, and 34 per cent, a college education.

The response to the questionnaires was very good. There was a return of over fifty per cent. Many comments were given explaining the difficulties in each area. Responses that were incomplete were discarded and those cases were eliminated in which only one partner of the marriage responded. After such eliminations the responses of 409 couples were used for the analyses. The information was put on punch cards and an analysis made by the length of time required to achieve adjustment in each area. In addition, the data on length of time required to achieve adjustment in each area were analyzed by years of education, years of marriage, age at marriage, and church attendance. Happiness ratings of the marriage were also analyzed by these same factors.

LENGTH OF TIME REQUIRED TO ADJUST IN SEX RELATIONS

Husbands and wives agreed that it took longer to achieve a satisfactory adjustment in sex relations than in any other area in which adjustment had to be made. Slightly over one-half of the couples felt that they had made a satisfactory adjustment from the beginning. Of the husbands an additional 15.2 per cent felt that there had been a satisfactory adjustment from the beginning, while a further 8.8 per cent of the wives felt there had been a satisfactory adjustment from the beginning. In these cases, however, the other spouse did not agree. The disagreeing spouse stated that it had taken months or years, or that a satisfactory adjustment in sex relations had never been made. It will be noticed that the husbands more frequently than the wives stated that the sex adjustment was satisfactory from the beginning. Approximately 12 per cent of the men and women reported that they had made a satisfactory adjustment within the first year, and ten per cent in from one to 20 years, the average being six years. Twelve per cent of the individuals felt that there had never been a satisfactory adjustment, and six per cent of the couples agreed on this point. Four per cent of the wives and seven per cent of the husbands made statements that conflicted with those of the other spouse on sex adjustment. These two groups stated that a satisfactory adjustment had never been achieved, while their spouses stated that the adjustment had been satisfactory.

TIME TO MAKE ADJUSTMENTS ON SPENDING
THE FAMILY INCOME

Husbands and wives agreed in stating that the second most difficult area of adjustment was in the spending of the family income.[1] There were no significant sex differences in the time the individuals reported that it had taken to achieve a satisfactory adjustment other than that the men were slightly more optimistic in reporting that everything was satisfactory from the beginning. It will be noticed that 56 per cent of the couples agreed that they made the adjustment from the beginning and that in the cases of an additional 11 per cent of the couples one spouse or the other thought it had been satisfactory. In about equal percentages the disagreeing spouses said that it had taken one year, several years, or that they had never made the adjustment. Approximately nine per cent felt the adjustment had been made within the first year and 13 per cent within one to 20 years, the average number of years required being seven. One couple reported that it was 34 years before they reached a satisfactory adjustment. About ten per cent of the men and women stated they had never made a satisfactory adjustment, five per cent of the couples agreeing. In the other cases one spouse felt that no adjustment had been made, while the other usually felt that the adjustment had been made from the beginning. It is interesting to note, in these cases of disagreement, that the one spouse who thought the adjustment was satisfactory from the beginning also checked the statement "it is satisfactory for both of us."

TIME TO MAKE ADJUSTMENT IN SOCIAL ACTIVITIES

The area which was listed as ranking third in length of time required to make the adjustment was the area centering around social activities and recreation. It is not as serious as making an adjustment in sex and spending the family income, standing about half-way between the two extreme areas of least difficulty and most difficulty. Of all the couples, 66.8 per cent agreed that they had made the adjustment from the beginning. In nine per cent more cases one spouse thought it had been satisfactory from the beginning; a slightly larger percentage of the husbands feeling that the

---

[1] "Spending the family income" included earning, spending, saving, insufficient income, and budgeting.

adjustment had been satisfactory from the beginning. Four per cent of the men and women stated that an adjustment had been made within the first year, 5.6 per cent said it took from one to twenty years, and 13.6 per cent said there had never been a satisfactory adjustment in this area. A larger percentage of women reported that they had never made a satisfactory adjustment in the realm of social activities than in any other single area. The 45 men and women who reported that they had reached a satisfactory adjustment in from one to twenty years gave an average of seven years.

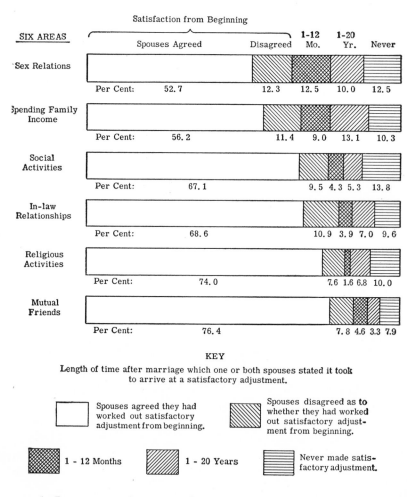

FIG. 1. *Percentages of 409 Couples Reporting Various Periods of Time After Marriage to Achieve Adjustments in Six Areas; Sex Relations, Spending the Family Income, Social Activities, In-Law Relationships, Religious Activities, and Associating with Mutual Friends.*

TIME TO MAKE ADJUSTMENT ON IN-LAW RELATIONSHIPS

Approximately the same percentage of the couples, 67.3 per cent, reported a satisfactory adjustment on relationships with in-laws from the beginning as on social activities. In 10.7 per cent more instances, one spouse felt that the adjustment had been satisfactory from the beginning. Within the first year 3.8 per cent achieved an adjustment, and 6.8 per cent in from one to twenty years; the average being eight and one-half years. Those feeling that they had never made a satisfactory adjustment in relationships with their in-laws totaled 9.4 per cent.

TIME TO ADJUST IN RELIGION

Making an adjustment in the religious life of a couple required less time than in most other areas. This may be because many churches discourage "mixed marriages." Parents also encourage their children to marry those of the same faith so that young people are more awake to the problems in this area than in other adjustment areas of marriage. A satisfactory adjustment from the beginning was achieved by 73.6 per cent of the couples. In 7.6 per cent more cases, one spouse felt that the adjustment had been satisfactory from the beginning. Again, the husbands were a little more liberal in stating that the adjustment was satisfactory from the beginning. Among the remainder, only 1.5 per cent said they had worked out an adjustment in the first year, and 6.9 per cent in from one to 20 years, with an average of approximately six years. Almost ten per cent stated that they had never arrived at a satisfactory adjustment. A larger percentage of the women than the men felt that the adjustment had never been satisfactory.

TIME TO MAKE ADJUSTMENT WITH FRIENDS

The area in which the 409 couples found the least difficulty in adjusting was in choosing and associating with friends. Seventy-six per cent of the couples agreed that their adjustment in this area had been satisfactory from the beginning. In 7.7 per cent more instances one spouse thought it had been satisfactory from the beginning. Approximately five per cent of the couples stated that they had made the adjustment during the first year, 3.3 per cent in from one to 20 years, with an average of five and one-half years, while 7.7 per cent felt that there had never been a satisfactory adjustment. Again more women than men reported that the adjustment had never been satisfactory.

We have seen that the sexes agreed in rating the six areas in the same order of difficulty. They agreed fairly well on the length of time required to make the adjustment or in stating that they had never made the adjustments. There was a tendency for a larger percentage of the men to state that the adjustment had been satisfactory from the beginning in all areas and, with the exception of sex and income, for fewer to state that they had never made the adjustment. This supports the conclusion that in our culture the wife has to make a greater adjustment in marriage than does the husband. She knows the situation is not satisfactory but she must adjust herself to the domination of the husband in the marriage relationship. The husband is frustrated more by failure to make the adjustments in sex relations and spending the family income, while the wife is more frustrated because of the failure to make a good adjustment in religion, in associating with friends, or in social activities.

STATE OF ADJUSTMENT IN EACH AREA

To see just what adjustment the couples had achieved in the six areas under discussion, each person was asked to check one of eight statements which described his present adjustment. It will be remembered that in each of the six areas, approximately ten per cent of the husbands and wives said they had never reached a satisfactory adjustment. The statements checked indicated that from 18 to 37 per cent of the couples had not achieved an adjustment "satisfactory to both" in the six areas. The largest group, 37 per cent, had not achieved a mutually satisfactory adjustment in sex relations, and the smallest group, 18 per cent, in associating with mutual friends. These husbands and wives reported that an adjustment had been made, but that it was satisfactory to one and not to the other. Some gave one of the other statements describing the adjustment. (See Table 1.)

TIME REQUIRED FOR MAKING ADJUSTMENT IN
RELATION TO EDUCATION

As was noted earlier, 23 per cent of the 818 spouses were grade school graduates, 43 per cent high school graduates, and 34 per cent college graduates. No consistent relationship was found to exist between increased years of education and the length of time required to adjust in the six areas. In working out an adjustment in social activities there was a slight positive association between increasing years of education and length of time to adjust; in sex relations, spending the family income, and in-law relationships there was a very slight negative association; and in religious activities and associating with mutual friends there was no difference in the length of time required to adjust.

TABLE 1. PERCENTAGES OF 409 COUPLES REPORTING VARIOUS DEGREES OF PRESENT ADJUSTMENT IN SEVEN AREAS

Present Adjustment	Sex Rela-tions	Social Activi-ties	Child Train-ing	Re-ligion	Spend-ing the Income	In-law Rela-tionships	Mutual Friends
Satisfactory for me but un-satisfactory for my spouse	4.8	3.0	2.4	3.4	2.6	3.0	1.5
Satisfactory for my spouse but unsatisfactory for me	3.5	3.2	3.4	2.6	2.7	2.6	1.6
Satisfactory for both of us							
Spouses Agreed	63.1	72.1	70.7	75.8	77.0	76.5	82.1
Spouses Disagreed	16.2	9.8	13.1	8.3	7.5	8.4	7.1
Unsatisfactory for both of us but working toward a better adjustment	2.4	3.4	5.8	2.6	6.0	1.9	3.0
At a standstill in adjust-ment	2.2	2.4	.5	2.5	1.2	.7	.9
Have many quarrels over it	.9	.7	2.8	.2	.6	.2	.6
Never discuss the subject	3.9	2.1	.7	3.2	.7	3.0	2.0
Think we will never reach a satisfactory adjust-ment	3.0	3.3	.6	1.4	1.7	3.7	1.2
Total	100.0	100.0	100.0	100.0	100.0	100.0	100.0

CHURCH ATTENDANCE AND LENGTH OF TIME TO ADJUST

The relationship between the frequency of church attendance and time required for making adjustment was considered. There was found to be no consistently reliable relationship between those who go to church regularly and occasionally or never and the length of time required to adjust in marriage.

ADJUSTMENT AND AGE AT MARRIAGE

The length of time required to make satisfactory adjustments in the various areas was analyzed by age at marriage. The age at marriage was of significant importance in determining how soon people achieved a satisfactory adjustment in the different areas. With one exception, religion, those married under 20 made a poor adjustment when compared with those who married over 20. Again, with two exceptions (in-law relationships and the choice of mutual friends) those who were married at 30 years or older made a better adjustment than those married at any other age. The greatest dif-ference was found in the adjustment in the area of sex relations. Only 47 per cent of the men who married under 20 said the adjust-ment was satisfactory from the beginning, while 83 per cent of the men who were 30 and over when they married said the adjustment was satisfactory from the beginning. There was a great sex difference in these two groups. Both men and women who married under 20 had difficulty in adjusting in sex relations, but it was especially the men who experienced difficulty. Of those who married over 30, it was the men who reported the greatest degree of success rather than the women. The men who married at the age of 30 or over included fewer who never made a satisfactory adjustment in sex relations than any other age group. In this same group, however, there were more women who had never adjusted in sex relations than there were in any other age group.

Although the percentages were different, the same pattern existed with relation to the age of marriage among males and spending the family income. The men who married under 20 had the greatest difficulty, while those who married at 30 and over had the least difficulty.

In the realm of social activities, the same pattern also appears, with the exception that the sex difference is not present. Both the men and women who married under 20 reported the highest percentage of failures at the beginning and both reported the greater success among those who married when 30 or over. The men who married under 20 seemed to have much more difficulty in making the adjustment with the in-laws from the beginning than did those who married later. This might be explained by a greater tendency for parents to interfere or to attempt to supervise when very young people marry. However, the women who married between 15 and 29 got along as well with the in-laws as did those who married later. The women who married at 30 or over included more who failed to get along with the in-laws from the beginning and more who had never adjusted with the in-laws. When the age of marriage was related to the time required to make the adjustment in religion and with mutual friends, no pronounced difference was found in the age groups. Those who married when 30 or over had a slightly better chance to make an adjustment in both areas early in marriage and, in addition, there were fewer who never made the adjustment. Again, it was the men who married under 20 who had the most difficulty.

NUMBER OF YEARS MARRIED AND ADJUSTMENT IN SIX AREAS

Since the questionnaire was answered by people who had been married from one to 40 years, the question arose as to whether those who had been married 30 years or more might have forgotten the difficulties they experienced in the earlier years of their marriage and that those who had been married under ten years might exaggerate the problems of early marriage. Therefore, a breakdown by ten-year periods was made to learn whether the duration of the marriage had affected the responses given. The analysis showed that all four ten-year groups rated the areas in the same order. It is true, however, that those who had been married from 30 to 40 years reported a greater percentage of successful adjustments from the beginning and in general fewer said that they had never made an adjustment. The exception here was in sex relations in which those married from 30 to 40 years reported a greater percentage of failures than any other group.

Studying the relationship between the duration of the marriage and the time required to make adjustments showed that the greatest difference was in adjustment in sex relations. Only 56 per cent of the spouses who had been married from one to ten years said the adjustment had been satisfactory from the beginning. The percentage increased by about five per cent with each successive age group, so that 70 per cent of the spouses who had been married 30 years and over said the adjustment was satisfactory from the beginning. Of those who have never made an adjustment, there were the most failures among the women who had been married under ten years and among the men who had been married over 30 years.

A study of the relationship between the duration of the marriage and the adjustment in spending the family income, in social activities, and in the area of associating with friends showed little variation with the exception that as noted above, there were more who made successful adjustments from the beginning and fewer who never made a satisfactory adjustment among those married 30 or more years. In the area of religion the largest percentage of successful adjustments from the beginning was reported by those who had been married from one to ten years. The couples who reported greatest difficulty in adjusting to in-law relationships from the beginning had been married from one to 20 years.

HAPPINESS OF MARRIAGE

After completing the questionnaire, each person was asked to check a phrase which most nearly described his marriage: very happy, happy, average, unhappy, or very unhappy.[2] Since these marriages have lasted an average of 20 years, one would not expect to find many unhappy marriages. Forty-eight per cent said the marriage had been very happy, 34.6 per cent happy, 16.4 per cent average, and .8 per cent unhappy or very unhappy. There were no sex differences in the rating of the happiness of the marriages. A very close relationship existed between the length of time required to adjust and the rating of the happiness of the marriage. A greater percentage of those who made their adjustment from the beginning

[2] The same five degrees of happiness were used by Burgess and Cottrell. In that study 42.6 were very happy, 20.5 happy, 14.4 average, 13.5 unhappy, and 8.0 very unhappy. Since there were divorced people in the Burgess-Cottrell study, one would not expect so many happy marriages as were found in this study.

in each area rated the marriage as very happy. There was a gradual decrease in the percentage of very happy with the increase in time required to make satisfactory adjustments.

The question arises as to whether a marriage can be very happy if there has never been a satisfactory adjustment in some area or areas. Of those who made an adjustment from the beginning in sex relations, 53.3 per cent said they were very happy, 35.3 happy, and only 11.4 per cent said they were average in happiness. On the other hand, of those who had never made an adjustment in sex, the figures are reversed. A rating of very happy was given by 11.2 per

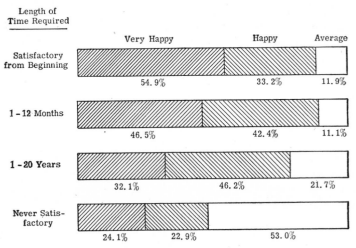

FIG. 2. *Degree of Self-Rated Happiness of 409 Couples Reporting Various Lengths of Time Required to Make Adjustments in Spending the Family Income.*

cent, happy by 36.7 per cent, and a rating of average by 53.1 per cent. In general, the same pattern existed in all areas: those who never made a satisfactory adjustment in an area were more likely to consider their marriage average in happiness. (See Figure 2.) There was a sex difference, more women than men saying their marriage had been average if there had never been an adjustment concerning friends or in social activities. On the other hand, more men than women said their marriage had been average if the adjustment had never been satisfactory in sex relations or in spending the income.

FAILURE TO ADJUST IN MORE THAN ONE AREA AND HAPPINESS

If spouses agreed that they had failed to make adjustments in any two areas, approximately four out of five of the marriages were classified as average or unhappy. If they failed to adjust in three or more areas, all were in the average or unhappy classification. Only one couple agreed that they had never adjusted in as many as five areas. This would be expected since this is a study of successful marriage. Some couples were contemplating divorce who had failed to adjust in from two to five areas. (See Figure 3.)

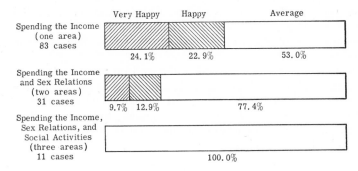

FIG. 3. *Happiness of Marriages in Which Couples Had Never Adjusted in One, Two, or Three Areas.*

AGE AT MARRIAGE, INCOME, YEARS MARRIED, EDUCATION, HEALTH, CHURCH ATTENDANCE, AND HAPPINESS

When an analysis was made of happiness ratings of the marriages by the age at which men and women married, it was found that a smaller percentage of those who married under 20 years reported their marriages as being very happy, the men experiencing the greater difficulty. Of the husbands the largest percentage of very happy marriages was among those who had married at the age of 30 or over, of the wives those who had married between the ages of 20 to 24. An analysis of the happiness rating by income showed that those who had incomes of $5,000 and over were more likely to be found in the happy group and a smaller percentage found in the average group than those who had less than a $5,000 income. An analysis by number of years married indicated that those who had been married under ten years reported the largest percentage of very happy marriages and the smallest percentages of average marriages, while those who had been married 30 to 40 years reported the fewest very happy marriages and the largest percentage of average marriages. The reporting of fewer happy marriages in the older age group would seem to be an indication of a somewhat different outlook on life rather than evidence that marriages become less happy as people grow older. A significant relationship existed between health and happiness in marriage. Of those who had very good health, 63 per cent said the marriage was very happy and only eight per cent termed it average, while of those with poor health

46 per cent said the marriage was very happy and 19 per cent average. Those who were regular church attendants rated their marriages as very happy in greater numbers than those who attended church occasionally or never. A slightly larger percentage of those having a college education rated their marriage as very happy and a smaller percentage rated the marriage as unhappy when compared with those who had a high school or a grade school education. The amount of education was more closely related to the happiness of the women than it was to the happiness of the men.

Husbands and wives agreed fairly well on the happiness rating of their marriages. When there was disagreement the spouse tended to place the marriage on the next higher or on the next lower rating with only 16 of the couples disagreeing to the extent that one spouse rated the happiness of the marriage as very happy while the other rated it as average.

SUMMARY AND CONCLUSION

Husbands and wives, regardless of age at marriage, years married, or years of education, reported it had taken more time to work out adjustment in sex relations than in any other area. They agreed in listing the rest of the areas in the following order: spending the family income, social activities and recreation, in-law relationships, religion in the home, and associating with mutual friends.

There was a very close relationship between the length of time required to adjust in marriage and the happiness of the marriage.

If couples failed to work out adjustment in three or more areas, they classified their marriage as average or unhappy.

The study confirms the findings of others that age at marriage, education, income, and health are associated with happiness in marriage.

A similar study representing a cross-section of the population would be desirable. This is a study of successful marriages among the parents of college students.

Five · *Predicting Adjustment in Marriage*

ERNEST W. BURGESS
Sociologist, University of Chicago

LEONARD S. COTTRELL, JR.
Sociologist, Cornell University

Reprinted below * *are the major findings and inter-pretations of Burgess' and Cottrell's study of marital adjustment. The statistical findings of their study of 526 couples are used in the marital prediction test which grew out of this research.*

AT the conclusion of a study the three following questions are almost always asked, and they are always well worth attention:

1. What, if any, contributions have been made to knowledge?
2. What is the significance of these contributions?
3. What further research is indicated?

An attempt will be made in this chapter to answer the first two questions by summarizing briefly the major findings of the study and by indicating their significance for an understanding of the way in which men and women adjust to each other in marriage.

Wives make the major adjustment in marriage. An outstanding, if not the most significant, finding of this study is that the background items of the husbands are much more important for adjustment in marriage than are the background items of the wives.

Why should the premarital characteristics of the husband be so much more closely correlated with marital adjustment than those of the wife? Perhaps in marriage the wife, on the average, makes much more of an adjustment to the husband than he makes to her.

On first thought the explanation that wives in the United States make the major adjustment in marriage is directly in contradiction to the American conception that marriage is a "fifty-fifty proposition" in which husband and wife make equal adaptations to one another. It might have been assumed that husbands in this country more than anywhere else in the world are disposed to cater to and comply with the wishes, attitudes, and even whims of their wives. European visitors to the United States are quick to point out the dominant position of the American wife in the home and the subservient or secondary role of her husband.

---

* Reprinted from *Predicting Success or Failure in Marriage*, by Ernest W. Burgess and Leonard S. Cottrell, Jr., New York: Prentice-Hall, Inc., 1939, pp. 341–349, by permission of the authors and publisher.

The findings of this study regarding the relatively greater weight of the characteristics of the husband in determining marital adjustment suggest that too much emphasis has been placed upon the superficial aspects of the American marital relationship. These aspects appear greater by contrast with the obvious and definite subordination of woman to man in Old-World marriages. Where the mores decree that the wife shall be submissive to the husband, as in Germany and to a lesser extent in England, all couples manifest a uniform pattern of behavior which corresponds to the approved forms.

In the United States, where the mores sanction equality in the marriage relation, the superficial forms of the husband's behavior may hide the actual situation. Since the mores do not demand the obvious display of the husband's dominance, wide individual differences in the marital relations are apparent. In many unions the wife is in fact, and not merely seemingly, superordinate. The domineering wife and the "henpecked" husband, to mention an extreme illustration, are much more evident in the United States than in Europe. The dictatorship of wives, however, is undoubtedly limited to a relatively small proportion of marriages. The majority of wives must still achieve their aims in subtle and indirect ways which evidence the dominant position of their husbands.

The statistical findings of this study deal with averages and obscure individual differences. Our problem is, then, to explain why so great an average discrepancy exists between the greater inferred adaptability of the wife than of the husband.

Two explanations are at hand which may operate independently or in conjunction. First, it may be assumed that the new mores emphasizing equality of the sexes in marriage have not as yet entirely displaced the old attitude that the husband should be dominant. Second, it may be asserted that the trait of dominance is, on the average, more marked in the male, and that of submission in the female. To the extent that this is true, the wife would be disposed to be subordinate and the husband superordinate.

To state that at present in American society dominance is in general a male, and submission a female, trait is not to imply that this difference is necessarily biological. It may, in fact, be social, not in the sense that it is commanded by the mores, but in that it persists in the attitudes arising out of our self-consciousness of sex differences and our conception of what is expected in the behavior of boys and girls, men and women.

Further research will be necessary to clarify the points raised by the discussion of these findings. If they actually measure present differences in the amount of adjustment made by man and woman in marriage, then it should be possible to determine the varying differences in adjustment between the husbands and wives in different sections of the United States. Comparative studies might be made to verify assumed differences between the East and the West, the North and the South, or between different districts within the city, as between equalitarian-family areas, semipatriarchal immigrant districts, and the matricentric suburban neighborhoods. It would be assumed, for example, that the Southern wife makes a greater adjustment in marriage than the Western wife, and that the immigrant wife living in the semipatriarchal-family neighborhood is more submissive to her husband than is the wife who is herself gainfully employed and residing in the apartment-house area with its equalitarian standards of family life.

The affectional relationships of childhood condition the love life of the adult. The response patterns of relationships established in childhood appear to be the dynamic factor determining the expression of affection in adult life. This finding is derived from the examination of 100 case studies in this investigation. It corresponds more or less closely to the conclusions reached by other workers in their clinical analysis of material obtained over a prolonged period by intensive psychiatric interviews. It is corroborated by the statistical evidence provided by this study.

Two general effects of the familial affectional environment upon the adjustment in marriage of young people have been independently established by Terman's study and by the present research:

1. Happy marriages of parents are correlated with happiness in the marriage of their children. This relationship is the outstanding association noticed in the study of the relation between background items of both husbands and wives and their adjustment in marriage.

2. Close attachment in childhood to father and mother and absence of conflict with them is positively correlated with the person's adjustment in marriage.

These two conclusions indicate the general correlation that obtains between a happy family relationship in childhood, with close attachment between parents and children, and a satisfactory adjustment as an adult in the marriage relationship itself.

Our case-study data enable us to proceed a step further and to make a specific formulation of a theory of childhood affectional attachment in relation to marital adjustment, as follows:

1. In childhood the person builds up a response relationship to the parent of the opposite sex which markedly influences his response to and selection of a love object in adult life.

2. If the childhood affectional relation to the parent of the opposite sex has been a satisfying one, the person will tend to fall in love with someone possessing temperamental and personality characteristics similar to those of the loved parent.

3. If the childhood affectional relation has been unsatisfactory, he is more likely to fall in love with a person of opposite temperamental and personality characteristics. An exception occurs where the relation in childhood has been one of frustration rather than of

conflict, so that as a consequence of idealization the person seeks all the more in a loved one the personality type of the parent of the opposite sex. Where the attitude is ambivalent, then there may develop alternating attitudes of love and hatred toward the affectional object.

4. The childhood response fixation is generally, but not always, upon the parent of the opposite sex. It may under certain conditions be centered upon the parent of the same sex or upon a brother or sister.

5. The actual complex of attitudes in affectional relationships in adult life tends to reproduce all the significant response patterns of childhood. Thus the adult unconsciously strives to act in his love life not only his childhood role with regard to his sex-opposite parent but also his childhood roles with regard to his parent of the same sex, to his older brother or sister, and to his younger brother or sister. Where the relation has been ambivalent, as in the case of submissive and rebellious behavior, this pattern also tends to be expressed in the marital relation.

This theory of the nature of early childhood affectional relationships as determining the dynamics of adjustment in marriage is of such great significance, if correct, that systematic effort should be made to verify or disprove it by objective methods. Its validation would greatly simplify the understanding of a great field of behavior that otherwise seems to be hopelessly complex, complicated, and often contradictory.

Socialization of the person is significant for adjustment in marriage. A group of background items constituting what may be called the social factor in marital adjustment is found to be significantly related to success in marriage. Among these items are: higher level of education; objective evidence of religious activity, such as duration and frequency of attendance at Sunday school and church; the number and sex of friends; participation in social organizations; and residence in neighborhoods of single-family dwellings. These items taken together may be regarded as an index of sociability, or of socialization in respect to the degree of participation and achievement of the person in the activities of the community and its chief cultural institutions—the family, the school, and the church.

The impress of social institutions upon a person may be measured in terms of his conformity to social rules, his respect for conventions, and his stability of character. The socialization of the person which results prepares him for adjustment in marriage.

The economic factor, in itself, is not significant for adjustment in marriage. A finding quite unexpected by the writers, and almost certain to be surprising to the public, is the virtual disappearance of the premarital economic items from the group of items significant in marital adjustment. It is true that several economic items such as moderate income, savings, occupations characterized by stability and social control, and regularity and continuity of employment are positively correlated with adjustment in marriage. But all these combined add very little to the effectiveness of the prediction that can be made without them. In fact, by the method of partial correlation whereby other factors are held constant, the discovery is made that the correlation of the economic factor with the prediction score is only .04 in comparison with .20 for the psychogenetic factor and the response factor, respectively; .18 for the socialization factor; and .14 for the cultural-impress factor.

The explanation for the very low weight to be assigned to the economic items in marital adjustment is that they add very little to the items included under psychogenetic, cultural-impress, social-type, and response factors. It may, indeed, be argued that the economic behavior of the person, at least so far as it affects adjustment in marriage, is an expression of these noneconomic factors. Economic items such as moderate income, savings, occupations characterized by stability and social control, regularity and continuity of employment, may all be taken as indicating a stabilized and socialized personality which readily adjusts to the marriage situation. But this is a type of personality which is also strongly indicated by psychogenetic, cultural-impress, social-type, and response factors. The economic behavior of the person may therefore be thought of as the resultant of these noneconomic influences. In fact, the trait of personality which all our items are measuring may turn out to be *adjustability* or *socialization* that makes for adjustment in society, in industry, and in marriage. However, it must be remembered that the sample on which this study is based does not cover the entire range of economic groups in our culture.

With the majority of couples, sexual adjustment in marriage appears to be a resultant not so much of biological factors as of psychogenetic development and of cultural conditioning of attitudes toward sex. This finding is derived from case studies and, while rather clearly indicated, should not be taken as conclusively established. It is in harmony with the obvious generalization that the biological growth and maturation of the individual takes place in association and interaction with his emotional, intellectual, and social development. The understanding of any one of these aspects of human growth is necessarily to be arrived at in the context of the others.

Prediction before marriage of marital adjustment is feasible, and should and can be further developed through statistical and case-study techniques. This study has demonstrated the feasibility of predicting adjustment in marriage and has indicated the course of future research to improve the accuracy and significance of prediction.

With present methods it is entirely practicable to indicate the risk group into which any engaged person will fall, with a definite statement regarding the statistical probabilities of success or failure in marriage. This is, however, group prediction, as with life-expectancy tables which are used by life-insurance companies. But the prediction of marital adjustment has one advantage over that of a life-expectancy table: our study indicates that statistical prediction for all practical purposes can be applied to particular individuals at the two extremes where all, or at least 99 out of 100, persons assigned to the highest and to the lowest risk group will either succeed or fail in marriage, according to the predictions.

The most practical use of prediction will, however, undoubtedly be with individual cases. It is, therefore, the aim of research to increase the precision, reliability, and significance of prediction in individual cases.

In conclusion, a recapitulation of the findings of this study shows the following:

1. Contrary to prevailing opinion, American wives make the major adjustment in marriage.

2. Affectional relationships in childhood, typically of the son for the mother and the daughter for the father, condition the love-object choice of the adult.

3. The socialization of the person, as indicated by his participation in social life and social institutions, is significant for adjustment in marriage.

4. The economic factor in itself is not significant for adjustment in marriage, since it is apparently fully accounted for by the other factors (impress of cultural background, psychogenetic characteristics, social type, and response patterns).

5. With the majority of couples, problems of sexual adjustment in marriage appear to be a resultant not so much of biological factors as of psychological characteristics and of cultural conditioning of attitudes toward sex.

6. Prediction before marriage of marital adjustment is feasible, and should and can be further developed through statistical and case-study methods.

In short, the outstanding factors in marital adjustment seem to be those of affection, temperamental compatibility, and social adaptability. The biological and economic factors are of less importance and appear to be largely determined by these other factors.

These six major findings represent the outstanding contributions which the present study makes to our knowledge of marital adjustment, particularly as adjustment may be predicted before marriage. In this study, as in many others, the most significant contribution is not to be found in any one finding, nor even in the sum total of findings, but in the degree to which the study opens up a new field to further research.

Six · *Learning to Live Together*
—A Case

ANONYMOUS

*An anonymous student contributes the following anal-
ysis of his own progress in marital adjustment. His discussion points
up some of the research findings previously reported.*

THIS paper deals with the adjustment my wife and
I have made in the several areas of marriage. I have discussed these
areas with my wife and we fully agree as to our present state of
adjustment in each of the areas. We both rate our marriage as very
happy.

My parents were both foreign born. They were married not long
before they came to America. In his native country my father was
the son of a wealthy land owner and never had to contend with
financial problems. His family's social position was of the upper
class. My father clung to his old concepts and could not accept the
new system of values in America. My mother on the other hand
took the acculturation process much more readily. Their marriage
was not happy and they were divorced when I was a child.

My wife's father was also born and reared in Europe while her
mother was a native American. Her mother was the dominating
factor in the family, the father being submissive to her control in
everything. So both my wife and I had the background of a mother
dominated family that was all or partly in the process of acculturation.

During the first months of our marriage my wife had a strong
tendency to dominate, identifying with her mother, while I reacted
in a passive way, identifying with my father. The pattern of our
parents' marriage was beginning to repeat itself in our marriage.
However, this did not prove to be a satisfactory relationship as I
had always resented my father's submissiveness to my mother's
wishes. So after a time we both agreed that we had to compromise
in our attitudes because my wife was playing the role of her mother
and I the role of my father, and antagonisms were beginning to
mar our relationship. Since then we have achieved a better balance
in equally sharing the responsibilities of finances and in making
of plans and in discussions of family problems. We both feel that
we have made a very satisfactory adjustment or readjustment in
this area of our marriage.

In matters of religion, friends and social life we are in full accord and this is especially true of companionship. We like the same

people. We have solved the problem of in-laws by keeping our relationships as impersonal with them all as possible.

In our attitudes toward sickness we are again sometimes at odds due to our diverse family conditioning. My wife's mother as well as my father had both used illness as an attention-getting device. Both complained of vague organic disturbances which brought them attention and sympathy. My father habitually used illness or aches and pains in order to stay home from work. In matters of health my wife has tended to accept the pattern of her mother. During minor illnesses she wants a lot of attention, affection and sympathy. Since I was antagonistic toward my father, I grew up associating illness with malingering behavior. So I find it hard to give enough sympathetic attention to health problems of my wife. We now both realize that our attitudes had their origin in our family environment and in the reaction of our parents to illness. We feel that it is therefore not a lack of sympathy or concern on my part or an over anxiety for attention on the part of my wife but simply that we both are the products of our respective families. We are both trying to change.

Our most serious conflict lies in the adjustment in the sexual sphere of our marriage. My wife's family never mentioned sex or its functioning. She was impressed with the belief that girls should not be friendly with boys or show any interest in sex or mention this taboo subject. By the time any information reached her it had gone through a process of interpretation and reinterpretation that completely distorted it. Thus it was that she entered marriage with a limited and distorted idea of the sex phase of marriage.

My own background was much the same. If sex was ever discussed when I was a child it was dwelt upon in a negative way. My mother stressed the idea that I should not take any interest in girls until I was through high school. She was always afraid that I would marry and not finish my education. Any friendship that I had with girls was strongly disapproved. From her constant warnings I developed a distrust and fear of sexual functioning.

At present our sexual relationship is about 20 per cent satisfactory. Our main difficulty lies in my strong inhibitions which hamper my sexual adequacy, and in my wife's cyclical swings in desire. My inhibited attitudes create a certain amount of irritability in my wife, which in turn accentuates my fear of sexual impotence and represents itself in hostility toward my wife. As this cycle progresses I experience anxiety about my own virility.

We know that our bringing up is back of many of our problems in sex adjustment. My mother's constant admonitions to "be careful" and her indirect inferences that sex was something to be rejected rather than fully accepted affected me. And my wife's attitude toward sex is much similar to mine. She has always approached it with fear and apprehension. In addition her responsiveness is affected by occurrences in her work and in her other activities. In myself the desire swings are not as broad as hers. Further, her mother had great difficulty in child birth and speaks of that period as a time of great physical pain. This attitude toward child bearing has affected my wife and she greatly fears pregnancy and the birth process. A baby at this time would also conflict with my plans to finish college. We use reliable birth control methods but can never put complete faith in their efficiency. This also affects our adjustment.

I had known my wife a year before we were married. We have now been married for a year and a half. Before marriage we were in full accord on all the questions that we thought important. We shared the same interests and found in each other a companionship and love that we agreed was to last us for the rest of our lives. We still both feel as we did when we married. But marriage is a completely new experience for us, family ties are broken, new responsibilities have been undertaken. This shift and the uncertainty of the new status we have assumed may account for many of our difficulties. We find that our sexual adjustment is now immeasurably better than it was during the first months of marriage. We have also established a reciprocal relationship in other matters which was largely absent at the beginning of our marriage. We understand each other better and can meet each other's personality needs better, so we are happier than at first. We feel that as we become more accustomed to marriage we will be able to overcome most of the obstacles that lie in the way of a rich marriage relationship for us.

Seven · Occupational Factors and Marriage

MEYER F. NIMKOFF
Sociologist, The Florida State
University

Does the occupation one enters affect his chances for a stable family life? Or are certain personality traits found more often in those who choose certain occupations, indicating that these personality traits rather than the occupation are a factor affecting marital adjustments? Meyer Nimkoff investigated a sample of people in "Who's Who" to determine the relationship between occupation and marriage success.*

* Reprinted from *The American Journal of Sociology*, 1943, 49: 248–254, by permission of the author and the University of Chicago Press.

RECENT discussions have developed the theory of the relation of occupation to marital adjustment. One phase of the theory is that occupations characterized by marked physical mobility and by slight group control tend to show a high degree of marital instability, whereas occupations subject to stationary employment and community supervision have low rates of marital maladjustment. Mobility is thought to be bad for marriage because it means (1) frequent uprooting of individuals, which attenuates group ties, (2) the separation of family members, and (3) the development of divergent patterns of behavior. When the happiness ratings of husbands in a considerable number of occupations were examined, it was noted that the proportion of happy marriages was very high among schoolteachers and very low among traveling salesmen. These ratings are explained in terms of the theory that traveling salesmen are among the most mobile and the least supervised persons in our population, while teachers are among the least mobile and the most highly controlled. The two factors of physical mobility and social control are not unrelated, since it is difficult to exercise control over individuals whose work keeps them on the move.

The theory expounded above leads to the question as to whether occupations are selective of personality traits. For instance, does the occupation of traveling salesman in general attract persons who have habits and attitudes which distinguish them from those, let us say, who go into teaching? If such selection does occur, the further question may be asked: What significance, if any, do the selected traits have for marriage? Terman has presented some evidence showing that the happily married are more emotionally stable and more highly socialized than the unhappily married and Winch's studies suggest that these attributes are probably of premarital rather than of postmarital origin. If occupations are selective of personality traits, as some believe, then the effect of the occupation itself may be largely limited to reinforcing an already existing tendency in the individual toward marital stability or instability. In the possible selective influence of occupations we thus have a second highly important aspect of the theory regarding the relation of occupation and marital behavior.

The influence of occupational factors upon marital behavior is further examined in the present study, covering a hundred cases in each of six different occupations in Who's Who, 1942–1943, or a total of six hundred cases in all.[1] The occupational groups selected

[1] The cases, matched for age, are selected from a random 20 per cent sample of the six occupational groups in Who's Who, 1942–1943. The use of biographies in Who's Who may be presumed automatically to afford some control over the factor of income; not that all persons included have the same incomes but that they are probably all, or nearly all, economically secure. It would have been desirable to match the cases for church affiliation, but information on this question was generally lacking in the biographies.

for study (artists, business executives, college professors, engineers, military officers, and physicians) were chosen from a list of occupations represented in *Who's Who* because they were assumed to vary sufficiently in respect to such factors as mobility, social control, and personality traits as to make possible some analysis of the relation of these factors to marital behavior. Military officers are engaged in work characterized by relatively great mobility, as are also certain groups of artists, such as actors and concert musicians. Artists are subject to relatively little social control of their sex conduct, partly because of the general feeling that they are temperamental (the personality factor), and therefore strict conformity to the general family mores is not to be expected of them. College professors and physicians, by contrast, remain comparatively stationary in their work and are subject in their moral conduct to considerable community control. The characterization of business leaders and engineers is not so clear, but they are thought to be subject to somewhat more moderate control because they are not so much in the public eye as are teachers and doctors and do not serve so extensively as "models." Since these characterizations of the six groups are based not on measurements but only on consensus, they are not set forth here as certainly valid. Many questions can be raised about them which, in turn, tend to reflect unfavorably upon the utility of the theories expounded in the first paragraph. Indeed, one purpose of this paper is precisely to raise such questions.

MARITAL STATUS

The data in *Who's Who* make possible a comparison of the proportions of single and married persons in these six occupational groups. The findings on marital status are given in Table 1, which shows the number who are single, the number married once, and the number married more than once. It is not known what percentage of the marriages represent unbroken unions, because the data on reported divorces are probably inadequate. In this six-hundred-case sample, which includes 553 persons who were reported as married at least once, only five divorces are recorded. While it is likely that this group has more than an average number of unbroken marriages, it is unlikely that the number would be as low as is suggested by the reported number of divorces. Indeed, the high rate of remarriage shown in Table 1 suggests the contrary, since it is not likely that the opportunity for remarriage would in so many instances be accounted for by the bereavement of a mate, even if we make allowance for the fact that *Who's Who* is selective of older people. The evidence suggests concealment of information regarding divorce, which is interesting because it shows that divorce is still felt to be an embarrassing experience, despite its increasing acceptance, which we note in the rising divorce rate.

TABLE 1. MARITAL STATUS OF 100 PERSONS IN EACH OF SIX
OCCUPATIONAL GROUPS IN *Who's Who,* 1942-1943

OCCUPATION	MARITAL STATUS			TOTAL
	Single	Married Once	Married More than Once	
Artists	15	65	20	100
Businessmen	5	83	12	100
College professors	5	84	11	100
Engineers	3	83	14	100
Military men	12	83	5	100
Physicians	7	77	16	100
Total	47	475	78	600

Since the persons listed in *Who's Who* are those who have achieved occupational distinction, an interesting question is whether promise of exceptional achievement acts as a deterrent to marriage. The evidence in Table 1 suggests that the answer is "No." Only 8 per cent of these noted persons are unmarried, as compared to around 10 per cent of the general population of about the same age. Unfortunately, there are no comparable data available for an unselected group representing the six occupations.

When the records for the different occupations are examined, they show that two of the groups, the artists and the military men, exceed the rate of bachelorhood in the general population. The artists contribute one-third of all the single persons in the sample, or about twice their share, and the military are not far behind with one and one-half times their share. Physicians have just about their share, while college professors, businessmen, and engineers are underrepresented among the unmarried, but the differences between these groups are not so significant as are the differences between all of them, on the one hand, and the artists and military, on the other.

AGE AT MARRIAGE

It is known that the probabilities of marriage are affected by the age at marriage, the chances of marriage falling with an advance in years. Artists and the military, we have seen, have a relatively large proportion of single persons. Does this mean that they marry at a later age than doctors, college professors, engineers, or business executives? The data in Table 2, showing the distribution of marriages by age at marriage for the six occupations, indicate that the answer is "No." In spite of first impressions, there is not much difference between the different groups. In all cases the means and the medians fall in the twenty-six to thirty age group, and for five of the six groups this is also the modal class. Only in the case of the businessmen does it drop below—to the twenty to twenty-five age group. This is probably explained by the fact that a business career does not so often require preliminary extensive schooling as does college teaching, medicine, or engineering. In business, too, the monetary rewards probably come more quickly where there is outstanding ability than in the case of the other occupations.

TABLE 2. AGE AT FIRST MARRIAGE OF 536 PERSONS IN SIX
OCCUPATIONS, *Who's Who,* 1942-1943

OCCUPATION	AGE								TOTAL
	Under 20	20–25	26–30	31–35	36–40	41–45	46–50	Over 50	
Artists	3	19	28	7	11	7	1	3	79
Businessmen ...	4	33	28	19	8	2	0	1	95
College professor:	0	17	42	23	8	3	1	1	95
Engineers	0	26	38	13	8	8	2	1	96
Military men ...	0	12	43	18	4	5	1	1	84
Physicians	0	18	36	18	11	2	2	0	87
Total	7	125	215	98	50	27	7	7	536

An interesting fact is that only seven of these distinguished persons were married under twenty years of age, or only a little more than 1 per cent of the total sample of 536 cases. How these figures compare with those for the rank and file of the same occupational groups we do not know, although it is known that professional groups tend to marry later in life than the general population. In the United States in 1920, 6.5 per cent of males under twenty were married, and nearly one-half (48.8 per cent) of the twenty-five-year-olds likewise, as compared to about one-quarter (24.6 per cent) of the twenty-five-year-olds in *Who's Who* under consideration. It is interesting to find that persons who show promise of success do not marry early. The finding is perhaps not so surprising for the four of the six professions which do not have a single marriage for persons under twenty, namely, college teaching, engineering, the military, and medicine, because all these require considerable preliminary training. It is, however, interesting to find that only four business executives and three artists in this sample were married before they were twenty, for these fields do not so often require long periods of preparation.

REMARRIAGE

The data on remarriage bring out the highly interesting fact that these exceptionally successful professional people are, as a group, not exceptional in the number of remarriages they make. Only 13 per cent were married more than once, whereas, of white men in general marrying in 1939, 15.5 per cent had been previously married. These figures are interesting in view of the belief held in some quarters that the marriages of famous people are less stable than those of the generality of mankind. It is said that fame turns their heads and makes them difficult to live with. If this is so, it does not show in the statistics of remarriage.

The artists have the greatest number of remarriages, one-quarter of the total number, or 50 per cent more than their share. Business leaders, college professors, and engineers have just about their share, while doctors have one-fourth more than theirs. However, the most striking finding in this connection concerns the military, whose remarriage rate is only 5 per cent, which is less than half that of college professors and businessmen and less than a third that of physicians and surgeons.

OCCUPATIONAL MOBILITY AND MARITAL STATUS

How shall we account for these variations? Consider first the possible influence of the factor of mobility. According to the theory stated in the first paragraph, currently viewed with favor, the occupations characterized by the highest degree of mobility would be expected to show the lowest number of marriages. The artists and the military do have the highest proportions unmarried, and these are commonly thought to be the two most mobile groups under consideration, hence the least subject to conventional control. The evidence therefore appears to give some support to the theory.

However, further examination of the data reveals certain irregularities and inconsistencies. The military, like the artists, have a high rate of nonmarriage; why not also, then, a high rate of remarriage, to agree again with the artists? Actually, as we saw, the military have the smallest number of remarriages of any of the six groups. Why this should be so is not clear. The military may be better adjusted in their marriages, or they may be less inclined to remarry after divorce or bereavement than the other groups, or the military code may frown on divorce. If the mobility of military life furnishes a welcome respite from the tension of unhappy marriage when it occurs, then the military would have less need for divorce. The armed services also take care of the physical needs of the men for food and shelter, and they have less need to remarry on this score. If the public is also tolerant of unconventional sex behavior where the military is concerned, this too would be a factor.

The above argument, based on the theory of mobility, is not entirely convincing, however. If the mobility of military life succeeds in greatly limiting remarriage, why does it not also more effectively prevent marriage itself? Table 1 shows that, for the military, the rate of "married once" is equal to that of businessmen and engineers and higher than that of physicians. It is possible that those military men who marry are highly stable. This could be explained in two ways. First, the high rate of nonmarriage among military men may mean that those who do marry are highly selected types, well suited to marriage. Second, marriage for the military seems to involve "marriage against odds," in that the policy of the services is not to encourage marriage, and the occupation itself is not particularly conducive to family life. These factors might act as deterrents and result in the selection of the best prospects for marriages.

Thus it appears that the theory of the relation of occupational mobility to marriage, while of value, is weak in part because there are varieties of mobility, with different effects, which the theory as currently stated does not recognize. The mobility of the military would seem to be unlike that of the artists in this important respect, that it is physical without being social. That is to say, the military officer in his movements from place to place is more likely to maintain social relations with those of his own class, while the artist may move on a variety of social levels. The effect of such a difference would be to subject the military man to a greater measure of social control, exerted partly by society in general and partly by his own group, which has a code of its own. In other words, high physical mobility need not mean little social control.

The problem is further illuminated by the finding that physicians have the second highest rate of multiple marriages, suggesting possibly a relatively high rate of marital instability. The physician in his sex life is subject to considerable community control, since he is regarded as a public servant, and the effect of such control might be expected to stabilize his affectional life. On the other hand, it is generally acknowledged that the practice of medicine, with its irregular hours, calls away from home, and close physical contact with members of the opposite sex, is not especially conducive to family solidarity. In this case we have a considerable degree of mobility, of a kind different from that of the actor or the military man, and the mobility is linked to considerable social control, the two influences tending perhaps to neutralize each other.

Our discussion to this point may be summarized by saying that the problem of the relation of occupational mobility and social control to marital behavior is complicated by the fact that there are not just one type of mobility and one type of social control. There are, rather, several types of each, which means there is considerable variation in the possible patterns of interrelationship between the two factors. For this reason, the theory of the relation of mobility and social control to marital behavior, when stated in simple, generalized form, tends to be somewhat unrealistic.

Let us consider also the theory of occupational selection of personality traits as related to marital behavior. In terms of this theory we might seek to explain the high rates of nonmarriage of artists and military men by saying that these occupations recruit a disproportionate number of nonmarrying types, that is, persons not emotionally suited for marriage. For example, it may be speculated that the military services, being one-sex groups, attract a large number of single men who contract habits of the single life for a long time. As for the artists, they have a reputation for being "temperamental," by which is meant, presumably, that they are often relatively emotionally unstable, and there is some evidence to support this belief. There is also some evidence that, in general, the emotionally more stable men tend to marry and that the less stable tend to remain single. The high rates of nonmarriage of artists may thus reflect high rates of emotional instability.

The theory that occupational differences in marital behavior may in some important measure be ascribed to the selective influence of occupations is an intriguing theory, but one that is subject, in the present state of our knowledge, to a number of serious limitations. The first is the difficulty of determining what manner of selection actually takes place in a particular occupation. Although a considerable literature has grown up around the attempt to meet this problem, the results are not very satisfactory. There are studies purporting to show that members of different occupations differ in intelligence and in opinions, interests, attitudes, values, and the like. A number of vocational-guidance tests aim to determine the extent to which one's interests agree or disagree with those of successful men in a given occupation. One striking defect of these tests is the rather arbitrary generalizing of traits on the basis of a few noted responses. The subject is tested in only a few selected situations, and even here the testing is done on a symbolic or verbal level rather than on a behavioral one. Failure to recognize the above considerations makes most present personality tests of doubtful validity.

If accurate measures of personality traits were available, the further problem of determining the significance of these traits for marriage could be tackled with greater confidence. An interesting beginning has been made by Terman, who reports correlations between marital happiness and a number of personality test items; but again the difficulty lies in the questionable validity of these items. Considerable improvement in personality testing will be required before the relation of personality traits to various types of marital behavior can be stated in measurable terms. This approach, however, appears to hold great promise.

Eight · Social Class and Marital Adjustment

JULIUS ROTH
ROBERT F. PECK
Human Development, University of Chicago

Marriages across social class lines are often highly publicized in the American press. The study reported below * *investigates husband-wife adjustments in such marriages.*

IN any stratified social order, marriage usually implies equality of status. Although the American class structure considered in this paper is not so rigid as the caste system discussed by Kingsley Davis in "Intermarriage in Caste Societies," the fact remains that strata exist and the family is placed in the class structure as a unit. This means that if a man and woman of different social levels marry, there must generally be a shift of status for one or both of them.

The question arises: Does this necessary shift of status affect the subsequent adjustment of the spouses? Ruesch, Jacobson, and Loeb point out the feelings of stress, frustration, and confusion which often accompany the acculturation of immigrants. The greater the degree of culture difference, the greater the maladjustment of the individual is likely to be. The differences in the characteristics of the social classes in our society indicate that these classes are different cultural groups. A person moving from one class to another must go through a process of acculturation similar to, though perhaps not so extreme as, that of an immigrant.

A fairly large group of cases which had some rating of marital adjustment and some good indication of the subject's social class was needed in order to examine these problems. The schedules Burgess and Cottrell used in their study of marital prediction provided such a group of cases. Each of their 526 cases had a marital adjustment score which they had worked out with the help of sta-

---

* Reprinted from the *American Sociological Review*, 1951, 16: 478–483, by permission of the authors and the *American Sociological Review*.

tistical techniques. Most of the cases had data which made possible an estimate of the social class level of the subjects.

SOCIAL CLASS DIFFERENCE AND MARITAL ADJUSTMENT

In over half the cases in this study in which the difference or similarity of the social class of the spouses was established, the spouses were of the same social class at the time of marriage. Burgess and Cottrell state that marriage tends to take place within a given cultural group and this has probably been the common finding in studies of marriage.

Although most of the marriages take place within a given class, a substantial number of cross-class marriages are represented in the study. How do they compare in adjustment to same-class marriages? According to the hypothesis, cross-class marriages are likely to cause greater stress to the persons involved. How does this reflect on their relative adjustment? The percentage distribution shows that the adjustment scores tend to be higher in the case of same-class marriages. Testing this relationship by the Chi-square method shows a significance at the 1 per cent level. This result suggests that the stress of a rapid shift in class values required by a cross-class marriage has a negative influence on the adjustment of that marriage.

In a cross-class marriage either the husband or the wife may be of the higher social class at the time of marriage. Does the effect on marital adjustment differ with the sex of the spouse of superior status? In a direct comparison of all the cases in which the husband was of the higher class at marriage, with all those in which the wife was of the higher class at marriage, the wife-high cases seem to be more unfavorable to marital adjustment than the husband-high cases, although both show a tendency to lower scores than same-class marriages. Using the Chi-square technique we may test the hypothesis: Cross-class marriages in which the husband is of the higher social class generally show better adjustment than those in which the wife is of the higher class. The level of significance proves to be very low ($0.30 < P < 0.50$). The relationship is obscured by the fact that the class differences represented can have different origins. For example, a woman may have been mobile before marriage past the level of her future husband or she may have acquired her higher status from her parents. This problem will be further discussed in the section on mobility patterns.

Despite the low statistical significance of the relationship between wife-high and husband-high cross-class marriage, the relationship is in keeping with findings on this point in other studies. McMillan finds that in the case of marriages across class lines, it was most often the wife who "married up" the status ladder. To put it another way, the men seemed to be more willing than the women to accept a lower status spouse. Terman found that in his subjects the wives who were markedly superior to their husbands in education had low happiness scores, while the scores were much higher in cases where the husbands were markedly superior in education. James West points out that in all of the cross-class dating in "Plainville" the boy is of the higher class. A boy dating a girl of a lower class is frowned upon, but "for an upper-class girl to have a date with a lower-class boy would be inconceivable."

Why is adjustment smoother when the man enters marriage at the higher status than when the woman does so? An important finding of Burgess and Cottrell gives a clue for further study on this point. The major adjustment, in fact almost the entire adjustment in most marriages, is made by the wife. Since an upward shift in class status carries some rewards and also entails fewer punishments than a downward shift, we would expect less stress in those cases where the wife had to move upward (that is, the husband-high marriages) than in those where she was expected to shift her values downward (that is, the wife-high marriages).

In the case of differences in class background the results were unexpected.

The results indicate that the difference in the parental social status *per se* does not affect the marital adjustment of the spouses. This is a direct contradiction of the finding of Burgess and Cottrell that the closer the similarity of the family background, the better the marital adjustment of the spouses. Why the difference? It is important to note that Burgess and Cottrell used a method of estimating parental status level which is different from the one used in this study. The latter uses Warner's social class concept and relies largely on the Index of Status Characteristics with the items: occupation, source of income, and education. Burgess and Cottrell used a numerical index of similarity in family backgrounds based on the weighted items: parents' religious preference, their church participation, their education, the father's occupation, the respondent's rating of their economic status, and the respondent's rating of their social status. The last two items are subjective ratings which appeared rather unreliable when compared to the objective data provided by the schedules. Some attempt was made to examine the biases in the methods of determining status level to account for the apparently contradictory results. This examination was inconclusive. The difference in the results of the two studies probably lies in a difference of classification of occupation, education, and religion and a different weighting of these factors.

Nine · Adjustment of the Divorced in Later Marriages

HARVEY J. LOCKE
Sociologist, University of Southern
California

WILLIAM KLAUSNER
Sociologist, University of Redlands

*Little is known about how the marital adjustment of divorced people in subsequent marriages compares with that of people married only once. Reprinted below * is a summary of an exploratory study on this subject.*

THE present paper is a report of an exploratory study of the problem: do divorced persons constitute good or bad risks in subsequent marriages? An answer to this question was attempted by comparing the marital adjustment scores of a group of forty-seven divorced persons who were *married to new mates* with scores of a group of sixty-four persons *married only once.*

The cases were obtained from the Los Angeles metropolitan area through members of sociology courses, who distributed questionnaires to persons of their acquaintance who were married but who had had previous marriages which had been terminated by divorce and also to persons who had remained married to their first mates.

The hypothesis was that there is no difference in the degree of marital adjustment of divorced persons in subsequent marriages and persons married only once.

The social characteristics of the divorced-remarried and the married-once-only groups were fairly comparable in religious faith, educational attainment, level of yearly incomes, sex distribution, and nationality. Both the divorced-remarried and the married-once-only groups were predominantly Protestant, 60 and 61 per cent, respectively, whereas 14.9 per cent and 11.0 per cent were Catholic. Four per cent of the divorced-remarried group and 6 per cent of the married-once-only group were Jewish, and about one-fifth of each group claimed to have no church affiliation. The median for years of education of the divorced-remarried group was 13.4, and the median for the married-once-only sample was 14.3 years. A yearly family income of less than $3,000 was obtained by 48.7 per

---

* Reprinted from *The Proceedings of the Pacific Sociological Society,* 1948, 16: 30–32, by permission of the authors.

cent of the remarried group and by 54.8 per cent of the married-once-only persons. The sex distribution was fairly equal, as males constituted 44.7 per cent and 48.4 per cent, respectively, of the two groups. About 61.7 per cent of the divorced-remarried group and 70.3 per cent of the married-once-only group were American-born of American-born parents, and about one in 25 and one in 10, respectively, were of foreign birth.

Adjustment scores, on which the analysis was based, were secured by the employment of the Burgess-Cottrell marital adjustment scale. Three types of comparisons were made: (1) the men and women combined of the divorced-remarried group with the men and women combined of the married-once-only group; (2) the divorced-remarried women with the women married only once and a like comparison of the men; and (3) the men of each group with the women of the same group.

The first comparison indicated that those in the divorced-remarried group achieved as high a degree of adjustment in their present marriages as the persons married only once. The respective mean scores were 149 and 151. The distribution of the scores of the two groups in terms of "good," "fair," and "poor" adjustment also were not significantly different. The divorced-remarried and the married-once-only groups showed 44.7 per cent and 50.0 per cent, respectively, in the "good" adjustment category, 38.3 and 39.1 per cent in the "fair," and 17.0 and 10.9 per cent in the "poor" adjustment category.

The second comparison was by sex. When the scores of divorced-remarried and married-once-only women were compared, the mean scores of 157 and 151, respectively, did not differ significantly.

Thus far the data verified the original hypothesis. For men, however, the verification did not hold, in that men who had been divorced and had remarried did not achieve as high a degree of adjustment in their subsequent marriages as did the men who continued in their first marriages. The mean adjustment score of those men who had had prior marriages terminated by divorce was 138 as compared with 159 for those who had been married only once. The difference of 21 points in the means is probably significant, as the critical ratio of 2.33 indicates that the difference in the degree of adjustment is probably a real one and not due to chance. No statistical significance was found between the two groups of men in any one of the three categories—"good," "fair," and "poor"—but when "fair" and "poor" were combined, the critical ratio of the difference between the percentage of divorced-remarried and married-once-only men was 2.18, so that the difference was probably a real one.

The third comparison showed that the adjustment scores of the married-once-only husbands did not differ significantly from the scores of the married-once-only wives, the respective means being

159 and 151. However, there was a 19-point difference between the means of the divorced-remarried husbands and the divorced-remarried wives, the respective means being 138 and 157, with a critical ratio of 1.88. Though this is not significant on the five-percent level, the failure to get a statistically significant difference may be due to the smallness of the sample. The critical ratio is large enough to support the tentative conclusion that divorced men and divorced women differ in their adjustment in subsequent marriages.

On the basis of these three comparisons a new hypothesis has been developed, namely, divorced-remarried women are as good risks in their subsequent marriages as women who marry only once, whereas divorced-remarried men are not as good risks as those men who marry only once. This modification of the original hypothesis is being subjected to possible verification or refutation by research now in process.

VIII · MIXED MARRIAGES

One · Marriages of Mixed and Non-Mixed Religious Faith

JUDSON T. LANDIS
Sociologist, University of California
at Berkeley

Marriages across faith lines are common in America. The next selection * discusses some problems of inter-faith marriages and the divorce rate of inter-faith marriages.

MIXED marriages have been defined as marriages in which there are significant, obvious and unusual differences between the spouses, other than sex. Differences in faith, race, and nationality are the ones usually considered as falling under the definition of mixed marriages. Sometimes differences in intelligence, education, age, social and economic status, physical size, and difference in previous marital status are listed as factors constituting mixture. It is usually assumed that extreme differences in background foster marital discord rather than marital rapport. However, the research that has been done indicates that some of these factors cannot properly be said to have an adverse effect upon marital adjustment. Research by Terman and Hamilton and our research revealed that husbands in marriages in which the wife had more education than the husband were happier than the average husband. In an analysis of the divorce rate by educational differences in 3,796 marriages we found the lowest divorce rate in marriages in which the wife was older than her husband. Available research emphasizes how little is known about contrasts in spouses and the possible effect of such contrasts upon marital adjustment.

This paper is not reporting a study of all types of mixed marriages; it deals specifically with inter-faith marriages. The need remains for further study of other types of mixed marriages.

Catholics, Protestants, and Jews have frowned upon mixed marriages and have done much to discourage their young people from entering mixed unions. Some young people feel that the discouraging of mixed unions among the followers of the different faiths is largely a battle for souls and that there is no practical reason why

* Reprinted from the *American Sociological Review*, 1949, 14: 401–406, by permission of the *American Sociological Review*.

they should not enter mixed marriages. Many young people today are probably not much interested in the struggle for souls, but they are interested in knowing whether a mixed marriage has less chance for success than marriage within a faith.

In an attitude study among 2,000 students 50 per cent of them said that other things being equal with respect to the prospective spouse, they would marry into a different faith. There was little divergence between the responses of Catholics and of Protestants. One-third of those who would marry outside their faith would be willing to change to the faith of the partner. Protestant students were more willing to change than Catholics. The attitude expression of students on inter-faith marriages is quite in contrast to the feeling of most church leaders, both Catholic and Protestant. Edgar Schmiedeler, director of the family life bureau of the National Catholic Welfare Conference, says, "Since courtship is the beginning which leads ultimately to a marriage contract, the sound starting point toward this goal will be to avoid courtship with any and all non-Catholics."

In spite of the strong Catholic stand on the matter, Clement S. Mihanovich of St. Louis University recently reported, after a survey of all dioceses, that 25 per cent of Roman Catholics married outside the faith.

To gain more information on the success or failure of marriages of mixed and nonmixed religious faith we collected, for 3 years, information on their parents' marriages from the students in our marriage lecture sections. Early in the course and before the subject of mixed marriages had been discussed, each student was asked to complete a questionnaire which gave several facts about his parents' marriage, such as age when married, occupation, education, religion, present marital status, whether either parent changed religious faith at or after marriage, who took the responsibility for giving the religious training, how much conflict over religion had been evident to the children, and the eventual faith chosen by the children.

This discussion is a summary of the information gained on religion in the parent families. We have the histories of 4,108 families. Of these, almost two-thirds, 2,794, were both Protestant. Almost one-third were either Catholic (573) or Catholic non-Catholic mixed (346). Of the 1492 individual Catholics in the study, 346 or 23 per cent had married outside the Catholic faith. In 192 of these 346 marriages, each spouse maintained his or her own religion after marriage; in 113 either the Catholic or the Protestant changed to the faith of the other; and in 41 marriages the Catholic had married a person with no religious faith.

Because of the method used in collecting the information, the evidence given will shed light only upon mixed marriages in which there are children. Approximately two out of three couples who divorce do not have children. A study of childless mixed marriages might show entirely different results than are revealed in this study. In fact, the results of our study among couples with children would lead us to believe that if there are not children, the Catholic-Protestant marriage has few elements which would make marital adjustment difficult. It is the presence of children in the home which makes for marital conflict in the Catholic-Protestant marriage.

Table 1 summarizes the divorce and separation rates in our study of marriages of mixed and non-mixed religious faiths and compares the findings with the findings of the studies made in a similar manner in different regions of the country. H. Ashley Weeks made an analysis of 6,548 families of public and parochial school children in Spokane, Washington, and Howard Bell analyzed 13,528 families in Maryland. Weeks and Bell did not make all of the breakdowns that we have in our study. These more detailed breakdowns have revealed some interesting material on mixed marriages. Our information on the divorce and separation rate in Catholic, Jewish, Protestant, and mixed marriages confirms the two earlier studies. This might not be expected, since our sample was taken from people who have children in college, while the other samples were more representative of cross sections of whole communities.

TABLE 1. PERCENTAGE OF MARRIAGES OF MIXED AND NON-MIXED RELIGIOUS
FAITHS ENDING IN DIVORCE OR SEPARATION AS REVEALED BY STUDIES
OF MARRIAGES IN MICHIGAN, MARYLAND, AND WASHINGTON

Religious Categories	Number	Landis study in Michigan (N-4, 108) Per Cent	Bell study in Maryland (N-13, 528) Per Cent	Weeks study in Washington (N-6548) Per Cent
Both Catholic	573	4.4	6.4	3.8
Both Jewish	96	5.2	4.6	—
Both Protestant	2794	6.0	6.8	10.0
Mixed, Catholic-Protestant	192	14.1	15.2	17.4
Both none	39	17.9	16.7	23.9
Protestant changed to Catholic	56	10.7		
Catholic changed to Protestant	57	10.6		
Protestant father-Catholic mother	90	6.7		
Catholic father-Protestant mother	102	20.6		
Father none-Mother Catholic	41	9.8		
Father none-Mother Protestant	84	19.0		

Approximately 5 per cent of the Catholic and Jewish marriages had ended in divorce or separation, 8 per cent of the Protestant marriages, 15 per cent of mixed Catholic-Protestant, and 18 per cent of the marriages in which there was no religious faith. On further analysis, we found that it makes a difference whether the mother is Catholic or Protestant in the mixed marriage. The divorce rate had been highest of all in marriages of a Catholic man to a Protestant woman. Twenty-one per cent of these marriages had ended in divorce, while only seven per cent of the marriages in which a Protestant man was married to a Catholic wife had ended in divorce. It is also interesting to note that when a Catholic woman marries a man who has no religious faith the divorce rate is relatively low, 10 per hundred, when compared with other types of mixed marriages. However, when the Protestant woman married a man with no religion the divorce rate was higher, 19 per one hundred. More research is needed on the latter type of marriage. It is our theory that this type of marriage would more nearly fall within the classification of both no religion.

We recognize that using the divorce rate as an index of success or failure in the mixed religious marriage does not necessarily give a true picture of marital happiness. To illustrate, the divorce rate could be low in cases in which the wife is Catholic, and yet the marriages could be unhappy. In the United States three out of four divorces are granted to women. If the wife is a good Catholic she cannot take the initiative toward divorce, although the marriage may be unhappy. On the other hand, the Protestant wife is free to ask for a divorce if the marriage is unsatisfactory. We found, however, that there are fewer factors making for disharmony in marriages in which the mother is Catholic than there are if she is Protestant.

FACTORS MAKING FOR DISHARMONY IN CATHOLIC-PROTESTANT MARRIAGES

When a Protestant marries a Catholic the Protestant must sign the Ante-Nuptial Agreement in which he promises that the marriage contract can be broken only by death, that all children shall be baptized and educated in the Catholic faith even though the Catholic spouse dies, that no other marriage ceremony than that by the Catholic priest shall take place, and, further, that he shall have respect for the religious principles and convictions of the Catholic partner on birth control.

Of all the differences between Catholics and Protestants the one making for the greatest conflict seems to be the one over the religious training of the children. There is considerable publicity about the use of birth control but this does not seem to be a very serious problem. Studies have revealed that some Catholics do not follow the teachings of the church on this point. If the wife is Catholic and opposes the use of birth control, this may not result in serious conflict since she is the one who has to bear the children. In the families studied, Catholic women married to Protestants had had 2.2 children; Protestant women married to Catholics, 1.9 children; both Catholic, 3.6 children; both Protestant, 2.7; and both

Jewish, 2.1. If the use of birth control is related to the size of the family we might conclude from the above that the Catholic woman married to a Protestant uses birth control since she has a much smaller family on the average than when two Catholics marry.

Our research supports Baber's conclusion, after his case studies of mixed marriages, that the chief source of friction centers around the religious training of the children. Although the young couple agree before marriage that the children will be baptized in the Catholic faith, they may find they cannot follow through on this agreement in marriage. It is impossible for the Protestant member to project himself into the future and to know how he will feel as a parent. When the children arrive the couple must then face the issue in the light of their present feelings, and they often break the agreements which they sincerely made during the period of courtship. In support of this statement we may look at the religious faith of 392 children who were reared in families of mixed Protestant-Catholic faiths. Half of the children had been reared in the Protestant faith, 45 per cent in the Catholic faith and 5 per cent had no faith. The most common tendency seems to be that the children, especially the daughters, follow the faith of the mother. Approximately 65 per cent of the boys and 75 per cent of the girls follow the faith of the mother.

TABLE 2. PARENTAL POLICY ON RELIGIOUS INSTRUCTION IN
192 CATHOLIC-PROTESTANT FAMILIES
(Per cent distribution)

Policy	Father Protestant Mother Catholic N-90	Father Catholic Mother Protestant N-102
Mother took all responsibility for the religious training	42.2	33.7
Our parents told us about both faiths but let us decide for ourselves when we were old enough	22.7	33.7
Responsibility was equally divided	22.7	19.1
We took turns going to both the church of my father and my mother	6.8	6.8
Father took all responsibility for the religious training	1.1	5.6
Some of us went with my father to his church and some went with my mother to her church	4.5	1.1
Total	100.0	100.0

The children who were the products of these mixed marriages were asked to check one of six statements which best described who took the responsibility for religious training in their homes. Table 2 presents a description of the policies and the percentages following each policy. It will be observed that the most common policy was that "mother took all responsibility for the religious training." The next most common policy was that "our parents told us about both faiths but let us decide for ourselves when we were old enough." Both of these policies are contrary to the agreement made before marriage. When parents face reality they are more likely to follow one of these courses.

As to how much of a handicap differences in religion had been to their parents' marriages, the children believed that the greatest handicap had occurred in marriages in which a Catholic man married a Protestant woman.

In the American home the mother is more likely to be a church member and is more apt to take the responsibility for the religious instruction of the children. When a man who has no faith or is a Protestant marries a Catholic woman, he signs the ante-nuptial agreement and does not find it difficult to abide by the agreement when his children are born. He expects his wife to be responsible for their religious training. There is then no great cause for conflict in this type of a mixed marriage.

If the mother is Protestant the marriage seems to have many more serious problems. The Protestant mother has agreed that the

TABLE 3. CHILDREN'S STATEMENTS OF THE DEGREE TO WHICH RELIGIOUS
DIFFERENCES HAD HANDICAPPED THE PARENTS' MARRIAGE IN
MIXED AND NON-MIXED MARRIAGE OF RELIGION
(Per cent distribution)

Degree of Handicap	Both Protestant N-721	Both Catholics N-103	Father Protestant Mother Catholic N-90	Father Catholic Mother Protestant N-102
Not at all	85.7	87.4	59.2	45.2
Very little	11.4	8.8	21.0	20.5
Somewhat	2.7	2.8	13.2	23.3
Great	.2	1.0	5.3	5.5
Very great	—	—	1.3	5.5

children will be baptized Catholic, and yet she can hardly bring up her children in a faith which she herself does not accept. Since the major responsibility for religious training falls upon her, she will probably bring the children up in the only faith she knows and believes in. This means that the agreement made before marriage must be scrapped. The Catholic husband is more apt to be a church member than the Protestant husband who marries a Catholic. It may be quite a blow to him to find that his wife will not have the children baptized into his faith. Conflict results since many Catholic fathers cannot give up without a struggle. The Catholic father not only has his own conscience to live with but he is constantly aware of the attitude of his church and of his family when they see his children being brought up in the Protestant faith.

An additional source of trouble in the mixed religious marriage is the serious and sometimes emotional interest which the in-laws take in the marriage. The two grandmothers are on the alert to see which faith will claim the grandchildren. The Protestant grandmother sometimes gives up when the son marries a Catholic because she figures that the children are lost from the beginning. On the other hand, the Catholic grandmother does all she can to see that her son's children are brought up in the Catholic faith. A careful study of in-law frictions in marriage would probably find more intense friction in cases where the children have made a mixed religious marriage.

In general, priests try to discourage mixed marriages in which the non-Catholic is strong in his faith. They may exert less pressure against the marriage if the non-Catholic is weak in his faith. The highest divorce rate was in marriages in which the largest percentage of husbands and wives were church members, i.e., the Catholic father-Protestant mother combinations. Seventy-five per cent of these husbands and wives were church members, while only 48 per cent of the husbands and 91 per cent of the wives were church members in Protestant father-Catholic mother marriages.

CHANGE TO FAITH OF SPOUSE

In two out of three of the mixed marriages the spouses maintained their own religious faith. In the other third of the mixed marriages one partner changed to the faith of the spouse. In 56 of the marriages the Protestant member had changed to the Catholic faith, and in 57 marriages the Catholic member had changed to the Protestant faith. What evidence we have shows that the marriage has a better chance for success when both spouses accept the same faith, that is, when one changes to the other's faith. The divorce rate had been 10.6 per cent in this type of marriage, but higher when the Catholic wife had changed to the Protestant faith (15.6) per cent and when the Protestant husband had changed to the Catholic faith (16.7 per cent). When a Protestant wife changed to the Catholic faith the divorce rate was 7.9 per cent; when Catholic husband changed to Protestant it was 4.0 per cent. Part of the explanation for the lower divorce rate is the lack of conflict over the religious training of the children. In these marriages, from 90 to 95 per cent of the children followed the religion of the faith adopted by the couple.

CONCLUSIONS

Marriages between Catholics and Protestants entail more hazards than do those between members of one faith. Although couples discuss before marriage the problems arising from religious differences, they can find no final solution to the problems and the differences do not usually decrease with the passing of time after marriage.

The divorce rate varies according to whether the wife is Catholic or Protestant in the mixed Protestant-Catholic marriage.

Children are important factors in the conflict in mixed marriages. Children tend to follow the religious faith of the mother.

Two · A Study of 48 Inter-racial Marriages

RAY BABER
Sociologist, Pomona College

Ray Baber pioneered in the study of mixed marriages. The following selection * giving his findings on inter-racial marriages is taken from a longer article on different types of mixed marriages.

FOR four years the writer has been collecting mixed marriage cases personally known to his students in the course on "Marriage and the Family." There are now 325 cases complete enough for tabulation purposes, making a large enough sample to show something of the variety and nature of such marriages. There is no control group with which they can be directly compared, but subgroups can be compared with each other and some aspects of behavior noted. Finally, some of the special hazards of such marriages can be analyzed.

INTER-RACIAL MARRIAGES

There are 48 cases of marriages between races.

When only *sex* and *race* are considered the five combinations (using the simple three-color classification) are as follows:

White × Yellow	2	White — Yellow	20	
Yellow × White	18			
Black × White	18	Black — White	25	
White × Black	7			
Yellow × Black	3	Yellow — Black	3	
	48		48	

N.B.—Throughout the article the symbol "×" is used to designate a marriage classified by sex, the male always being given first. The symbol "—" is used to designate marriages not classified by sex. For example, the 25 Black—White marriages include both the black men marrying white women (B×W), and the white men marrying black women (W×B).

* Reprinted from the *American Sociological Review*, 1937, 2: 705–716, by permission of the author and the *American Sociological Review*.

It will be seen that the bulk of the sample is made up of black and yellow men, in equal numbers, marrying white women. The yellow men are mostly Chinese and Japanese (7 each), with 3 Filipinos and 1 Javanese. The yellow women are 1 Chinese and 1 Japanese. The mixture is almost entirely between whites and non-whites, the 3 yellow-black combinations being the only exceptions.

It is interesting to note that the males are preponderantly non-white, the ratio of non-whites to whites being more than 4 to 1. The women are mostly white, the ratio being almost 3 to 1. As far as this sample goes, black and yellow men marry white women *four times as frequently* as white men marry black and yellow women, there being 36 and 9 cases respectively. One possible reason for so few white men marrying yellow women is that there are so few of the latter in this country, and these few are in demand by the males of their own race, who outnumber them enormously. But the same does not hold true of Negroes. The supply is plentiful either way, yet only 7 white men married Negro women, while 18 Negroes married white women. Of these 7 white men only 2 were born in the United States, the others being from Greece, Italy, Germany, England and Barbados. But of the 18 white women who married Negroes, 10 were American born. Surely there is no more stigma attached to the white man who marries a Negro woman than to the white woman who marries a Negro. Is color difference in the mate less repulsive to the white woman than to the white man? It can scarcely be a lack of men of their own color that leads white women to marry colored men, for in New York City the sex ratio for the white population was 100.6 in 1930, which year allows approximately for the median duration of the marriages. And since the Negro sex ratio in New York City for the same year was only 91.1, Negro men were certainly not driven to look for non-Negro women. On the other hand, the Oriental races have a paucity of women in this country, and it is probable that in the Y×W marriages the Oriental men are forced to seek non-Oriental wives. Possibly the smallness of the sample is to blame for the disparity between the colored×non-colored and the non-colored×colored unions, but the difference appears too great for mere chance. Some of the reasons back of these particular marriages will be given further on.

Of all 48 marriages 16 were childless, only 5 of which were of 3 years or less duration. For marriages with a median duration of 10 years this seems a rather low birth performance. Undoubtedly one reason is the realization of the hardship imposed upon the children of such unions, for such comments as "they didn't feel that they should have any children," "they agreed that they ought not to have children," or "they are definitely against having children," occur frequently. One Jewess of a good family who married a Negro lawyer against the protests of her heartbroken parents promised her mother that they never would have any children.

The success of marriages being commonly judged by the degree of happiness of the husband and wife, they were rated separately in each case on the following five-point scale: very happy, moderately happy, neutral or "so-so," moderately unhappy, very unhappy. In tabulation it was necessary to assign arbitrary weights to these categories if a numerical scale were to be devised. After trying several systems of weightings the following seemed to give results fairly consistent with the total pictures presented in the case stories: very happy, 100%; moderately happy, 75%; neutral, 50%; moderately unhappy, 25%; very unhappy, 0. Using this scale the happiness ratings were as follows, both sexes combined:

	Number of Cases	Type of Mixture	Happiness Rating
	18	Black × White	57
	7	White × Black	39
Both combinations	25	Black — White	52
	18	Yellow × White	67
	2	White × Yellow	100*
Both combinations	20	Yellow — White	71
	3	Yellow × Black	75*
All combinations	48	B—W—Y	62

* Sample too small to be significant by itself.

As might be expected, the average happiness rating for the total group is not high, being only one-half step above neutral. This is lower than the rating for intermarriages involving both nationality and religion, and still lower for those involving religion only, as will be seen presently. It will be noted that the W×B marriages are much lower on the happiness scale than the B×W marriages, and that both are much lower than the Y—W marriages. The greater the color difference the smaller the chance of happiness—at least in these cases. In a small sample there is always the possibility that such a seeming correlation is the result of chance combinations of other factors.

The children of interracial marriages are particularly handicapped, for they literally have no race, frequently being rejected by both the races from which they come. Such terms as half-breed, half-caste, mulatto, and Eurasian usually carry disapproval and sometimes scorn. In America, part of this is due to the implication that, because of our laws against intermarriage, many such persons must have somewhere in their background a history of illegitimacy, but much of it is due to unreasoning race prejudice. Not only are the children subject to ridicule and sometimes ostracism at school and on the playground, but also the chances of intrafamily strife are increased.

In one case (W×B) the boy is white and his two sisters dark. They quarrel a great deal, his most effective technique being to call them "nigger," which infuriates the girls and stirs up both the parents. In another (Y×W) the six-year-old daughter is called "chink" by her playmates at school. Her parents are ostracized by whites, and her Chinese father is "beaten up" periodically by her mother's brothers. The mother in another case (W×B) hates the daughter because she is light like her father, and will not let the girl marry a dark person. In one instance (Y×W) the wife had a daughter by her first marriage with a white man, and now in this second marriage the white daughter resents having a Chinese stepfather and half-brother. Misery attends the mother in another union (B×W) because her little daughter hates her for being white and loves her father because he is black like she is. Her little brother, however, loves his mother, and hates his sister for hating and striking his mother. The mother "has no friends." Still another mother in a mixed marriage (W×B) is hurt because her daughters avoid introducing her to their friends as their *mother,* but are eager to introduce their father and show him off.

Why do people marry with the storm signals of race prejudice set against them? In some cases the reasons are the same as in ordinary marriages—love, propinquity, mutual interests, etc.

In one case a white girl of excellent family worked in the office of a Negro lawyer, fell desperately in love with him, and finally married him, though it sent her family to the depths of despair. The couple achieved a moderate degree of happiness, but her family ties were never happy thereafter. In another case a beautiful and brilliant coed in an eastern university, much sought after by the opposite sex but determined upon a career rather than marriage, met a Hindu who had studied in Europe and was continuing with graduate work in the United States. Soon these two were "deeply in love," and seemed to have a perfect intellectual affinity, as well as strong sex attraction for each other. They lived for years as common-law husband and wife both in America and Europe without ever letting her family know. They were devoted to each other, but their happiness finally broke on the rock of her conscience, plus the maneuvering of a "friend" who managed to bring about a misunderstanding. He married another woman and she is starting her life over.

In some cases the couples achieved a reasonable degree of happiness and in a few instances they were very happy. The very fact

that two persons of different race are willing to brave the unyielding opposition of all about them in order to wed may be evidence
of an unusually strong personal attraction. Furthermore, such opposition makes them fully aware of the difficult adjustments ahead,
and may result in early and determined efforts to justify their decision. Such factors are favorable to adjustment, and occasionally
they outweigh the heavy hand of prejudice.

In one marriage (Y×W) the Polish-born but American-nat-
uralized wife learned to cook Chinese food, and the Chinese
husband learned to like American cooking. In another case
(Y×W), in which both partners were cultured, the family was
left almost entirely to itself until the little son was old enough
to go to school. When he began to bring his playmates home
with him, and they returned to their homes with tales of the
beautiful Chinese things they had seen, various parents were
soon coming also and the isolated couple acquired an entirely
new and satisfying social status.

SUMMARY

Taking the study as a whole the happiness rating may seem too
high for a representative group of mixed marriages. Combining the
"very happy" and "moderately happy" groups, and also the "very
unhappy" and "moderately unhappy" groups, the happy marriages
outnumber the unhappy 3 to 1. There are at least two possible
sources of error here. First, there is some evidence of unconscious ·
selection of cases by the students. In spite of specific instructions
to take the cases exactly as they came, there may have been an unconscious slighting of divorce cases, whether from personal bias or
from a feeling that a continuing case would be more valuable.
Furthermore, they were somewhat less likely to be in touch with
cases in which divorce had occurred some years previously than
with those marriages which had continued their normal social contacts. A second possible source of error is the disposition of outside
observers to rate a couple's happiness too high. It is usual for couples to compose their differences in the presence of others and do
their quarreling in private. Their friends may know they are not
entirely happy, but they do not always suspect the extent of the
trouble. There seems to have been some tendency to rate a couple
"very happy" if the observers knew of no definite conflict. This
possible error is not serious in this study, for we make no comparisons with an outside group rated differently. Finally, no attempt
should be made to generalize from this relatively small sample. The
findings herein presented are meant to *apply to this study only.*

IX · FAMILY REPRODUCTIVE BEHAVIOR

One · Spacing of Births in Graduates' Families

W. A. ANDERSON
Sociologist, Cornell University

How soon after marriage does the average couple who are university graduates have their first child? An examination of the histories of 944 university graduates * has provided some conclusions about child spacing and family size.

THE study is based upon information obtained from the graduates of the classes of 1919, 1920, and 1921 from Cornell University. Our sample includes 81 per cent of the 1,840 holders of Baccalaureate degrees for those years, who provided data on their date of marriage and on the date of birth of each child born to them, together with other information. The analysis of child-spacing is based on the intervals between the births of 2,147 live-born children to the 944 graduates who have one or more children and who provided the date of their marriage and the date of birth of each of their children. Of the 554 graduates not included, 166 are single, 250 are married but have no children, while 138 did not furnish exact dates of marriage or birth so that they could not be included. This study is based on families in which the childbearing process is over. That this is true is shown by the fact that 99.6 per cent of all husbands and 99.1 per cent of all wives are forty-five or more years of age. The likelihood of any additional births in these families is, therefore, very small.

The period between marriage and the birth of the first child averaged 32.9 months, or 2.7 years, in the families of the male graduates and 31.3 months, or 2.6 years, in the families of the female graduates.

These average periods between marriage and the first birth do not vary greatly in our male and female graduate families.

The 261 first births in the 1921 men's families came, on the average, 38.4 months, or 3.2 years, after marriage, while the 59 first births in the families of the women of this same class came after 35.5 months, or 2.9 years. This is a first-birth interval of 8–10 months

---

* Reprinted from *The American Journal of Sociology*, 1947, 53: 23–33, by permission of the author and the University of Chicago Press.

longer for men and 3–6 months longer for the women of the class of 1921 than for the men and women in the classes of 1919 and 1920.

Of the 943 first births, 20 per cent, both to the male and the female graduates, come in less than 12 months after marriage. In the male graduate families, 32 per cent, and in the female graduate families, 38 per cent, of the first births come between 12 and 23 months after marriage, or in the second year of marriage. Thus 52 per cent of the first children in the families of the men graduates and 58 per cent of the first children in the families of the women graduates are born within the first two years of marriage.

In our male graduate families, 19 per cent, and in our female graduate families, 14 per cent, of the first births come between 24 and 35 months of marriage, or within the third year of marriage. The remainder of the first births, 29 per cent in the male graduate families, and 28 per cent in the female graduate families, come after three years of married life, while 13 per cent and 12 per cent respectively, come after five years of marriage.

If nearly 30 per cent of all first births occur after three years of marriage, then it can be suggested that the proportion of long intervals between marriage and first births is relatively large.

A study by Rockwood and Ford gives information on the preferences of 364 Cornell University students of the years 1940 and 1941 relative to the interval they desire between marriage and parenthood. While these students are unmarried, still in school, and more than twenty years younger than our 1919–21 graduates, and while attitudes may have changed in this period, it is of interest to note how their desires relative to first births compare with the experiences of the graduates we are studying.

Of these students, 11 per cent want their first child in the first year of marriage, 58 per cent in the second, 25 per cent in the third, and 6 per cent in the fourth or fifth years of marriage.

Actually, more of the 1919–21 graduates, 20 per cent, have their first child in the first year of marriage. Considerably fewer, 32–38 per cent, have their first child in the second year. Many more, 29 per cent, have their first child after the third year of married life.

The average length of the intervals of the births following the first, both in the male and in the female graduate families, is, in most instances, longer than the interval between marriage and the first birth, until the family numbers six children. There are only 20 families of six or more in the total 944, however.

The percentage distributions of the successive births show that the largest proportion of these take place within two, three, and four years after a preceding birth. Relatively few occur after five years from a preceding birth. Where there are more than four births, practically all take place within two to three years of the preceding one.

Of the students interviewed by Rockwood and Ford, 60 per cent believe children should be spaced two years apart; 25 per cent think two and one-half to three more desirable; and 14.6 per cent, one to one and one-half years. Only 1.1 per cent think there should be more than three years between children. The desired intervals are, in the main, shorter than those which we actually find in our completed university families.

A look at the average length of the intervals in months between births in the families that we are studying, by the number of children in these families, suggests several generalizations.

The first is that the average length of the interval between marriage and the birth of the first child is longest in one-child families and shortest in the largest families and that the average length of this interval decreases regularly as the size of the family increases.

The same regularity of decrease takes place as the size of the family increases between the first birth and the second birth and between each succeeding birth, in both the male and the female graduate families. For example, the average length of the interval between the first and second births decreases uniformly from 47.2 months in the families of the male graduates with two children to 21.5 months in families of five children. In the families of female graduates, the decrease is from 48.7 months where there are two children to 25.1 months where there are five children.

One of the intriguing conjectures that comes from the determination of these birth intervals is their possible use in predicting the probable size of the family. It may be possible to point out to a family, for example, that if a first birth does not occur until 40–50 months after marriage, there probably would be no other births or only one or so at most. If the first birth occurred between 25 and 35 months after marriage, then the chances of there being more than one or two more children in the family would appear slight. Of course, it is not even inferred that this present study, without further supporting research, makes any such predictions possible.

It was thought that the pattern of the spacing of children might show some differences where the graduates were reared in different environments or married at different ages. The regularity of the pattern of spacing is the same, however, no matter where the persons were reared. Whether the parent was reared on the farm or in a city of 100,000 or more inhabitants, analysis showed the pattern of the timing of births to be the same.

A detailed table not included here, constructed for different ages at marriage, reveals the same general uniformity that is found in the other relationships. It appears that no matter what the age at marriage, where there are children the pattern of spacing is much the same.

When the data for this study were obtained, no information was obtained relative to the extent to which efforts were made in these families to control the number of births and, as a consequence, to influence the length of the birth intervals. It is obvious, therefore, that it cannot be stated whether the spacing of the children is the result of biological or social factors or both. The study simply reveals the pattern of spacing as it actually occurs, no matter what the factors are that determine it.

Two · Maternal Mortality *

METROPOLITAN LIFE INSURANCE COMPANY

THE mothers of America have reaped great gains from the recent advances in medical science, the developments in public health administration, and the rise in our general standard of living. This progress has saved the lives of many thousands of mothers and their infants; it has also strengthened family life by reducing the current chances of death for husbands. The present favorable conditions are undoubtedly reassuring to the annual corps of more than 3,500,000 mothers, particularly to those having their first baby.

The progress which has been made in safeguarding maternity constitutes a significant chapter in the history of American public health. Today the hazards incidental to pregnancy and childbirth are at a level which seemed Utopian not many years ago. As recently as 1935 the maternal mortality rate in the United States was 58 per 10,000 live births, the lowest recorded up to that time. Currently the rate is appreciably under 10 per 10,000 nationally, and in large sections of the country it is even less than 5 per 10,000 live births.

Safer maternity has resulted in part from the increasing proportion of women utilizing hospital facilities and the services of a physician at childbirth. In 1935 only 37 percent of the births in our country were delivered in a hospital; by 1949 the figure had risen to 87 percent (see the chart on the next page). At the same time the proportion of women attended by a midwife dropped from nearly 13 percent to 5 percent.

About three-fifths of the births in our country are to women in their 20's. Motherhood at these young ages has distinct advantages for both the mother and the child. For one thing, the hazards of maternity are at a minimum at this period of life. Then, too, the chances are very high that a young mother will live to bring up her

* Reprinted from *Statistical Bulletin*, 1951, 32: 1–2, by permission of the Metropolitan Life Insurance Company.

children to maturity. Each year over one-fourth of the married women at ages 20–24 have a baby. The proportion decreases rapidly with advance in age; it is one-eighth at ages 30–34, but only one-fiftieth at 40–44 years. The highest birth ratio is found among married teen-agers. Not far from one-half of them become mothers in any year, but because of their limited number they contribute only about one-eighth of the total births annually.

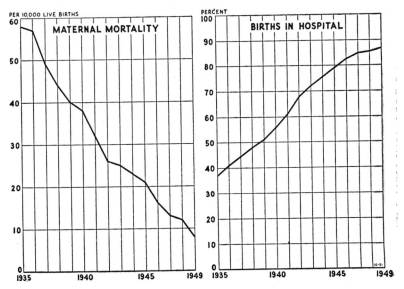

FIG. 1. *Maternal Mortality and Hospitalization of Births—United States, 1935–1949.*

Motherhood has enjoyed a much greater popularity in the past decade than it did in the depression decade of the 1930's. Recent years have seen record-breaking numbers of births, largely as a result of the great numbers of newly married couples; those married longer are encouraged by favorable economic conditions to increase the size of their families. The birth rate has risen markedly at virtually all the childbearing ages, and especially among women in their early 20's. Recent surveys by the Bureau of the Census indicate that women living in urban areas have shown the largest increase in fertility since 1940; farm wives, however, have recorded almost no change in their birth rate. For the first time in about four decades enough babies are being born in the cities to maintain the urban population without relying on migration from the rural areas.

Over the years, more and more mothers have been spared the tragic experience of seeing their children die early in life. The mortality among babies under 1 year of age has been reduced by more than one-third since 1940 alone, the rate dropping from 47 per 1,000 live births to just under 30 per 1,000 currently. The loss of life among children at the preschool and school ages has declined to remarkably low levels. At the same time the chances that the mother would lose her husband while there are dependent children have been reduced appreciably.

These favorable developments have greatly benefited American family life and augur well for the future of our country.

Three · The Frequency of Plural Births *

METROPOLITAN LIFE INSURANCE COMPANY

THE Dionne quintuplets made medical history when they overcame the serious hazards of early life, and have continued to add a page to that remarkable story each birthday. Since the birth of the Dionnes, just one other case is known of quintuplets who have survived infancy—the Diligenti children born in Argentina in July, 1943. It is rather singular that the only two authenticated cases of this kind in all medical history occurred within less than a decade of each other.

Quadruplets, while not as rare as quintuplets, are still very unusual. There were on the average only 1.6 cases of quadruplets per 1,000,000 confinements in the United States during the period 1934–1947; these figures include only cases in which at least one infant was born alive. Triplets are far more common than quadruplets—in fact, 66 times as frequent. Thus, in this study involving nearly 36,000,000 maternity cases, one set of triplets occurred every 9,400 confinements, whereas quadruplets were reported only once in about every 620,000 confinements. Twins, of course, account for the large majority of plural births. In the period under review, there were nearly 392,000 cases of twins reported in our country, or one pair in every 92 confinements.

The likelihood that a confinement will result in a multiple birth depends upon various factors. Age of the mother is one of them. The frequency of plural births increases progressively with advance in age of mother to a maximum at ages 35–39, and then falls off somewhat. The chances are better than 17 in 1,000 that the confinement of a woman in her late 30's will yield a plural birth. For teen-age mothers, the chances are only 6 in 1,000.

At every age period, the chances of multiple birth are greater for nonwhite than for white mothers. For the greater part of reproduc-

* Reprinted from *Statistical Bulletin*, 1950, 31: 6, by permission of the Metropolitan Life Insurance Company.

tive life, at ages 20 and over, the chances are about two-fifths greater for the nonwhite mothers. The difference in the frequency of plural births in the two racial groups, moreover, increases with the number of children born at one confinement. Thus, twins were relatively about 1¼ times as frequent among nonwhite mothers as among the white; triplets were 1¾ times, and quadruplets 4½ times as frequent. The higher proportion of plural births generally among the colored is accounted for entirely by the experience among Negroes; the rates for the other nonwhite races are lower than those for the white.

Four · The Rh Blood Factors

CURT STERN
Zoologist, University of California

New knowledge about the Rh factors means that many babies who formerly would not have lived, now will have a chance of survival. Some doctors now make tests for the Rh factors a routine part of prenatal and premarital examinations.

The following explanation of the Rh factors * *by Curt Stern is written clearly and comprehensively for the non-medical person.*

THE RH BLOOD FACTORS

IT has been assumed that the genetic causes of abnormal embryonic development either resided in the mother or the child. In recent years, certain congenital abnormalities have been shown to result from mutual interaction of maternal and filial genotypes. The foremost of these interactions is related to the now famous *Rh* locus.

In 1940, Landsteiner and Wiener, by injecting rabbits with the blood of Rhesus monkeys, obtained an antibody against an antigenic property of the Rhesus blood. When this antibody was mixed with the blood of human individuals, it was discovered that the blood cells of about 85 per cent of these persons became agglutinated, while the blood of 15 per cent of them remained unaffected. Apparently, the majority of the human individuals tested contained an antigen, Rh, which is identical with, or similar to, the antigen

---

* Reprinted from *Principles of Human Genetics*, by Curt Stern. San Francisco: W. H. Freeman and Company, 1949, pp. 313–320; 570–571, by permission of the author and the publisher.

present in Rhesus monkeys; and a minority did not contain this antigen.

It was soon demonstrated that the presence or absence of the antigen is heritable. Marriages between two "Rh-negative" persons yield only Rh-negative children, while marriages between two "Rh-positives" or between an Rh-positive and an Rh-negative individual may produce children of both types. The proportions of these two types of offspring in the two kinds of marriages fit a simple single factor interpretation according to which Rh-positive individuals are either homo- or heterozygous for a dominant allele, *Rh,* and Rh-negative individuals are homozygous for a recessive allele, *rh.*

It was found, later, that the *Rh* locus is represented in human populations by many more than two alleles, *Rh* and *rh.* We shall discuss below the problems connected with this multiple allelism but, for the present, shall treat the case as if only the two alleles, *Rh* and *rh,* existed.

Erythroblastosis Fetalis. Soon after the discovery of the Rh factor, Levine recognized that it was involved in the occurrence of the disease of newly born or unborn, known as *erythroblastosis fetalis.* It consists of an anemia due to hemolysis (breakdown) of the fetal blood and consequently results in jaundice. One aspect of the disease, which has given it its name, is the presence of immature red blood cells, the erythroblasts, in the blood stream. Normally, these immature cells are found only in the bone marrow and other organs but not free in the circulating blood. Frequently, fetal erythroblastosis leads to abortion or stillbirths but, in case of recovery, completely healthy children usually develop.

The disease was known to have a familial occurrence, showing a high frequency among the sibs of propositi, as well as among their more distant relatives. In spite of various attempts to formulate a genetic interpretation, the hereditary mechanism had remained unknown until the Rh antigen was found and its mode of inheritance determined. Then, Levine noticed that more than 90 per cent of the erythroblastotic children were Rh positive and had Rh-negative mothers. He concluded that, apparently, the blood cells of the Rh-positive newly born were hemolyzed by an antibody provided by the Rh-negative mother. The existence of such an antibody was then demonstrated in the serum of Rh-negative mothers who were, or had been, pregnant with Rh-positive offspring. It was lacking in most of the Rh-negative women who had never been pregnant or had only nonaffected children. However, the antibody was present in the serum of a few such women, and, in every case, it was found that the women had received repeated blood transfusions. These transfusions were given for various reasons and sometimes many years earlier.

These facts led to the following explanation of the origin of erythroblastosis. Normally, human individuals lack specific anti-bodies against the Rh antigen, but the antibodies may be produced in Rh-negative persons by repeated transfusions with Rh antigen. This iso-immunization, the production of antibodies in the same species, man, from which the antigen is obtained, is comparable to the experimental production of antibodies by injection of blood from different species into rabbits or other animals. When an Rh-negative woman carries an Rh-positive fetus, the Rh antigen from the latter may penetrate the placenta, reach the body of the mother and cause the production of an antibody. No harm is done by this antibody to the blood cells of the Rh-negative mother, since they lack the antigen. When, however, the antibody finds its way, again through the placenta, to the Rh-positive fetus, an immunological reaction occurs between the antibody and the red blood cells of the fetus, resulting in erythroblastosis fetalis.

It may be wondered why iso-immunization does not occur in the inverse case—that of Rh-positive mothers carrying an Rh-negative child—for the antibody should be formed in the fetus and, finding its way into the body of the mother, should lead to agglutination and hemolysis of her blood cells. It is possible that this process does, indeed, take place, occasionally, but on a scale which does not cause any noticeable symptoms. The main reason for this lack of an effect of an Rh-negative fetus on an Rh-positive mother lies in the fact that the antibody-forming mechanism of a child does not usually mature until about six months after birth. Therefore, no antibodies against Rh-antigens will be produced in the fetus. Fur-thermore, even if some antibodies were formed, they would, after passing through the placenta into the mother's body, be reduced so greatly in concentration due to the large volume of the mother's blood as compared to that of the fetus that no ill consequences would result.

Since erythroblastosis fetalis usually occurs in Rh-positive children born to Rh-negative mothers, the fathers of affected children are Rh-positive, since they are responsible for the *Rh* allele present in their affected offspring. The frequency of erythroblastosis fetalis among all pregnancies is related to the frequency of the *Rh* allele in the population. The frequency of the *Rh* allele, p, and that of the *rh* allele, q, can be determined by the use of the Hardy-Weinberg Law. Rh-negative individuals are *rh rh*. Their frequency is q^2. Therefore, the allele frequency of *rh* is equal to the square root of the frequency of Rh-negative individuals. In a White population, this frequency is close to 16 per cent (0.16), so that $q = 0.4$ and $p = 0.6$. From this, it follows that homozygous *Rh Rh* individuals occur in the frequency $p^2 = 36$ per cent, and heterozygotes *Rh rh* in the frequency $2 \cdot p \cdot q = 48$ per cent.

Rh-positive pregnancies in Rh-negative women result from the following two kinds of marriages: *rh rh* (females) $\times$ *Rh Rh* (males) and *rh rh* (females)$\times Rh$ *rh* (males). The frequencies of these marriages are $p^2 \times q^2 = 5.76$ per cent and $q^2 \times 2pq = 7.68$ per cent. In the first kind, all pregnancies result in the production of an Rh-positive fetus but only one-half of the children in the latter type of marriage are Rh positive. Thus, the sum of all unfavorable pregnancies in the population becomes $5.76 + 3.84 = 9.60$ per cent, or about one-tenth of all pregnancies.

The incidence of the disease is very much lower than the incidence of potentially unfavorable pregnancies. It is estimated to occur once in 200 to 500 pregnancies in White populations, that is, only in 1 out of 20 to 1 out of 50 of all potential cases. The reasons for this fortunately low occurrence of the disease are not fully known. It is partly due to the fact that the disease is rare in the earlier pregnancies of women because the mother has not yet built up a high level of antibodies. Partly, it may be due to individual differences in the permeability of the placenta, the organ which permits the Rh antigen to pass from the fetus into the mother's circulation. The mechanism of this passage is not clearly understood at present, and there may be genetic differences among individuals controlling placental permeability.

If the disease has once occurred during pregnancy, it recurs, often to a more severe degree, in every succeeding pregnancy in which the genotype of the fetus is the unfavorable *Rh rh*. This means that all succeeding pregnancies lead to illness of the child if the father is homozygous *Rh Rh*. If, on the other hand, he is heterozygous *Rh rh*, there is a 1:1 chance of either a healthy *rh rh* child or another affected *Rh rh* one being born. It is possible, by immunological methods, to determine whether an Rh-positive individual is homozygous or heterozygous for the *Rh* allele but the serum necessary for such a test is very rare. Such serum can be obtained only from certain rare immunological types of pregnant women so that such tests are not readily available at large.

The practical consequences of the immunological and genetic understanding of erythroblastosis are great. Immunologically, it is clearly indicated that Rh-negative female patients should not be given blood transfusions with Rh-positive blood, since they may build up antibodies which may react in a later pregnancy with an Rh-positive fetus. The treatment of serious cases of erythroblastosis in the newborn consists of blood transfusion primarily to replace the affected red blood cells. In very severe cases, transfusion may be carried out with the object of replacing all of the child's blood which contains the antibodies derived from the mother. Otherwise, transfusion need only add blood free from antibodies. Obviously, no blood should be administered which contains Rh antibody. Thus, the mother is excluded as a donor.

Genetically, determination of the Rh constitution of prospective parents permits a prediction regarding the possible occurrence of the disease in the offspring.

In many American hospitals, it is routine procedure to test a pregnant woman for the presence or absence of the Rh antigen. If she is Rh positive, no special precautions are required. If she is Rh negative, the husband is tested and note is taken in case he is Rh positive. Even if he is Rh positive, the chances that the child will be well are very high, since erythroblastosis, as we have seen, occurs in only a small fraction of Rh-positive pregnancies in Rh-negative mothers.

The Rh Alleles. As stated, more than two alleles are now known at the *Rh* locus. They are distinguishable by the fact that several antigens are controlled by these alleles. Each allele of the *Rh* locus, it appears, controls, simultaneously, the production of three different antigens, called C, D, and E. An allele may produce antigen C or an alternative c, and, in addition, antigen D or an alternative d, and antigen E or an alternative e. In contrast to the antigens C, D, and E, which have been called Rh antigens, their alternatives c, d, and e have been named Hr antigens.

The threefold Rh status is dependent on the existence of eight different *Rh* alleles. In heterozygotes, all alleles act additively, so that, for instance, $Rh^{CD} \cdot /Rh^{cdE}$ individuals possess antigens C, D, and E. In addition to the eight *Rh* alleles listed, several more alleles have been found. These "intermediate" alleles control the production of such antigens as C^w or D^u, which are different from either C and c, or D and d, respectively. C^w or D^u are alternates to C–c, or D–d, that is, a gamete possesses, in addition to E or e, either C, c, or C^w, and either D, d, or D^u, but never more nor less than one of each class.

Two of the eight alleles, Rh^{CDE} and Rh^{CdE}, are very rare in all populations and the six more frequent alleles have different frequencies in different groups. In most White populations, the six combinations of the three alleles, Rh^{CDe}, Rh^{cDE}, and Rh^{cde} account for about 93 per cent of all genotypes. In these populations, the general allelic designation Rh includes primarily Rh^{CDe} and Rh^{cDE}, and rh corresponds to Rh^{cde}. The frequencies of these alleles in Whites are approximately: Rh^{CDe} 0.41, Rh^{cDE} 0.15 and Rh^{cde} 0.41.

The existence of so many different *Rh* alleles permits a very fine immunologic and genetic subdivision of human populations. In medico-legal investigations, the use of Rh properties in cases of doubtful paternity leads to a greatly increased probability of exclusion.

The control, by the *Rh* locus, of three separate kinds of similar antigens has been interpreted by Fisher as a consequence of the existence of a complex of three separate *Rh* loci which are closely located next to one another in a chromosome. In the absence of evidence by means of which this interpretation can be tested, it is equivalent to the assumption that a single locus is capable of controlling three antigenic properties. The latter assumption, held by Wiener and others, is the basis of the nomenclature employed in the preceding pages.

Erythroblastosis fetalis may occur whenever the fetus carries an *Rh* allele which produces antigens not present in the mother. The terms Rh-positive and Rh-negative do not take into account the great diversity of antigenic constitutions. While the majority of pregnancies with erythroblastosis are the result of presence of the antigen D in the child and its absence in the mother, the disease may also be produced by presence of any one of the other Rh antigens in the child—e.g., C, E, or even c, d, and e—and absence of the respective antigen in the mother. Thus, an exceptional family has been reported in which an Rh-positive mother had an affected child. Examination showed the presence of antigens C, D, and E in the child and of C and D in the mother. Accordingly, it was suspected that the E antigen was responsible for the disease, and this hypothesis was proven correct by finding antibodies against E in the mother's blood.

The medical literature contains some instances of erythroblastosis fetalis caused by mother-child interactions of the A-B-O antigens. Children belonging to group A, developing in an O mother, may induce an increased production of anti-A antibodies in the mother's blood; a corresponding situation may arise with B children. Very rarely, the concentration of these antibodies becomes so high that sufficient amounts diffuse into the embryo's blood to cause damage.

The interaction between the genotypes of pregnant mothers and their unborn children may not be restricted to the *Rh*, or, very rarely, the *I* alleles. It has been suggested that similar interactions may be responsible for the *toxemias* (blood poisoning) which sometimes affect pregnant mothers. There is, however, no specific evidence available which serves to support or refute this hypothesis.

RACE MIXTURE AND THE RH BLOOD FACTOR

In this connection, a very special case may be recalled, that of the Rh incompatibility between pregnant Rh-negative mothers and their Rh-positive embryos. If two isolated human races existed, one isogenic for the allele *Rh*, the other for *rh*, the pathological phenomenon of Rh-determined erythroblastosis fetalis would not be known in either race. If the two races intermarried, many disharmonious mother-child combinations would appear, resulting in a disease which might then be called typical for miscegenation. Races do exist, the Mongoloids for example, which have a frequency for the allele *rh* of 0.0. No race is known where the allele frequency for *rh* is 1.0, but intermediate frequencies occur. In the Caucasoids, the frequency of *rh* is approximately 0.4. These different allele frequencies are the reason why erythroblastosis seems absent in Mongoloids but present in Caucasoids.

At present, we shall consider the consequences in regard to the antigenically disharmonious mother-child combination after miscegenation between, for instance, Chinese and Whites. Let us imagine the immigration of Whites into China and of Chinese into a country inhabited by Whites, and the miscegenation of the immigrants with the native race. In China, no erythroblastosis fetalis will occur in the first generation of intermarriages between Chinese women and White men, since all Chinese women are Rh positive and not subject to Rh iso-immunization. However, in the marriages between White immigrant women and Chinese men, the disease will affect some of the children, since about 16 per cent of White women are Rh negative and can be iso-immunized by fetuses who all have inherited the *Rh* allele from their fathers. In later generations, the relative frequency of erythroblastosis in the population of China, now of mixed Chinese-White origin, will be less than in the first generation, since the frequency of the *rh* allele and, therefore, of *rh rh* women will be lower than among the original Whites due to the decrease of the frequency of *rh* after dilution with the *Rh* allele of the original Chinese. Still, the frequency of the *rh* allele will be *higher* than it was before the White immigrants came. Hence, *rh rh* women will occur as expected from random mating, and some of them will have erythroblastotic pregnancies. Thus, from the point of view of the Chinese, and judged purely from Rh incompatibility, miscegenation will have had permanently bad effects.

It is very different in the "White country" with its Chinese immigrants. None of the Chinese women married to White men will add to the fetal disease, but Chinese men married to White women will cause the appearance of a higher frequency of erythroblastotic children than among marriages of White men and White women. In later generations, the frequency of the *rh* allele in the White population, now of mixed White-Chinese origin, will be *lower* than before the *Rh Rh* immigrants came; the frequency of *rh rh* women will be correspondingly less, and the incidence of the disease will be lower. Thus, again, judged purely from Rh incompatibility, miscegenation will be found to be permanently beneficial.

Five · Effects of First Pregnancy on Sex Adjustment

JUDSON T. LANDIS
Sociologist, University of California

THOMAS POFFENBERGER
Sociologist, Oregon State College

SHIRLEY POFFENBERGER

Does pregnancy aid or hinder in working out a good sex adjustment in marriage? What effect does pregnancy have upon the sex desire of husband and wife? Does fear of pregnancy and childbirth hinder the sex adjustment? The next reading * *sheds some light upon the general pattern of sexual adjustment during pregnancy.*

IN an attempt to get some basic information on first pregnancy and the effects of the pregnancy experience upon husband-wife relationships this research was done with the cooperation of a group of couples who had recently gone through their first pregnancy. During the Spring of 1949, 228 couples who lived in the barracks village at Michigan State College were interviewed and asked for their cooperation. The study was anonymous. Questionnaires were distributed to the couples by the research team [1] who later returned with a box with a slit in it for collection of the questionnaires. All couples living in the village whose first child was not more than $2\frac{1}{2}$ years old were included in the sample. Husbands and wives were given separate envelopes containing questionnaires to be filled in independently. Each spouse was to seal his completed questionnaire and then the two were to be placed in a large envelope. In this way it was possible to compare the responses of husbands and wives on certain questions. There was no way of knowing how many couples discussed their questionnaires as they filled them out. All but 7 of the couples interviewed cooperated in the study and 212 out of 221 questionnaires handed out could be used in the final tabulation.

Educationally those in the study do not represent a cross-section or sample of young people who experience pregnancy today since

* Reprinted from the *American Sociological Review*, 1950, 15: 767–772, by permission.

[1] Thomas and Shirley Poffenberger lived as graduate students in the Barracks village and collected the data for this research as partial requirements for the Masters' degree.

all the husbands were in college and half of the wives had had some college education. They represent the majority of people experiencing first pregnancy only in that they were young and in the early years of marriage.

Of the 212 wives in this study, 37.2 per cent had become pregnant within the first six months of marriage and 59.8 per cent had become pregnant by the end of the first year of marriage. Two and eight-tenths per cent reported being pregnant at the time of marriage; 23.2 per cent became pregnant after one to two years of marriage and 14.2 per cent had been married three or more years at the time of conception.

To the question, "What effect, if any, did pregnancy have upon your sexual adjustment?", husbands and wives as a group were in agreement in their answers. More than half (58 per cent) indicated that pregnancy had had "no effect" upon their sexual adjustment; 25 per cent of the wives and 23 per cent of the husbands felt that the effect had been "unfavorable," while 17 per cent of the wives and 19 per cent of the husbands felt that the effect had been "favorable."

In order to evaluate further the effect of pregnancy on sexual adjustment, responses to the above question were compared with responses to a question rating sexual adjustment during three periods of marriage: before pregnancy, during pregnancy, and since the birth of the child. The results were the same. The responses of 50 per cent of the sample indicated relatively constant patterns of adjustment in these periods. Most of the persons in the group having had good sexual adjustment before pregnancy had much the same adjustment following the birth of their child.

The group of couples who said the pregnancy had a favorable effect upon their sex adjustment had tended to have a poor adjustment before conception. Only 15.6 per cent of the wives in this group had a very good adjustment before pregnancy while 50 per cent reported a very good adjustment after the birth. On the other hand, those wives who reported an unfavorable effect had had significantly good adjustment before conception; 36.4 per cent of these reported very good adjustment before pregnancy and only 6.8 per cent reported very good adjustment since the birth. (Significant at the one per cent level.) The husbands showed the same trend but with less variation in their ratings of sexual adjustment.

Some of the reasons given for the improvement of sexual adjustment were that the couples had not "had sufficient time to achieve good sexual adjustment before pregnancy occurred;" the "husband was more considerate of wife after the birth of the child;" the "wife tried to be more tolerant of husband's sex needs;" "improvement of wife's physical condition after having a child;" and "a better understanding with regard to sex." In general, as was found in our earlier research, it takes time to arrive at a good sexual adjustment. The additional time which had elapsed, although the wife had been pregnant, had resulted in some couples reaching a better understanding regarding sex. The close identification of the husband with the wife during pregnancy might have helped him gain a better understanding of her sexual nature. On the other hand, if there had been no pregnancy, it is possible that these couples might have made as rapid progress toward an understanding of each other's sexual natures and needs with the lapse of time.

The couples who reported a poorer adjustment as a result of the pregnancy explained it largely in terms of the added responsibilities which came with parenthood. The wife had to spend more time taking care of the baby, and in general was too tired for sexual enjoyment. The most frequent reason given was that there had been a general lessening of desire on the part of the wife.

It is generally believed that the sex desire of men is relatively periodic. One study shows sex desire in women to be more common

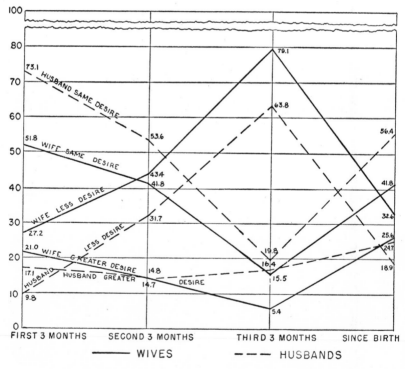

FIG. 1. *Percentages of Husbands and Wives Rating Sexual Desire in Three Periods of Pregnancy.* (Total Responses: First three months, 209 husbands and 211 wives; second three months, 210 husbands and 211 wives; third three months, 206 husbands and 207 wives; since birth, 203 husbands and 206 wives.)

just before or just after menstruation while there is no time of the month when there is an upsurge in sex desire among men. However, when couples in the sample of the present study rated their sexual desire, it was found that 21 per cent of the wives said they had more desire the first part of the pregnancy, but 27.2 per cent reported less desire and 51.8 per cent said they noticed no change in sex desire. Figure 1 summarizes the self rating of sex desire during pregnancy by husbands and wives. There is a significant reduction in desire for both husbands and wives since the birth of the child. The percentage of those who said their desire was the same as before pregnancy decreased for the wives from 51.8 per cent in the first part of pregnancy to 41.8 per cent in the period since birth, and for the husbands from 73.1 per cent to 56.4 per cent respectively.

It might be expected that as a result of progressive physiological and psychological changes, sexual desire might diminish for the wife. A change in glandular functioning might also have something to do with her change in sex desire. However, the fact that the husband's desire seems to follow a general pattern of decrease as the pregnancy progresses, suggests that there may be a psychological basis for the decrease in sex desire of both the husband and the wife.

The concept of the husband empathizing or identifying with the wife is exemplified among some primitive people who practice the "couvade," i.e., the various lying-in practices through which at childbirth the father symbolically substitutes himself for the mother. There is evidence in this study to indicate that in a way many husbands of today practice a psychological "couvade" during the wife's first pregnancy. The wives were asked whether they noticed any change in their husband's attitude toward them after they became pregnant. Almost half, 47 per cent, said that they did notice a change in attitude and of those who commented, 93.6 per cent reported that the husbands were more thoughtful and considerate. Comments of the wives were: "He was very understanding and seemed more settled;" "He became more interested in how I was feeling and was always looking after me when we went places;" "When I went places by myself he was always warning me to be careful;" "He became more affectionate and closer to me;" "He was overly helpful and thoughtful and we were very close;" "He helped me more around the house;" "More gentle in manner and speech;" "He babied me a lot especially toward the last part of pregnancy;" "He thought and acted as if I were now a woman, no longer a child." It is logical that some of the husband's lessening of sex desire is a result or accompaniment of his identification with the wife and her experiences during first pregnancy. One might question the viewpoint of those who believe that the male glands function in such a way that they require periodic release from sexual tension regardless of psychic or cultural factors. This study suggests that so-called glandular functioning which calls for periodic sex release is somewhat dependent upon psychological factors and cultural conditioning. In this study we asked for a rating of general sex desire and not for sexual outlet. It seems reasonable to assume, however, that a study of sexual outlet during pregnancy would show that it would follow the same curve as decrease in desire.

Further, the responses in this study brought out several culturally produced reasons for a decrease in sex desire on the part of husbands during the wife's pregnancy. Ten per cent of the husbands said they ceased having intercourse because "it didn't seem right" or "I didn't enjoy intercourse." A larger percentage of husbands than wives gave the reason that "it didn't seem right." Although a significant reduction in desire as pregnancy progressed was reported, when sex desire is compared to happiness in the same period, a consistent tendency appeared for those husbands and wives who did have more desire to be happier than those who had either the same degree of desire or less desire.

PLANNED AND UNPLANNED PREGNANCIES

Wives were asked whether they had planned the pregnancy. Slightly over 38 per cent of the wives indicated that they had tried to avoid pregnancy; 26 per cent more had neither tried to avoid nor planned their pregnancy, while 35.8 per cent said they had planned their pregnancies. The responses would seem to indicate that only about one-third of the couples actually planned to have their child when they did. Of those who were trying to avoid pregnancy, 61 of the wives reported that a mechanical or chemical contraceptive was used and 12 indicated they were using rhythm or withdrawal methods.

Following first births, there was a significant increase in the use of mechanical and chemical contraceptives; the percentage jumped from 28.8 per cent for the entire sample to 65.2 per cent.

Of those couples who indicated they were using contraceptives since the birth of their first child, 38.4 per cent of the wives mistrusted the method while only 20 per cent of the husbands mistrusted it, the difference being significant at the one per cent level. (The findings suggest that wives' distrust is related to fear of another pregnancy.)

To determine what effect distrust of contraceptive methods may have had on sexual adjustment during the period since birth, the responses to the questions were compared. It was found that those wives who distrusted their contraceptive method, and who feared another pregnancy, had a significantly poorer sexual adjustment than those who trusted their methods.

Fewer husbands distrusted the contraceptive method being used, and for those who did distrust it, no evident effect in relation to sexual adjustment was noted. While many husbands may identify with their wives during pregnancy, it appears that this identification is not strong enough to create sufficient fear of pregnancy so that the husband does not enjoy sexual intercourse later.

HEALTH DURING PREGNANCY AND SEXUAL ADJUSTMENT

In this study 56 per cent of the wives said they noticed no change in their health during pregnancy; 33 per cent said that their health was better; and 11 per cent said that their health was poorer. Of those wives who said their health was better than before pregnancy, 36.9 per cent reported very good sexual adjustment since the birth of the child. Of those who rated their health the same as before, 33.6 per cent reported very good sexual adjustment and 32.3 per cent average or below, while only 13.6 per cent of the "poorer health" group reported a very good sexual adjustment and 63.7 per cent reported "average or below."

Thus the difference between 36.9 per cent and 13.6 per cent can only suggest that poor health during pregnancy sometimes has a negative effect upon sexual adjustment following birth of the child.

FEAR OF CHILDBIRTH AND SEXUAL ADJUSTMENT

Of those who feared another labor and childbirth 22.5 per cent had a very good sexual adjustment, while 39 per cent of those who had no such fear had a very good adjustment. The sexual adjustment was considered average or below by 46.3 per cent of those who feared another labor and childbirth, but the same rating was given by only 33.6 per cent of those who had no such fear.

Distrust of contraceptives and fear of another labor and childbirth are apparently representative of similar attitudes, so it would be expected that if one were found significant, the other would also be significant. The fact that both were found to be significant strongly indicates the negative effect on sexual adjustment of fears related to having another child.

SUMMARY

This study indicated that:

(1) In general, the couples studied who had a good sexual adjustment before pregnancy had a good sexual adjustment during pregnancy and following the birth of the child.

(2) In a minority of the cases, couples who had a poor sexual adjustment before pregnancy seem to have had an improved sexual adjustment after pregnancy; and in another minority of cases, those who had a good sexual adjustment before pregnancy had a much poorer sexual adjustment after pregnancy.

(3) The percentages of husbands and wives reporting the same

sex desire as before pregnancy decreased with each trimester of the pregnancy; the percentages reporting less desire increased rapidly with each trimester. The general level of sex desire reported by husbands and wives was somewhat lower after the birth of the child as compared to before the pregnancy.

(4) Wives who had confidence in the contraceptive being used experienced better sexual adjustment following birth of the child.

(5) Fear of another pregnancy and childbirth was a hindrance to good sexual adjustment.

(6) Wives whose health was better than usual during pregnancy had a somewhat better sexual adjustment after pregnancy than those who were in poor health during the period.

Six · Artificial Insemination

JOSEPH H. GREENBERG
Sociologist, University of Colorado

A sociologist relates factors in the social background of students to the attitudes that the students express toward artificial insemination. *

DESPITE popular misconception, human artificial insemination is actually not a dramatically new phenomenon. The first recorded instance of its use occurred in 1790, when it was performed in England by the British physiologist and surgeon, John Hunter.

Dr. Alan F. Guttmacher of Johns Hopkins University, one of the outstanding American pioneers in the field of human artificial insemination, defines it as "the non-sexual deposition of the male semen, previously collected, within the reproductive tract of the female." There are two types of artificial insemination: A.I.H., and A.I.D. In A.I.H., the husband's semen is used. This procedure has a certain degree of effectiveness in cases where pregnancy is difficult or impossible under normal conditions because of a defect of some sort in the wife or husband. The artificial insemination process, by placing a relatively large quantity of sperm cells within the female reproductive system in an area where conception is most likely to occur, raises the normal chances of pregnancy.

A.I.D., on the other hand, is artificial insemination using a semen

* Reprinted from the *American Sociological Review*, 1951, 86–91, by permission of the author and the *American Sociological Review*.

donor (usually very carefully selected by the physician, and unknown to the couple) who is not the husband. Its practice is ordinarily confined to cases where the husband is sterile or possesses harmful hereditary traits, yet where the couple have decided to have a child that biologically is half theirs—that is, the wife's. Along this line, it has been estimated by a leading American urologist that there are at least one and a half million involuntarily childless marriages in the United States, easily a third of which are attributable to deficiencies of the husband. Another prime factor in the growing popularity of A.I.D. is the shortage of babies for adoption in many areas of our nation.

It is in regard to A.I.D. rather than A.I.H. that opinions have been strongest. Some moralists have become alarmed by the practice, while visionary eugenicists have hailed the prospects for a brave new world of super-people. The Roman Catholic Church and the Church of England have perhaps been most vehement in their condemnation of A.I.D. Many notable persons, however, have spoken up in approval of it.

Despite the current controversy regarding artificial insemination, no scientific study of attitudes towards A.I.H. and A.I.D., to the author's knowledge, has been attempted. Yet interesting questions for research suggest themselves: Is there actually any difference in persons' attitudes towards A.I.H. and A.I.D.? Do variations in attitudes towards A.I.H. and A.I.D. exist among different social groups? To answer these questions, the author examined the attitudes of two hundred and forty-seven men and women students at the University of Colorado during the summer sessions of 1949 and 1950, the two periods being chosen so as to reduce temporary influences on the sample. Anonymous questionnaires were distributed during the class period to two Lower Division and two Upper Division classes. These were later analyzed as one large sample after the four classes or samples were found to be sufficiently similar for combination.

Because of the many misconceptions concerning artificial insemination, the author, preliminary to the distribution of the questionnaires, informed the students as to what the process of artificial insemination was, and distinguished between A.I.H. and A.I.D. without expressing his attitude towards either.

The two basic questions on the questionnaire, specified as applying to the students themselves in their own or hypothetical marriage situation as husbands or wives, are as follows: [1]
1. "Would you yourself make use of artificial insemination, with

---

[1] An interesting project for comparative research might be to investigate the attitudes of a sample of married adults only, where the situation would be somewhat less hypothetical, or the actual behavior of a group of involuntarily childless couples who are aware of artificial insemination.

husband as donor, if you wanted a child and could not have one by
normal sex relations?"

Yes (   ); No (   ).

2. "Would you yourself make use of artificial insemination, using
an unknown donor, if you wanted a child and the husband was
sterile?"

Yes (   ); No (   ).

Question 1 tests attitudes towards A.I.H.; Question 2, towards
A.I.D. No opportunity was given for an "Undecided" or "No Opinion" answer, in order to force a positive or negative response.

In addition to Questions 1 and 2 above, the questionnaire asked
for information regarding sex, age, religious preference, region of
home residence, year in college, size of home community, marital
status, and undergraduate grade average. For various reasons, however, not all of the two hundred and forty-seven students gave information and opinion in every case.

FINDINGS

The results of the questionnaire discussed above show a striking
difference in attitude revealed towards A.I.H. and A.I.D. The Chi-
square value in this case is 86.3, which far exceeds the 1% level of
significance, indicating that the difference between acceptance (or
rejection) of A.I.H. and A.I.D. is statistically highly significant. The
identity of the donor appears to be the crux of the matter in regard
to attitudes concerning artificial insemination. Less than 10% rejected A.I.H., whereas close to 50% rejected A.I.D. One may conclude from these findings that rejection of artificial insemination,
for our sample at least, is directed not so much towards the phenomenon itself, but rather towards the person acting as donor.

But what of the variables considered in their relation to attitudes
concerning A.I.H. and A.I.D.? Differences in age, sex, marital status,
region of home residence, year in college, undergraduate grade
average, and size of home community were tested as to acceptance-
rejection of A.I.H. No statistically significant variations were revealed, although differences in attitude towards A.I.H. by size of
home community did approach the 5% level of significance. We
may conclude that the various age, sex, marital, regional, college
year, grade average, community, and religious groups are quite
similar in their attitudes toward A.I.H.

Slight curvilinear trends are revealed for age, year in college, and
size of home community. Students in the youngest and oldest age-
groups are a little more willing to accept A.I.H. than are the age-
groups in between; juniors and seniors accept somewhat more fully
than do freshmen and sophomores and graduate students; and stu-

dents from small and medium-size cities stand higher in acceptance than do those from farms and villages or those from large cities. Yet these trends should not be construed as highly important, inasmuch as the differences are slight, the number of groups in each case is not large, and the number of cases in some groups (some of the age-categories, for example) is rather small.

As was the case in regard to A.I.H., a great consistency exists between the various age, sex, marital, regional, college year, grade average, and religious groups in their attitudes towards the A.I.D. phenomenon. One variable, however, appeared to be of distinct importance. This was the ecological factor, "size of home community." Differences in acceptance-rejection of A.I.D. between students from communities of various sizes are statistically significant.

No distinct, clear-cut trend (either in one direction or curvilinear) in acceptance-rejection of A.I.D. is apparent for the various age and college-year groups. Nor is the slight tendency for the "B" students to reject A.I.D. more fully than do the "A" or "C" students important statistically or socially. But for size of community, although no well-defined trend in acceptance-rejection of A.I.D. manifests itself, the exceptionally high acceptance of A.I.D. among students from small and medium-size cities and the significantly high *rejection* among students from very large cities is of distinct interest. Human artificial insemination is to most persons something new, different, radical. In one sense, therefore, acceptance-rejection of artificial insemination, particularly of A.I.D., may be considered an index of general conservatism and resistance to social change. The significantly high rejection of A.I.D. among students from very large cities, therefore, even higher than among those from farms or villages, questions the validity of the long-cherished generalizations concerning the metropolis as a place where innovations are most welcome and social change proceeds at a rapid pace.

As a corollary to the main subject of our study, it is interesting that the students' written comments on the questionnaires revealed that both acceptance and rejection of A.I.D. rested essentially on psychological factors. In general, those willing to utilize it felt that it was psychologically better than adoption both for the child and parents, whereas those rejecting it stated that too many psychological difficulties would arise.

What may account for the extreme reluctance to resort to A.I.D. among persons from very large cities? Religious affiliation (Catholics and Jews cluster in large cities) has appeared statistically insignificant, despite the injunctions of some religious groups against the practice, so one must look elsewhere for an explanation. May it hinge somewhat on the expense and inconvenience of rearing children in the metropolis? In any event, the fact that the ecological element of community size related significantly to attitudes towards A.I.D. merits further study.

*Seven • Effect of Adoption
on Fertility*

FREDERICK M. HANSON, M.D.
JOHN ROCK, M.D.

*Two physicians have turned the light of scientific in-
vestigation upon the question, "Will adopting a child enable a
childless couple to give birth to a child of their own?" The report
of their findings follows.**

PHYSICIANS and laymen have long thought that it is
quite common for couples who have previously been childless to
have a child of their own following adoption. Many people can cite
one or more cases they know of personally, and when asked will
preface their statement with a remark that the phenomenon is well
known. Yet we find no report of an accurate survey of how often
this sequence occurs nor, assuming its frequence, of what is its
etiology. The theory grows among physicians that psychogenic disturbances play an important part in reproductive physiology and
may influence conception. Proponents of this theory assert that
adoption relieves the inhibiting psychogenic factor and allows the
conception. A limited survey of the possible occurrence of this relationship and of what effect adoption may have on other related
reproductive functions has been made and is reported in this paper.

The literature contains little that is directly concerned with the
cause of these possible phenomena, although several papers have
definite bearing upon the subject. None has given any percentage
of frequency of occurrence. In 1936 Perkins reported a study made
over a five-year period in which he approached people through the
medium of a magazine article asking for voluntary responses to his
questionnaire. Two hundred seventy-three people reported that
having adopted a child they subsequently had normal pregnancies,
ranging from one to fifteen children. No percentage of frequency
can be calculated from this study since no one reported adoption
without subsequent pregnancy, although the stated purpose of the
author was to find "whether infertility is ever or often affected by
the decision to adopt." He discusses as provocative decisive factors
bringing about the infertility, excessive mental strain, worry over
financial matters, guilt feelings due to puritanical upbringing, or
perhaps subconscious guilt feelings because of past indiscretions.

* Reprinted from the *American Journal of Obstetrics and Gynecology*, 1950,
59: 311–319, by permission of The C. V. Mosby Company.

Thus, in this early study of the problem itself, a psychiatric basis is proposed and discussed. Perkins postulated that perhaps "an imbalance of endocrine influence may be balanced by adoption whereas just the desire to adopt is not sufficient." Actual adoption then is the particular factor, according to him, which permits conception and parturition.

Dunbar in 1938 summarized the work of Sellheim, Mohr, and A. Mayer done between 1925 and 1930, and stated, without acceptable proof, that "psychic influences associated with a vivid but unsatisfied desire for a child, may stimulate the ovaries to pathological growth. It is possible that this may result in premature maturation of the follicles and discharge of the ova which are not yet ready for fertilization, and consequent sterility. That there are peculiar cases of first conception after 15–20 years of married life may be explained by the fact that as a woman gradually becomes reconciled to her sterility this injurious influence on the follicular apparatus disappears."

Orr in 1941 reported a case of "Pregnancy Following the Decision to Adopt," which he attributed in large part to psychosomatic causes. Both members of the couple had had over 500 hours of psychoanalysis which brought out evidences in each member of conflicts dealing with repudiation of femininity and masculinity. Their decision to adopt was followed immediately by a normal conception, which ended in normal delivery, the last menstrual period occurring eleven days following the time the application to adopt was made. The baby was chosen fifteen days after the onset of menstruation and the wife had no further periods. The pregnancy followed a period of ten years of infertility, seven of which were because of controlled conception. Prior to the decision to adopt, a period of three years of infertility without contraception passed, during which pregnancy was desired and attempted. It must be stated, however, that associated in this case is a history of pelvic endometriosis for which the wife was treated surgically 13 months prior to the normal conception, at which time a Fallopian tube and ovary were removed. There are many cases of infertile patients with pelvic endometriosis, however, who, by surgical treatment, have been enabled to conceive, usually within two years following surgery. This must be remembered as a possible cause of the conception in this case, adoption then only incidental. Here, again, however, a psychosomatic cause of infertility is proposed.

We quote at length from Knight (1941). "We are all aware of the frequency of 'conscious' opposition to having children in married couples, so that they take extreme precautions to avoid conception. This conscious opposition is attributed to the conviction that they cannot afford children, that they do not want to have their social life and freedom from responsibility interfered with, or so on—in such couples it may happen that after some years they decide to have a child and then find that they cannot bring about conception. The conscious opposition has been changed by considerations such as the realization of the barrenness of their childless home or a growing feeling that the marriage is nearing the rocks and a child is needed to bind them together again. The unconscious opposition, however, has not changed and still operates to prevent pregnancy. It is obvious that a couple who have recently changed their attitude in regard to having children are thus open to the suspicion that the strong opposition still lingers, and this opposition may be manifested by their prolonged indecision as to just when they will carry out the adoption or by excessively rigid specifications which a prospective adopted child must meet in order to be acceptable to them." Here is proposed the basic question in a study of the effect of adoption on fertility: can a psychogenic factor, of itself, cause the infertility that exists before adoption and disappears afterward? Knight accepts such a relationship and describes how he thinks the effective cause is made manifest.

William Menninger states that probably the most prominent factor in psychogenic sterility is fear of the inability to become pregnant. He lists three cases in his own personal experience which he proposes as cases of psychogenic infertility relieved by adoption, and lists as well, in verification, Orr's case (previously discussed) stating it to be a similar case, making no mention, however, in his résumé of the case history, of the pre-existence of the endometriosis. Robbins in 1943 reiterated the possible underlying psychogenic conflicts which bring about infertility and stated that "a promising opening for psychologically oriented investigation of problems relative to conception is the well-known phenomenon of conception in a previously sterile woman after she has adopted a child. Unfortunately, accurate statistics of the frequency of such events are not available but inasmuch as almost everyone knows of one or two such incidents they must occur frequently." We feel, however, that perhaps those cases that do occur are so well publicized that the relative frequency of the occurrence is in turn overemphasized. Weiss discusses these factors as well.

Karl Menninger states also (1942) that the unconscious wish not to have a child may exist even though conscious appearances deny it, and claims the disturbance may be due to a repudiation of femininity, but more frequently is based on a tremendous unrecognized fear. Further he states that "we should logically expect that the significant alterations in functions or structure related to the repudiation of femininity would be connected with the reproductive organs. Frigidity and vaginismus represent physiological rejections of the feminine role in intercourse and cannot exist over a long period without some corresponding structural changes, such as (at least) the atrophy of unused tissues and glands." This last statement may be seriously questioned. Disuse has not been shown of itself to cause atrophy of the vaginal tissues or any of the reproductive organs or glands. He states further, however, "sterility is somewhat comparable to frigidity: it represents the failure of normal biological functioning. That it occurs far oftener among human beings than among animals, should have suggested before now that something in the spirit of our civilization interferes with a process generally regarded as beyond psychological control." He mentions also the reported cases of "reorganization of the psychic life (e.g. psychoanalysis) of a woman resulting in pregnancy 10, 15, and 20 years after marriage," and that "moreover, pregnancy frequently follows the adoption of a child." Evidently he feels that this is a very common occurrence, since he writes that "such phenomena as the occurrence of pregnancy following the adoption or decision to adopt a child are frequent enough to belie the explanation of coincidence for even the most organically minded doctors." Statistical evidence of sufficient frequency to "belie the explanation of coincidence" is not given.

In the literature thus far quoted we find no definite proof of a psychogenic influence on reproductive functions, and feel that those instances of possible examples are only speculative in nature.

Helene Deutsch discusses the role of psychogenic factors in the production of sterility and gives an excellent account of conflict patterns and personality types which one encounters in the psychoanalytic study of these patients. She states, however, that "every form of psychogenic sterility is only relative—that is to say, it can be eliminated if the psychic conditions are changed (provided the organic situation permits), and that the same psychic factors may manifest themselves only in later phases of the reproductive function without disturbing its first phase, fecundation." She continues, "in general it can be said that the most frequent cause of (psychogenic) sterility is unconscious fear. This fear may relate not only to reproductive function, but to everything sexual, thus eliminating any possibility of physical motherhood by exclusion of the sexual experience." Yet, "seen as a functional disorder, psychogenic sterility in woman is a very complicated and stubborn phenomenon; its initial cause is usually difficult to discover, even though modern methods of investigation can find the disturbances in the hormonal messenger service. Yet, strikingly enough, the symptom (sterility) frequently persists despite favorable treatment of the hormonal defect, because, in our opinion, it continues to be fed by psychic energies."

That psychogenic factors may play an important part in other aspects of endocrine dysfunction than failure of conception, also is possibly true. That frequent anovulation with or without amenorrhea affects fertility is self-evident. Benedek and Rubenstein have studied and summarized the correlation between psychodynamic processes and ovarian activity in general. Ripley and Papanicolaou studied how frequently menstrual disorders are encountered in the various psychoses and found a high percentage. Many cases of amenorrhea following nervous strain or fatigue are reported. Especially during World War II this was found to occur in the wives of military men during periods of great anxiety.

Thus one may for the moment accept the prevalent opinion that there exists a definite connection between psychogenic factors and endocrine dysfunction in the woman. But how the effect of psychogenic factors is mediated is yet a matter of speculation. We believe that the equally prevalent opinion that adoption may relieve infertility is questionable.

METHODOLOGY

Through the aid of adoption agencies a study was made of 202 couples who adopted, approximately between 1938 and 1948. The cases of adoption in the six to twelve months immediately preceding the survey were not included as it was felt that sufficient time had not elapsed since adoption to make evident its possible effect on fertility. The couples were approached by means of a questionnaire asking whether or not they had had children following adoption, and other pertinent information. Advantage was also taken of the opportunity to discover what we could on the possible influence of adoption on some other aspects of reproductive physiology. Eighty-five of the 202 were studied by a more detailed questionnaire as to the etiology of their infertility. Of these eighty-five couples, eighteen wives were within the age group 20 to 29 years, sixty-three within the thirties, and four within the forties, with a high of 44 years.

RESULTS

Pregnancies were reported in fifteen cases out of 202. Eleven of these fifteen were studied as to the cause of the presumed infertility and how it was relieved. Table 1 includes those reasons given by the involved couples as to the cause of their pregnancies.

Of the 85 cases studied (including the aforementioned eleven cases from among those in whom pregnancy followed adoption), the following facts are of value. Seventy-four adopted because of childlessness alone, two because of a limited number of natural children already in the home, four because of neonatal deaths, three because conception was avoided due to the existence of constitutional disease in the wife, either renal or cardiac, which contraindicated pregnancy, and one because of psychologic disturbance diagnosed before fertility had been tested. Thirty-five of the 85 couples reported pregnancies prior to adoption that failed to reach term. Sixty-five had had sterility surveys of varying completeness.

TABLE 1

CASES	REASONS GIVEN BY ADOPTIVE COUPLES AS TO CAUSE OF THEIR PREGNANCIES FOLLOWING ADOPTION
A.	Further infertility study and treatment after adoption (donor insemination)
B.	None
C.	"Greatly increased love, understanding, and appreciation of children since having them in our home."
D.	None
E.	None
F.	"Release of mental strain. Prior to adoption, outside activities had exhausted me [wife] mentally, was extremely run down."
G.	"Tension of wanting baby relieved by adoption—only matter then of producing one of our own, once we had adopted and producing one no longer in our minds."
H.	None
I.	None
J.	"We were very happy and probably more contented. I think that anxiety has a lot of influence in this matter. We have now had two normal children since adoption."
K.	"Complete relaxation from the tensions caused by our great desire for a child."

Fifty-one of these sixty-five knew of apparent causes for their sterility.

Forty-five of the 85 submitted to operations in treatment of their infertility or of existing pathology. These included the common operative procedures such as tuboplasty, myomectomy, dilation and curettage, uterine suspension, and oophorocystectomy. Contraceptive practices included all of the usual devices, the vaginal diaphragm being used in most instances, though only for a relatively short period of time. As evidenced most couples adopted well within the reproductive ages. Occupation seemed to have no effect on fertility in any instance.

Following adoption, nineteen of the 85 couples reported changes in menstruation, the most common change being loss of premenstrual and menstrual discomfort. The next most common change was in the length of the cycle, with two reporting change in the amount of flow during menses. One reported more regularity of menses of a twenty-eight-day type with slight pelvic pain and midmenstrual spotting on the fourteenth day, possibly denoting in this patient a beginning of ovulation, or at least, more regularity of ovulation. Twenty-two couples reported sexuality changes, mostly on the wife's part, the majority reporting less tension with intercourse, more ease of act, and more enjoyment. Two reported less interest in intercourse, due to, as they describe, cessation of interest in having natural pregnancies. The remainder of the 85 reported "no change" in both menstruation and sexuality, which is of no value in interpretation.

Is adoption frequently followed by pregnancy? Fifteen, or 8 per cent, of the 202 adoptive parents achieved a subsequent pregnancy. This figure of 8 per cent is not remarkable compared to statistical surveys in general, since ten per cent of spontaneous cures are to be expected. Therefore, we can say adoption is not followed by normal pregnancy to any remarkable degree.

One may ask, however: Can adoption in any of these fifteen be considered as effecting the subsequent pregnancy? Unfortunately we know details of sterility in only the 85 cases previously mentioned as having returned comprehensive questionnaires. Eleven of the fifteen pregnancies fall within these 85. Let us eliminate from the 85, six cases of bilateral salpingectomy, six of panhysterectomy, and three of azoospermia, a total of fifteen. Of the remaining seventy couples with potential fertility, eleven, or 15.7 per cent, reproduced.

It is instructive to consider the available information in these eleven. Five couples had uncompleted pregnancies prior to adoption. In two of these five there was oligospermia. There exists the very strong possibility that the pregnancies following adoption in these two cases were a matter of chance, not uncommonly encountered in oligospermia. The other three cases could possibly be explained on a similar basis. Whether or not psychogenic disturbances played a part is speculative. Possibly the adoption acting as a cure for psychogenic disturbances allowed in some way a pregnancy to be carried to term. We feel that even less possibly adoption acting again in the same way may have eliminated whatever disturbances existed which caused the oligospermia. Certainly, we have very little if any proof for these speculations. Spontaneous cures in habitual abortion and oligospermia without adoption are not rare. We feel that the burden of proof lies with psychogenic disturbances, since in these five cases adoption is not clearly the curative factor.

One of the cases of infertility in this group was reportedly due to a juvenile uterus and anovulation. Here, again, we feel that chance plays a part since perhaps ovulation had always been infrequent and only now after a short four-year exposure period was conception possible regardless of adoption. We could speculate again in this case that adoption in some way was responsible for more regular ovulation. It seems that there are many proponents of this theory from the literature reviewed here. We think the theory may be right, but we cannot prove it.

The history most clearly suggesting a psychogenic factor involved in pregnancy following adoption would be one in which a long period of infertility existed even though the husband and wife had been shown by present examination methods to have no defects, and in whom adoption was followed very shortly by a normal pregnancy. Only one of the eleven cases conforms to this ideal, in which eleven years of infertility were followed nine months after adoption by a normal delivery, indicating, as in Orr's case, that the conception occurred at the time of adoption. This strongly suggests an underlying psychogenic disturbance relieved by adoption, although what the physiologic counteraction was, is impossible to determine. This case also contains a history of an oophorocystectomy. What part this played in the conception is also difficult to determine, especially since we do not know when the operation was performed in relation to the adoption.

Three other couples showed a similar history of pregnancy occurring relatively soon after adoption but with a shorter exposure time than in the case above. It is interesting to note that each of these four cases described above (F, G, J, and K in Table 1) in which possibly a psychogenic factor existed attributed their normal pregnancy to the adoption, which acted, as they describe, by relief of mental strain connected with childlessness.

It should be mentioned that in one of these eleven cases we have proof that donor insemination was responsible for the pregnancy. In such an event, of course, this case should be excluded from the group.

What evidence have we that adoption affects other reproductive functions? We have mentioned previously that twenty-two couples out of 85, studied in detail, reported sexuality changes, mostly on the wife's part, and nineteen reported menstrual changes. The most commonly reported effects on sexuality were less tension and more enjoyment during intercourse and more ease of act (perhaps denoting less pain in intercourse). Two reported less interest in intercourse, for reasons previously given. These changes all seem easily explainable on a better psychologic outlook following adoption. The most common menstrual change reported by nineteen couples of the 85, loss of menstrual discomfort, also could be explained on the same psychological basis. Of the eleven cases in which pregnancy followed adoption, only two were reported as having had changes in sexuality described above. In only one case pregnancy followed a marked improvement in menstruation.

Therefore, we feel that no correlation can be made with improvement of either menstruation or sexuality that might be considered effective in bringing about conception. No greater percentage of changes was reported in the group in which no pregnancy followed adoption than in the other group. There seems, in fact, to be no significant physiologic factors on which this phenomenon could be explained. All this then perhaps suggests an underlying undetected factor which possibly may have some bearing in psychosomatic activity. We have pointed out also four cases of pregnancy following adoption in which psychogenic factors may have played a part judging from the evidence given. Most of the menstrual and sexuality changes reported, of course, are psychological by definition.

SUMMARY AND CONCLUSIONS

The literature affirming the therapeutic effect of adoption on infertility is quoted and discussed. It is all speculative and without proof.

A survey of 202 adoptive couples revealed subsequent pregnancy occurring in fifteen (8 per cent). Spontaneous cures of infertility without adoption are generally considered likely in 10 per cent.

A more detailed study of 85 of the 202 couples was made. In fifteen of these the wife had been sterilized or the husband azoospermic. Eleven of the fifteen pregnancies, or 15.7 per cent, fell in the remaining group of seventy cases. One followed donor insemination because of oligospermia. There was oligospermia in two other cases. Isolated or widely separated pregnancies are not uncommonly achieved by men with exceedingly low sperm concentration. In two cases with oligospermia and in three others there had been abortions previous to adoption. Malpas reported successful delivery after three abortions as occurring in 27 per cent of such cases, and in 62 per cent after two abortions. Eastman calculated successful delivery in 16.4 per cent of cases with three previous abortions, and a similar figure to that of Malpas in cases with two abortions. In these five instances then adoption seems not to be the definitive curative factor.

Of the remaining five cases, in one there had been previous anovulation. That adoption relieved this condition is purely speculative, for spontaneous inexplicable ovulation often occurs in the habitually anovulatory female.

In the residual four cases, adoption was followed by improvement in the wife of the emotional tone, and there is no other explanation for cure of infertility. These pregnancies also were conceived very closely following adoption. As these contribute only 7 per cent of the seventy cases of potential fecundity, we believe they do not prove that adoption is a likely cure for sterility.

Of 85 women, twenty-two (26.2 per cent) reported improvement in sexuality, and nineteen (22.6 per cent), more normal menstruation following adoption. The causal relationship is problematical.

The authors gratefully acknowledge the invaluable aid given in this research project by Miss Madeleine Hoagland of the Children's Friend Society of Boston and Miss Constance Rathbun of the Children's Aid Society of Boston.

This study was aided by a grant from the Committee on Human Reproduction of the National Research Council.

Eight · *Birth Control, The* Fortune *Survey*

ELMO ROPER
Public Opinion Analyst

Despite laws, official statements from religious groups, and other pressures, Americans tend to form their own conclusions on matters that they consider important to their personal lives.
A Fortune Survey * reports upon the attitudes of a representative sample of American women toward birth control.

THIS installment of the Survey nails down an important shift that has been going on in opinion for some years and has already been explored by others. The spread of information about birth control is gaining the approval of growing majorities. In 1936 the FORTUNE SURVEY found 63 per cent of the general public approving. Today similar percentages of young women believe that such information should be given to the unmarried as well as the married.

Do you believe that knowledge about birth control should or should not be made available to all married women?

	All women	College women	Grammar school only	Catholic women
Should be available	84.9%	92.6%	70.2%	69.0%
Should not	10.0	4.9	18.2	24.4
Don't know	5.1	2.5	11.6	6.6

(If "should" above) Do you believe that knowledge about birth control should or should not be kept away from unmarried women?

	All women	College women	Grammar school only	Catholic women
Should be withheld	23.3%	15.5%	33.6%	33.6%
Should not be	69.8	78.5	55.3	58.9
Don't know	6.9	6.0	11.1	7.5

* Reprinted from *Fortune,* Survey of Public Opinion, 1943, 28: 24, 30, by permission.

It is clear that overwhelming majorities of women of all persuasions favor the availability of birth-control information to all married women. Comparing the two tables, it will be seen that 59 per cent of all the women (69.8 per cent of 84.9 per cent) believe that unmarried women should not be kept in ignorance of birth control.

X · FAMILY INTERACTION—PARENTS AND CHILDREN

One · How Family Forces Affect the Individual

O. SPURGEON ENGLISH
Psychiatrist, Temple University
Medical School

Psychiatry has contributed much to the understanding of the effects of early conditioning upon the later life of the individual. A psychiatrist now raises some pertinent questions about the functioning of the democratic family, and offers some suggestions about what may be expected of parents. *

THE dynamic psychology of the last half century which has focused the spotlight of its attention on the psychosexual development of the child as containing the nucleus of personality, plus direct observations of children themselves, has thrown the family as a social unit into sharper relief. It has made the defects of family life more glaring, and in so doing it has also served to make the exposed family members glare right back at the spotlight-holders.

In fact, some have even seized the spotlight and turned it round upon these researchers, with the result that one articulate mother wrote the following lines in protest:

My thesis is that while psychiatry considers the home of tremendous importance, the root of probably all psychiatric difficulties and almost the only place where most of these difficulties can be resolved, it has not thought of the problems of the home itself. I think current teaching on child-rearing tends to alter the center of gravity of the home, making the child the center, the king, and, too often, the tyrant.

Certainly, a child needs security and love. But I suspect the definitions of these words have gone a little astray. We should not eliminate consideration of other members of the household. I see people who were the recipients of love and tenderness, care and concern, who were the center and the

* Reprinted from *Bulletin of the Menninger Clinic,* 1950, 14: 66–74, by permission of the author and the publisher.

delight of the home. And now, grown and married, they will
settle for nothing less. They were never asked to give concern
or be considerate or enjoy seeing someone else succeed. So
now they consider the husband (or wife) cold and without
understanding, and the children dull and unpleasant, because
they are not the center of a constantly admiring audience.

No, the loving tender care that makes the child the center
of the home is a dangerous preparation for being an adult.

Now we think all fair-minded psychiatrists would admit that
these lines are penetrating and realistic and no more a caricature of
the psychiatrist's position than they themselves have used on occasions in their portrayal of the injured child without explaining why
the parents must inevitably so injure him. But as our friend contrasts her position with that of the psychiatrist, we are enabled to
see the extremes much more clearly and are, therefore, better able
to see the middle ground also. We are better off for seeing both the
needs of the child and the needs of the parent and that these must
inevitably conflict with each other.

It seems a sad and unconstructive discovery to learn that the
home is a place of conflict, but if it must be so, it is much better
that we *know* it is so in order that we may begin to do something
about it, if we can. Furthermore, in spite of the truth and justification for the mother's quoted remarks, we have to return to the fact
that any improvements which can and will be made must be made
largely by the parents. The child can or must cooperate, but it will
be the parents who initiate improvement in family life. They have
both the power for control and supposedly also the intelligence
for leadership.

The family is a very complex unit of people, even when functioning at its very best. When we think of the well-functioning family,
we envision a man and a woman about the same age, healthy,
capable, with well-rounded interests, many of which they share in
common, who appreciate and enjoy each other and each other's
friends and who take considerable pleasure in sharing their lives
with several young children.

However, if we consider merely our high divorce and separation
rate, we must realize that a great many families in this country are
those containing divorced parents, widows, widowers and step-
parents.

Then if we add the presence of mothers-in-law, fathers-in-law
and grandparents, we can see that this picture of the supposedly
simple family pattern becomes complicated by the presence of a
great many other people. Also must be considered foster parents
and parents who have adopted some or all of their children, not to
mention other possible departures from the ideal one in which the
mother, father and offspring remain together in relative harmony.

When we consider the forces which affect family life, it seems we must also put this family in a certain perspective, historically and politically.

The whole development of democracy, bringing to the individual dignity, freedom of speech, the value of love and liberty for liberty's sake, has been a development that is not so many centuries old. In spite of our devotion to this concept and its own popularity, we must remember that a countertrend has sprung up in the last 30 years and that totalitarianism, with its subservence of the individual to the state, its absolute authority, its pageantry and its telling everybody what to do, has made great strides. Whether we like it or not, a large part of the world's population has seen fit to swing back.

Certainly, psychiatrists advocate democracy in the family, and with a large output of literature have been advocating its furtherance for some time. Some of our critics are asking, however, possibly with reason, whether as a result we are making children happier and whether we are decreasing the number of maladjusted and unhappy adult people.

There is one trend which the philosophy of democracy and family life seems not to have taken enough account of and that is the difficulty of bringing about concerted action in family life. This does not mean the kind of concerted action resulting from a father-dictated family policy. Yet, with the passage of time and with every family member demanding and being given his individual rights, the result is often a divided and neurotic personality coming from a family in which he has neither received discipline for its sake from the parents nor has he been able to formulate any satisfactory goals or satisfactions in living, as a result of his own freedom to choose.

This is not to say that the changing and modern approach is wrong, but it does indicate that we haven't arrived at the eventual solution of the secret of producing large numbers of stable and happy and useful personalities.

Let us examine, therefore, what might be expected from every family. By family, we mean largely the adults who populate the home.

WHAT SHOULD BE EXPECTED FROM THE FAMILY

Seriously, the challenge to the grownups seems to be that of knowing how parents can provide:

More time to spend with children.

More patience with the child's difficulties in growing up.

More knowledge of the nature of human emotional growth.

More affection to meet the tremendous love demands of every child and adult.

More resourcefulness in absorbing and redirecting aggression.

Better techniques for eliciting cooperation and enhancing the pleasure of group living.

More opportunities for participation in a variety of home and social activities.

Opportunity for their children's exposure at periodic intervals to a variety of thinkers and speakers on the subject of human destiny.

An ever-increasing knowledge of how to create a better marriage and home atmosphere.

More participation in the emotional and educational dynamics of family life by fathers.

TIME AND TEACHING

The first eight points we stressed in regard to the family's responsibility to the children concern time. We think it can be generalized that there is a tendency for so-called "busy people," "important people," people who are "in demand," to fail to find time for their children. In such people, this is to some degree understandable not only because of the satisfaction which comes to them from participation in social progress, but also because of the satisfaction ensuing prestige brings.

However, it is perhaps more to be regretted that the very people whose abilities make them so busy or those who are so aware of social problems or those who are adept at some special skills or possess special knowledge cannot or do not take the time to share this with the younger generation both in and out of the home. Their zeal to save the world or do all the work in sight by themselves may represent some escape from dealing with the education of the young, but we think it most often is because they haven't been sensitized to the fact that every person has so much to learn in his youth and he needs so much teaching from every interested person, especially the parents.

Some parents who are not busy and have time on their hands do not *have time* in the sense that they want to *give that time* to their children. They need to be shown how they can prevent, through working with their child in the present, later despair, maladjustment, family friction and ill will. Among this group are many fathers who make a large financial contribution to family life, but a very small contribution emotionally, socially and educationally. Many problems arise in families with capable parents who knew how to live their own lives with some degree of success, but never took the time and interest to make sure their children learned it, too.

Now, of the people who take the time to spend with their children and try to teach them, *there are some who have little patience.* This is often because they are essentially impatient people, but it is also sometimes due to the fact that they know too little of the nature of the child they would teach. They neither know the nature of the child's needs nor the proper timing whereby he should receive gratification for them.

For example, a child has a need to engage in both work and play with adults, in order to get a feeling of pleasure associated with these activities which he will use again and again all his lifetime. But when he tries to make this need known at, say, the age of two and a half years, he may be regarded as too young or a disturber of parental routine and receive rejection and discouragement.

The needs of children and how and when these needs should be met will not be repeated here except to make one point about the giving of affection. We still have to educate people to be unafraid that affection will spoil and weaken and become a force inimical to discipline. Actually, discipline is easier in a setting of affection. And affection given freely and properly balanced with demand, strengthens rather than weakens.

However, in this greater dilemma of proper blending of affection and discipline, we feel the approach on the part of the parent should be, "I'm happy to give the affection, and I know you will meet most of my expectations when I need you to do so," and not, "I expect you are going to be pretty hard to control, but in case you do conform the way I want you to, I'll be nice to you."

We believe, in other words, that the family has some obligation to show the example of faith, trust and confidence early and continuously.

AGGRESSION

In the matter of meeting and handling aggression, the family has a great responsibility—one it has met inadequately up to the present time. If this sounds like undue criticism of the American parent by a psychiatrist, let us hasten to share the blame and say that psychiatry, psychology and child education have not shown the parent enough ways to understand and handle aggression.

The aggressive nature of human make-up is most generally accepted, so we turn our attention to what to do about it. There are probably few parents who actually want their children to be over-aggressive, since even the toughest of parents have a suspicion that they will feel the effect of this aggression turned upon themselves some day. But there are a great many who fear their children won't get along in the world and be able to take care of themselves if their expressions of aggression are actually diminished in intensity or shunted into socially accepted channels. There are, furthermore, some who know all too little about the techniques of good will, tact and kindness, and if they do know about them, will tend to consider them weaknesses rather than strengths.

However, let us return to those who do not like aggression, who want peaceful, considerate offspring and actually do not seem to know how to accomplish this.

No discussion of molding aggression in the young could be complete without saying a word about counter-aggression in the present. Certainly, children are not likely to benefit from a limp and long-suffering parent or a devalued or depersonalized one. And here psychiatrists are getting a fair amount of censure, whether they deserve it or not, because they have emphasized so much the dangers of frustration by parental dominance. The same mother from whom we quoted in the beginning says:

> There has been too little emphasis on what parents can do in a positive way to create, mold and develop, and too much on simply being a reservoir of patience, affection and understanding. Certainly, we must be these last three things: They are the true foundation, but they are not the only needs.
>
> The words authority and discipline have fallen into disrepute, but I feel they must reside with father and mother. We have been frightened away from them by the threats of father-mother dominance and 'momism,' but these things are only the excesses of two very good things. There is great security to the child in the knowledge that his father and mother will protect him from behaving badly and will teach him what they feel to be right.
>
> If they will do these things from love of the child rather than from a need to prove themselves, I think it is the greatest security of all. Because it will show the child how to earn the love and respect and approval of a world that gives love, but insists that something is due in return.

Since the author couldn't put any more clearly his thoughts on the proper setting of the home climate for blending (a) the child's needs, (b) the parents' limitations and (c) the necessary social sublimation of aggression, we have let this mother's words speak through this paper what we feel to be some important truths in a very fundamental parent-child relationship.

A child needs someone who loves him and who can also outline a plan of development around which he can discipline himself. The young do not see much of the best in life unless it is placed before them in some organized form.

SOCIAL VALUES

Too few people know how to entertain themselves or someone else. A family should teach the young ones to converse amiably and interestingly with older people. This can begin with the family group at mealtime by cultivating the art of conversation, rather than allowing the dinner hour to become a time for all and sundry members of the family to air grievances and criticisms.

Moreover, adults can help in this by showing an interest in conversing with the children about their activities and friends. Art, music, collecting, photography, sports or any other activity help not only to bring the young one to have pleasant memories associated with nature and with people, but enhance those emotional ties which insure security from loneliness, isolation and boredom, and which, incidentally but importantly, lead to the best social usefulness of aggressive impulses.

We have suggested that the young be exposed periodically to those who will discuss human destiny. No doubt such a plan would subject the youth to a great many platitudes and clichés, for it takes an unusual adult to expose to the young his *real* beliefs, share his weaknesses with them and admit the humble sources of his strengths. But perhaps a third of the time a person would appear with wisdom, humility, sincerity and a gift for talking to the young, and the idea would be worth the effort.

Such a forum would be a community activity sponsored by the home and from which parents themselves would have to agree to stay away, so the speaker could with greater ease be himself with the young. The wholesale accumulation of knowledge in the classroom needs to be leavened with a visiting mind who can talk to the young and make them think of how to utilize in a more effectual way what they are receiving from life and from books.

THE DYNAMICS OF FAMILY FUNCTIONING

Finally, there is the great secret of what makes the family function. How many parents convey to their children by deed or word that the pleasure of living together and having children is of greater emotional intensity than the worry about them and the responsibility and expense of raising them? And if they could answer in the affirmative, would they be able to convey to their children what goes into this desirable state?

Our title is "How Family Forces Affect the Individual," but in many instances there has been a conspiracy on the part of the adult leaders of families to see that family forces did *not* permeate the child's consciousness. If they had to scrimp to send him to a certain school or buy her certain clothes, they concealed the fact because their own pride would be hurt to confess it. Although they would have had only a problem in economics to explain, they seemed to fear criticism for not having been born rich or being good moneymakers or better managers.

They wouldn't be seen by their children hugging or kissing each other or talking of their devotion to or their need of each other, lest this seem weak, childish or immoral, and might conceivably invite some question which would lead to a discussion of sex. The result of our hypocrisy is that most children find their way through dating, courtship, marriage, lovemaking and family-rearing all too much alone and make the same mistakes over and over again.

It must be remembered that a great many children are the result of the fact that the sex act is such a pleasurable human performance. As the children become older and begin to present problems calling for patience, good will and wisdom, the parents somehow have lost much, if not all, of the pleasure they had in each other's being together. They no longer enjoy each other or find a source of happiness and rejuvenation in each other. They have become burdened with their respective responsibilities, and their emotional attitudes toward their children are fairly ambivalent.

Considering the many changes which take place in the human personality between the time of the honeymoon and the next 15 years, it would be superhuman if they could manage things so as to devise adequate satisfactions for themselves in life and achieve with any consistency that continuous desire to help others, including, of course, the children.

This calls for the family to ask that the school system assist it in the matter of sex education and preparation for marriage. Theoretically, these things should be taught in the home. The home should be able to teach family life best. But it hasn't accomplished this so far, and we doubt that it will, left to itself.

The school system is a more stable repository of knowledge which the family needs to help it in this important task. Any random couple who set out to rear a family can be entirely too capricious, inhibited or prejudiced to help their young with the important business of being good parents-to-be themselves. If the schools get ready to give this problem a steady impetus from year to year, the family can be a good or bad ally, but in any case the growing individual gets something of the necessary knowledge and inspiration for the task of parenthood.

It is true that not many teachers, schools or parents are yet ready to have the schools help to study family life and give it the place of dignity and value in our minds that it deserves. But the idea is growing and will eventually become a reality, we believe.

In conclusion, the family has much to learn. It needs to find sources of strength over and beyond state and government subsidies. In our rapidly moving world, we are in a race to make up in ideas (psychological science) what originally existed in a home, because formerly the family were perforce thrown in close contact with each other and looked to each other for satisfaction and security. In spite of the increasing speed of our existence, it appears doubtful if we will prosper unless we learn the importance of pausing frequently to come in touch with each other more tenderly and wisely. The family has always been the place for this phenomenon, and society has always blessed it.

We must be careful not to squander this heritage. It is the common denominator of the best kind of living of the past and the precepts of modern dynamic psychology.

Two · *The Practical Application*
of Basic Mental Hygiene Principles
by the Cornelian Corner

LEO H. BARTEMEIER, M.D.

The earliest experiences that an individual has in his relationship with his mother are believed to form the basis of all his later human relationships and to influence his total personality.
The Cornelian Corner, described below,* is an attempt to prevent malformations in personality by applying principles of mental hygiene from the moment of birth.

SOME time during the early months of 1942 two Detroit physicians, who regularly met each other for luncheon, began to engage in serious discussions about problems which had been concerning each of them for a rather long time. The pediatrician was preoccupied with the difficulties which so many mothers experienced in connection with the feeding and the care of their infants. It seemed to him that much of their anxiety and the obvious dissatisfactions of their infants were unnecessary and unnatural. In his effort to solve this problem he had broken with the traditional procedures and had advised the mothers to feed their infants as often as they seemed to want nourishment and to let them have as much as they would take. The results had been most gratifying. The mothers' anxieties diminished and the infants were appreciably more contented. This departure from the rigidity of feeding schedules was contrary, however, to what he had been taught and not in keeping with the practice of his colleagues.

The psychiatrist with whom he discussed this matter had been particularly concerned about the difficulties he had experienced in treating patients who suffered from severe mental disorders which often required long periods of hospitalization. He knew that their illnesses stemmed from intense dissatisfactions they had repeatedly suffered in their infancy and babyhood. He was intrigued with the contentment and satisfaction of both mothers and infants which

* Reprinted from *Bulletin of the Menninger Clinic*, 1948, 12: 113–116, by permission of the author and publisher.

the pediatrician had observed after he had allowed the infants to indicate how much and how often they should receive nourishment. In this radical break with traditional pediatric procedure the psychiatrist saw one possibility for improving the mother-child relationship and for lessening the incidence of the serious mental disorders of adult life. Like the pediatrician he was especially interested in preventive medicine.

These two physicians then began discussing their mutual interests with a few of their colleagues and learned that they too were concerned with the same problems. A small group, which included an obstetrician, an expert on nutrition, a registered nurse and a clinical psychologist, decided to continue and enlarge the original discussions between the psychiatrist and the pediatrician and to meet at regular intervals for the purpose of this collaboration. Accordingly, on November 12, 1942, they formed a small organization which they named the Cornelian Corner. The first Article of the Constitution which they framed at that time describes why they chose this name for their society. It reads as follows:

> This association shall be named after Cornelia, daughter of Scipio Africanus, the Elder, mother of the Gracchi and of Sempronia, the wife of Scipio Africanus, the Younger. On the death of her husband, refusing numerous offers of marriage, she devoted herself to the education of her twelve children. When asked to show her jewels, she presented her sons, and on her death a statue was erected to her memory inscribed, 'Cornelia, the mother of the Gracchi.' The sons, Tiberius and Gaius, devoted their lives to the welfare of their fellow men.
>
> When the kitchen was used by the family as a "living room" it was customary for the mother to face a corner of the room when nursing her infant. Thus her back was turned to others in the room and both she and the infant were more removed from disturbing influences.

During the early meetings of this small group their discussions were confined in the main to the cultural influences which have effected a near disappearance of the nursing of infants and how this natural procedure might be re-established in the American scene. As their discussions continued, their objectives came to include all those early parental influences which determine so importantly the favorable or unfavorable evolution and development of character traits. They outlined these objectives in Article II of their constitution which reads as follows:

> *Purpose.*—Believing that a program aimed at relief of the cultural tensions so frequently incident to feeding, toilet training, and child discipline represents the nuclear approach to the problem of mental hygiene, we dedicate ourselves to such a program.

The purpose of this association, therefore, shall be to promote healthy parent-child relationships.

We will strive toward the achievement of this objective:

1. Through research in the fields of child development and family life.
2. Through the education of parents, especially expectant mothers and fathers, as to the basic needs of the developing child.
3. Through the wide promulgation to professional groups of all pertinent information regarding the developing child and his environmental needs.
   a) We will strongly advocate the abandonment of the artificial practice of separating the newborn child from his parents.
   b) With the conviction that it is advantageous to both mother and child, we will encourage the breast feeding of infants with opportunity to nurse whenever the infant is hungry or anxious.

During the five years that it has been in existence the Cornelian Corner has won the interest and the enthusiastic support of a surprisingly large number of people. For the past two years it has conducted seminars for physicians and for the nurses in charge of the pediatric and obstetrical wards in the general hospitals of metropolitan Detroit and the neighboring communities. These seminars have been made possible through a grant from the Children's Fund of Michigan. They have been conducted by leading pediatricians, psychiatrists, obstetricians and other specialists in the field of child development. In addition to this educational project, the Cornelian Corner has gained the cooperation of five Detroit hospitals in its project to have infants remain in the same room with their mothers from the time of their birth. This has already been carried out in a number of instances and some valuable data have been collected which already demonstrates the desirability for such procedures.

Clinical investigations have repeatedly demonstrated that throughout the period of infancy and babyhood the entire existence of every child is dominated by two inherited strivings. One of these is the instinct of hunger and the other is the instinct for love and all that it implies at this period of development. Experiences which interfere with the gratification of either one of these instinctual strivings produce tension, discomfort and pain. The repeated occurrence of such states of tension gives rise to anxiety, to disturbances in digestion and to other interferences with the natural development of the child. Every infant, for example, in addition to the satisfaction of his hunger, also needs the gratification of his impulse to suck. No man-made schedules can adequately supply the satisfactions of these instinctual needs. They are inherited biological strivings which every good mother senses and knows how to satisfy. They vary in their intensity from one child to another—just as each infant even in the same family shows individual characteristics from the time of its birth. The need for a great deal of close proximity to his mother's body and all that we understand by the term mothering is just as important for the wholesome development of the infant as the need to be adequately fed. This natural mothering establishes the first human relationship which becomes the foundation for all other subsequent relationships and influences the character of the individual throughout his entire life.

The second objective of the Cornelian Corner is "the education of parents, especially expectant mothers and fathers, as to the basic needs of the developing child." The Cornelian Corner encourages the expectant father to accompany his wife on her first visit to the obstetrician and learn directly about her needs during the prenatal period so that he can share her experience with her and assist her to become a good mother.

Through its efforts to have the new-born infant in the same room with its mother from the time of birth the Cornelian Corner hopes to make it possible for the father of the child to visit as often as he can. It encourages him to hold his infant so that he, too, may begin to love his child as early as possible.

The Cornelian Corner is, therefore, a mental hygiene project which aims to promote better parent-child relationships from the very beginning of life.

Three · Child-Rearing and Social Status

MARTHA ERICSON DALE, PH.D.

In recent years anthropologists and sociologists have called attention to different values held by the different social classes within the same community. The short article below * presents a study designed to test the theory that the social class in which a child is reared is an important influence upon his personality development, and that there are systematic differences between child rearing practices of different social classes.

THE main problem of this investigation was to test the hypothesis that, since differing social classes present different learning environments for children, systematic differences in child-

* Reprinted from *The American Journal of Sociology*, 1946, 52: 191–192, by permission of the author and the University of Chicago Press.

rearing practices could be found. A secondary problem of the investigation was to study the effects of training procedures on the development of personality.

THE SAMPLE

The 48 middle-class mothers interviewed were relatively established in their class. These mothers were reached through nursery schools and through child-study groups. All were residents of Chicago. There were 107 children in this sample; all children whose histories were recorded were normal children.

The 52 lower-class mothers who were interviewed were relatively stable in status and were, for the most part, upper lower-class, and all were residents of Chicago. There were 167 children in this group. All children whose histories were recorded were normal children.

CHARACTERISTICS OF MIDDLE- AND LOWER-CLASS FAMILIES

The differences to be found between middle- and lower-class families are clearly group differences. There are unquestionably many families, both middle and lower class, which, upon closer examination, would deviate markedly from the central tendencies found in this study. The findings with regard to these two groups, however, are clearly enough differentiated to permit generalization.

In the middle-class families it was found that the educational level of both maternal and paternal grandparents was higher than that of the grandparents in the lower-class families. The educational level of the parents and of the parents' siblings was also higher than that of the lower-class families. The occupations of middle-class parents and parents' siblings fell into the first four categories (the highest) of the seven-point occupational classification developed for this study, while the occupations of the lower-class parents and parents' siblings fell mainly into the lowest three categories of the occupational classification.

METHOD OF STATISTICAL ANALYSIS

The data from the guided interview schedules were coded and recorded for punching on Hollerith cards. Some of the differences were not statistically significant; but it should be remembered that the sample was small and that these differences, in order to be reliable, had to be relatively large. The differences, therefore, were important ones.

RESULTS

The hypothesis which this study investigated was that systematic class differences in training could be found. The general areas explored were those of weaning, thumbsucking, cleanliness training, environmental exploration and control, and age and sex roles. Differences were found in certain areas; these were primarily in feeding, cleanliness training, environmental exploration and control, and age and sex roles. Middle-class families were generally found to be more exacting in their expectations. Training was generally begun earlier in the middle-class than in the lower-class families. In the middle-class families there was more emphasis on early responsibility, closer supervision of children's activities, and greater emphasis on individual achievement.

EARLY FEEDING EXPERIENCES

Significant differences were found in early feeding experiences of children. In the middle-class families, fewer children are breast-fed; where they are breast-fed, they tend to be breast-fed for a shorter time. Fewer middle-class children than lower-class children are completely breast-fed. Middle-class children also tend to be bottle-fed for a shorter period of time than are the lower-class children. Three times as many middle-class children as lower-class children were reported as thumbsuckers.

CLEANLINESS TRAINING

Significant differences were found in the cleanliness training of the children in the two classes. Middle-class parents begin training their children for bowel and bladder control earlier than do the lower-class parents, although the middle-class children do not achieve control earlier than the lower-class children. Boys in both classes were found to be more difficult to train than girls.

AGE EXPECTATIONS AND SEX ROLES

Several class differences in age expectations and sex roles were found. The main difference was that children in middle-class families were expected to assume responsibility in the home earlier than were the lower-class children. Middle-class girls are expected to begin cooking and sewing earlier than the lower-class girls. Middle-class boys and girls are expected to be in the house earlier at night than the lower-class boys and girls. Lower-class children begin going to the movies alone earlier than the middle-class children; and many more of the lower-class children are paid for errands and for working than are the middle-class children. Middle-class children, on the other hand, are expected to prepare themselves for some profession.

The results of this investigation thus show that there are systematic social class differences in training children in crucial matters. Middle-class children and lower-class children live in well-differentiated cultures. Even though training is begun earlier in the middle class, it is not achieved any earlier. Middle-class children are probably subjected to more frustrations in learning and are probably more anxious as a result of these pressures than are the lower-class children. Lower-class families tend to be more lenient in the training of their children.

Children in the middle-class families are taught to assume responsibility early, are more carefully supervised, and have less free time. We had anticipated that lower-class parents would expect the early assumption of responsibility in the home on the part of their children. This is, however, not the case; the lower-class children are not taught these tasks until an age at which the learning has become relatively easy. The latter probably do not meet as many frustrations as do the middle-class children.

This investigation confirms the theory that membership in a social class is an important influence on personality development and that there are significant differences in child-rearing practices between social classes.

Four · Ordinal Position in the Family as a Psychological Variable

ROBERT R. SEARS
Laboratory of Human Development
Harvard University

The environment of the child within a family is constantly changing. The first child lives in a world that is far different from the world of the second, third, or fourth child in the same family. Parental attitudes and methods change as parents become older, as other circumstances affect their lives, and as successive children are born. Is there an identifiable pattern in the changes that occur in parental practices with succeeding children? If so, what effects are observable in the traits of the children?

The following selection * deals with these questions.

THERE appear to be two main approaches to the study of the family. One describes the family as a group having certain properties that differentiate it from other groups. It has a certain kind of structure; it has a set of internal relationships that can be specified by reference to the roles of the family members; and, as a group, it has certain legal, economic and status relations

---

* Reprinted from the *American Sociological Review*, 1950, 15: 397–401, by permission of the author and the editor.

to other groups. Possibly not all sociologists would wish to identify themselves with this approach, but systematically speaking this is a sociological way of ordering the social events represented by the family and its activities; it is so because it takes the group as the unit of its study.

The other approach to the family, which is essentially psychological, takes the individual as the unit of its study. The family is conceived as creating a particular kind of social structure within which the individual is embedded, which acts upon him in diverse ways and on which he acts. The family is conceptualized as an environmental factor having the twin functions of instigator to behavior and manipulandum for behavior. It provides the main setting in early life for the learning of those behavior characteristics that have both individual and social reference, skills such as talking and feeding oneself, and motives and values. A description of the family, in other words, is a description of the conditions of learning for a child born into that family.

These two approaches supplement each other. Implicit in the sociological method is the assumption that there are regularities from one family to another in the basic characteristics of the different family roles. To the extent that this is true, there are therefore consistencies in the kinds of behavior performed in the family circle by these different members. For example, if the family structure in a particular society is such that the mother is the caretaker of infants, while the father is the economic buffer against the rest of the society, there will be allocations of responsibility within the family that would differ from those of a family belonging to a society in which an extended family provided the child-care activity and the mother had extra-familial economic duties. Furthermore, it would be expected that the child-care activities would be carried out differently in the two societies because different kinds of people with differing behavior potentialities would fill the role of care-taker. That this is true has recently been demonstrated by Whiting in a cross-cultural comparison of these two types of family structure. He found that societies in which grandparents customarily resided in the household and participated in child care had reliably more severe aggression and independence training than societies in which all care was done by young mothers themselves.

To the extent, then, that a society has a regularized family structure in which there are consistencies from family to family in the kinds of behavior required of each family role, the role itself may be used as an index of the occurrence of certain behavior and certain learning experiences. Ultimately, the explanation of an individual's behavior must be driven back to the exact circumstances of his rearing and of the immediate stimulational forces acting upon him, both biological and social, but for the discovery of regularities in personality development, the indices represented by family roles appear provisionally fruitful. The major task of science, after all, is the ordering of the events of nature in such a way as to permit generalized statements about antecedent-consequent relationships; it is not required to devote itself to the full and complete explanation of individual "naturalistic" events.

An interesting example of the relationship between a family role and presumably learned behavior characteristics is to be found among children who have different ordinal positions in the family. Dean investigated the personality characteristics of twenty pairs of children by having the mother in each instance make paired comparisons of her own two children on a large number of items. Each pair of children was of the same sex, eight of the pairs being girls and the remainder boys. In all the families there were but two children and all were under seven years of age. Children in the first ordinal position were judged by their mothers to be more dependent, to spend more time "just thinking," more worried, more excitable, to have their feelings hurt more easily, to be less demonstratively affectionate, and to be less effective in protecting themselves from verbal or physical attack. These differences suggested that the two ordinal positions in the family were in all likelihood accompanied by certain uniformities of experience that molded the personalities into what might be called "first ordinal position role type" and "second" type. It is evident, of course, that not all the differences are necessarily ascribable to role differences; other factors vary, too. For example, mothers are more experienced and more busy by the time a second child is two years old. In any case, the data suggest that there may be consistently different experiences for older and younger children.

In an effort to discover what some of these might be, data from another investigation have been examined. These data will be published in more detail elsewhere, but there are a few relationships that deserve description in the present context. Forty-two three- and four-year-old children in the University of Iowa preschool were observed under standardized conditions four hours each during a four month period. Among the measures taken were frequency counts of various types of nurturant and dependent behavior. The children were also rated on various types of dependency by their teachers. The mothers of the children were interviewed about their methods of child-rearing, the interviews being recorded and then transcribed for analysis.

The content of each interview was classified by a subject-matter index based on the Yale Cross-Cultural Survey, and each sentence or paragraph relating to each code number was retyped and appropriately filed. The interview material was ultimately in the form of separate slips of paper filed entirely by subject-matter. One file folder, for example, contained all the references by all the mothers to the problem of infant feeding, another contained everything on the weaning process, another covered the training of independence, another the methods of handling aggression, and so on.

In order to determine the nature of differences in child-rearing procedures used by the various mothers, it was necessary to convert this descriptive information to quantitative scales. Since this was a pilot study, it is perhaps not surprising that the interviews contained insufficient information on some points, and it has proved impractical to try to scale all the behavior dimensions that one might wish. However, a few dimensions permitted adequate rating, and some of these are relevant to the matter of ordinal position.

The majority of the children were either first or second children or only children; seven were from families with three or more. In spite of this skewed distribution, and the anomalous situation created by only children, there were two child-rearing characteristics that appeared to be related to ordinal position. One of these was the use of self-demand feeding in infancy. Second and later children were treated more permissively in respect to scheduling of feeding than were first or only children. Other aspects of infant nursing and weaning were also less frustrating for them. Secondly, the mothers provided less nurturance (affectionate care-taking and helping) at bedtime and slightly less worrisome cautioning about sickness and danger for the second and later children.

The correlations supporting these statements are small, but together with some other scales relating to total current nurturance, and certain qualitative materials presented in the interviews, it seems evident that something rather consistent in child-rearing changed between the first and second children. The mothers became less anxious about their own skills and less concerned about the health and well-being of their children. Pediatric advice requiring rigorous control of the feeding process was more disregarded; the child was allowed more weight in determining the treatment given him. Mothers evidently discovered that their anxieties about health were over-determined and they let the children have less-restricted play. Less ritual and ceremonial attention was given the child at bedtime; he was taken more casually and with less concern.

Doubtless other factors besides child-rearing experience and the changed family structure conduced to changes in methods of rearing later children. One factor that proved of considerable importance in the present study was the social mobility of the mothers. From interviews with the mothers, information was obtained that permitted an evaluation of their present class status and the class status attained by their parents. By comparison of these values, it was possible to identify those families that were reasonably stable in lower and upper middle class status and those who were mobile upward from lower middle to upper middle and downward mobile from upper middle to lower middle. There was a highly reliable relationship between mobility upward and the use of self-demand feeding. From an examination of the interviews, it appeared that this represented an attempt on the part of mobile mothers to adopt the currently fashionable permissiveness recommended by the more progressive and literate pediatricians. Mobile mothers read Spock. They follow the canons of modern advice on infant care.

It is interesting to note, however, that these same mothers, when left to their own devices, tended to be somewhat more punitive with regard to aggression. There was no difference between the stable groups of upper and lower middle class mothers in this respect, but the upward mobile mothers evidently took the control of aggression more seriously. In this connection it is worth noting that modern pediatric advice is considerably less specific, and has less of the simple recipe quality, about the handling of aggression than about methods of feeding. So, while the mobile upward mothers were able to absorb the notion of permissiveness in feeding, the tension and strain that appear to go with upward mobility led to greater punitiveness of aggression. That anxiety over status leads to more directive and severe control of children was clearly demonstrated in a laboratory situation by Merrill. These upward mobile mothers demonstrated it in their real life behavior.

The effects of adding younger children to the family, then, seem to be in the direction of a reduction of severity in nursing and weaning and a reduction of bedtime ceremonial. Doubtless there are other factors that change, too, and these will eventually be discovered by further investigation. In the meantime it is interesting to note certain kinds of behavior in these children. In general, on the basis of the teachers' rating scales, the second and later children were somewhat less dependent than first and only children. The differences are small and not statistically reliable, but they are consistent through a number of scales and direct observations. However, the correlations of the child-rearing characteristics with ordinal position were relatively small, too. This is always likely to be the case when one uses an operationally defined variable from one systematization of events, at one level of complexity, as an *index* of another kind of variable at another level of complexity. In the present instance, ordinal position role is a sociological variable, and we are trying to use it as an index of certain psychologically consistent events in the learning experience of the child.

The next question must ask what are the effects on child behavior of those child-rearing methods of which ordinal position is an index. The relation of those methods to behavior can be examined without reference to ordinal position.

The first of these factors, degree of frustration in connection with nursing and weaning, is positively related to dependent behavior in the preschool. Correlations of the frustration scale with such scales as "seeks help from teacher," "seeks help from other children," "seeks praise," "seeks attention from teacher," and with the raw total of dependency incidents observed in the Gewirtz study, are all in the .30 to .45 range. Interestingly enough, there is no relation between nursing and weaning frustration and the total frequency of overt aggression in the preschool, but there are two teacher rating scales related to inhibited aggression that correlate with early frustration: "exhibit displaced attacks" (+ .38) and "threatens teacher" (+ .23).

The second correlate of ordinal position, degree of bedtime nurturance, is unrelated to any of the measures of child behavior in the preschool situation. This suggests that the nursing and weaning frustration in infancy is the factor responsible for producing the slight but positive correlation between early ordinal position and dependency behavior.

This hypothesis gains some support from a theoretical analysis of the origin of dependency behavior. The infant is entirely dependent on the mother for sustenance, for the food that can satisfy his primary—and urgent—hunger drive. During the first few months of life he must learn to control his mother and to secure what he wants through her. If her rigidity of scheduling of feedings and her method of handling the weaning process are such as to decrease the child's ease of gaining satisfactions, he would be expected to suffer, over the long term, an increase in his anxiety with respect to both food-getting and control of his mother. The increased strength of total drive produced by this anxiety would strengthen the motivation underlying the behavior that has as its aim the controlling of the mother, i.e., the dependency behavior. Through stimulus generalization, this type of behavior would then be expected to occur in any social situation involving unsatisfied needs and/or the presence of persons like teachers who represent mother surrogates. In effect, the anxiety originally produced by nursing and weaning frustration would serve as the facilitating instigator to whatever behavior had been predominant in those infant situations in which the anxiety was aroused. In the case of nursing and weaning frustrations, this behavior would be mother-controlling, attention getting, and food getting. Unfortunately the present data include no information concerning the details of the children's eating behavior, so the latter expectation can not be tested.

In sum, it appears that second children are somewhat less dependent than first. Dependent behavior is related to a history of frustration in nursing and weaning experiences, and the mothers of second and later children tend to be somewhat less frustrating than the mothers of first children. It is not clear from the present study whether this difference is related to some basic difference in the family structure and the roles composing it, or to greater experience of the mother and her decreased anxiety about the child, or to her social status mobility upward. Variation in frustration of nursing and weaning is related to all these three factors and further investigation will be required to isolate the constant variable. In any case, this type of research involves the interpretation of the family as a learning situation for the children in it, and potentially provides a way of bridging the gap between sociological and psychological approaches to the field of family research.

Five · *Maternal Over-Protection and Rejection*

DAVID M. LEVY
Psychiatrist

In the selection below * *David Levy treats a special type of parent-child relationship and the effects of this relationship upon the developing personality of the child. The discussion shows how husband-wife adjustments may affect parental attitudes toward and treatment of children. It notes also that an early lack of affection may lead to an individual's later failure to function adequately as a parent.*

AN analysis of maternal overprotection was made by selecting from large numbers of overprotected children, twenty cases in which the overprotection was obvious—pointed out both by lay observers or professional workers, and in which the patient was clearly a wanted child. Our object was to select a human relationship in its simplest and most complete form; then, to think through all the significant facts known about the parents and children involved in the relationship in terms of our study. In contrast with other cases of maternal overprotection, the twenty selected for this special investigation were referred to as "pure" forms.

The term "maternal overprotection" was accepted as synonymous with excessive maternal care of children. It comprises such terms as babying, oversolicitude, too much mothering, overindulging, and a host of similar expressions indicating that the mother exceeds the "normal" in her care of the child. According to our clinical findings, the excess may be formulated in terms of: (1) excessive contact, *e.g.*, a mother sleeping with her fourteen-year-old son; (2) prolongation of infantile care, *e.g.*, breast feeding to age four years; (3) prevention of development of independent behavior, including such descriptive terms about the mother-child relationship as, "she

* Reprinted from *Journal of Nervous and Mental Diseases*, 1931, 73: 65–70, by permission.

won't take any risks," "she always fights his battles"; (4) lack or excess of maternal control, shown in overindulgence of the child in regard to privileges or possessions, disregard on the child's part of eating time, sleeping time—in general, doing what he pleases, undeterred by the mother's commands or pleadings. This is in contrast with excessive maternal control in which a relative over-modification of infantile traits is manifested in undue obedience on the part of the child.

All factual data on maternal overprotection, when formulated by this plan, show much dovetailing; nevertheless, the stress is found often greater in one group than in another. It appears so far that overindulgent overprotection yields aggressive-egocentric behavior of varying degree in the offspring, whereas dominating overprotection yields submissive and effeminate behavior. Since in our cases the patterns of the mother-child relationship appear to be well established in infancy, and by a series of factors operating in the mother before the birth of the child, the mother-child relationship is considered primary; all other factors (patient's relationship with other adults and children, physical and intellectual factors, special abilities and disabilities) as secondary modifying influences, exaggerating or diminishing the influence of the primary relationship. Consider the case, for example, of a child who is treated by his mother more like a baby, is held closer to her, and is more dependent on her for aid in his school work and in social contacts than are other boys. At seven and one-half years, he is referred to the institute for symptoms of irresponsible, dependent and immature behavior, in keeping with the overprotective relationship. He presents a series of submissive and aggressive traits, though largely the former. His teachers note his docility. He takes his four-year-old brother's lead in play, and likes to indulge in baby talk. This docility is in contrast with his wish to dominate the group, yet he runs to the mother for protection from other boys. Although in the primary relationship, such findings are easily discerned and anticipated, yet they are influenced considerably by the following factors in this patient: developmental delay, inadequate muscular strength, coördination and intelligence. Besides these factors, there are an interfering, indulgent mother-in-law, a father who favors the younger brother, and much brother rivalry. In this case, as in all others of "pure" forms, the events following infancy are affecting, in this case intensifying, an overprotective relationship previously established.

After classifying the symptoms of overprotection as they are objectively manifested in the mother-child relationship and working through the behavior pattern of the child, as its direct outgrowth, all factors in our social-psychiatric investigation are evaluated in terms of the primary relationship and in the order that follows:

1. Period of anticipation of pregnancy and childbirth of patient:

All conditions which delay the coming of a wanted child in the form of relative sterility, miscarriages or stillbirths, obviously compel the mother to go through periods of anticipation and frustration. The maternal attitude towards the child following such experiences will be more apprehensive and protective than if the child's birth occurred in the usual time. Such experiences occurred in our series eight times.

2. Extra Hazard: The illnesses of infancy and childhood were evaluated in terms not of their actual seriousness but of maternal response. It was found that frightening illnesses or accidents in which the child "looked dead," as in fainting and convulsions, from whatever cause, stimulated more overprotective response than familiarly known though serious diseases. Protective and infantilizing care and prevention of the usual training of children may be occasioned, for example, by frequent "colds," as also by all operative procedures, as well as actual deformity. An only child or first child, who, however long, is an only child, represents a greater risk than a child who is one of a large family. If it is known or assumed by the parents that an only child represents or is an only pregnancy, the hazard is presumably increased. A combination of events such as a relative sterility or a succession of miscarriages, followed by a viable child, after which pregnancy is considered impossible, is a frequent pattern in our series.

3. Maternal factors: Satisfactory sexual and social life with the husband set up a number of conditions that operate against a mother-child monopoly. On the other hand, sexual incompatibility and lack of social interests in common with the husband intensify the mother-child relationship. The child must then bear the brunt of the unsatisfied love life of the overprotective mother and absorb all her social activities. Such findings are especially frequent in our group. Sexual incompatibility occurs in every case.

In the early life of our overprotective mothers, two factors stand out clearly: inadequate affection and early responsibility. The responsibility is shown in regard to early self-support or contribution to family earnings, and also in occupying an authoritative position over other siblings. It appears plausible that mothers in our group, affect-hungry since early years, try to satisfy their incomplete lives almost exclusively in maternal relations. Attaining that state, they entrench themselves in a mother-child monopoly through an aggressive offensive against all intruders, including the husband. Frequently submissive to the wife, the husband may not interfere at all in matters pertaining to the child and frequently is not consulted. The wife is competent, takes responsibility readily, is often derogatory of her husband. Such findings apply to fourteen mothers in our series. In the remaining six, the overprotection is but of the submissive, dependent type—by mothers who, divested of other social relationships, cling together with the child, as though in a hostile environment. Such mothers are in contrast with the larger group of aggressively overprotective mothers. The picture of the latter group is that of mothers, independent and competent, who, attaining their love-object in an offspring, push away everyone in the effort to create a mother-child monopoly. In the case of the dependent overprotective mother, the situation is reversed, though with a similar result. She is in a passive relationship with the social environment—the mother-child monopoly is created for her.

4. Paternal factors: The following characterization is consistent for the fathers in our series: responsible, steady workers, submissive to their wives, dependent on them for family decisions, exerting little influence on the patient or adding to the overprotection. The fathers in our series do not exert authority in the family, are not looked up to by the wife for family decisions, òr do not aid in disciplining the child; hence, they do not help in mitigating the effects of the maternal overprotection. When the paternal rôle is weak or negligent, the maternal rôle is unmodified. Given an inadequate or indifferent father, it is assumed that, out of necessity, the mother would play a more important rôle with her child. This holds especially where no paternal influence exists, as in the case of widows or divorcees.

5. Other factors modifying overprotection: Of these factors, relatives chiefly were considered. Some cases, as in our series, are complicated by a mother-in-law who lives in the home and whose rivalry with the daughter-in-law is manifested in an overprotective attitude to the grandchild.

6. Problems of the patient: General attitudes of our patients may be classified, according to behavior manifestations, as aggressive, submissive, or indifferent. All forms may be represented in any given case. Most frequent of all forms are the aggressive, and also most readily understood as an expression of the dynamics of the mother-child relationship. The attempt to dominate every situation, and its corollary, the refusal to yield to others, results in a series of complaints from teachers and parents that are well comprehended under the heading "rebellion against authority." This includes various forms of disobedience, impudence, temper tantrums, bullying and general undisciplined behavior. The freedom of action and speech which parents allow these children is often extreme. In a number of cases the point of tolerance is reached. The typical attitude of the mother towards the child is that as a reward for all her devotion, she has raised a monster who makes life intolerable for herself and her husband.

The irresponsible behavior of both the submissive and aggressive child is explained on the basis of unmodified and overmodified infantile experiences. In the aggressive, it is understood as a throwing off of responsibility, a refusal to do one's share; in the submissive, as an immaturity, an infantile expectation of help from others.

Consistent for all cases is difficulty in making friends. The most frequent reason for this is the attempt on the patient's part to always be leader, to boss the game, to give orders, to quarrel and fight. A small number keep away from friends because of timidity or refusal to join in rough sports. A number of patients have been entirely restricted to adult society until school age; a number have not been allowed to go with other children in the neighborhood.

Difficulty in making friends is understood as a carry-over of the mother-child monopoly. The inability to make friends reinforces maternal overprotection. It compels the mother to bear the brunt of the child's unpopularity. With the absence of friends, an important mitigating influence of maternal overprotection is lost. The group of boys, insofar as it puts a value on independence and courage, is an antidote to infantilization. It strikes out against mother dependency. For our patients, the value of the group in developing freedom from maternal overprotection is lost.

When difficulties occur in the class room they follow closely the overprotective pattern, mostly in the form of attention-getting behavior. Our patients for the most part, however, are good students, a few of them excellent. School work, as well as secondary interests, evaluated in terms of maternal overprotection, are seen as helpful agents in the development of "independent" success on the part of the child. School failure throws a further burden on the mother-child relationship. The excellent adaptation to the class room on the part of some of our patients is explained in terms of satisfaction of achievement, made easy by natural abilities; in some cases, it is response to the authority of the school teacher, when it is consistent; and for the most part, it is an identification with the educational values of the mother. It has been shown that for certain objectives, overprotective mothers sacrifice all their indulgences and become stern, unyielding and effective. The child then learns to surrender when all the artifices, used successfully in eluding most responsibilities, fail.

Of the "vegetative" adaptations, our patients show more frequent bladder control than the general group, though more feeding problems. This is consistent with the careful bladder training by the overprotective mother, in contrast with negligent methods who have a correspondingly greater number of problems in this regard. In eating and sleeping, the acts become socialized through excessive contact with the mother, and hence, more frequently a difficulty.

Developmental data show nothing significant in regard to motor or speech development that is not consistent with the intelligence of the children. Overprotected children in this series average nine months on the breast, in contrast with children of rejecting mothers, who average four months on the breast. Check groups for this study have been made on two hundred other cases at the Institute, taken seriatim from the records, weeding out the overprotective cases. Frequency of sexual incompatibility was compared with normal samplings and with other groups.

Six · Adolescent-Parent Adjustment
—Rurality as a Variable

IVAN NYE
Sociologist, Bucknell University

The farm has been looked upon as the ideal place to rear children. The reading below * *questions the validity of this folk belief and reports findings favorable to city families.*

OF the folk wisdom that continues to dominate large areas of sociological thinking, perhaps none is more persistent than the idealization of every aspect of the farm family. In the more limited area of adolescent-parent adjustment this has been as true as for the rural family as a whole. The researches of Cavan and Stott which suggest poorer adjustment for farm adolescents, appear to have affected the thinking of sociologists very little. Burgess and Locke term those findings inconclusive.

The present study indicates very significant differences between farm and city families, with the differences favoring the city families, as measured by an Adolescent-Parent Adjustment Scale of sixty-eight items. Thirty-seven of the scale items favored the city. Of the five interaction areas: (1) feeling of being loved and accepted by parents, (2) parents' trust and confidence in the child, (3) child's feelings about the personalities of the parents, (4) socialization of the child, (5) adjustment to groups outside the family, all show differences favoring the city families. Differences are particularly great in the feeling of being loved and secure, and in feelings about the personalities of the parents.

The sample in the study consisted of 1,472 adolescents from grades eight and eleven of fifteen of the public schools of Michigan. It included farm 423, open country non-farm 183, village 238, small town 173, fringe 208, and city 216, and 5 who did not indicate residence. The instrument was administered in the classroom of classes taking required subjects. A combination of high motiva-

* Reprinted from *Rural Sociology,* 1950, 15: 334–339, and from the *American Sociological Review,* 1951, 16: 341–349, by permission of the author and the publishers.

tion with use of class time made it possible to secure a hundred per cent return, of which 99 per cent were usable.

The items in the scale were taken from previous research and from suggestions by other researchers. Its original construction began in 1946 in Salem, Oregon, where the city high school was experiencing a "wave" of vandalism, insubordination and absenteeism. The teachers felt that most of the adolescents' school adjustment problems could be traced to unsatisfactory adjustment in the home.

A check list of parental behavior items was prepared, but what proved to be more significant was a number of open-ended questions such as: On what subject would you like more freedom from parents? More information? More advice? More direction? Finally, and most productive, What advice do you think most important to give to parents of children your age?

Of the mass of information secured from the above questions there was little indication which behavior and which attitudes were really important to adolescent-parent adjustment and which were perhaps annoying or common, but not important. To test its significance, each attitude and behavior item was formed into an objective multiple-choice question. The resulting questionnaire was administered to 572 high school students in six Washington high schools. Each of the items was tested for association with the adolescent's evaluation of his relationship to his parents as measured by the question, "Do you consider your relationship to your parents: Ideal......, Very satisfactory......, Satisfactory......, Unsatisfactory......, Very unsatisfactory......?"

After the elimination of non-significant behavior and attitude items, an objective form for the measurement of adolescent-parent adjustment was constructed, consisting of 31 adolescent-mother, 31 adolescent-father, and six adolescent-parent items. For convenience these were grouped into the five general areas listed above. A number of tests of validity were employed both for individual scale items and for the scale as a whole.

SUMMARY

The study of adolescent-parent adjustment of the 1,472 adolescents in these Michigan public schools indicated that city families enjoy better adolescent-parent adjustment than farm families as tested by the scale used. This is indicated by: (1) higher mean adjustment scores, (2) higher distributions on individual scale items, (3) larger percentages in the highest quartile and lower percentages in the lowest quartile.

Adolescent-parent adjustment tends to decline with increased rurality (city, fringe, small town, village, open country non-farm, to farm) with the exception of the small town which ranks below the village and almost as low as the farm.

The inadvisability of lumping all rural populations together is demonstrated.

The findings stop at the question of *why* are farm adolescents comparatively more poorly adjusted to parents than city adolescents. Some hypotheses to explain this fact might include: (1) . While city adolescents grow up in a social world resembling that which their parents lived in, that is not true of the farm adolescent. Social change is proceeding so rapidly that it is a different world. Particularly significant is the change from a world dominated by primary groups to one dominated by secondary groups. This makes particularly severe adjustments in the areas of (a) social values and ways of gaining status, a passing of the values on work, production and reputation to those of money and consumer goods appropriate for making good first and casual impressions in the secondary group, (b) change from "great family" to the small immediate family bringing necessity for intensifying the bond between parents and children as the size of the group declines from which family members can draw their emotional security, (c) transition from one in which duties, privileges, and satisfaction of needs centered in the family to one in which, to a great extent, they must be owed to, conferred by, and satisfied by the school, the adolescent group, and the community. (2) He is in increasing contact with urban children who work less and receive more freedom and more material things. (3) The farm adolescent feels that (in the eyes of the total society) he belongs to an underprivileged and an inferior group, and this feeling of lack of success and recognition affects his feelings toward and his adjustment to his parents.

Partial support is given these hypotheses by the findings in this study that the highest socioeconomic level farm group were about as well adjusted as the comparable city group. They have more nearly completed the social transition to the secondary group, have less work and more things, and feel less (if any) inferiority toward other groups.

Seven · Some Neglected Areas in Family-Life Study

JAMES H. S. BOSSARD
ELEANOR S. BOLL
WINOGENE P. SANGER
Sociologists, William T. Carter Foundation
University of Pennsylvania

James Bossard and his associates have made a special contribution to a study of the family by calling attention to the implications of many taken-for-granted facets of family life. They have studied family interaction patterns under different situations to observe how these situations affect children involved. The following article * gives a brief summary of several aspects of their research.

MOST of the forces playing upon the contemporary family have made for the individualizing of the life of its members, and this fact has correspondingly influenced the literature dealing with family life. Important as this individualistic emphasis may be, the essential fact remains that a family is a project in group living, and the stability of the family calls for the promotion of techniques in the co-operative functioning of its members. It is our contention that this approach has been unduly neglected in the recent literature on family life, as well as in the teaching of students in preparation for marriage. This article seeks to present in summary form six factors whose role in the promotion of successful family living seems wholly obvious and highly important. They are (1) the family meal as a form of family operation, (2) family patterns of conversation, (3) family entertaining and visiting, (4) household pets, (5) family rituals, and (6) the family council.

THE FAMILY MEAL

There are two places where the family spends most of its time as a group. They are the dining room and the living room. The relative importance of these two varies, but it seems safe to say that for most American families, the dining room takes first place. It is here that the family members meet regularly, repeatedly, and in

---

* Reprinted from *The Annals* of the American Academy of Political and Social Science, 1950, 272: 68–76, by permission of the authors and *The Annals.*

intimate participation with each other. In lower-class families it is particularly the dining room that is the social center of the household.

From this it follows that the family meal is a recurrent and fundamental aspect of the family's life. And what happens is more than a dietary procedure. It is while seated around the table that the family is at its greatest ease, both physically and psychologically; is held together for definite periods of time; becomes engrossed in common objectives; and has fewer distractions than at most other times. There are, to be sure, many purposes which the family meal is made to serve in the life of the family. Firsthand studies made under the auspices of the William T. Carter Foundation at the University of Pennsylvania identify four common types of family meals.

1. Some are hurried meetings which appear to be regarded by the family personnel as unavoidable periods of family refueling. Food tends to be served as if eating were a mere physiological compulsion, and gulped as if the time required were a wasteful form of biological maladjustment. Conversation is scant, often blunt and direct, and the meal is terminated as soon as possible.

2. Other family meals are devoted largely to recurrent domestic warfare. The children are taken to task for past or present misdeeds, parents quarrel with each other, the food is criticized or its preparation is depreciated. There are families in which few meals are completed without a family quarrel, or without some member of the family leaving the table in tears, anger, or disgrace. Or there is constant nagging about table manners.

3. Some family meals, particularly at selected class levels, become occasions for interesting conversations. Information on various topics is exchanged; triumphs, disappointments, and various other experiences are shared; family programs or projects are evaluated; public issues are discussed; and intellectual interests tend to be stimulated. All, even the children, are encouraged to take part. Each one who participates is recognized for what he or she contributes to the group discussion.

4. Still other family meals become occasions for family rituals. They are characterized by order and impressive decorum. Prayers may be said by way of prelude, candles may gleam, mother may preside as conventionalities are observed, there are servants perhaps to serve the food, and coffee in the living room may follow. The meal here becomes a "private communion" for the members of the family group.

The specific nature and role of the family meal in any particular home is a matter both of circumstance and of choice. In one respect, it is the product of the kind of people that compose the family—their occupations, and their attitudes toward life and toward one another; but in many ways, the family meal becomes a factor which determines the foregoing in some measure. Families make family meals what they are, but it is equally true that family meals make families what they are.

To emphasize the family meal as a factor in family stability means that conscious thought should be given to its systematic cultivation. This involves, of course, many things. The physical setting of the family meal is important. It can be served now in the dining room, then perhaps on the lawn, or on a card table before an open fire or window. Particular occasions, such as birthdays, family days, and holidays, may be observed with special meals, and at special places. Attention to impressive details, like eating by candlelight, the use of colorful china, color combinations of food, and dining room furnishings, is possible in many—perhaps most—families in this country today. Finally, there is the creation of "atmosphere," with attention to the observance of etiquette. This, assuredly, is available to everyone.

FAMILY MODES OF EXPRESSION

Language is so important a factor in human relationships that it is difficult to understand why its role in family life should have been neglected so generally. Language is many things that are basic in family life. It is a form of behavior, and a particularly revealing one, for each individual member of the family; it is the medium of their interaction; and it is the vehicle through which ideas and attitudes are transmitted. In addition, it is also a form of behavior for the family as a whole, and it is this organic aspect that is being emphasized here.

A study of family conversation in eighty-two families, made by the Carter Foundation, reveals a number of striking facts. First, most families show a specific totality or pattern which is characteristic of that particular family. This pattern is a product of many aspects of the family's life—the occupations of its members, their religious affiliation, the geographic areas in which they have lived, their social status, their age and sex, and the like. As a pattern, it reveals the life, past and present, of the family. For this reason the pattern is persistent and distinctive for any given family.

It is striking to observe, in thus studying objectively a number of family patterns of conversation, how readily they can be typed. For instance, some families talk chiefly about themselves: their experiences, achievements, misfortunes, plans, and problems. Other families, by way of contrast, talk mostly about persons or events outside of the family. As these conversations are reduced to written form and analyzed, it is noteworthy how largely they are of one kind or another in the foregoing respect.

Similarly apparent is the contrast between family patterns of conversation that are analytical or evaluating. The first-named are those which consist chiefly of the analysis, description, and interpretation of persons, objects, or events. The interest is to tell about the subject under discussion. One has something to tell here, and the overtones may be those of humor, mystery, drama, or simple recording. Over against this type is that where the underlying motif is that of passing judgment. Motives are impugned, purposes are evaluated, persons and events are "placed in their proper light." These are the family conversations devoted to "talking about someone." Comments are chiefly critical, depreciatory, belittling. The boss is flayed, a competing neighbor's child is depreciated, the teacher is criticized, a social rival is ridiculed, a relative is castigated, a public official is denounced, the children are nagged, or the food is declared unpalatable.

Somewhat akin to this latter type is the pattern where conversation comes to be a kind of exhibitionism, or showmanship. The emphasis is not so much on expressing a thought as on giving a performance. The aim may be at cleverness, and may achieve that purpose or degenerate into mere smart-aleckiness; or the conversation may partake of the nature of a sadistic performance, where the purpose of hurting expresses itself in cutting speech; or the objective may be primarily that of holding the floor, so to speak, with a juggling of verbal balls, sometimes of gold but more often of tinsel. In most cases, this type of speech seems designed basically to call attention to the speaker, and may be related to a deep-seated inferiority complex.

Other contrasts in these family patterns of conversation are to be found in their tonal qualities. At one extreme are those conversations which abound with "snarl words," and much of the talk consists of spasmodically throwing verbal bits at one another as one throws sticks at a dog. In contradistinction are those family conversations which suggest a Sunday afternoon symphony concert. Instead of loud noises, wrangling, and constant interruptions, there is a quiet and polite exchange of ideas, even allowing for disagreement in conviction. People are allowed to finish a sentence. Even the children are allowed these courtesies.

One important by-product of this study is the impression one gains of these patterns as unconscious, even if persistent, habits of family living. That is to say, the families studied had no awareness, seemingly, of the extent to which their patterns of conversation conformed to a given type. There was no awareness or thought either of their nature or of their role in the development of the child members or in the relations between the adult family members. One cannot but be impressed with the possible human salvage that could be achieved by some judicious attention to the cultivation of family language patterns. One wonders, too, what the diversion of but a minor part of current instruction in family living to family patterns of conversation might accomplish in this respect.

FAMILY ENTERTAINING AND VISITING

Family entertainment of guests, and visiting in other homes in turn, constitute an important part of the life of many families. Authors of autobiographies who write of their own family lives, either of childhood experiences or of the marital relations of their parents or themselves, devote much space to the subject of guests and of visiting. Perhaps the reader will agree that many of his or her own most abiding and meaningful family life experiences have been of this kind. But here again one finds that almost no attention has been given to this phase in the literature of family life.

Our own studies reveal a wide range of family consequences. The coming of guests may precipitate family planning and behavior as a group: a family conspiracy to appear to be what it ordinarily is not, but perhaps would like to be; or a concerted effort to deal with a guest with harshness or with humor. Experiences with guests often become a part of the family heritage: "Do you remember when so-and-so stayed here that week end?" Or the guests lift the family out of the doldrums, infusing new life and enthusiasm into relationships and routines that have begun to pall. Again, with the coming of guests, members of families reveal themselves to one another: father acts foolishly with that young blonde; mother's fawning attitude toward Mrs. Smith obviously belies her constant critical comments about her.

Entertaining becomes at times an enjoyable family enterprise; elsewhere and on other occasions, it is the time when one member indulges a selfish interest or turns foolish or unpleasant. It may be exploited for business or professional purposes, or it may be reserved for delightful variations in the family program. It may be overdone, turning the home into a miniature Grand Central Station; or it may be a controlled and selective expression of family group values. At any and all events, family entertaining is an aspect of family living which may contribute to family unity and stability, or it may become a factor in the creation or intensification of its conflicts and disorganization.

Family visiting is a complementary phase of family living. A recent study initiated by the senior author, while not yet complete, casts the shadow of forthcoming conclusions. The study covers thus far a total of thirty-four cases, ranging in age from 19 to 27, and includes past experiences and impressions resulting from the role of guest in someone else's home. Three conclusions may be noted briefly. About half the cases definitely reported that they had gained an insight into other families—their pretenses, social ambitions, ways of rearing children, husband-wife relation, and various oddities in family living. Some of these insights were labeled as disillusioning; others were identified as distinctly educational. Another group were led, through seeing other families in action, to a greater appreciation of their own families. They concluded, as a result of such visits, that their own home life was more pleasant, and that their own family members were better-mannered or more intelligent or more considerate than those whom they had visited. Finally, there were those who, through contact with other families, were made aware of deficiencies in their own background. In some cases such awareness was accompanied by discouragement; in others, by a determination to improve things in their own family setting.

HOUSEHOLD PETS

One in every four big-city families has a dog. Dogs are found in three out of every four farm families. The dog population of the United States was estimated in 1948 at 20,000,000, an all-time high. Cats are about half as popular as dogs. Approximately three out of every five families in the country as a whole have either a dog or a cat. In addition, all sorts of other animals, ranging from ducks to snakes and from lion cubs to lizards, serve as household pets. Not only are these animals found in a majority of American households, but, as is obvious to every observer of the family scene, they constitute an integral part of the family's life. The lack of recognition of their role in the literature on the family constitutes one of its most glaring omissions.

One study published several years ago, and based on a collection of original case studies, explored the various ways in which dogs affect the lives of family members. Briefly summarized, the conclusions of this study follow.

1. The dog is an outlet for our affection. This is its basic service and the chief reason for its presence in most homes. The manifestations of this affection may vary from an occasional friendly cuff to the most tender solicitude, but in most families it is open and frank, with general agreement that the dog receives more attention and affection than any other member of the family.

2. The dog serves each family member according to his or her particular need. This relationship often develops a deep and abiding quality, as evidenced in numerous tributes of older adults to the canine companions of their youth.

3. The dog contributes to the development and integration of the family the challenge of a continuing responsibility, and this obviously is one of life's major and maturing experiences.

4. The dog is one of the best vehicles for parents to use in the training of children in toilet habits. Self-discipline evolves as an accessory before the fact of imposing a discipline upon someone else.

5. The dog is possibly the best available vehicle for parents to use in the sex education of their children. Promiscuity and its re-

sults for the female dog present a natural opportunity to discuss similar tendencies, and problems, in the human female.

6. The dog is a satisfactory victim of personal needs for ego gratification and ego satisfaction. When things have gone wrong, in the office, at the club, or on the playground, and you feel like taking it out on someone, there is Waldo waiting for you.

7. Akin to this is the fact that the dog satisfies the very human longing or desire for power. The wish to dominate someone seems fundamental, and the dog offers an outlet that may save other members of the family.

8. A dog accustoms one to the idea of the normality of physical processes, thus making for the lessening of certain inhibitions in the area of natural and intimate family contacts.

9. By the time one has walked a dog a few months, one is sure to have increased markedly the range of one's acquaintances, even in the most impersonal city neighborhood. A dog thus serves as an effective social aid, particularly for the younger members of the family.

10. Similarly, a dog serves as an effective and continuing subject of family conversation, particularly helpful because he stands mute. In many families marked by intellectual aridity or perennial tensions, such service may be of major importance.

11. Finally, a dog offers companionship, to each according to his needs. And in the contemporary small family, with its individualized life and the mobility of its members, this function often meets a real need.

A summary of reactions to this publication over a five-year period is significant apart from the personal satisfaction to the author. A total of 1,035 letters were received expressing interest in or approval of the article, a possible record response to an article published in a scientific journal. The authors of these letters varied from high Federal Government officials, through New York City bank presidents, to lonely farm boys on far western states. A relatively large number of these letters were from doctors, psychiatrists, and other professional persons dealing with human beings and their problems. Perhaps the following extract from a letter from the publishing editor of the article is the most apt evaluation of the role of the household pet.

"The Mental Hygiene of Owning a Dog" has been just about the most successful article we have ever published. I think there is a lesson somewhere in that—I am not quite sure what, but perhaps it is that we have too much of a tendency to present mental hygiene as something unusual and complicated—involving psychiatrists, psychologists, psychiatric social workers and such—while really it is made up of elements as simple and everyday and easily available as the sunshine and fresh air and clean food and water that are the basis of physical hygiene.

To all save the hopelessly esoteric, it should be obvious that household pets are an integral part of many family groups, enriching the range of their activities, broadening the scope of their responsibilities, integrating the relations of their members, and promoting the family hygiene.

FAMILY RITUALS

In analyzing family life from within, our attention came to focus some years ago upon certain forms of family behavior so recurrent as to suggest the term "habit," and yet having aspects of conscious rigidity and a sense of rightness not generally associated with mere habit. We have come to think of these as family rituals, and, speaking specifically, we define them as patterns of prescribed behavior, arising out of family interaction, which are directed toward some specific end or purpose, and which acquire rigidity and a sense of rightness as a result of their continuing. Thus conceived, rituals develop in connection with many aspects of family life, but cluster chiefly around such things as holidays, anniversaries, meals, vacations, religious worship, and collective ways of using leisure time. Perhaps an illustration will clarify our concept.

The Night Before Christmas Ritual. When Kay S. was three years old, her father held her on his lap and read to her on Christmas Eve Clement Moore's well known poem, "The Night Before Christmas." Each Christmas Eve thereafter this has been repeated. When Kay was five years old, her sister Jane was born, and during the succeeding years the reading of this poem on Christmas Eve became more and more of a ceremonial event. As the two daughters became older, they would sit on either side of their father on the family sofa, and mother and other relatives would be present. After the reading, refreshments came to be served, and talk would follow about Christmas celebrations of former years. As time went on, the ceremony became more and more elaborate. Candles were lit while other lights were extinguished; the conversational aftermath lengthened. Nothing ever deterred Kay and Jane from being at home on Christmas Eve; dates with boys, even after their engagements had been announced, were not made; once Kay did not accept an invitation to a much desired trip so that she might be at home for "the reading." After Kay's marriage, she and her husband came to her parents' home on Christmas Eve in order to be present for the event. This practice has been continued down to the present time, both by Kay and her husband and by Jane and her husband. Last year, "father" read to both daughters, their husbands, three grandchildren and grandmother.

Our study of family rituals covers a period of about eighty years and includes data from almost four hundred families. Some of the conclusions which emerge from this material are as follows. (1) Family rituals have been an integral part of family life during the entire period included in the study. (2) They seem quite definitely to be on the increase. (3) An increasing proportion of these rituals have to do with the secular rather than the religious. (4) Education and economic ease make for their development, but decreasing size of the family unit acts contrariwise. (5) Obvious differentials exist on the basis of social class. Lower-class rituals tend toward expediency; as one moves upward, classwise, they are more concerned with the niceties of living.

But the outstanding conclusion is that of ritual as a relatively reliable index of family integration. Family rituals tend to unify the diverse elements of a family group into a harmonious unit. They both reflect and promote the common interests of the members of the family as a group; they stimulate a sense of group participation; they foster family pride; they encourage refinements in personal relations; they serve to control the behavior of family members; they are an incomparable medium through which newcomers, such as children, are grooved into the pattern of family life. Most of the rituals which we studied arose as group efforts to achieve some common purpose. The trend from the authoritarian to the democratic family, which modern students have emphasized increasingly in recent years, facilitates the development of this type of ritual and increases its importance as an index of family organization. This naturally leads to the final phase with which this article deals.

THE FAMILY COUNCIL

The family council, as a more or less formalized meeting of a family group and with regulatory powers over its members, seems to be as old as the human family. In primitive societies, and in the earlier stages of civil society, its organization was more formal and its powers were more prescribed. It had a relatively high status among various immigrant groups coming to this country, and particularly so among the French who settled in Louisiana. In contemporary times, with the prevalence of smaller family groups and with the greater role of public agencies in family matters, a more simplified and informal type has come to prevail.

In terms of formalized definition, then, the modern family council may be regarded as a gathering of the family group to discuss matters of common family interest, to advise, deliberate, and if possible agree. Its basic implications are that the family is a unified group of interacting personalities, in which each member has his rights, roles, and responsibilities. Occasionally one hears of modern family councils which are organized on a more pretentious basis, with a definite time, place, and procedure, with rules and regulations. Father may be the presiding officer; there is a secretary to keep a record of the proceedings; decisions are made formally by majority vote. More and more, however, the contemporary family council dispenses with formalities of this kind and becomes an informal get-together of the family group for joint discussion of its common problems.

There are at least five reasons for a growing emphasis on the family council and its role in the promotion of stability in the contemporary American family. First is the decline in the size of the family, thus permitting greater ease in family conference and fuller voice to all its members, with particular reference to the younger ones. Second is the growing isolation of the immediate family, which eliminates the interference of relatives. Next is the decline of parental authority, particularly the domination of the father, and the rise of the democratic idea as applied to family group living. Fourth is the growing diversification in interests and occupations of the family members, which makes for increased richness, variety, and at times conflicts in the family background. Finally, one needs to recall here the growing emphasis in family life upon the personality development of its members, particularly its child members.

Based on current uses of the family council, certain tentative conclusions concerning its values are stated here in summary form. (1) It may serve to acquaint all members of the group with the family's needs and problems. Personal problems are merged into a group problem, and each may see his or her problems and needs both in relation to those of each other member and also in relation to those of the group as a whole. (2) Wiser decisions are possible because all members can present pertinent information and particular interests. (3) There is the important fact that group decisions tend to be supported by group authority. The authority of the group is more acceptable than the authority of just a single member. (4) Emotionally, perhaps the most significant value inherent in the family council idea is the sense of security which it may give to the individual family member. Here is not just a family into which he is born and in which he must remain, subject to regimen and complete conformity. This is *his* family, in which he has his say and in which he co-operates in doing his part. The successful family council involves a strong "we feeling," a sense of belonging, of oneness and unity with the family.

CONCLUSION

The general assumption underlying this article is that stable and successful family living is something that must be achieved. It does not come by accident, inheritance, legislative fiat, priestly blessing, or as a result of the ordering and forbidding technique. It is not the creation of university lectures or sermons from pulpits or denouncements in the daily press. From these and other agencies may come counsel and guidance, inspiration and suggestion, but at best these are but threads which each family can weave into a large fabric as the loom of its daily life shuttles back and forth in the continuing give and take of group living.

XI · FAMILY PROBLEMS AND CRISES

One · The Bereaved Family

THOMAS D. ELIOT
Sociologist, Northwestern University

Bereavement is an inevitable family experience. Many people turn away from any recognition of the inevitability of the death of loved ones in the belief that such recognition is morbid. Americans tend to attach taboos to any discussion of death, except in the abstract or in relation to individuals far removed from one's own personal circle.

In studying social behavior, however, some sociologists have observed that there are patterns, both social and individual, in the facing of the crisis of bereavement. A constructive analysis of the ways in which families and individuals meet bereavement follows.*

LET death rive out a member from a group bound in a functional unity of affectionate interaction—the experience of the survivors is bereavement. Outside of primary groups—in the sense of groups involving affective attachments—one does not find bereavement in any true sense. Outside the circle of personal acquaintance one may experience degrees of "shock" depending upon one's capacities for one or another type of identification and sympathy, or upon the existence of other than affectional interests or habits disturbed by the death. One may also observe rituals and simulations of bereavement, required by the culture. And, within the family, death may occur without the phenomena of bereavement. Nevertheless it is clear that bereavement is typically a *family* crisis.

CRISES AND RESPONSES

Crisis, in the sociological sense, is the state of affairs in which the habitual behavior patterns, personal and cultural, are suddenly inadequate to the resolution of tensions in the situation. At such junctures the processes of readjustment involve emotional excitement and efforts in the organism to respond in some way that will relax its unpleasant state of tension.

* Reprinted from *The Annals* of the American Academy of Political and Social Science, 1932, 160: 184–190, by permission of the author and *The Annals*.

Whether these efforts are "successful" or not is as yet a matter of more or less subjective evaluation. The response may be more or less "intelligent" in the sense of voluntary attempts to adapt means to an end. In unprecedented crises the organism may fail entirely, even disintegrate; or it may compensate effectively through the more or less accidental or deliberate discovery or invention of new behavior patterns, which may then be recognized and accepted into the culture of the group as folkways.

When a crisis is one of a kind for which there is ample precedent in the social heritage of the group, the group culture usually includes a special set of *mores*, rituals, and attitudes, which are supposed to deal with such crises satisfactorily if gone through by those most concerned.

The purpose of the present paper is merely to analyze and classify some of the ways in which families and their members have responded to the crisis of bereavement. The types of response described could all be illustrated from case studies if the space allotted for the article permitted. Elsewhere I have pointed out the tremendous importance of this eternally new but universal problem as a possible field for sociological research and eventual helpfulness, but also its difficulties because of resistances and taboos. Were it possible to secure records in which the history is reported by each member of the group and by one or more observing outsiders, such a multidimensional representation of the event (*gestalt*) would, of course, be far more significant.

It will be a long time, however, before a series of such cases can be secured. One way to shorten this time may be to make such groping efforts at interpretation of partial data as are now possible, and to publish them in such a way as may stimulate those in a position to prepare more thoroughgoing studies. If we accustom ourselves to the considerate facing of this common-uncommon experience of bereavement, we may gradually break down the isolation which exists in our culture between the bereaved and the never-bereaved, which is now supported not only by convention, stereotype, and taboo, but also by the general tendency to repress the disagreeable in our own past or prospective experience.

IMMEDIATE EFFECTS OF BEREAVEMENT

The effects of bereavement may be divided very roughly into immediate and later, or primary and secondary.

Among the immediate or primary effects of bereavement I have noted several as typical:

    (1) Abandon

    (2) Refusal or rejection of the facts (including dissociation of emotion, or sense of unreality)

(3) Preternatural or detached calm
(4) Shock, in the neurological sense
(5) Exaltation
(6) Self-injury
(7) Repression
(8) Blame of self or others, revenge
(9) The intense longing of grief

The first eight occur in various sequences and combinations with the last. Without grief (it may be assumed) the others would not arise. Ordinarily, however, the word "grief" is used so loosely, to cover all these phenomena, that it has little specific descriptive value. In the present paper we are concerned with *family interaction,* and shall pass over such immediate responses of bereavement as involve a minimum of interpersonal conditioning and subsequent family behavior. Refusal to believe the death; the degree of shock; the mental content or interpretation of one's temporary dissociation or exaltation; the particular form, degree, or circumstances taken by the impulses to hurt or destroy oneself—all these are indeed subject to influence by the current beliefs, cultural forms and models, and sanctioned folkways. But their organic or physiological basis, like the longing for the lost one, does not directly and inevitably require or imply any social relationship other than those which existed between the bereaved individual and the deceased individual. In the impulse to project upon god, devil, self, or other human beings the blame for the death, one gets the first response directly dependent upon the existence of others, and, in some measure, a return to interaction with other survivors.

It should be noted, however, that behavior of any of the sorts noted in our above list, while not themselves requiring stimulation from others, may be increased by the behavior of other members of the family, through (more or less involuntary) imitation, or by contrast; also that, even though not roused by others' behavior, such responses as incredulity, prostration, ecstasy, suicidal or murderous attempts, and so forth, tend to set up marked reactions of compensatory or imitative nature in other members of the family.

SECONDARY REACTIONS

From a psychiatric point of view, the organism's efforts to deal with the shocks and strains of bereavement may be further analyzed. The following types or classes of response have been noted, corresponding to certain of the well-known "mechanisms" of the psychoanalysts:

(1) Escape, or attempted escape from the conflict. E.g., use of drugs, moving of residence, suicide, social distractions, or illusions.

(2) Defense and repression. E.g., removing all reminders, deliberate forgetting, postural self-control, or certain "mental diseases."

(3) Compensation (in the narrower sense). E.g., rationalization, beliefs and cults, rituals of guilt or contrition, perpetuation of memory of deceased or of wish or supposed will of deceased, revenge, penance or "overdetermined" grief.

(4) Masochism and exhibition. E.g., voluptuaries of grief, recluses, ascetics, and the like.

(5) Identification (introjective). E.g., stepping into the rôle of the deceased, or "carrying the spirit" of the deceased.

(6) Transference and substitution (involving projection). E.g., reattachment of affections to new mother, child, or spouse; espousal of charities or causes.

Most of these behavior patterns take time and social interaction for their development: they are not immediate and primary, but secondary and socially conditioned. Some *mores* of bereavement correspond to and offer channels (or correctives?) for these mechanisms.

It will be noted that many of the above reactions may prove successful or unsuccessful, depending upon the inner resources and the current social situation. A classification based upon degree of success in readjustment may therefore cut across the psychiatric classification. For example, it may leave among the failures some efforts to substitute a love object, while other such reattachments may be spontaneous and highly successful.

It should also be noted that while the psychiatric classification stresses mechanisms or *processes,* a classification according to degrees of success will naturally stress *results*—i.e., cross sections of processes at a given time. To the extent that case studies have been drawn from recent bereavements, the results cannot be considered conclusive, as the processes of readjustment or failure may be incomplete.

Degrees of success in readjustment cannot be measured but must be roughly (and perhaps subjectively) evaluated, and then grouped. And there is a further difficulty—the danger of cultural subjectivity. That is, an adjustment which might be individually successful, such as remarriage, may be so frowned upon in a given place or time that it may turn out unhappy and thus prove a failure, or it may be misjudged as failure through moral prejudice. A refusal to commit suttee would have been considered failure in Hindu culture. Nevertheless, it seems worth while to attempt an empirical arrangement of people's social and secondary reactions to bereavement, in order of their apparent success. The nearest I can come to an objective definition of such success is a condition in which there is acceptable evidence that the unpleasant tensions have been relaxed or reorganized into some tolerable or more satisfactory pattern.

INDIVIDUAL EFFECTS OF BEREAVEMENT

A. *Total failure to readjust*
  (1) Suicide
  (2) Early death
  (3) Insanity
  (4) Moral disintegration
  (5) Obsession

B. *Partial failure*
  (1) Eccentricities
  (2) Physical illness or prostration
  (3) Aboulia, purposelessness
  (4) Isolation
  (5) Embitterment, misanthropy, cynicism
  (6) Reversion to or recurrence of griefs
  (7) Self-blame or personal hates
  (8) Fears
  (9) Loneliness

C. *Partial success*
  (1) Resignation, "God's will," etc.
  (2) Stoicism
  (3) Stereotyped formulæ of immortality, misery escaped, etc.
  (4) Sentimental memorials
  (5) Effective repression of memories
  (6) Intensification of affections
  (7) Extension of affections
  (8) Deliberate absorption in distractions or duties
  (9) New or fantasied love objects

D. *Conspicuous success*
  (1) New love object
  (2) Thoroughgoing religious rationalization
  (3) Spontaneous forgetting, relaxation of tensions
  (4) Devotion to life work
  (5) Identification with rôle of deceased
  (6) Creation of constructive memorials
  (7) Transmutation of the experience into a productive reinte-
gration of the personality.

Obviously, the most frequent results are the infinite combinations of B and C above—partial success and partial failure.

These types of individual compensatory behavior have been listed in this paper because they undoubtedly influence the pattern of family behavior during the bereavement and post-bereavement periods. Like the immediate or primary responses to the death, these behavior patterns are contagious; but they are more consciously imitated or resisted than are the immediate impulsive responses. They may be based upon models and may serve as models for imitation. In fact, one finds persons worrying in bereavement because their own feelings do *not* correspond to some preconceived or admired model or code; or accusing another member of the family of indifference because of his easier readjustment or more effective repression.

In a simple culture it may be that grief is more or less sincerely standardized. The net impression from current studies in our own fluxing culture is that of the amazing differences in both the inner and the outer manifestations of grief, to be observed everywhere.

HOW BEREAVEMENT AFFECTS THE FAMILY

Neither the psychiatric classification nor the types of success and failure listed above represent responses of the family as a whole. Allport's theory to the contrary notwithstanding, there is a difference between the individual responses and the constellation and interactions thereof in the family relationship.

Even more than individuals' feelings, the behavior of the family may be affected by the financial gain or loss incident to the death. It is difficult to isolate the true bereavement features from the socioeconomic features which have been so extensively studied by social workers. For the social psychologist, however, the latter are of interest only as they influence personal attitudes and family interactions.

Turning, then, to what is more strictly the topic of this paper, let us note some ways in which families have been observed to change as a result of bereavement.

(1) The rôle of a family member exists in relation to the configuration and functioning of the family as a unit. A death tends to disturb this unity. The shifting of the rôles of the various members under bereavement represents a reshaping of the configuration.

(2) The consensus of the family in respect to these rôles, i.e., in respect to its own pattern, may result; or, family conflict may develop as a sequence to incompatible conceptions of the rôle of certain members under the new conditions.

(3) Such conflicts or jealousies, or the lack of a common personal or domestic object or symbol of affectional attachment (conditioning stimuli) may result in decreased family solidarity.

(4) Acceptance of new interpersonal responsibilities may increase family solidarity.

(5) Removal of authority, of habit-stimuli, of home, or of support may lead to revision of family folkways.

(6) Maturity of children who lose their parents may lead to individualism or turning to their own families.

(7) The will, or personality, of the deceased, acting psychologically as a dynamic complex in each member's memory, and reënforced by consensus, may activate the behavior of the entire family.

No one case will display all the patterns, individual and social, that have been suggested above; but it may be of value to present such parts of a single case as will illustrate the sort of material being brought to light, and the manner of its analysis.

NARRATIVE FC 10 (DISGUISED)

Analysis

This is the story of two cases of bereavement in the family of a professional man. No attempt will be made to give a comprehensive account—merely enough to offer a glimpse of what these experiences meant to me.

At the age of 25 I was happily married to a woman whose previous life had been in some respects very different from my own, but who brought to me the things that I had missed in the past. We were alike chiefly in having been brought up in clergymen's families and (naturally) in not having much money. Our first year was badly broken by the War. . . .

We were both eager for children and looked forward with happy anticipation to the coming of our first-born. She arrived a year later and fulfilled our fondest hopes. She was a healthy, happy baby. And then, a year and a half later a second child was born. We were delighted with the thought that our first would not have to grow up alone, but would have a playmate almost her own age. But we were doomed to disappointment. The second baby was undernourished and partly paralyzed. For a long time, in fact so long as he lived, we knew not what day his life might be snuffed out. He cried "constantly," until both parents were worn out with worry and lack of rest. We took him to the best medical men available, spending our time, our money and our strength until it seemed we could do no more. After nine months of struggle, we accepted the inevitable. We realized that he would never grow up and that the strain of caring for him was more than we could bear. So we secured a nurse who kept him for a time and later placed him in a hospital school. He lived for six years, and in all that time there was not a week, in fact scarcely a day, when we did not half expect word that he had slipped away. We visited him, because he was our baby, but one

Affectional bond documented.

The child's illness prolonged, the death expected; probably and naturally hoped for at times.

Reaction to expected death: desperate and loyal efforts.

NARRATIVE FC 10 (DISGUISED)

could hardly say that these were happy visits. When at last he passed on, it gave almost a sense of relief, and yet there was a terrible longing for the lad that he might have been.

Immediate reaction to death: relief. Secondary reaction: longing.

After we had been married about six years, my wife was found to have a tumor which it seemed necessary to remove. So she went to the hospital, confidently expecting to be back home in a couple of weeks. But on the operating table another tumor was discovered, whose removal was exceedingly difficult. Even so she seemed to be regaining strength when peritonitis set in and within ten days she was gone. The shock was something I cannot possibly describe. I could hardly eat; I had a constant feeling of nausea. Mentally I was full of self-accusation for not having taken the whole case more seriously and provided more adequately. (Not for three days did I get her a special nurse, since the physician did not advise it.)

Unexpected death of wife. Immediate reactions: acute shock; and self-blame.

Fortunately I was able to sleep, and gradually my appetite returned. Within a week I forced myself back to my work. I devoted much time to my six-year-old girl.

Sleep as an escape? Gradual and spontaneous relaxation of acute tensions. Deliberate distraction through meeting duties; partly successful. Transference or intensification of affection.

Friends were thoughtful and quietly expressive of their sympathy. My mother spent a couple of weeks with us. But for weeks I went about in a sort of daze. I was luckily able to secure a good housekeeper, who quietly fitted herself into our household, learned our ways, said little, but assumed responsibility and became very fond of the small girl. This woman was with us for over two years.

Comfort in friends' contacts and attitudes. Aboulia? Deeper levels of shock not healed. Affections not fully compensated. Routine reëstablished — with change of folkways.

It should be said that the second child was still living at this time, and was an added cause of distress throughout. He died about a year after his mother. Outwardly we seemed to have made a

Analysis
Child not readjusted.

good adjustment, but the girl missed her mother, grieving secretly. At no time since her death has she been willing to mention her. Several times I have talked to her about her mother, but she would never bring up the subject of her own accord, nor would she ever say much when I opened the conversation. She clung to me and feared that I would leave her.

Repression.
Fears.

Once when we were in a store together I went into a booth to try on some clothes; missing me she started for home crying as hard as she could. She did not want to go visiting or to have me go away. However, she has gradually changed in these respects and seems now to be quite normal.

Increased solidarity between survivors.
Gradual readjustment and relaxation of tensions.

For myself, I was inexpressibly lonely. The housekeeper did her work admirably, but she was a woman of limited education and could not be a companion. I drifted into a correspondence with an old friend, visited her, and for a time was quite sure she was the one to fill the gap in my life. However, I cooled off and realized that she might provide only sympathy and companionship for a time. When I thought of the one who was gone and asked myself, "What would she think?" there was only one answer. I broke off and decided that it was much better to "go it alone."

Loneliness as partial failure to readjust. Inadequacy of economic substitute for wife.
Unsuccessful substitution of love object. Memory and wish of deceased as an active and inhibiting complex.

Still later a real affection developed between me and a woman five years my junior, who had lived with us when the small girl was about a year old. She was a charming person, who had gone through the experience of losing·her father and making a very happy adjustment to her stepfather and stepbrothers and sisters. We decided to get married, and have for over a year been living happily together.

Apparently successful substitution of love object.

The past is not wholly buried, but my daughter has a good mother and I have a lovely wife. Everything seems on a firmer footing than ever before. We are facing the future with hope and courage, knowing that there is plenty to do, accepting our daily problems as they arise.

Identification in bereavement and in readjustment to "steps."
Frank admission that process is not complete, but prognosis good.

I think the fact that the two women were fond of each other, and the fact that the girl and her stepmother are getting on so

Child finds substitute love object.

	Analysis
well have contributed enormously to my own readjustment. When I look back I feel that I have been through hell, but for the most part I look forward and keep rather happily busy in the present.	*Recurrent memories successfully assimilated.* *Distractions in current duties and in change of scene.*

It may be noted, as a point in method, that cases such as the above have been secured as spontaneous narratives, with only general oral suggestions as a basis. They are therefore less detailed and comprehensive than studies based upon a formal outline or schedule, but have the advantage of preserving the spontaneous emphases felt by the bereaved in his own experience and memory; and they lend themselves to treatment as a series or sequence of situations as the configuration changes.

Two · Mourning Customs and Modern Life in Bengal

D. N. MITRA

The following description of the mourning customs in Bengal,* and an enlightened and thoughtful man's attitudes toward the customs, contributes to our understanding and evaluation of American ways and attitudes. This article is more meaningful when read as a companion piece to "A Hindu Marriage in Bengal," and "A Hindu Wife," by the same author, presented earlier in this book.

ACCORDING to the prevailing custom, a certain period of mourning for the deceased has to be observed by Hindus, and at the end of the period some religious rites (*Sradh*) have to be performed. A good feast for the Brahmins and for relatives and friends has also to be provided. The Brahmins should be fed a day earlier, and their menu must not include any preparations of fish or meat.

The period of mourning varies in different communities. The Brahmins observe a period of ten days, the Vaidyas twelve days, and we, the Sudras, a month. Some Sudras, claiming that they are the Kshatriyas (warrior class), have of late begun to observe a

* Reprinted from *The American Journal of Sociology*, 1947, 52: 309–311, by permission of the University of Chicago Press.

period of twelve days instead of a month and have taken holy threads like the Brahmins and the Vaidyas.

There are many restrictions imposed on mourners which, again, vary in different communities and also in the relationship of the mourners to the deceased, the chief of these being the prohibition *against* fish, meat, eggs, and some other articles of food. There are further prohibitions against cutting hair and nails, shaving, wearing shoes, covering the body with any kind of garment except a thin sheet of cloth (*urani*)—this being applied to the members of the family who are younger and very closely related to the dead—sending dirty linens to the washerman, etc.

There are many restrictions with respect to cooking the food, particularly for the sons and unmarried daughters of the dead. They have to prepare their own food in separate ovens made of bricks only, without clay or any other mortar. Vessels must be made of earth called *malsas* and must not be covered. Fuels must not consist of any other firewood than dried jute sticks and dried cocoanut and other leaves. The food, consisting of rice and of certain vegetables all of which are boiled together in the same vessel, is called *habisanya*. New *malsas* are to be used daily. Mourners have to sleep on the floor on only a blanket, without a pillow or even a mosquito curtain. The *habisanya* is the chief meal for the day, and only some fruits, sweets, etc., are allowed in the evening. Mourners are also not allowed to change their clothes. They must have the same cloth for the entire day and night after their daily bath, and that cloth must be borderless.

The whole idea is to undergo all sorts of hardship and privations and to avoid all luxuries and pleasures as a mark of respect to the deceased. Mourners are not allowed to use oil—not to speak of soap —napkins, etc., at the time of bath and are not permitted to comb their hair.

To begin with, this difference in the periods of mourning has always agitated my mind. Is the love or respect of the Brahmins toward the dead less than that of the other communities? Why, then, this difference?

I was told by some with whom I discussed it that, if the Brahmins had to observe a period of one month's mourning, worship of the deities by them and their attendance at other religious ceremonies would have been very greatly dislocated, because during the period of mourning they were prevented from doing these acts for the well-being of the other communities. This argument was not at all convincing to me.

Nor could I get any satisfactory answer to my question: "Why should the Vaidyas and Kshatriyas then observe a period of twelve days' mourning?" I do not know the Sastryas, but my honest conviction is that in this priest-ridden country it was the priests who were responsible for this convention, for their own convenience and in order to dominate the other communities as superior beings.

I had a series of bereavements in my family, in quick succession, some twenty-five years ago, when I was about thirty years old, and I had to observe a period of one month's mourning in each case and was required to abide by all the injunctions of the Hindu society during each period. It affected my health.

Sir Prafulla Chandra Ray, a great Bengali, a great scientist, and a great man, who had a very soft corner for me in his heart, felt very much for me and asked me to wear shoes, to put on adequate clothes, and to take proper food, in disregard of the prevailing custom. He explained to me that, in ancient times when these social rules were made, the people used to live in the villages in their own homes, living on the produce of their lands, and that it was not difficult for them to observe these injunctions of the priests. But times have changed considerably since and are still changing fast, and we should adapt ourselves to the changes of the time.

"You will have to attend office," he added, "and you will have to travel from one corner of the province to the other [I was then a touring officer] to earn your bread. How is it possible for you to move about from place to place bare-bodied and with bare feet and to observe the restrictions about your food without any detriment to your health and work?"

He cited the example of his mother and said that, when his (Sir Prafulla's) father died, he was suffering from diarrhea and that his mother gave him a proper diet including fish soup. She did not follow the restrictions at all and was taken to task very severely by the Hindu society. But she did not budge an inch from what she thought best for her son at the time, and her bold reply was that she had done exactly the same thing as his (Sir Prafulla's) father would have done had he lived. If she had given him the *habisanya,* his father's soul would not have rested in peace. This incident occurred about seventy years ago, when the social laws were more rigid and strict than at present. She was a bold, courageous, and sensible lady, and it is no wonder that a son like Sir Prafulla was born to her.

I did not venture to act according to Sir Prafulla's instructions then, as my elders would not allow me to relax any of the rules. But a few years ago, when my aunt died, I had to attend office regularly and also to move about from place to place. I put on proper clothes and wore canvas shoes, but I observed other injunctions strictly.

Even then I was criticized very unkindly by my relatives, who are highly educated and cultured. I told them that I regarded my aunt as my mother, that her death was equally a great shock to me, and that my regard and love for her were not less than that of her own sons. If I had been converted to Christianity, my love and respect would have remained the same, and in that case I would not have been criticized by them in the manner in which I am being censured now for wearing clothes, shoes, etc. They may regard me as a Christian for the time being, but my attempt to convince them was altogether fruitless. This incident caused a misunderstanding between me and many of my near relatives, and that misunderstanding still persists.

My wife died about a year and a half ago. Against the wishes and sentiments of many of my relatives and friends, I made up my mind to observe a period of twelve days' mourning and to perform the *Sradh* ceremony at the end of this period. When I proposed it to him, my priest sanctioned it, but a day or two later he came and said that personally he had no objection to my proposal but that he had been advised by the other priests not to do it, as I had not taken any holy thread like the Kshatriyas.

With great difficulty I had to secure the services of another priest from a different locality to enable me to act according to my mind. But a vastly learned Brahmin with a university education and with all the degrees of the university refused to read some chapters of the Gita (our Bible) on this occasion on the grounds that I was performing the *Sradh* ceremony after twelve days of mourning— and he is a professor of a first-class government college in Calcutta.

A friend of mine, a Brahmin, who also possesses high university degrees and is a professor of the University Science College, however, agreed to read the Gita out of his respect toward my wife, whom he knew.

Then, according to the prevailing custom, I was not very willing to feed the Brahmins and also to feed my relatives and friends. I said that I was not going to save the expenditure on this item, since I would feed the poor instead. But that was not to be.

In this case I had to yield to the custom and to the mandates of my relatives. The house did not look like one of mourning but rather like a house of merry festival, with the relatives, both men and women, coming and going in cars, gharries, rickshas, etc., and with the cooks and servants busy preparing a heavy menu.

As stated above, the Brahmins had to be fed a day earlier, and their menu must not include any preparations of fish or meat. But the relations and friends must have a sumptuous feast with plenty of fish preparations, because the mourners would be permitted on that day to eat fish for the first time since the period of their mourning.

Leaving aside our grief and sorrow for the departed, we had to be busy and anxious about securing the foodstuffs in these days of rationing, about the proper reception of the guests, etc. We had to pay the taxi or gharry hire for all who kindly came and obliged us, as this is also the custom.

Of course, those who came and dined expressed their sorrow at the death of my wife, and some close female relatives also shed tears for a little while.

The whole thing was repulsive to me. There was no difference between a house of marriage festival and one of *Sradh* ceremony. Moreover, it was a great strain on my grief-ridden sons and daughters, who had not yet recovered from the shock of their terrible loss. One of my daughters who is a graduate and who had to bear very largely the brunt of the whole thing remarked that all the relatives came to the "festival" and that, if a small fraction of them had kindly come when her mother was lying seriously ill and helped us a little in nursing her, we would have appreciated their sympathy more deeply. She is a very outspoken girl and is therefore not liked by many of her relatives.

Three · Class Differences in Family Reactions to Crisis

EARL L. KOOS
Sociologist, University of Rochester

*An experience that would constitute a crisis in one family might have no crucial significance at all in other families. Questions concerning such problems as how families in different positions in the class structure meet crises, differences in what constitutes a crisis, and frequency of occurrence of crises in families of different social classes are discussed in the next selection.**

AS we approach the subject of class differences in the effects of crisis upon the family, I find a number of facets calling for discussion. Crisis in relation to family living needs to be broken into its components; these we shall discuss individually.

First, what is a crisis? Many of us have called attention to a fact which needs constantly to be kept in mind—*that crisis is relative to a number of things*—first of all, to the cultural and social heritage of the individual family. We need not be cultural determinists to recognize that the whole background and social *milieu* of the family dictates strongly to it what it shall regard as crisis. For one of us it would be stark tragedy to be without employment and to see nothing ahead for some months but relief. It is with this idea in mind, probably, that a middle-class father said: [and meant it]

---

* Reprinted from *Marriage and Family Living*, 1950, 12: 77–79, by permission of the author and the editor.

"I'd shoot myself before I'd go to the county welfare office and apply for help." This contrasts sharply with a lower-class father's statement: "There's never been a time when I could be sure that I could care for my family. And my father was that way before me, too." Certainly a family living as did the latter, in a subsociety for which unemployment and the seeking of relief is an accepted part of the pattern of living, can hardly be expected to consider events in the same light as do those of us to whom security is something very much to be taken for granted.

Crisis is relative, too, *in terms of the ideas and ideals we have regarding family life*. The greater degree of institutional structuring and the greater rigidity of roles found in the lower-class family both determine very much the way in which the family will regard events in its life. When a lower-class mother, for example, says that "we're born into this world to live this way" she is indicating a different attitude toward family crisis than does the middle-class mother with her statement that "no one has to accept their lot in life —we all can change."

Both of these factors operate, then, to create class differences in crisis causation. This brings us to a brief consideration of what the class differences are. We have earlier called attention to the fact that in our research experience low-income families have a broad range of disruptions; so broad, in fact, that they cannot be thought of as occurring in any one special area of family life. We have as yet found no limit to what may cause crisis in the lower-class family. This is in sharp contrast to the recorded experience of families in the middle class. In the latter, crises involving financial difficulties have been conspicuously absent; crises involving interfamily relations are similarly infrequent in their occurrence. The superior financial position of the middle-class family and the sense of competence that goes with having money may well explain the absence of crisis situations related to money; the explanation of the absence of interfamily crisis situations seems to lie in the greater importance —for the middle-class family—of its position in its local situation.

What then, is the focal point of crisis in the middle-class family? It is intrafamily to begin with, but more important, it appears from our developing knowledge to be centered in the interpersonal relationships of husband and wife or of parents and children. Most important is the fact that crises resulting from strained parent-child relationships occur more than twice as often as do those resulting from strained husband-wife relationships. This is not to say that lower-class families do not have interpersonal crises; the evidence is to the contrary. It is to say that the special threat to the middle-class family lies in this area, and that there is no such special threat to the lower-class family.

The second major question to be raised involves the frequency of crises in middle- and lower-class families. From a variety of evidence, both research and empirical, we know that trouble and disease tend to occur most frequently in a small number of illness-prone and crisis-prone low-income families. No such selective characteristic has yet been seen in the middle-class families. Of even greater significance is the fact that middle-class families *have more crises per family than do those in our lower-class families.* This, I believe, is not difficult to explain. Since middle-class families have—on the whole—higher levels of aspiration, and since they are under greater pressure to maintain these levels, it may well follow that the middle-class family is more sensitive to the frustrations of modern living than is its lower-class counterpart. Also, the lesser degree of institutional structuring and the lesser rigidity of roles mentioned earlier appear to give the middle-class family a greater sensitivity to factors in its environment and consequently a lower threshold. This is not to disregard differences among families in relation to their adequacy. There can be no question but that crises vary in frequency as family adequacy varies, but when matched for degree of adequacy the middle-class family's greater sensitivity is clearly seen.

We have by now examined in detail at least one crisis in each of nearly 2,000 families, and have found the beginnings of an answer to the third question: *Is there a variation in the length of time a family suffers from a particular crisis and in the crisis profile?* There is a variety of patterns of behavior in crisis; similarly, there is great variation in the length of time the family suffers disruption of its pre-crisis behavior or until it settles down to a new pattern.

I can only indicate here one summary judgment on our materials: first, that *middle-class families more often react more severely to crisis than do low-income families, but that they recover their earlier interaction patterns more readily,* and second, that *they are more likely to come out of the crisis with some benefit to themselves.* There seems little reason to question the validity of this, since in general the middle-class family has far more to lose in the way of *morale* than does its counterpart in the low-income group; in general, too, it has much more opportunity, and much more with which to reestablish itself after the crisis is over.

One additional question is ever-present: *how does the family meet its needs in crisis?* It is this question that those concerned with marriage counseling must face very realistically. Even though some middle-class (and fewer lower-class) families come out of a crisis more conscious of family values, better able to work together, with a greater resiliency, and with a deeper understanding of human problems, we can realistically ask whether allowing the family to face crisis unnecessarily is the best means of attaining good family life. If it is not, then we have—in our concern for the family—somehow to provide help in preventing and meeting crises.

It is significant, I think, that we find more than one-half of the lower-class families turning to outside help in meeting their crises.

To be sure, these are not all "the best possible sources." Most are nonprofessional, many are truly commercial, some are downright unethical. Many lack any but the single quality of friendliness.

But where do the middle-class families turn? The answer is: They don't! For most there is even shame in turning to the home-and-school counselor, to the school psychologist, to the minister, for to do so is to admit failure in the family and, as Margaret Mead has said, "The one thing Americans fear is failure." Less than one in ten among the middle-class families goes outside itself, in our experience, in search for ways of meeting its crises.

All of this is by way of introduction to the special emphasis of this paper. My special concern is with how families already in existence, already functioning as interpersonal groups, meet the problems they incur, and upon what we—as proponents of good family life—need to recognize and to do if families are to weather the storms which seem inherent in what we term "The American way of life."

We have seen, within the last two decades, the development of quite remarkable institutional aids for the family with financial problems. While we have by no means reached an optimum position, and while this development is uneven from state to state, we must admit that our society has moved far in the direction of meeting the family's needs as regards financial help in times of trouble. Our unemployment insurance, old age assistance, retirement and survivor's insurance, and other programs, have moved ahead rapidly in the last years. This meets, however, only part of the need, and it is my personal belief that it meets the lesser part. It is of course true that no family can function adequately if it has to face financial need; it is more true, I believe, that even though it may have financial aid in time of crisis, such aid is inconsequential if the family is not helped in areas other than financial.

If we look at the ways in which families "muddle-through" in the solution of their crises, we find first, a tremendous lack in the services which are available to families. Public welfare agencies have little time and few personnel for dealing with the interpersonal problems of the families with which they deal; they have, further, in most cases, actual directives against doing anything with the family that aims at other than financial assistance. Permit me to quote from a letter written by the Commissioner of an urban county welfare department:

> We see our job as that of relieving financial need, whether it is in the case of an old person no longer employed, a family whose working member is laid up with illness, or a child to be cared for with public funds. *It is not our job to meddle in the personal affairs of such people.* [italics mine].

It is highly significant, in this connection, that the rules in this welfare department state that "families shall be visited often enough to insure that they are receiving only such assistance as is required under the law."

It is not my intention to prove inadequacy in meeting low-income family needs by these quotations; it is my intention to show that in our *public support* of the family in its hour of crisis we tend to see the problem only as one demanding the giving of relief in money or kind.

There is a similar lack in our services to the family in the realm of the private agency. As relief has become the responsibility of governmental agencies, the private agencies which were formerly the depositories of such responsibility have shifted their goals to the meeting of interpersonal problems. This is all to the good, but let's be realistic about this shift. Has the private agency shifted also its philosophy—has it moved in the direction of removing those barriers which have militated, over the generations, against the acceptance of "help" in the solving of family problems? There is much evidence which cannot be denied; evidence that there is—in the middle-class family especially, and in the low-income family as well —a resistance to being helped. I need not take time to prove this point other than to say that one finds the family—regardless of its class—turning either to untrained, unskilled, and often unethical sources of help, or turning to no one—keeping its problems essentially within its own limits.

Robert S. Lynd coined the nice term "the unable," by which he meant those in need of help from society. I am sure that he would agree with us that "the unable," in a society such as ours, has come to include—under certain circumstances—all of us, and that concern for the family necessitates our developing patterns of support which are acceptable to all families.

This is no simple problem! We have, in all frankness, too few available personnel to meet the needs of our families, just as we have too little consciousness on the part of society as a whole of the need for providing such services. We are, however, making strides; there are increasing numbers of psychiatrists, marriage counselors, skilled social workers, and others coming off the educational production line. There are increasing awarenesses on the part of communities that counseling for marriage and the family is a *sine qua non* of modern living. This part of our task is moving—albeit, slowly —toward meeting the needs of the family.

But this is not enough!! Nor is it ever going to meet our family needs. From the analysis of the problem of the family in our society, it appears that the very emphasis of our education for good family living *must include* an indoctrination with the idea that the family cannot do its job alone; that it is no sign of weakness if the family turns to professional help in its attempt to do its job; and that responsibilities of the family are so great in the doing of its job today that it is negligent if it does not use these services.

Four · The Stepmother

WILLIAM C. SMITH
Sociologist, Linfield College

Increasing divorce, especially among people with children, coupled with the fact that divorced people have a high remarriage rate, means that more families than ever before in the United States must adjust in step-relationships. Some special problems and characteristics of step-relationships are examined in the reading * *below, and in the following selection on the step-child.*

SOME writers paint most doleful pictures of the stepmother—she cannot possibly succeed, no matter how good a person she may be. According to Erich Wulffen, hatred of the stepmother for her stepchild is, doubtless, rooted in sex. The child reminds the stepmother of her husband's love-joys with his first wife, and she is sexually jealous of the dead woman. The stepmother's hate toward the stepdaughter is particularly venomous when the latter is more beautiful than the woman's own daughters. That, again, has an underlying sexual motive.

Fritz Wittels, another German writer, is unduly pessimistic about the steprelationship. According to him,

There is an immemorial folk-prejudice against the woman unlucky enough to marry a widower with young children. Some say it is the outcome of the anti-stepmother attitude aroused in children by the tales they have heard about wicked stepmothers from their earliest years. The fact is, however, that the structure of the human family is of a very peculiar kind, with the inevitable result that a second wife cannot do right by the children of her predecessor, even when animated by the most earnest desire to be a true mother to her stepchildren. If she has herself been married before and has had children by her first husband, she will, by force of nature, give them the preference. . . . If she has not been married before, or has had no children by her first husband, she will want to

* Reprinted from *Sociology and Social Research*, 1949, 33: 343–347, by permission of the author.

bear children of her own. Should she remain childless, she will have a sense of inferiority to her predecessor, and this will react on her relation towards her stepchildren. If, as usually happens, the second wife brings children into the world, she would have to be an angel from heaven not to feel more loving towards the fruit of her own womb than towards stepchildren who are, in any case, prone to regard her as an interloper.

According to these two writers, it would appear that behavior in connection with the steprelationship is quite rigidly fixed in the germ plasm. Helene Deutsch gives support to this position when she declares that in all cultural milieus, "the term 'stepmother' automatically evokes deprecatory implications."

A study of the steprelationship in other cultures, however, does not support this point of view; there is considerable variation from culture to culture. The small biological family characteristic of the United States is not found everywhere. In many societies there is a sharp distinction between the reproductive unit of parents and children and the authentic institutional family; and frequently the small reproductive unit plays an insignificant role, while other social groupings carry on much the same functions as the American family. In some places the reproductive unit is almost totally ignored— the father is almost completely excluded from the family, and the mother is only one among several women responsible for the care of the child. In such a situation the child is born into a rather large group where from the very outset he must make adjustments to a number of relatives who exercise considerable influence over him. If a stepchild is a member of a large group where the reproductive unit is of slight significance, he will not be unduly disturbed by the loss of a biological parent, because he has membership in the larger group where he has already made adjustments to his potential stepparents. Families like ours, which are organized on a conjugal basis, have certain disadvantages. If an adult member of this small group dies, or leaves for any reason, the functioning of the unit is usually disrupted and the remaining members have to make new adjustments, oftentimes abrupt ones. On the other hand, the larger consanguine family persists for several generations. The loss of any one individual member does not disorganize the whole unit, and the several members are not subjected to severe emotional disturbances due to some sudden change. In the large consanguine family the situation of the stepmother is far different from that in our relatively impermanent conjugal family system.

Where polygyny is practiced the situation differs widely from that in our society. Under such a system it is the usual practice for all children to call all the wives "mother" so long as they live with a common husband. If one of the wives dies and the man marries another wife, she does not come into the family circle as a stepmother to the dead woman's children, but as another mother to *all* the children. The children already have several mothers and the coming of an additional mother brings little change in the course of their lives, for she has no more to do with the motherless children than with any of the others whose mothers are still living.

Where the sororate is practiced the dead wife's younger sister is expected to step into the breach. This is established custom; she knows that she may some day become stepmother to her sister's children and they know who will become their new mother in the event their own parent dies. The sororate provides a favorable situation for the steprelationship. The surviving mate does not have to go about blindly in search of a substitute parent and in desperation bring home a new mate who is a total stranger to the children. Where the mother's younger sister must become the father's second wife, there will be no attitude of resentment toward her on the part of the children, nor will she try to drive the children out of the home.

According to the classificatory kinship system, under which a number of persons are included in a single category of relationship, the real mother and all her sisters are called "mother" by the child. It is highly probable under such a system that one's attitude will be different toward the mother's sister if she is called "mother" rather than "aunt"—but we must not be too dogmatic on that point. Doubtless, the kinship terminology of a classificatory system does something to generate attitudes which are not found in our culture. Where it is the accepted behavior for a child to run up to any one of several nursing women and suckle at her breast, or seek comfort and help from her, then to all intents and purposes she is his "mother"—he does not stop to ask her if she is his flesh-and-blood mother. This system tends to widen the family circle and draw into it many who in our society are on the periphery. Where a characterizing term such as *stepmother* is used, attention is directed to the fact that such a person is *different* and, consequently, differential treatment may readily be accorded such a person. The classificatory system tends to erase, rather than accentuate, differences.

We must bear in mind, however, that in simple societies there are fewer difficulties to face than in our complex life. In a nonliterate group all children are molded by practically the same pattern. Likewise, there is great homogeneity among adults because all are subjected to a single, standard set of influences. Because of that condition there is less danger of personality clashes between a stepmother and a stepchild than in our society, with its heterogeneity of culture patterns and its wide range of personality types.

In some areas children are considered group children and are not the private property of their biological parents. They belong to the group and the group as a whole is responsible for them. Under such a system blood ties are not considered highly important. In fact, biological kinship relations are all but erased where the practice of exchanging children, either immediately after birth or later, is followed. In such situations a steprelationship brings no new problems, so there is slight opportunity for conflicts to arise if a stepmother appears on the scene. In the main, it may be said that the lot of the stepmother in most non-Western cultures is better than it is in our culture. If the status of the stepmother depended on the biological factor as Wulffen, Wittels, and Deutsch would have us believe, then there should be very little difference between situations in any of the cultures, because the biological differences between the various groups are insignificant. We must conclude, then, that the position of the stepmother depends on the cultural milieu in which she finds herself.

It seems that in our society a stepmother must be exceptional before she is considered good. The stereotype of the stepmother presents her as being inconsiderate and lacking in motherliness. Then, when a woman goes through a marriage ceremony and becomes a stepmother, she is automatically placed in a definite category which defines and characterizes her. We define her first and then make her fit the definition. We forget all that the psychologists and educators have taught us about individual differences; we make no realistic examination of the total personality concerned but react to the generalized category, even though it does not accord with actuality. This hangs a millstone about the neck of the stepmother and makes her role an exceedingly difficult one. Rarely does a foster mother have any such onus heaped upon her; she is usually considered kind and motherly. A comment on an adopted child was heard recently: "Isn't Robert a fortunate child to have such a home!" It is usually assumed that adoptive parents will be good. The stepmother stereotype, on the other hand, holds such sway that it distorts the judgment of old and young. A young woman said of herself: "When I was a little girl, if my parents disciplined me, I would say that they were stepparents because real parents would not treat me that way." A woman must be a first-rate diplomat to succeed at the job of being a stepmother.

Nevertheless, we see on every hand instances where the steprelationship has worked out in the best way possible, and in many instances the coming of a stepparent has brought a decided improvement. The newspapers, however, do not publicize such cases. We need not stretch our imaginations far to conclude that the stepmother provided a better home for two children concerning whom their mother said after the divorce that she did not want "either of them damned children."

Even under the most favorable circumstances, however, the role of the stepmother is a difficult one. When childless persons marry, the bride has to make adjustments to her husband and, at times, to some in-laws. When the marriage makes her a stepmother, however, she must adjust to a husband who may be different in the home from what he was in courtship, because the children's reaction to their new mother may bring unforeseen changes in him. The in-law situation may be more highly problematical because of deeply interested maternal grandparents who may resent her assumption of the place left vacant by the death of their daughter. She must adjust to children who have grown accustomed to the care of another. She may come with the best of intentions to be a good mother, but at the very outset some seemingly insignificant matter may give the new relationship a bad beginning. The stepmother may do something no worse than the real mother would do, but, due to the stepmother stereotype, the child reacts more unfavorably to her than he would have to his own mother. A stepmother may be of high grade and the children may be well-mannered, but still they will not adjust to each other, simply because the stepmother is different from the real mother. The children, accustomed to their own mother, ordinarily do not even notice little episodes that acquire special significance when a stepmother is involved.

Five · The Stepchild *

WILLIAM C. SMITH
Sociologist, Linfield College

THE idea prevailing in folklore is that in the end retributive justice is meted out to the cruel stepmother, while the stepdaughter, despite harsh treatment, emerges from the ordeal with angelic whiteness. Facts, however, do not support these generalizations.

We cannot accept the traditional ideas relative to the stepmother, neither can we concur in those relative to the stepchildren. Contrary to the folk-tales, not all stepdaughters, like Cinderella, marry charming princes and live happily ever after. Many stepchildren are exceedingly unhappy, many develop warped personalities, and many become delinquent.

As yet there is no adequate statistical measure of the number of step-relatives in our population. Some inadequate samples indicate that about six per cent of children have step-parents. It would seem that this group is sufficiently large to merit some attention.

Basically the family is an agency devoted to the care and sociali-

* Excerpts from the *American Sociological Review*, 1945, 10: 237–242, by permission of the author and the editor.

zation of children. It does not seem, however, that the child's biological parents need necessarily be included in the family circle.
Psychological bonds may be close and intimate even where the
physical relationship is lacking. It appears to be of paramount importance for the child to be on sympathetic and confidential relations with the adults in his immediate world. All other things being
equal, however, the child in the home with an unbroken family
structure usually is most advantageously situated. When a break
comes, either through death or divorce, the child is subjected to an
emotional upheaval which may have far-reaching results. Many attempt to reorganize the broken homes through the introduction of
a substitute parent. How well, we may ask, does the family with a
step-parent succeed in carrying out its basic functions so far as the
children are concerned? Do any warped personalities come out of
this situation or are they all well balanced and wholesome?

The step-relationship seems to be a factor in juvenile delinquency. Some researchers have presented data which make it appear that the presence of a step-parent in the home is in some way
related to juvenile delinquency. But we must not be dogmatic in
our conclusions. We cannot be sure to what extent a step-parent in
the home is in itself a factor contributing directly to juvenile delinquency. On the basis of a number of studies it would appear that
there is no positive correlation between family structure and the
behavior of children. The *character* of parent or step-parent is of
greater consequence than his presence or absence in the home. It
is the subtler aspects of family life—the attitudes and personal relationships—rather than the formal and external aspects which are
significant.

Many children must make one or more intermediate adjustments
in the period between the break-up of the first and the establishment of a second home. A child may be under the care of housekeepers or live with relatives to whom attachments may develop
because of which adjustment to the new home becomes the more
difficult. One girl resented the coming of a stepmother because a
housekeeper whom she liked was thus crowded out. When a child
has to deal with a succession of strange housekeepers, who know
little and care less about directing him in his habit formation, he
resents having the accustomed inconsistency disturbed by a stepmother who tries to bring order out of chaos. One boy interpreted
his stepmother's efforts at discipline as an interference which amply
justified his belief that stepmothers, in general, were mean and
cruel.

Frequently children live with grandparents by whom they are
pampered. After living with an overindulgent grandmother, the
pampered child will resent any restrictions imposed by a stepmother.

In addition to the mind poisoning by folktales and gossip, there is the interference by relatives. One grandmother told her grandson that his stepmother was not a good mother and that he could come to her whenever he wished to do so. Another boy would hear these words from his grandmother, "Oh, you poor unfortunate child! How you must miss your own dear mother!" In such situations, the step-mother may readily develop a dislike, even a hatred, for the grand-mother and this may react unfavorably on the child.

When a divorced parent, who has custody of the children, re-marries, the other parent often schemes to turn the children against both the ex-mate and the step-parent.

Oftentimes the departed parent is idealized and the substitute parent cannot possibly measure up to this standard. At times when the father dies or leaves while the child is a mere infant with no memory of the parent, if things do not go well at home, the child builds up an ideal parent and projects that construct upon the ab-sent one. It is not surprising that a child idealizes his departed parent, for usually he has an unequal chance of having a second home as good as the first one. If his mother has died and there are several children, the father needs a housekeeper, but his range of choice is more limited than at the time of his first marriage—pro-spective wives hesitate about assuming responsibility for someone else's children. Because of this the second wife may come from a lower social stratum than the first and so not be readily accepted by the children.

The second marriage is often a business proposition; help is needed in caring for the children. But desirable caretakers are not numerous, and frequently a widower with children finds a widow who has children of her own who need a father. This, then, becomes more a merger than a marriage. The situation becomes increasingly complex where there are *his* children, *her* children, and *their* chil-dren.

The introduction of a substitute parent into a home may become a serious liability to the child, unless the new parent is able to win his confidence and respect without, at the same time, interfering with the child's relation to his real parent.

It behooves us to be guarded when drawing conclusions relative to the behavior of the stepchild because there are so many com-plicating factors in the situation. The child's age, for instance, must be taken into consideration in any attempt to account for his atti-tudes. An infant will make adjustments to a stepmother more read-ily than an adolescent. "I was only a year or two old," wrote a college girl, "when mother remarried and I grew up thinking Daddy Ben was my real father. I loved Daddy Ben. He was always good to me." But age alone does not tell the whole story. One girl who acquired her stepmother at the age of three and one-half years became bitter against her. Probably her six older sisters had con-siderable influence over her.

By way of conclusion, we may state that the stepchild has all the problems of any other child and usually has them in larger dosages. In addition he has problems which stem directly from the step-relationship as it manifests itself in our modern, urban culture. A number of stepchildren have become delinquent and criminal but, in many instances, on the basis of available data, no part of it can be charged to the step-relationship. There are, also, conditions conducive to delinquency in homes with unbroken family structures. Parallel situations are found in "split homes" where there is good and sufficient cause for delinquency wholly apart from the step-relationship. There are, however, factors in the home with a step-parent which are more problematical than in other homes. There is, for instance, a greater incidence of emotional insecurity with its disorganizing influence. Favoritism is often found in an unbroken and so-called normal home, but the home with a substitute parent is particularly conducive to the expression of partiality. Some children are unwanted by one or both parents, but the probability of being an unwanted child in a home with a step-parent is even greater. Problems of discipline are not absent from unbroken homes, but usually they are attended by more complicating factors in the "split home." Nevertheless, many stepchildren have made adjustments which are no less wholesome than those of children in unbroken homes. In some instances, the coming of a step-parent has been to the advantage of the child, for the new parent has been able to enter into a more sympathetic intimacy with the child than his own parent.

Six · Excessive Drinking and its Relationship to Marriage

ROBERT STRAUS
Sociologist, Section on Alcohol Studies
Yale University

The effects of excessive drinking upon the family was one of the arguments used by prohibitionists to bring about prohibition. Yale University, through its section on Alcohol Studies of the Laboratory of Applied Physiology, is pioneering in the scientific study of alcohol and the effects of its use. The selection below * contains some of the conclusions of the Yale research.

* Reprinted from *Marriage and Family Living*, 1950, 12: 79–83, by permission of the author and editor.

THE relationship between excessive drinking and the marital association will be considered in terms of a three point thesis. It will be shown first that excessive drinking and particularly characteristics which are usually present in the excessive drinker tend to preclude marriage; second, that married life and excessive drinking are incompatible; and third, that the destruction or disruption of the marital association frequently results in the onset of excessive drinking. Finally, some implications which may prove useful to the marriage counselor will be suggested.

We must differentiate between the ordinary moderate user of alcoholic beverages and the excessive or problem drinker. There are in the United States today approximately 65 million adult persons who are users of alcoholic beverages. The vast majority of these are moderate users, who drink because it is customary for them to do so. Whereas these moderate drinkers will, for the most part, stoutly defend their right to drink when they please, alcohol for them presents no particular problem. With the exceptions to be noted below, they control the amount which they drink and if alcohol were to be taken away from them their reaction would be resentment more than a craving for a physical or mental necessity.

Unfortunately, among these 65 million users of alcoholic beverages there are some four million who drink not in moderation but to excess, and for whom drinking constitutes a very serious problem. In speaking of excessive drinking, the intention is not to imply a specific amount which represents excess quantity, but rather that amount which for any particular individual leads to problems such as physical injury, arrest, loss of job, marital discord, or other maladjustments of a social, physiological, or psychological nature.

The four million drinkers who constitute America's problem drinking population are not all alcohol addicts, nor does their drinking stem from any single cause or type of causes but rather from a variety of etiological factors. Perhaps three types should be distinguished because of basic differences in motivation or in overall characteristics. In one type uncontrolled drinking is accompanied by severe psychological or personality dysfunction, by a variety of physiological disorders, by obvious maladjustment to the social environment, or by a combination of these factors.

A second type of problem drinker may display fairly normal outward responses, get along well with his family and friends, hold a good job, and appear essentially as a well-oriented member of society, and yet still suffer from periodic uncontrolled drinking.

A third type, sometimes called the social misfit drinker, may drink excessively to the extent that it leads to all sorts of difficulty and yet may be perfectly capable of controlling the frequency or amount of consumption. In this category we find many of the drifters who populate our missions and jails, and others with a low level of intelligence or ambition. They are people who find themselves so limited in their sources of gratification or so alienated from the fast moving society around them that they seek a pleasant form of escape through alcoholic intoxication. These social misfit drinkers do not drink because they are compelled to do so, but rather because they want to.

The true alcohol addict is characterized by the fact that although he may possess a variety of very fine traits which endear him to his family and friends and make him a potentially productive and respected citizen, he is suffering from a compulsion to drink. He is driven by his compulsion to repeated states of inebriation despite the fact that he is fully aware that his drinking is destroying all that he values in life. In addition he can no longer drink moderately. It is said that the alcoholic has no terminal facilities for his drinking, for one or two drinks almost invariably lead to a full-fledged bender. He is in the sad position where, despite his desire to stop, he finds that he cannot alone help himself. His position is further complicated by the fact that his drinking behavior cannot as yet be predicted and thus preventive measures are severely restricted. If it were possible to tell in advance just what characteristics predispose an individual to alcohol addiction, the field of preventive therapy would become well defined. Predisposed persons could be made aware of the impending danger before they become so victimized that they are powerless to change the course of their drinking behavior. Although such predictive factors have not yet been isolated it is possible to describe certain psychological and sociological factors which characterize persons who seem more likely than others to become alcohol addicts. The isolation of identifying physiological factors is the object of considerable research now under way. While prospects of success are promising, the existence of a physiological basis for alcohol addiction has not yet been determined.

In approaching the identification of persons who may become problem drinkers from the psychological viewpoint, it is appropriate to describe an experiment conducted by Massermann in which a group of cats were first taught to associate the presence of food and the act of eating with an electric light and with buttons which they learned to press to produce the light. After the cats had become well conditioned to these processes, the experimenter introduced a complicating factor in the form of an electric shock or an air blast which greeted their button pushing and acted as a block to their enjoyment of food. After repeated punishment and frustration, the cats refused to push the buttons or to eat food in their cages. They even came to associate the painful air-blast so closely with food that they refused to eat under any circumstances. The cats had become what may be called neurotic; they were victims of a conflict—a conflict between a hunger drive and a drive to avoid pain. And this conflict which they could not themselves resolve acted to paralyze their entire behavior pattern. What should have meant a normal pleasant experience had become associated, instead, with a mysterious pain.

Massermann then gave the cats some alcohol by injection and found that when mildly intoxicated the cats would hop around, eat, and push light switches. When the effects of the alcohol had worn off they lapsed into their apathetic condition, refused to eat, and the effects of their conflict were again evident. Next, the cats were introduced to milk containing alcohol and they learned to value it to a point where plain milk was completely rejected. As long as they were mildly intoxicated the difficulties of their hunger pain conflict were not manifested, but when the effects of alcohol were not present they again lapsed into inactivity.

The cats had thus become dependent upon alcohol intoxication; they had become addicted to alcohol; they had come to feel that they needed the alcohol in order to go on facing life. As a final stage of the experiment, the cats were retrained so that the act of eating was no longer associated with an air blast or shock, and when this reconditioning had taken place they reverted to an earlier demonstrated dislike of the alcohol milk mixture. That is, their conflicts were resolved and they were rehabilitated from their alcohol addiction.

With certain elaboration and refinement, this is the story of why men and women become addicted to alcohol too.

Like the frustrated cats, human beings today find themselves in a highly complicated society. Life is competitive and impersonal. Mistakes are easy, and everyone makes his share. There is keen competition with respect to employment, sexual satisfaction, social position and prestige. In everyone, mistakes and wounds suffered in social living produce a certain amount of anxiety, tension, frustration, and guilt. Yet, despite these difficulties most people manage to make a fairly satisfactory working compromise with life.

Certain individuals, however, are not so fortunate. For them, these anxieties, tensions, frustrations, and guilt feelings are like the blast from the air hose or the electric shock to Massermann's cats. Whenever they try to satisfy ordinary needs, they feel pain. Some of these people suffer from unreasonable frustrations in every sort of situation. At home, at work, in schools, in the church, these individuals are constantly suffering tension, embarrassment, and distress. Some of them try to hide their distraught condition, others are unaware that anything particular is wrong. They just know that life is one painful experience after another, and that they seem to live in constant friction with the world. These people are maladjusted; like the frustrated cats who couldn't resolve their conflicts between hunger and pain, these people are neurotic.

To avoid the charge of oversimplification in comparing neurotic humans with cats in which a neurosis-producing conflict is conditioned by laboratory experiment, it should be pointed out that cats, of course, have no means of realizing their problem or of making an intellectual or an emotional effort to adjust their difficulties. Likewise, recourse to alcohol for the cats does not involve family, marital, employment, legal, or other difficulties.

However, just as the neurotic cats were conditioned to associate their basic need of hunger with pain, so neurotic human beings associate with pain such essential human needs as companionship, associating with others, giving and receiving affection and many more.

Since alcohol is basically a depressant and an anesthesia, its immediate effects on the human organism are to relieve anxieties, and fears, and to alleviate the pains of tension and conflict. It also acts to depress inhibitions of certain forms of socially disapproved behavior, thus allowing the individual to release his pentup aggressions or repressed desires. For the neurotic individual who fears associations with other people—who detaches himself from society —alcohol can be used as a means of either reinforcing this detachment (that is, without alcohol he is lonely and needs people, but with it he can afford to become morose and solitary) or it can help him to break through this detachment (that is, it depresses his inhibitions against associating with others and allows him to mingle freely without feeling the pains of anxiety). Alcohol may also provide temporary solutions for conflict by repressing one of the conflicting elements. For the neurotic who feels the need for self-aggrandizement, alcohol allows him to act the part of his self image. No difficulty is insurmountable for him. He makes great claims on society and on himself; he feels that he is entitled to anything he asks. It is behavior such as this which tends to make the alcoholic and his demands almost impossible for others to live with. They also make it hard for him to live with himself, for since his impossible demands cannot be met, he constantly feels that he is abused, hurt, disappointed, and indignant. He goes around with a tremendous feeling of hostility and resentment. Without alcohol he cannot express these hostilities because of his need for love and affection from others. When under the influence, however, he need no longer repress them.

At this point it should be stressed that neurosis is itself merely a matter of degree. We live in a highly complex society in which all individuals are faced with a wide variety of conflicting situations at all times. The neurotic is the person who more than others finds it difficult to resolve these conflicts and who in his attempts to do so hits upon pseudo-solutions which in themselves serve merely to increase the neurotic anxieties and pain.

Of course, not all neurotic persons become alcoholics, but it can be said that it is very unlikely that the well-balanced, well-integrated personality will become a compulsive drinker, while it is not unlikely that the individual who suffers from deep neurotic conflict and anxiety may, upon the introduction of alcohol, find in it one of those pseudo-solutions which in the end can have no other effect than to increase his neurotic pain.

Turning now to a sociological consideration, a broad categorization which fits most alcoholics is that of undersocialization. Undersocialization can be defined as a syndrome which includes a wide variety of atypical conditions and relationships with normal society. Usually, undersocialization is the result of a failure to adjust to normal social ways and this, in turn, is frequently the result of a deficient process of socialization. The concept, socialization, describes the conditioning of the individual to the ways of society, including expected or desirable behavior and social taboos and prohibitions—in other words, the ways of getting along with people and of sharing social experiences. Deficiently socialized persons or desocialized persons are usually deprived of the opportunity of sharing experiences with others, of belonging to social groups and participating in social activities. They are also deprived of such important personal needs as affection, prestige, the feeling of security, and the rewarding aspects of identifying with others. The satisfaction of these needs is usually achieved only through association with other people. Because they have not learned the ways of society, undersocialized persons are insecure, and acts of sharing become distasteful, difficult, and even dangerous for them. For this reason they often seek to avoid such associations as are normally found in the family, in schools, in employment situations, in church participation, and in community life.

Thus, going hand in hand with neurotic anxieties, we find that the alcoholic, either preceding or directly resulting from his alcoholic condition, is a person who is isolated from the normal channels of social intercourse. People who are deficient in their learned ways of getting along with others or who forget some of these techniques appear more apt to become alcoholics than individuals who are well integrated in their social environment.

It should be stressed at this point that neurotic conflict and undersocialization are by no means isolated entities. As a matter of fact, one would never expect to find one condition present without some degree of the other. On the one hand, the insecurity, the fears and anxieties which accompany neurosis tend to preclude normal social relationships, thus isolating the individual from institutional participation. On the other hand, the individual who has never learned or has forgotten the techniques for sharing social experiences, getting along with others, giving and receiving affection and the like, will be faced with severe anxieties over his inadequacy for meeting social situations in ways which will be socially acceptable.

Now that we have outlined certain broad characteristics for persons who can be said to be more likely than others to become alcohol addicts, we are ready to consider these in the light of the contemporary status of the institution of marriage in America.

During the last century the function of the marital institution has undergone revolutionary change with development of a more specialized society. Economic, governmental, educational, religious, and recreational institutions have all expanded greatly with the assumption of functions formerly assigned to the family. Accompanying specialization, there has been a growing tendency toward impersonalization in all of these institutions except the family. The result has been that a primary function of the American family has come to be the satisfaction of such personality needs of the individual members as affection, prestige, self-respect, and sexual expression. The family is also the seat of personality development and of socialization. Thus, the individual who comes from the parental family bearing characteristics of neurotic personality or social isolation which make him prone for becoming an excessive drinker is likewise ill equipped for the sharing of interpersonal relationships and the close reciprocal intimacies demanded in the marital family.

We can now consider the three-point thesis mentioned at the beginning of this paper. Point one of the thesis suggested that the same characteristics which make the individual prone to excessive drinking also tend to preclude marriage. Point two suggested that these characteristics are incompatible with the marriage association.

Two general characteristics of the excessive drinker, neurotic anxiety and undersocialization, have been described. To the neurotic, undersocialized individual whose psychological and sociological maladjustments may manifest themselves in a variety of emotional and behavioral instabilities and abnormalities the association of marriage with its severe demands on intimate, reciprocal personal relationships and on the sharing of emotional and social needs and gratifications seems most foreboding, repulsive, and even dangerous. He is poorly equipped on both the psychological and the social level for acts of sharing and for participation in group experiences. As a result, he will carefully avoid any or all situations which demand such sharing. He will particularly avoid marriage and, if he should marry, the marital association with its uncompromising demands for giving of the self will most likely prove so intolerable to him that, consciously or unconsciously, he will seek its dissolution. Hostility toward the incompatibilities of marriage may even result in the excessive use of alcohol as an expression of aggression toward the uncomfortable state of marriage or toward the marital partner whom he probably will blame for his condition.

The considerations just suggested can now be subjected to empirical examination by considering data dealing with marital status taken from two studies [1] which have been made of particular categories of excessive drinkers and expectancy data for comparable groups of the general population.

Table 1 indicates by percentage distribution the observed marital status of a group of 1,223 arrested inebriates and the expected distribution for comparable members of the general population.

TABLE 1. MARITAL STATUS OF 1,223 ARRESTED INEBRIATES

Observed (%)		Expectancy (%)
53.1	Single	19.6
22.9	Married	71.9
11.5	Separated	3.5
7.5	Divorced	1.2
5.0	Widowed	3.8

Here it is seen that while 80 per cent of the general population group had married, only 47 per cent of the arrested inebriates had ever entered into a marital relationship; while 72 per cent of the general population group were still married and living with their wives, only 23 per cent of the inebriates had kept their marriages intact. In Table 2 similar comparisons are made between a group of 203 homeless men, of whom 177 were excessive drinkers, and a comparable general population group.

Here the discrepancies are even sharper than those for the arrested inebriates. Fifty-five per cent of the homeless men had remained single as compared with an expectancy of 15 per cent. As might be suspected, only one man in the homeless group had a

TABLE 2. MARITAL STATUS OF 203 ITINERANTS *

Observed (%)		Expectancy (%)
55.6	Single	15.0
0.5	Married	74.9
16.8	Separated	3.9
13.8	Divorced	1.0
13.3	Widowed	5.2

* Seven of the men were reported as non-users of alcoholic beverages, 17 as moderate users, the drinking habits of 2 were unknown, and the remaining 177 were classified as excessive drinkers.

marriage which could still be called intact as compared with a normal expectancy of 75 per cent.

Tables 3 and 4 indicate comparative percentage distributions of

[1] Bacon. "Inebriety, Social Integration and Marriage." *Quarterly Journal of Studies on Alcohol*, 1945, and Straus. "Alcohol and the Homeless Man." *Quarterly Journal of Studies on Alcohol*, 7: 360–404, December, 1946.

marital status for only those men in each group who had ever been married.

TABLE 3. PRESENT MARITAL STATUS OF 574 ARRESTED INEBRIATES
WHO HAD MARRIED

Observed (%)		Expectancy (%)
48.8	Married	89.4
24.6	Separated	4.4
16.0	Divorced	1.4
10.6	Widowed	4.8

TABLE 4. PRESENT MARITAL STATUS OF 90 HOMELESS MEN WHO
HAD MARRIED

Observed (%)		Expectancy (%)
1.1	Married	88.0
37.8	Separated	4.6
31.1	Divorced	1.2
30.0	Widowed	6.2

Here the factor of marital incompatibility comes into sharper focus. It is seen that the arrested inebriates were divorced 12 times and separated 6 times as often as expected, while the homeless men were divorced 25 times and separated 8 times as often as expected.

An additional phenomenon demonstrated by these data is not related to the preclusion of marriage or incompatibility in marriage but rather to the third part of our introductory thesis (e.g., that disruption or destruction of the marital association frequently results in the onset of excessive drinking). It is seen in Tables 3 and 4 that the drinking groups exceed the expectancy in incidence of widowhood by ratios of over 2 to 1 for the arrested inebriates and of nearly 5 to 1 for the homeless men.

In seeking an explanation for this relationship, we must again consider the function of the marital association in fulfilling intimate personal needs. Life outside the family has in many instances become so impersonal that there are many marriages in which the partners, particularly those who are not too emotionally stable to begin with, become abnormally dependent upon each other for emotional security, and for stimulation and cues to behavior. Such persons develop few interests outside the home and lose touch with techniques for making or gaining gratification from associational ties. Upon the sudden death of or sudden separation from the partner around whom the whole life pattern has become centered, the survivor finds himself disoriented and isolated both socially and emotionally at a time in life when there are few opportunities and incentives for forming new interpersonal relationships and group associations. Life imposes a meaningless and drab existence for such an individual, and, should he be introduced to alcohol, the chances are not remote that he would find it a gratifying form of obliteration or a helpful crutch.

In conclusion I would like to suggest an implication contained in the thesis and the characteristics which have just been described. It is an important implication not only for the marriage counselor and for all others concerned with the conservation of marriage and the family but also for the public at large, since public opinion frequently plays an important part in the eventual interpretation and disposition of such situations.

It is a human failing in approaching problem situations of all kinds to think in terms of single cause and effect relationships which lead to hasty deductions concerning etiology. In the analysis of situations in which marital discord and excessive drinking both appear, there is and has been a great tendency to concentrate attention on determining whether the excessive drinker became addicted to alcohol as a result of an unbearable marital situation or whether the marital relationship has "gone on the rocks" because of excessive drinking by one of the partners, and to blame one situation on the other.

Excessive drinking is a spectacular factor of behavior; it is not easily concealed and it is not infrequently present along with marital discord. We have tried to show that whereas one condition may intensify the other, excessive drinking and marital incompatibility are in reality both manifestations of the same type of underlying psychological and sociological abnormality. The widower who becomes an alcoholic appears on the surface to have turned to excessive drinking as a means of burying his sorrow, when in reality his drinking is more likely to be a form of pseudo-adjustment to a situation caused by an emotional overdependence on his late wife for which he can find no substitute through available, socially accepted channels of behavior. The bachelorhood of the excessive drinker who never married may well be blamed on his drinking and the fact that "No decent girl would want him," whereas if the truth were known a good many fine girls may have longed for a chance to marry him (each thinking, of course, that she could reform him). He, on the other hand, may have avoided matrimony for the very same underlying reasons that he drinks to excess. In a similar vein the large number of divorces and separations which are attributed to excessive drinking are no more the result of this single cause than the problem drinking of many married persons is the result of incompatibility with the marital partner. In each case, one must look to refined levels of behavior and realize that the relationship of excessive drinking to problems of marital association is almost invariably one of multiple joint causation and most rarely one of direct cause and effect.

Seven · *War and the Family*

JAMES H. S. BOSSARD
Sociologist, University of Pennsylvania

Throughout history war has been a family disorgan-izer and a cause of family crises. The next reading * explores effects of war upon family life in the past as well as in modern times.

STUDIES of the effects of war have concerned them-selves in the past chiefly with its economic and political conse-quences, somewhat less with its social reverberations, and to a rather minor extent with its meaning for the family. This paper deals with this last named, relatively neglected, relationship.

PRELIMINARY CONSIDERATIONS

Four considerations should be noted by way of preface. *1. The first of these is the recurrence of war.* For centuries, among most peoples, war has been a customary pursuit, as normal a condition as that of peace. Warfare was both constant and inevitable among tribes subsisting upon the free products of nature. The role of con-quest was predominant in the ancient world. War for the Greeks was a business enterprise, it existed by "nature," peace had to be established by special treaty. To Rome, an inland city, war was the only possible form of business expansion. The Germanic tribes glorified war with naive directness while Rome was busy cloaking her squabbles with plausible pretexts. Under feudalism, war was the respectable method of business investment. For centuries, a war with France was the only method by which an English gentleman could become rich. The division of booty was like the contemporary declaration of dividends. In the period of the origins of nationality, war was the established mechanism of nation making. Nations are seldom born except in the travail of battle. The commercial wars of the 17th and 18th centuries were incidental costs of the legiti-mate maintenance and pursuit of trade.

Obviously, our problem must be considered in the lengthened perspective of the centuries, which reveals both the frequency and the persistence of war. Modern students must guard against the kind of zealous mistake which advocates of prohibition made a quarter of a century ago: they must not prove too much. If alcohol

* Excerpts from the *American Sociological Review*, 1941, 6: 330–344, by permission of the author and the *American Sociological Review*.

were as destructive as its foes of that era alleged, the human race
would have drunk itself into a state of inebriate impotence long
ago; similarly, if war were so destructive of family life as some
modern students contend, mankind could not have survived its own
history.

2. *The Specificity of the Problem.* All social problems are specific
—as to time, place, and particular combination of circumstances.
In turning, then, to the effects of war upon the family, one asks:
the effects of what war, in which country, upon what kind of
family?

(a) Each war is peculiar to itself and its meaning for family life
in its most concrete and significant aspects will vary with its dis-
tinguishing features. Some wars are fought with large armies on
land; some, with far-flung navies at sea. One war involves danger
to large proportions of the population; another, extensive equipment with relatively few persons engaged in actual combat. The
World War of 1914-1918 was a war of men, organized in large
armies, with an unbelievably high casualty rate; World War II was
a war of machines, of elaborate equipment, and with relatively low
casualty rate. There have been wars, fought chiefly between armies;
there are wars which are totalitarian. Some wars are fought chiefly
in terms of blockade, and counter blockade, with resultant malnu-
trition and an aftermath of widespread disease; others are fought in
part in psychological terms, with a strategy of terror and deception.
Finally, one might distinguish between wars in which the chief
losses are from bullets and those where the human costs take the
form of large losses in military and civilian populations because of
disease. The British in the Crimea lost twenty-five times more men
from disease than from bullets. By the end of the Thirty Years War,
one-third of the population of the Palatinate had succumbed.

(b) The effects of war vary obviously from one country to another, dependent upon the role it plays and the fate it meets. The
effects of war upon the family in an invaded Poland differ from
those in a victorious Germany.

(c) Finally, what war means to the family depends upon the
family. What is the effect upon new families, i.e., families formed
as the war begins or during its continuance? Over against these are
older, established families, where the husband or son is withdrawn
for military service. There is the unhappy family, in which war
offers an honorable and socially acceptable way out of a difficult,
and often seemingly hopeless, situation. Over against such cases are
those families which may be termed happy, as well as that large
number in which the emotional tone of the relationship is, figuratively speaking, neither black nor white, but shows intermediate
shades of indefinite gray.

3. *Direct and Derivate Effects.* War, like all major social changes,
has its immediate, direct effects and its subsequent, derivative

effects. The distinction is an important one, and emphasizes again the necessity of maintaining a long-range point of view. By way of example, it is interesting to contemplate in the objective retrospect of the centuries, the chain of consequences of the Punic Wars in the third century B. C. First, for the thirty or more years of actual warfare, a large proportion of able-bodied Romans saw service in the field. Husbands were away from home years at a time.

As a consequence, the management of estates and households devolved upon their wives, many women receiving a training in self-reliance and efficiency in responsible position. This in turn led such women to submit with ill grace to the restrictions in their daily lives and interests that their husbands imposed upon them on their return from the wars. Before long, the *Manus,* i.e., the power of the Roman husband over his wife, came to be indicted by these women as a tyranny. After the second Punic War, the controversy was compromised, and the practice of marriage without *Manus* grew up. It was this sad circumstance which led the elder Cato to remark: "We Romans rule over all men, and our wives rule over us."

But the end is not yet. In due time, the Roman matrons "deliberately sought to become learned and clever." In the age of Cicero, a band of brilliant and often unscrupulous women were not only versed in the learning of their time, but became also a power in politics.

4. "Multiple Effects." The effects of war upon the family are numerous and varied. Modern students speak of the "multiple effects" of important social changes. Still continuing with the Punic Wars, one can see clearly, in the perspective of more than two thousand years, the range and diversity of consequences of war for the family. As a result of the triumph over Carthage, many Romans became wealthy. This made fathers unwilling to release their control over their daughters and their dowries. Free marriages grew up without the *Manus* and with the girl remaining under the control of her family. Women retained their own incomes. With financial independence came demands for other privileges and rights. The marriage rate began to decline. Roman men resented the attitude of women. "Why have I not a rich wife?" asks the poet Martial, "Because I do not wish to be my wife's maid." Also, the wars of conquest brought many subject women into the Empire. Many of these were attractive. Mistresses were easy to obtain. The birth rate began to decline. Children involved too irrevocable a tie-up between a man and his wife. Divorce became popular and easy. By the time of the Augustan age, its frequency had attained the proportions of a public scandal. Seneca says that the women of his day counted their years not by consuls but by husbands, and Juvenal charges some women with divorcing their husbands before the marriage garlands had faded on the lintels.

WAR AND THE FORMATION OF NEW FAMILIES

Most obvious are the effects of war upon the formation of new families. Four such effects are noted. (1) When war becomes imminent, an immediate effect is the acceleration of the marriage rate. Such acceleration is usually temporary. Some marriages already planned are moved forward; others indicate cautious young men choosing the lesser danger of matrimony. The prospect of conscription acts like a shot in the arm of Dan Cupid. The number of marriage licenses issued in August, 1940, in New York City, for example, was more than 50 percent higher than for the same months in the preceding year.

(2) Following this preliminary flurry, the marriage rate falls during war periods: first, because it takes marriageable males of susceptible years out of circulation; second, it creates uncertainty and insecurity not favorable to the assumption of supposedly life-long obligations. Marriage rates fell markedly during the first World War, in France, for example, from 7.7 to 2.3. On the whole, the drop was most pronounced in the invaded countries, less in those that were not, least in nearby neutral countries. When the war was over, there was a swift recovery in the marriage rate: in France from 4.8 in 1917 to 16.0 in 1920. The rebound was similarly striking in other belligerent countries. Comparing the rates for the five years after the war with those prevailing before 1914, it is significant to note that the postwar excess more than counterbalanced the losses of the war years. War, then, tends to postpone marriage. The marriage rate apparently is a relatively resilient demographic characteristic.

(3) War increases the relative number of hasty and ill-advised marriages. Such marriages are always occurring. Gin, coincidence, glandular disturbances, and many other factors are involved. In every society, there are those persons who act with unreasoned impulsiveness, even in regard to the major problems of their lives; the highly charged emotional atmosphere which war engenders increases both the number of such persons and the scope of their irrational behavior. After World War I, one heard a great deal about war marriages, and the term came to carry with it a sort of left-handed justification for whatever happened. They were marriages that were consummated under the emotional excitement and the abnormal conditions of the war period and which in most cases would not have been made under normal circumstances.

(4) Marry-and-run marriages constitute another form of war phenomena; like hit-and-run accidents, they often are rather tragic occurrences. By marry-and-run marriages are meant those legal weddings which are not followed by continuing cohabitation. The couple marry. After a day, a week or two together, they separate, to resume the accustomed tenor of their respective ways. In war

time, it is usually at the call of military duty that their life together is terminated. Now the essential danger in such marriages is that the couple do not have the customary opportunity to make the gradual unbroken transition from romantic bliss to prosaic adjustment which is the basis of continued domestic accord. Happiness in marriage, according to the experts, is an achievement, not a discovery. It comes as a by-product to successful experience in living together. Beginning their life together on the romantic level, and with the help of the romantic aura, married couples learn to compromise as they cohabit. It is this normal process which is lacking in marry-and-run marriages. The romantic glow may fade, or be dimmed, during the separation, while each shares different life experiences. When, as, and if, they unite later, and they do not always do so, there are shadows in their relationships which the glow of the honeymoon could have dissolved.

EFFECTS OF WAR UPON ESTABLISHED FAMILIES

1. War separates for uncertain periods of time the members of families already established. Married men rally or are called to the colors, persons of all ages and both sexes leave their accustomed homes to engage in some activity tributary to war. The basic fact is that of separation under the psychological conditions which war engenders. (a) There are two overshadowing aspects of such separations. One is that between parent and child, usually in times past, between father and child. This is always a serious matter of far reaching consequences. The absence of the father means the loss of his contribution, whatever it may be, to the continuing personality development of his child. It means, particularly in many families, the removal of the chief disciplinarian. This loss comes at a time when the other members of the family, particularly the mother, are already disturbed and preoccupied. Students of the effects of the World War, 1914–1918, both in England and in Germany, refer repeatedly to the lack of discipline of children during the war years, due to the absence of the father and the preoccupation of the mother and other adults in the family. The general atmosphere in many families was one of hysteria and sentimentality, which obviously is not favorable for a rigorous inculcation of the group mores nor of the lesser conventions. At any rate, what discipline and training there are in many homes are wholly in the hands of the women of the household, thus carrying forward that feminization of child rearing which many students have noted in modern times.

(b) The other outstanding aspect of family separation during war is between husband and wife. This customarily means the wife stays in the home. The result of this is the break-up of a crystallized relationship, thus creating for both the problem of adjusting to a new nonfamily pattern of living for the time being. The term *mobility of the mores* is suggested to identify the process of the revaluation of the moral code which takes place when persons change their place or their status. We shall concern ourselves first with the husband who is withdrawn from his civilian setting, taken to a camp, and made into a soldier for the time being.

One of the basic elements in all wars is their effect upon the mores of the soldier who is withdrawn from civilian life. Let us examine this in terms of process. First he is removed from his primary groups—family, neighborhood, church—with their controls over his conduct. He shakes off, as it were, his identification with the erstwhile moral pattern. He goes into the army and thus achieves a certain anonymity. He loses his identification with the groups he has known. He enters a group in which there is occupational and psychological homogeneity. His new buddies are all engaged in the same pursuits, unusual, stirring, and with a possible rendezvous with danger or death at the end.

THE SOLDIER AND THE INGROUP

"You are in the army now." It is a man's world in which old-time and feminine controls are gone, at least for the moment. All soldiers are in the same boat. To drink, to engage in amours, is to behave as the group does. It is traditional for the soldiers to "cut loose." What the sociologists call an ingroup has come into being. No disgrace is involved in the assumption of certain liberties. A soldier's new ingroup approves, for the time being, new forms of conduct.

There are various factors which make for new patterns of conduct for this ingroup. Army life is rigid. It controls you, even your thinking, much of the time. It is a life of routine. When there is temporary release from the schedule, various vagaries of conduct become emotionally satisfying. Such sequence would be particularly pronounced among privates and non-commissioned officers. They are the underdogs. They take the orders. They do the actual fighting. An affair with a woman reestablishes status, just as does the ugly duckling with her illicit love affair compensate for the rivalry of her more lovely sisters. Again, the soldier's new military status gives him opportunity. There are no women folk to check the hours of his pursuits. The uniform has its own appeal in wartime. The government furnishes prophylactics. There is no local court to comprehend you. The girl knows you are in the army; she knows what to expect. Then, too, the soldier rationalizes his need. He is serving his country. Doesn't this girl owe something to him? In other words, the wearing of the uniform is rationalized to confer upon the individual a different set of moral precepts. Older, more stringent, inhibitive mores continue to have his approval, to be sure, but they hold for the folks who stay at home, particularly for his women folk. He is "in the army now" and the moral code has to be translated and changed to meet the needs of a unisexual group which is serving the country in time of crisis and with great danger to himself. He is serving his country, and he has his needs and the rights which the situation confers. When one is dealing with armies, and particularly armies on the move, one must face this transvaluation of the mores. Such transvaluation may be temporary; it may last only so long as he is in the army; when he returns to civilian life, he may take up where he left off; but this is what the situation tends to be as long as the ingroup persists. Obviously, there are many individual reactions to the ingroup, some wholly different from what has been outlined.

THE STAY-AT-HOME WIFE

Meanwhile the wife is at home. Her relative isolation from other women in the same position makes the situation different. No ingroup develops here; only isolation and the temptation of opportunity. Sooner or later, confusion and misunderstandings arise between the separated couple. Each tends to become uncertain about the other; each detects the air of uncertainty in the other. The next step may be a defensive coolness toward the other, or some degree of conflict. Nobody knows what the proper relationship is; for this very reason, conflict is apt to grow. There is uncertainty, and the temptation of freedom, for each from the other, against a general social background charged with high emotion. Adultery, and the thought of it, flourish upon opportunity.

Meanwhile, there is the immediate necessity for the wife to assume greater responsibility and leadership in the family. She must now "take over," as we say. Her first steps in this direction may falter but there is no other way. Moreover, the necessity may be long continued. The assumption of leadership is a habit which feeds upon itself. Reference has already been made to what the Punic Wars did to the Roman matron. Read what a recent witness says of the effect of the Civil War upon the southern wife.

> In 1860, the South became a matriarchy. The men went away from home to other battlefields, leaving the women free to manage farm and plantation without their bungling hindrance; whence they returned, those who had escaped heroic death found their surrogates in complete and competent charge and liking it. Four years had fixed the habit of command which, when I first began to know them, thirty had not broken.

War terminates many marriages. Husbands are killed in war; they die from disease. Some couples take advantage of the separation of war service to be divorced. Some men disappear. Some may appear out of the blue a long time afterwards. Some return physically disabled. War, in other words, creates on a large scale, the problems of widowhood, desertion, divorce, and the readjustment that physical disability of one mate often involves.

For all who are reunited, there is the task of reestablishing that peculiarly intimate relationship which is the essence of family life. This it is not always easy to do. Mates are not filed in secluded portfolios when war separates them. They go on living in their respective worlds. The significant fact is that these worlds have been different, often grossly, glaringly different. When, later on, men and their wives are reunited, both have their respective pasts behind them. There may be merely a shyness to overcome. There may be a hangover of pleasant but worrying memories. Many a married soldier (and conceivably his wife) who, in the excitement of war, takes lightly a commandment or two returns to his own fireside with a sense of shame and remorse. Internal struggle, which the psychiatrists call mental conflict, is often deep-seated and unconscious.

War affects established families through what it does to their planes of living both during and after a war. War is destructive of wealth. It redirects production to nonproductive ends. It alters the price level with detriment to families living on fixed incomes.

The effect of war upon the birth rate is obvious and measurable. Countries experience a fall in their birth rates during wartime and usually a temporary rise after the close of the war.

WAR AND SOCIAL CHANGES PECULIARLY
IMPORTANT TO THE FAMILY

(1) War cannot but affect the status of women. It is obvious that when the man is away, the woman must play—at being a man. Reference has been made to the improved status of Roman ladies during and after the Punic Wars and of southern women after the Civil War period. This process has been much accelerated in recent years as war has involved increasingly the efforts of women. The change in warfare from a clash between professional armies to a struggle between entire populations, the addition of economic to military phases of conflict, the development of totalitarian warfare, all have combined to make the efforts and contributions of women of greater importance. This involves the increasing employment of women outside of the home, their invasion of new fields of employment, the fading out or at least blurring, of class distinctions in the competitive contacts of the job, the earning of cold cash, and the enlargement of new horizons in many ways beyond the daily occupation. Air raids make her morale a basic line of defense.

Things obviously cannot stop there. When women work, earn, and spend like men do, they want the same rights as men do. This is certainly what happened during and after the first World War. War not only changed the employment of women "from a shameful business to heroism" overnight, but it put the finishing touches upon "the emancipation of women." But the right to behave like a man meant also the right to misbehave as he does. The decay of established moralities came about as a by-product. We call this a change in the mores.

This change in status and the change in the mores, particularly the sex mores, are of fundamental importance to the family. Equality in employment and in sex behavior means equality before the law in matters of divorce, desertion, and separation. They necessitate the democratic marriage. They encourage companionate marriage. The loosening of sex and family mores contributes to the increase of tension within the marriage bond. The challenge to time-honored sanctions results in insecurity, both in the home and outside. Increasingly, the hunt does not cease after the hare and the rabbit have been caught.

(2) There are counteracting and complicating factors in the changing sex ratio which war brings about. (a) There were in each warring nation after 1918, large numbers of women who could not expect to marry. (b) The bargaining powers of women were reduced. (c) The proportion of ill-fitting marriages was increased—women who in normal times would have rated an A husband had to make the best of grade C, older men marrying much younger girls, unmarriageable men marrying, etc. (d) The creation of sex antagonism, both within marriage and without.

(3) War involves the reorganization of the entire societal pattern. The simplest way of stating this is to say that most people stop what they have been doing and do something else. Population is redistributed. Some areas grow phenomenally, others contract correspondingly, problems multiply inevitably for both. Social services lag because of preoccupation with other tasks. Civil liberties are suspended or abridged. All this means that people are shifted from their customary occupations and preoccupations. They are taken away from their primary social groups. New judgments arise to meet new needs, which means that new folkways and mores appear. New forms of conduct are approved.

(4) War develops its own characteristic psychology—an accumulation of kaleidoscopic changes of ideas, impressions and emotions. Old household gods and possessions lose their value. So do old folkways and mores.

The customary relations between cause and consequence become uncertain and fallacious. There is no apparent relation between what a man does and what happens to him. Why then be limited by the old restrictions? Why then be inhibited by yesterday's virtues? Why educate the next generation to a set of principles which are now being disproved?

A final word. War, like all crises, is a selective factor operating on a gigantic scale. So far as its effects on individual families are concerned, some are therapeutic; some, just disturbing; others are disorganizing; a relatively few, plain demoralizing. It is easy, however, to point out the vagaries of conduct and philosophy that develop. Over against these is the fact that millions of men and women come through, not unseared, for the crucible of war does not permit that, but for the most part with a better understanding of life and one's fellows, a more abiding charity for their faults, a deeper respect for their virtues, and perhaps it is not too much to hope, with a keener understanding and perspective of one's self.

XII · DIVORCE

One · Statistical Perspective on Divorce *

KINGSLEY DAVIS
Sociologist, Columbia University

THE WIDESPREAD INCREASE IN DIVORCE

THE divorce rate, like the marriage rate, is characterized by fluctuations connected with war and the business cycle, but there is an unmistakable tendency for the rate to rise over a long period. In the United States this can be shown in two ways— in the census data on divorced persons and in the registration statistics on divorces as they occur. Table 1 shows that the number of divorced persons per 100 married was 0.54 in 1890 and 2.82 in 1949, representing an increase of 521 per cent; and the average number of divorces per 100 marriages was 5.56 during the 1881–90 decade and 25.89 in the 1940–49 decade, representing an increase of 466 per cent. Although the registration of marriage and divorces is inaccurate in the United States, the fact that both sets of data show the same rapid trend is proof enough of its existence.

TABLE 1. INDICES OF DIVORCE IN THE UNITED STATES, 1890–1949

Year	Divorced Persons per 100 Married (from *census* data)		Average Divorces per 100 Marriages (from *registration* data)	
	Number	Index	Rate	Index
1890	0.54	100	5.70	100
1900	0.72	132	7.56	133
1910	0.95	176	9.79	172
1920	1.18	217	12.02	211
1930	2.02	373	15.79	277
1940	2.40	443	18.36	322
1947	2.80	517	26.16	459
1948	3.17	586	26.59	467
1949	2.82	521	26.79	470

The rising rate of divorce characterizes not only the United States but all other countries touched by urban-industrial civilization. It is

* Reprinted from *The Annals* of the American Academy of Political and Social Sciences, 1950, 272: 15–21, by permission of the author and *The Annals*.

therefore not merely an "American" phenomenon, but is somehow related to the evolution of the family in western society in general. It is a consequence of the changing structure of the family—lowered fertility, loss of economic functions, absorption of women in the labor force, emphasis on personal gratification and "happiness" in marriage. This changing structure is in turn a consequence of the changing social system—the decline of the local community and its social controls, the acceleration of geographical and social mobility, the growth of large industries, cities, and so forth. These developments have all tended to make people less inclined to continue unions that seem unsatisfactory, and less restrained from getting out of such unions. Divorce laws have gradually become more liberal during the last century, but custom and opinion have changed much more rapidly than the laws, with the result that, regardless of the legal forms, the Western world is in fact achieving divorce by mutual consent.

INTERNATIONAL DIFFERENCES IN DIVORCE

However, neither the divorce rates nor their rates of change have been uniform in all western countries. Some of these countries, such as Italy, Spain, and Ireland, apparently do not permit absolute divorce at all. Others have strict or lenient laws or other traits or changes that influence the probability of divorce.[1] Furthermore, there are great differences in the incidence of divorce as between nonindustrial countries. India, for example, has rather little divorce, whereas Egypt has a rate that has generally exceeded that of the United States.

Such great differences as between countries of the same general type show that the rate of legal divorce depends in part on special conditions. The rates in western countries, for example, are not determined simply by the conditions of urban-industrial civilization. In 1945–47 the American divorce rate was almost six times that of England and Wales, yet the latter area is more urbanized than our country.

It should not be surmised, however, that differences in divorce rates necessarily represent true differences in the amount of marital dissolution. As we shall see in a moment, a legal divorce is only one way of breaking a marriage, and in the absence of opportunity for divorce, these other ways may play a compensatory role. Unfortunately, the causes of international differences in divorce rates have been little investigated, despite their importance for a sociological understanding of marital dissolution. Yet the generalization can be made that wherever in western countries divorce has been permitted, its incidence has tended to rise during the last century.

---

[1] The striking rise in the rate in England since 1940 is due to the liberalization of divorce laws in that country.

IS THERE A SATURATION POINT?

How high will the divorce rate eventually go? Did the United States figure of 40 divorces per 100 marriages in 1946 represent a permanent peak? Nobody knows the answers, but certain considerations suggest that the saturation point is at least in sight.

First of all, there is a theoretical limit to the divorce rate. Over an extended period there cannot be more divorces than marriages; in fact, there must always be fewer, because some marriages must necessarily end in death rather than divorce. More to the point is the fact that the rise in the divorce rate has on the whole been greater where the rate was formerly low, and less where it was high. For instance, the percentage rise in the rate per 100 average annual marriages between 1910–12 and 1945–47 is shown in Table 2.

Those countries that began with a divorce rate of less than 3 per 100 average marriages experienced by and large a fourfold to tenfold increase, while those beginning with more than 3 experienced in general only a twofold increase. This tendency for the rate of increase to be less in countries with an already high incidence of divorce suggests that the trend in divorce can be represented by a typical growth, or logistic, curve; and for some countries having a long enough series of data, this is the case.

TABLE 2. RISE IN DIVORCE RATE PER 100 AVERAGE ANNUAL MARRIAGES, 1910–12 TO 1945–47, SELECTED COUNTRIES [a]

	Three-Year Average Rate 1910–12	Per Cent Increase by 1945–47
England and Wales	2.2	3,867
Scotland	7.4	691
Belgium	19.4	301 [b]
Sweden	19.6	481
Netherlands	23.5	378
New Zealand	24.1	489 [b]
Denmark	38.8	391
France	50.6	225
Switzerland	58.6	108
United States	105.6	221
Japan [c]	137.5 [d]	−7 [e]

[a] Computed from Metropolitan Life Insurance Company, *Statistical Bulletin,* Vol. 30 (April 1949), p. 2.

[b] Average rate 1945–47 based on two years only.

[c] Computed from Ryoichi Ishii, *Population Pressure and Economic Life in Japan* (Chicago: University of Chicago Press, 1937), pp. 97, 100.

[d] Average annual marriages for preceding decade based on 1898, 1903, and 1908 only.

[e] Divorces based on 1946 only.

The significance of such a shape in the trend is that it clearly points to an eventual leveling off of the divorce rate. Whatever the forces in western society that have brought about the remarkable increase in divorce, they will not work indefinitely in the same direction. A new equilibrium is being established involving a divorce rate much higher than the preindustrial one, but not an increasing rate. Unless there is a major social revolution—such as the complete removal of child rearing from the family's functions—it seems doubtful that the divorce rate in any country will go far beyond the 1946 peak in the United States.

DIVORCE AND BROKEN HOMES

The rising rate of divorce has not meant, as is commonly assumed, a corresponding rise in the number of broken families. The latter is kept low, in the first place, by the capacity of the decline in mortality to compensate for the increase in divorce, and in the second place, by the tendency of most divorced persons to remarry and thus be absorbed into new families.

If the marriages broken by death are added to those broken by divorce, one finds that in the United States, with the exception of the two world wars, the total rate of marital dissolutions from these two combined causes was downward from 1890 to 1915 and relatively constant thereafter (Figure 1).

Along with the increase of divorce, the rate of remarriage has ap-

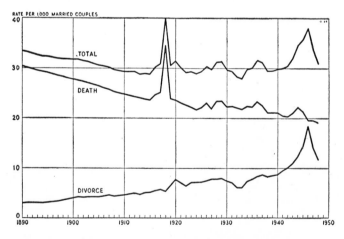

FIG. 1. *Marital Dissolutions by Death and Divorce—United States, 1890–1948.* (Source: Metropolitan Life Insurance Company, *Statistical Bulletin,* Vol. 30, Nov. 1949, p. 2.)

Note: The figures for divorce include annulments, and those for mortality include deaths overseas during World Wars I and II. Rates for 1948 are provisional.

parently been rising, at least in the United States. Census data show
that in 1940 the proportion of remarried women among those previously widowed or divorced was about one-sixth greater than in
1910. In the age group 25–34, more than three-fifths were remarried
according to the 1940 data, as compared with about one-half in
1910. A census survey in 1948, combined with registration data, revealed that approximately 75 per cent of those procuring divorces
during the five years from 1943 to 1948 were already remarried in
1948. Of those divorced earlier—between 1934 and 1943—approximately 86 per cent had remarried by 1948.

ANNULMENT, SEPARATION, AND DESERTION

Disproportionate attention is given to divorce as compared to
other forms of voluntary marital dissolution. The reason is partly
one of ignorance. While we know little enough about divorce, we
know even less about annulment, desertion, and informal separation. What we do know indicates that their combined frequency is
imposing, and in countries having little legal divorce they often
take the place that divorce would otherwise occupy.

In the United States as a whole, annulments constitute only a
small proportion of legal dissolutions. At their peak in 1946, when
almost 22,000 annulments were granted, they represented only 3.5
per cent of the total. But according to Jacobson,

> In California and New York, however, they were of much
> greater importance. Thus in California, annulments constituted
> somewhat more than one-ninth of all legal marriage dissolu-
> tions in 1948. In New York they were an even larger proportion
> of the total; almost one-quarter of the marital dissolutions in
> 1940, and since 1946 almost one-third. In at least five counties
> in New York, the number of annulments now exceeds the num-
> ber of absolute divorces.

From 1940 to 1948 the annulments in New York State constituted
almost one-third of all annulments in the nation. New York has this
high annulment rate because it grants divorce only for adultery but
gives annulments for any one of eight different grounds, many of
which are ill-defined.

Unfortunately there is hardly any statistical information concerning the number of desertions and informal separations in the United
States. Such information as we have suggests that the number is
quite high. In the 1940 census there were 3.1 million married persons not living with their spouses, which was more than twice the
divorced number of (1.4 million). By careful analysis of the characteristics of the separated persons, Ogburn concluded that a large
proportion of them might be permanently separated. "Separations
are more numerous among non-whites, in cities, in the young and

old age groups, in the service occupations, and . . . among the low-income groups of the laboring class."

Sample surveys made by the Census Bureau in 1947–49 show that, while the number of married persons and of divorced persons had increased, the number of separated persons had declined slightly. Thus, whereas the separated were 4.5 per cent of all persons ever married in 1940, they were only 3.4 per cent in 1949; and whereas they were more than twice as numerous as the divorced at the earlier date, they were only about a third more numerous in 1949. If accurate, these data suggest that divorces are being obtained by people who would formerly have merely remained separated. Since desertion and separation have been the main bulwark of the poor, this result could be expected with increasing real income and better education.

CONCLUSION

The long-run trends discussed or cited in this article amount to a major revolution in the family structure of industrial society. The combination of increasing longevity, a slightly earlier age at marriage, and a tendency to control fertility and bunch reproduction in ages below 30, has freed married women for economic pursuits and led to a new conception of marriage as a personal rather than a community or kinship matter. Marriage, divorce, and reproduction have accordingly become much more responsive to current conditions, almost like the swings of fashion.

Yet behind the fluctuations are abiding regularities, among them a rather constant tendency to enter matrimony ultimately, to remarry more frequently after divorce, and to have a family of modest size. Although legal divorce has experienced a general rise, it does not bring a commensurate number of broken families. Death has declined as a cause of dissolution, and remarriage has tended to reabsorb the divorced. Also, legal divorce has perhaps taken the place formerly occupied by desertion and informal separation. In any case, the new family structure seems to be integrated with the general character of modern society. Its main features will remain as long as that kind of society lasts, although it is a mistake to think that certain trends, such as a rising divorce rate, will persist indefinitely.

Two · Divorce and Size of Family *

PAUL JACOBSON
Vital Statistics Analyst, Metropolitan
Life Insurance Company

DIVORCE in families where there are children is more common than is generally realized. Of all the divorces (including annulments) granted in the United States in 1948, no less than 42 percent were to couples with children; this compares with 38 percent in the period 1922–1932. However, the average number of children in such families, namely, 1.8, has remained the same in both periods. This means that the number of children affected by divorce has increased even more rapidly than has the number of divorces. In 1948, about 313,000 children under age 21 were involved in the 421,000 absolute decrees granted. Thus, including the marital partners, there were almost 1.2 million persons in families dissolved by divorce; and this large number does not include individuals in homes broken by separation or desertion, for which data are not available.

The proportion of divorces involving children varies considerably with the duration of marriage. According to the experience in 1948, the proportion with children rises from about 10 percent for marriages ended before the first year to a peak of 65 percent in the 18th year of marriage. Beyond that, the proportion drops steadily as the children grow up and leave their families. It is noteworthy that in 1948, children were involved in more than one half of all divorces granted to couples married from 7 to 23 years.

As might be expected, the average number of children in families broken by divorce increases with the duration of marriage prior to dissolution. The average per parent-couple rises from 1.3 children (including those from previous marriages) for families dissolved the first year to a maximum of 2.5 for families broken about the 20th year of marriage.

Turning from averages to the total number of children involved brings out the important fact that divorce-orphans are concentrated in the early years of marriage. This is, of course, a consequence of the high proportion of all divorces that occur at early durations of marriage. It means, obviously, that a large proportion of the children affected by divorce are at the younger ages. National data on

* Reprinted from *Statistical Bulletin*, New York: Metropolitan Life Insurance Company, 1950, 31: 1–3, by permission. Summary of article, "Differentials in Divorce by Duration of Marriage and Size of Family," Paul Jacobson, *American Sociological Review*, 1950, 15: 235–244.

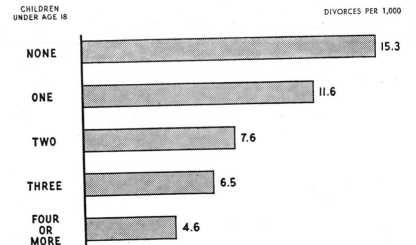

CHART 1. *Divorces Per 1,000 Married Couples, According to Size of Family—United States, 1948.* (Source: Basic data on divorces and annulments collected by Statistical Bureau of the Metropolitan Life Insurance Company from 19 states and 16 counties in other states.)

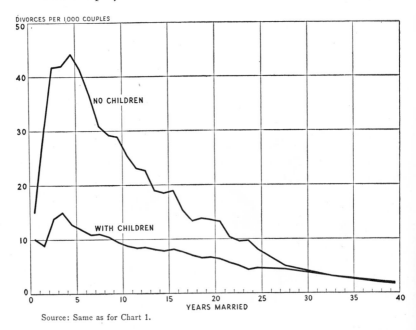

CHART 2. *Divorce Rate for Married Couples With and Without Children Under Age 18, According to Duration of Marriage—United States, 1948.* (Source: Same as for Chart 1.)

this point are lacking, but recent statistics for several counties indicate that fully two thirds of the children affected by divorce are under age 10.

The divorce rate varies inversely with the number of children under age 18 [1] in the family, as may be seen in Chart 1. For couples without children the divorce rate in 1948 was 15.3 per 1,000. Where one child was present the rate was 11.6 per 1,000. The figure thus continues to decrease, and in families with four or more children, the rate was 4.6. Altogether, the relative frequency of divorce for couples with children was little more than one half that for couples without minor children at the time of divorce.

The difference in the divorce rates between couples with and without children varies according to the duration of marriage, as is evident from Chart 2. For couples with children, the peak divorce rate, reached in the fourth year of marriage, was 15 per 1,000 in 1948. In childless families, however, the rate rose to a maximum of 44 per 1,000 couples in the fifth year of marriage, or to about three times the rate for couples with children. As the length of married life increases, the difference in the relative frequency of divorce between the two groups diminishes. By the 20th year of marriage the ratio was two to one; after the 30th year the two rates were practically identical.

These findings indicate that the relative frequency of divorce is greater for families without children than for families with children. Yet, the presence of children is not necessarily a deterrent to divorce. It is possible that in most cases both divorce and childlessness result from more fundamental factors in the marital relationship. Moreover, while some unsuccessful marriages may not be broken until the children have grown up, their number is less than is popularly believed in view of the small difference in the rate between the two groups at the later years of marriage.

[1] The discussion which follows is based on children under age 18, instead of under age 21. This change is made because the Bureau of the Census in 1948 provided data from which it is possible to estimate the distribution of existing marriages only according to the number of children under 18 years of age.

Three · Education as a Factor in Divorce

EDMUND deS BRUNNER
Sociologist, Columbia University

Is there a tendency for people with more years of education to seek divorce more readily than do those with fewer years of education? The next reading * considers this question and offers conclusions based upon an analysis of United States Census data from 1940 and 1947.

DOES education make for divorce? This question can receive only a partial answer for the simple reason that in a vast majority of the cases the purpose of divorce is the remarriage of one or both of the parties. Once remarried, such persons are, of course, removed from the category of divorced persons.

Divorce, moreover, is not the sole measurement of marital maladjustment. There are tens of thousands of separations, legal and otherwise. These are enumerated in the census under the category "husband absent." This category, however, also includes separations because of military service, long civilian absence because of work under certain conditions which prevent family residence at the point of employment, or institutional residence. There are strong reasons for believing that such circumstances account for a minimum of the separations reported by the Census.

Although the data are limited, they indicate that the better educated women tend to seek the solution of marital difficulties in divorce rather than in separation; the ones with less education, in separation rather than in divorce. The chief exception to this generalization is among the youngest groups of women, whose marriages were relatively recent and who may not have had time for a divorce to be granted. When figures for separations and divorce are added, it appears that between the ages of 22 and 35 a smaller proportion of better educated women than of those with less education reported broken marriages. This, to repeat, makes no allowance for remarried divorcees. Remarriage is very likely to be a factor in these years.

The higher incidence of separations among those with less education is doubtless due in part to economic status. These groups probably include couples with lower incomes, who are therefore less able to pay for divorce proceedings.

---

* Reprinted from *Teachers College Record*, 1948, 49: 7–9, by permission of the author.

The considerable rate of increase in separations and divorces since 1940 is proportionately about matched by the rate of increase in the number married. Again the remarriage factor is important. From 1940 through 1946, 5,500,000 persons obtained divorces, yet during these years the number of divorced persons of both sexes increased by only about 500,000.

In the main in 1940, the trends with respect to separation and divorce of men are similar to those for women, in the United States as a whole. The most significant difference is in the proportions involved. With respect to divorce, most educational and age categories show a sharply smaller proportion of men than of women. The differences usually run from 25 to 50 per cent smaller. This suggests that divorced men remarry more quickly than their former wives do.

Space limitations prevent the analysis of the Negro data. However, considerably lower percentages of Negro women with one or more years of college were married than of white; and 15.3 per cent of those between the ages of 25 and 34 ever married were separated or divorced, as against 19.3 for those with high school education or less.

Four • Divorce and Readjustment

ERNEST R. MOWRER
Sociologist, Northwestern University

, *Many discussions of divorce imply that divorce is always a traumatic experience for those involved. It must be recognized, however, that in many cases divorce is but the aftermath of marital discord. The divorce is a solution to problems in that it is the final legal termination of a previously broken marriage. Nevertheless, in the majority of cases, a more or less serious readjustment to life is necessary for at least one member of the divorced pair and certain problems are likely to arise for both partners. In the following reading * an attempt is made to explore the many areas in which adjustment may be required.*

THERE are few crises in the life span of an individual which produce a more severe strain upon the personality than

* Reprinted from *The Annals* of the American Academy of Political and Social Science, 1932, 160: 191–196, by permission of the author and the editor.

divorce. In a culture which has not yet adjusted itself to the eventualities of divorce, even death tends to produce less conflict in the individual, because of the presence of socially sanctioned forms of adjustment. Whatever may be the situation in the future, there is at present little provision for adjustments after divorce in American culture. The individual is left to muddle along as best he can, whether as a child whose parents have been divorced or as an adult whose marriage is thereby terminated.

Divorce is, of course, but the climax of domestic discord. It is accordingly only a convenient symbol of the beginning of the period of readjustment. Actually, the period of readjustment often has its beginning long before the divorce is granted, although it is not unusual for individuals to refuse to face the situation until divorce has closed the door to reconciliation. In other cases, however, either one or both principals to the marriage may have completely readjusted themselves to the situation.

The problem of readjustment obviously is not the same for all individuals. In fact there is the widest range of differences, depending upon a large number of factors in the life experiences of the individual. Some of these factors have to do with the type of domestic discord, while others are related to certain differentials in the attitudes of the two persons.

Domestic discord situations may be differentiated into two types, in terms of the basic conditions under which conflict arises. First, there is that group of cases in which discord is the result of the disorganization of either or both of the personalities involved. From the standpoint of this type of case, divorce simply means a change in the elements making for disorganization, since there has been continuous lack of adjustment throughout the life history of the individual. In this type of situation the intensity of mental conflict may vary from time to time, though such variations do not make disorganization less constant. Furthermore, at least one of the individuals may find in the marriage situation a partial solution of some of the perplexing problems of life. In so far as this is true, divorce adds complications to the life problems of that individual.

Where domestic discord arises out of the marriage situation, the problems of the divorce are likely to seem more cataclysmic in origin than otherwise. The result is that the individual who has previously seemed quite well adjusted may become completely disorganized in every phase of his social relations. He finds that even the simplest of problems, which previously he handled very proficiently, have now become enormously enlarged. The orderly world in which he knew his way around quite well has suddenly become topsy-turvy, and all his old techniques of adjustment appear weak and futile.

DIFFERENTIALS IN READJUSTMENT

The second group of variations grows out of differentials in the attitudes of the individuals involved. The problem of readjustment is, for example, quite different for one of the principals as compared to the other, unless the desire to terminate the marriage is mutual and for essentially the same reasons in each case. Situations of this latter sort, however, are relatively rare. What more commonly happens is that one individual has long ago lost interest in the marriage and has therefore readjusted to the changed situation, leaving his partner to the disillusionment so often associated with divorce.

Furthermore, the individual's conception of marriage is an important aspect in determining the nature of the crisis after divorce. For those individuals who go into marriage chiefly for practical reasons, the problem of adjustment after divorce is quite different from that where romantic ideas constitute the chief motivating factors.

Romanticism is in fact one of the causes of both divorce and the disillusionment which follows in its wake. The romantic code looks upon love as the only thing that counts in the selection of a mate. But how is one to know infatuation from love, which it resembles in every respect except that of lasting? The answer of the romanticist is that one must try, and, failing, try again. Divorce is the inevitable way out of a mistaken choice. But since so much emphasis is placed upon love, the disappointment is all the more keen, even though one is convinced that it was only infatuation. In the nature of such things, however, the love which has become infatuation to one is often still love to the other.

CONFLICT IN READJUSTMENT

Divorce inevitably gives rise to problems of sexual adjustment. Even though there was sexual conflict in marriage, it is seldom that such conflict prevented all sex expression. The tendency is to resort to sexual irregularity of one kind or another. Not uncommonly, at first the individual gives way to a reckless abandon, as though to get even with the mate who has betrayed him.

Sexual irregularity, however, is seldom a satisfactory solution of the need for sex expression. Even when there have been illicit sexual contacts during the period of marriage, it is not so easy to go against the sex *mores* of the group and be content with this sort of sexual life. During marriage, the individual could always shift the responsibilities for his irregular sex behavior to his marriage partner; following divorce, he can blame only himself. The result is that ordinarily the only satisfactory solutions are found either in remarriage or in some form of substitution or sublimation.

The mental tensions arising out of sexual irregularity are, of course, of various sorts. If a man's relations are with prostitutes, there is always the fear of disease and the feeling of degradation for having stooped so low. At first this latter feeling is not always an impediment, since the individual sometimes wishes to degrade himself for the sadistic pleasure he gains thereby. Revulsion tends to set in later, inclining the individual to seek other outlets. Relations with women who themselves are seeking sex expression give rise to mental conflict for fear that the individual may become pregnant and assert her legal claim upon him for support of her child.

For the woman, on the other hand, there is always the danger of pregnancy as well as that of contracting a venereal infection. Furthermore, her sexual nature is probably more diffused than that of the male and does not find as satisfactory expression in experiences which are largely upon a physiological basis.

Another form of tension is that which develops as the result of breakdown in habituation. Marriage inevitably develops a wide range of habits involving division of labor and reciprocal responses. The extent to which one's psychological economy is based upon these habitual reactions which constitute a large part of marriage relations is generally unappreciated until they have been interrupted. Unless there has been a gradual individualization of conduct prior to divorce, the individual tends to find himself suddenly faced with the necessity of reorganizing his behavior in many ways. The problem of reorganization tends to be aggravated by the distortion of perception which develops out of his feeling of depression and inadequacy.

EMOTIONAL DEPENDENCY HINDERING READJUSTMENT

Closely related to habituation is the emotional dependency which develops in married life. Not infrequently, especially where there is personality disorganization, one individual is highly dependent emotionally upon the other. Ordinarily, of course, this individual is not the one to seek a divorce, and hence it is he who suffers most. In some cases, for example, the individual was emotionally dependent upon a parent as a child. In marriage he transfers his dependency to his marriage partner. Divorce leaves him without any one to whom he can transfer this dependency, unless there are children. Even in this case, the transference is likely to be temporary and to give rise to conflict as the child grows older and makes other contacts.

In other situations emotional dependency finds expression in the tendency for one person to take parental attitudes toward the other. This tendency to shield the other and constantly to look out for his welfare may become so strong and result in so much pleasure to the individual that the loss of the marriage partner as the focus of his attentions create a severe strain upon the personality.

The importance of emotional dependency in producing tensions and stress following divorce is, of course, aggravated in modern life where premium is placed upon the response phases of marriage relations. This emphasis upon response as the basis of marriage facilitates the development of a high state of rapport in which every aspect of family relations is interlocked with every other aspect. In the early days of marriage, anything which threatens to disrupt this identification between the whole of the personalities of the two individuals is assiduously avoided because of its symbolical meaning. This tendency toward idealization often continues for one person even up to the granting of the divorce. Thereafter, the individual finds himself like a ship at sea in which the motor has been damaged beyond repair. If his problem were merely that of building up new habits, or of exercising any kind of rational control, readjustment would not be difficult. Trouble arises, however, because of the highly emotional basis of the tensions, which refuse to yield to conscious control.

Other factors in the strength of emotional dependency are whether or not the marriage is the first, and the age at which it was contracted. First marriages and those having their roots in the transition period between adolescence and adulthood have a way of going deeply into the emotional subsoil. Divorce leaves the individual highly disorganized, with little recourse other than to repress his emotions, only to have them reappear in disguise.

UNCERTAINTY IN SOCIAL RELATIONSHIPS

Divorce also tends to introduce certain ambiguities into one's social relationships. For the woman there is the problem of economic support which her husband had previously taken care of. Not infrequently the wife has had neither experience nor training which can be turned to account. She becomes dependent, therefore, upon alimony and the assistance of her relatives; or else she is compelled to lower her standard of living. She may even be harassed with the difficulties of finding any sort of work to do. The necessity of becoming self-supporting, the adjustment to which is normally made in the late teens and early twenties when the individual is more plastic, has been delayed by marriage, only to reappear when the person is less able to meet it.

Furthermore, one does not know how one's friends will react toward him. Even though the taboo against divorce and the divorcee has quite thoroughly disintegrated (as it has not in many groups), there is always the problem of whether or not one's friends will take sides in the controversy leading to divorce. Any reticence on the part of a friend, even though it arises only out of solicitude and fear of saying something which might embarrass the other, is interpreted as showing censorship and alienation. Undue solicitude, on the other hand, is quite as objectionable, since it suggests condescension and is a blow to one's pride. What the divorcee wants is to be treated as he has always been, when to do so is almost impossible, since all relations between the two persons have always included to some extent the marriage partner.

Where the taboo against divorce still holds, of course, this natural ambiguity in social relationships is aggravated. Not infrequently the individual feels that his only recourse is to make new contacts, leaving behind old friendships as a part of the marriage situation from which he wishes to escape. Self-reproach, resentment, disillusionment, and feelings of betrayal are accentuated because of this tendency to break the larger web of social relationships.

Jealousy also plays a part in the problem of readjustment, especially in the case of the woman who has not wanted a divorce. The greatest strain, however, does not come until the ex-husband marries or seems about to do so. The divorced wife feels her pride hurt that another woman can replace her and perhaps hold him longer than she was able to.

REMARRIAGE AND READJUSTMENT

Remarriage is, of course, both a part and the aftermath of readjustment to divorce. Here, however, one is concerned with remarriage as a phase of readjustment. Not infrequently it seems the only solution, and yet in other cases it leads only to complications. Where the individual has become wholly emancipated from his previous marriage so that remarriage means no more than the obtainment of satisfactions which are lacking in single life, a second venture into matrimony may lead to a more harmonious integration of personality. But how can one know when he has achieved such a high degree of emancipation?

What not infrequently happens in remarriage is that the individual finds himself making unfavorable comparisons between the new alliance and the old. Idealization of the past helps to erase much of the disappointment in the first marriage and to make of it a trying standard for comparisons. And though the individual may enjoy his contacts with his new marriage partner, he may still unconsciously wish for the old and feel that he is somehow betraying a love which is more real than the present one. In fact this ambivalence of attitudes is all the more trying where there is little to find fault with in the new alliance. If there were only opportunities which provided some semblance of justification for attitudes of hatred, these would provide outlets for the conflict and at the same time allow the individual to chastise himself.

Again, where the taboo against divorce is quite strong, the individual finds it difficult if not impossible to forget that he has been divorced and has remarried. The result is that his attitude toward his remarriage is always an apologetic one in spite of the fact that he finds it quite satisfactory. The person tends, accordingly, to keep aflame the resentment and the bitterness which were the aftermath of the termination of the earlier marriage, as a protection against any feeling of self-inculpation at having gone against the taboos of the group. His apologetic attitude itself indicates some lack of adjustment in remarriage.

Furthermore, if there were children by the first marriage, this tends to complicate the picture. Especially if the child happens to be of the opposite sex and to look like the divorced parent, the person may be much more fond of him than of children by the second marriage. The result is often a feeling that in his fondness for this child, he is being unfaithful to the present marriage. The individual may attempt to reassure himself and to prove his fidelity by mistreating the child, only to find that he has aggravated the situation by adding self-reproach for his parental negligence.

Children by the former marriage may further complicate the picture by causing the parent to doubt how well satisfied they are. Even though the child seems well adjusted to the foster parent, there is always the possibility of inner tensions. Furthermore, as the child becomes older, either as the result of contacts with his own absent parent or as a reflection of the attitudes of those with whom he is in contact, he may regret that his parents ever were divorced. Fear of this situation is perhaps the reason why parents so often try to build up attitudes of hatred in their children toward their former marriage partners, since this is the only insurance they have against possible tension in the future.

READJUSTMENT OF CHILDREN

Divorce, however, not infrequently requires readjustment on the part of children as well as on the part of the parents. Unless the child is very young at the time of separation, considerable mental conflict tends to arise out of the fact that contacts with one parent are relatively infrequent. If this parent happens to be the favorite, the conflict is all the more severe. But whether the favorite or not, contacts are usually under the most favorable circumstances, and thus tend to increase the child's affection for the absent parent.

Furthermore, in neighborhood contacts the child whose parents are divorced often feels himself inferior to his playmates, since they have two parents whereas he really has but one. He gets the idea, therefore, that his parents were somehow less capable than those of his friends and playmates, otherwise how did it happen that they were less successful in meeting the problems of marriage?

Further difficulties in personality adjustment develop out of the fact that parental contacts are chiefly of one sex. The daughter is handicapped by having no one to confide in during the trying experiences of puberty if the absent parent is her mother. The son whose father is gone finds himself surrounded by feminine patterns, with little or no opportunity for developing a masculine rôle.

When the parent with whom the child lives has remarried, conflict often develops between the foster parent and the child. The child not infrequently resents the presence of the foster parent in the home. He may even blame his own parent for the situation, thus leading to estrangement between the child and both the principles to the second marriage.

Divorce also not infrequently leads the child to take a skeptical attitude toward marriage. This skepticism, however, comes into conflict with the natural tendency to seek contacts with the opposite sex and to wish to marry. The result is that the individual tends to enter marriage in a highly skeptical frame of mind, only to find all that he has feared. Thus divorce is passed on from one generation to the next.

Not always, however, does divorce lead to disorganization of the child. Where remarriage occurs relatively early, so that the child is hardly aware that the foster parent is other than his own parent, the child may be quite as well adjusted in the family as he would have been had his parents never been divorced. What are the features making for successful adjustment in one case and unsuccessful in another is not entirely clear except in a genreal way. Much the same thing may be said about readjustment of the individual after divorce. Thus the foregoing analysis may be said to consist of a restatement of the problem for further research.

Future research in readjustment after divorce accordingly will keep in mind that the fundamental problem under consideration is that of personality development. Divorce is but one of the many crises in life which call for readjustment. The form which readjustment takes following any crisis depends upon two sets of factors: certain circumstances and conditions at the time of and following the crisis, and the background of personality development. Of these two sets, the latter is perhaps the more important, since the devices which have been used in the past in readjustment to crises will tend to function in the new situation. If these mechanisms are such as to facilitate adjustment, the situation is effectively and expeditiously solved. If, on the other hand, the personality does not show a high degree of integration, the individual is likely to be highly disorganized by divorce and to have considerable difficulty in finding any solution for his mental conflict.

Five • Children of Divorce

KINGSLEY DAVIS
Sociologist, Columbia University

*The reading below * considers reasons why divorce
in our culture involves for the children of the divorcing parents
more problems than are created by divorce in other cultures.*

THEORETICALLY the problem of the post-divorce
child is universal—not only because divorce itself in one form or
another is universal, but more profoundly because the child of divorce constitutes a potentially anomalous element in social organization. In most societies this potentiality is not allowed to express
itself; instead, social institutions exist which take care of the child
without undue turmoil. The peoples of Western civilization, on the
other hand, have developed a peculiar institutional system that
makes the problem very acute and hard to solve in practice. To
understand why this is true one must compare the position of the
child after divorce in different societies.

DIVORCE AND THE IMMEDIATE FAMILY

Since it dissolves the immediate family (now generally believed
to be always and everywhere a part of society), the act of divorce
usually offends the sense of order and fitness in social affairs. Hence
it is nearly always tolerated in fact but never approved in principle.
When children are involved the antagonism to divorce is greater,
because dissolution of the marriage runs counter to the main function of the immediate family—namely, the bearing and rearing of
children. Having formed a union which is socially defined, which
involves mutual rights and obligations, and which clearly has as its
main function the rearing of children, the parents separate and thus
deprive the child of its socially prescribed milieu. If he remains
with one parent he lacks the other—a real loss, because each parent
plays a necessary and complementary role in the child's life. If the
parent with whom he stays remarries, the child falls into a stepchild
situation. If he is shifted back and forth between the parents, he
must adjust to two different domestic milieus, possibly two different
stepchild situations, and must therefore run the risk of discontinuity
in his emotional and intellectual development.

* Reprinted from *Law and Contemporary Problems*, 1944, 10: 700–710, by
permission of the author, Duke University School of Law, Durham, North
Carolina. Copyright by Duke University.

This description seems extremely obvious, but it appears so only because it describes the situation *in our culture*. To millions of people living in non-Western societies the description would appear ludicrous—not because it fails altogether to fit their social systems, but because it fits them only in an abstract or analytic sense. Although the immediate family is a universal group, it is not instinctive; rather it is a cultural phenomenon, and as such its specific form, and above all its connections with the rest of society, vary tremendously from one social system to another. It happens that in countless societies the immediate family is so interwoven with other institutional groups that, in case of divorce, the children do not constitute a social problem. The break-up of the immediate family is the same as in our society, and the anomaly of the child's position is potentially the same, but actually the parents' relation to other persons—often to clansmen and joint householders—is such that the child continues largely under their care.

DIVORCE IN PRIMITIVE SOCIETY: THE IBO

The success of non-Western societies in solving the problem of the post-divorce child is explained by their wider use of kinship groups other than the immediate family. With them the immediate family is not the sole, nor even the most important kinship unit. Instead the clan, the extended family, and the joint household serve as important parts of social organization and perform functions which with us are left either to non-kinship groups or to the immediate family. Let us take as an example the Ibo society of Southern Nigeria, whose divorce customs have been ably reported.

The first thing to note is the nature of Ibo marriage. It is not an agreement between the two prospective mates, but rather a contract between the parents and more fundamentally the clans of the mates. Without the prior consent and agreement of the two parental families no marriage could take place. Secondly, the prospective groom or his family must pay a bride-price to the girl's relatives, without which the union would have no legal standing. Thirdly, in spite of the marriage, the husband and wife remain socially and religiously members of their respective clans. The wife joins her husband's family physically but not spiritually. She must participate in the economic activities of his household, and above all she must bear children for his clan. But her underlying allegiance remains with her own family, and she may at any time return to it. The bride-price is the compensation that her parents, having gone to the expense of rearing her, receive for the loss of her services. It is not the price of her person, as such, for she continues to belong to her clan, but the price of her services. In return she has obligations toward her husband and his family. He also has obligations toward her, and unless these are properly observed her services may be withdrawn. She does not share her husband's possessions, inherit any of them after his death, or hold any claim to the children borne by her. Her husband has the right to contract as many marriages as he or his family can afford, and since a man's prestige depends on his wealth, and his wealth is most effectively displayed by the number of wives, he will try to secure as many as possible.

Being a private contract between the two families, a marriage may be revoked at will by either side. If he is willing to forget the bride-price the husband may send his wife back for any cause whatsoever. On the other hand, the wife may not be able to leave her husband even for just cause if her family refuses to refund the bride-price. Only if she has good prospects of remarrying, which means that another man stands ready to pay her family the bride-price (which then is returned to the original husband), may she leave of her own free will.

One of the most frequent causes of the dismissal of Ibo wives is barrenness. If several years elapse without a child being born, the wife may be sent home and the bride-price recovered. If, on the other hand, the wife has fulfilled her duty by bearing at least two children, including one son, it is extremely difficult for the husband to return her to her parents and receive back the bride-price. The charge of barrenness often elicits the counter-charge of impotence. If the wife fails to conceive for some years after marriage, she or her family and possibly her husband may make arrangements for extra-marital relations. A child born under such circumstances is of course the property of the husband and bolsters the position of the wife.

Obviously in Ibo society there can be no question of the custody of the children when a marriage is dissolved. They belong to the husband's family. It was largely for them that the marriage was contracted and the bride-price paid in the first place. The question may be raised as to how they can be taken care of without their mother, but the truth is that the mother's care is not necessary. Since the household usually includes some of the husband's female relatives, perhaps other wives, there is little difficulty about rearing the children.

The case of the Ibo has been chosen because its handling of divorce is, in its major outlines, typical of that in many primitive societies. The marital relation is dominated by lineal kinsmen, and the custody and rearing of the children do not depend on the continuance of the immediate family. The fact that the Ibo are patrilineal in their clan organization means that the child is viewed primarily as a member of the father's clan. This is sometimes thought to be the most difficult case for post-divorce children in kinship societies, because of the young child's physical dependence on its mother. Actually in some patrilineal societies the children do remain with the mother while they are infants and are returned to the father at a later date.

In matrilineal and matrilocal societies the problem is easier. There, after divorce, it is the father who must leave; the child belongs to its mother's clan and hence remains in the mother's household. No conflict arises between the biological attachment of young children to the mother and their sociological attachment to the father. This is one reason why divorce is usually easier in such societies.

In societies where the emphasis on extended kin is bilateral rather than unilateral, or in which residence and descent are at variance, or in which other special conditions obtain, almost any conceivable rule may prevail with reference to the custody of children after divorce. Sometimes the children are divided equally, sometimes the boys are given to the father and the girls to the mother, sometimes the mother gets the younger, the father the older children. Generally, however, there is no major problem of adjustment, because, whoever gets him, the child is likely to live in intimate and stable relationship with other relatives, both male and female, who will perform the functions of the missing parent.

THE CASE OF THE CHINESE

Not only primitive but civilized societies may utilize kinship as an important principle of social organization. This was the case in China before the process of Westernization set in. The immediate family was subordinate in nearly every respect to the extended family. The mates were selected and the marriage arranged by the parents, and the couple usually lived with the parents of the husband. The young bride was subordinate to the older females in her husband's extended household, and the husband was subordinate to his grandfather, father, or older brother. The household was frequently quite large, so that the children were surrounded by adults other than their mother and father—notably by uncles, aunts, and grandparents. The husband could divorce his wife for numerous causes, of which one was barrenness and another disregard of his parents. The wife's right of divorce was virtually nil.

Divorce in China did not imply family disorganization in our sense of the word. Since the dominant kinship unit was the extended patrilineal kin, the dissolution of a particular marriage had little significance, for it took more than this to break up the entire kindred or even a particular household. Furthermore, concubinage and polygyny made divorce less disruptive, because if one consort were divorced the others could maintain the immediate family. In any case the child necessarily remained in the father's household, where he continued to find the milieu much as it had been before. If divorce seldom occurred in Chinese society it was not because the dissolution of wedlock was considered "bad for the child," but because marital harmony did not depend primarily upon personal likes and dislikes.

In a kinship society, whether primitive or civilized, the immediate family is hardly an independent unit. It is the extended family which exercises the main influence, which has the privilege of choosing the mate, determining the residence, controlling the property, watching the morals, and in general managing the affairs of the young couple. The married pair either live with or near their relatives, and the children consequently grow up with the latter. Therefore if one parent is lost through death or divorce the child's domestic environment is not seriously disturbed. He tends to remain in the same household, among the same intimate relatives, feeling just as secure and loved as ever. Also, what might be called the principle of kinship substitution usually operates—the principle that if one kinsman is lost, another is available to take his place. Such a principle is necessary if kinship is to form the basis of social organization, and it is embodied widely in the so-called classificatory type of kinship terminology, which calls different relatives by the same term (*e.g.* father and father's brother) because they may be functionally equivalent or capable of substitution. The principle means that the child is seldom left without some relative to function as a parent for him. Being familiar with this mechanism, he accepts it as a part of life. Also, since usually it is sociological rather than biological paternity that counts, the "stepchild" situation does not arise. Actually, so far as daily behavior is concerned, the child may have drawn little distinction between his parents and the other adults in the household anyway. It is therefore easy for him to make the adjustment when a parent is lost. Things remain for him pretty much as they were before.

DIVORCE IN THE SMALL FAMILY SYSTEM

One of the outstanding peculiarities of Western civilization, in contrast to the cultures discussed above, is the degree to which kinship has lost its social importance. At first sight this might suggest that divorce itself would have lost its importance, but such is not the case. The decline of kinship has affected the extended, not the immediate, family. The latter has lost some of its erstwhile functions in our mobile, urban, industrial society, but because it is virtually the sole remaining kinship unit it has acquired some of the functions formerly performed by other kinship relations. Its burden has therefore become heavy—perhaps too heavy for its inherently frail structure; and divorce, which dissolves the immediate family, has become a much greater problem, because it represents a threat to the family organization that remains.

With the principle of kinship substitution and the custom of the great household abandoned, the child of a deceased or divorced parent has as a rule nowhere to turn except to the other parent. He does not retain the balanced family life that a child in a kinship society is likely to have. He is therefore a "problem" in a much more pressing sense.

EMOTIONAL TENSION IN THE SMALL FAMILY

Having become the sole important kinship unit, the small family exhibits an unusual emotional concentration within itself. Its members, living apart from other kinsmen and surrounded by temporary acquaintances or strangers, can rely only upon themselves to share the feelings peculiar to blood relationship. The resulting intensity is sometimes extremely great, if not stifling. The loss of nonaffectional functions has further increased the importance of the family's emotional bonds at the same time that it has reduced the mutual cooperation in outside matters which would ordinarily support these bonds. Marriages, instead of being arranged by the elders on the basis of objective standards, are formed on the basis of romantic love and maintained on the strength of mutual likes and dislikes. The custom of having only one, two, or three children, plus the isolation of the parents from any other children than their own, increases the uniqueness and hence the emotionality of the parent-child relation. Consequently any marital discord not only affects the mates acutely but also involves the children. Husband and wife, as a compensation for marital unhappiness, unconsciously seek consolation, revenge, release, prestige, security, or what not in the children. The offspring in turn are victims of divided loyalty, emotional insecurity, and parental interference. This is why many experts believe that chronic discord is worse for the child than divorce; but the emotional intensity of the immediate family in modern society complicates divorce itself. It not only makes divorce more probable (because if things go wrong they go very wrong), but it also makes much harder the emotional readjustments of parents and children after divorce.

THE EQUALITARIAN PRINCIPLE AND CUSTODY

Our reliance upon the immediate family is connected with another trait that aggravates the problem of the divorced child—namely, the equalitarian principle in wedlock. In a society where clans exist the child belongs either to his father's or his mother's clan. He cannot belong to both. Consequently in case of divorce there is little question as to the child's custody and residence. But in our system the child does not automatically belong to one parent. Instead he may belong to either one, and it is up to the court to decide which one. Furthermore, because the estranged parents have a potentially equal claim, they often *compete* for the affection and custody (though not for the support) of the child. The court must assume the role of arbiter. It must exercise its "discretion," but finds itself with few rules on which that discretion can base itself. The welfare of the child rather than the claims of the parents is supposed to be the goal, but what is "welfare" to one judge is apt to differ from what is "welfare" to another.

That parents compete for custody of the children is suggested by the results of Marshall and May's study of cases in Maryland and Ohio. They show that the mother generally gets the children, but that this is because she is usually the plaintiff. When the father is the plaintiff he gets custody more often than she. There is thus a tendency to award custody to the "innocent" party, although this apparently has little to do with the welfare of the child. There is also a tendency for the mother to get custody oftener when the children are girls, the father when they are boys—a fairly frequent pattern in other societies. Less than five per cent of the Ohio cases involve division of the children between the parents, although provision is usually made whereby the parent not receiving custody may visit, or be visited by, the children, in which case there is a sort of de facto mixed custody. The facts indicate that a majority of the children of divorced parents in this country are living with their mother. This conclusion is substantiated by a study of high school students whose parents have been divorced. Thirty-two per cent of these students did not remember their father's occupation as compared to only 8 per cent of the students from non-divorced homes, indicating a surprising lack of contact with the father after divorce. Nevertheless, the parents have at the start an equal claim to the children, and the question of custody must be thrashed out anew in every case.

The competitive claims of husband and wife also emerge with reference to the support of the child. Since in our culture the father is supposed to support the child and the mother to care for it, the tendency of the court is to continue this division of labor after divorce. The fact that in a money economy a child can be supported at a distance, makes this arrangement seem convenient; but actually it presents an anomalous situation, because the father, deprived of the child's company, is nevertheless held economically responsible for him. The father thus receives an obligation without a reciprocal right. The one-sidedness of the arrangement is reduced, however, by the fact that woman's social role is more closely connected with the family than is that of the male, and that consequently his being deprived of the child's company entails less sacrifice than her being so deprived. Furthermore, the care of children is more burdensome and less easily evaded than their support.

THE FACTOR OF MORAL STIGMA

Although divorce in some form is permitted in all societies but encouraged in none, there are great differences in the degree of disapproval attached to it. American opinion has gradually changed from sharp to rather mild disapproval. The law, however, has retained in theory the older attitude; it bans divorce by mutual consent, stipulates that one party must have committed a wrong against the other, and thinks in terms of the "guilty" and the "innocent" partner. The moral condemnation of divorce has made, and still does make, the child's position more difficult than it would otherwise be.

To see the effect of moral stigma one should compare the child whose parents are separated by divorce with one whose parents are separated by death. The obvious difference that in one case only one parent remains alive while in the other both parents do, means that the divorce child may *theoretically* retain the contact and devotion of both parents. But this ideal possibility does not usually work out in practice, because the child, entangled by the closeness and intensity of the family bonds and the guilt complex of the divorce relation, is inevitably involved in the marital conflict. He is, after the divorce, the sole remaining link between the former mates, and consequently serves as the only instrument through which they can express their mutual resentment. The equalitarian principle which gives both of them rights in the child is conducive to his being used in this way, for if he divides his time between the two he must necessarily serve as a means of communication for them. A study of the divorce child in Nebraska showed that "often the part-time child is used as a weapon by one or both parents," that "in a few cases youngsters stated they had procured information for one parent against the other," that the situation afforded "the father an opportunity to find out how his former wife is spending his alimony, whom she is 'stepping out with,' and so forth," that "the mother may likewise question the child when he comes 'home' from father," and that in some cases "the child is bribed in order to get this information," and is thus taught by his own parents "to lie, spy, and blackmail."

Playwrights and novelists have seized upon the dramatic element in the situation, usually portraying the child as an innocent victim of parental folly, living an unnatural and lonely life. Some of the sympathy undoubtedly reflects the genuinely difficult situation of the child, but one suspects that a good deal of it also reflects a moralistic bias. Since divorce is sinful, the child's lot must be painted as badly as possible in order to make the sin (in its consequences for the *innocent* offspring) seem as terrible as possible. Thus the moral stigma attached to divorce not only makes the child's position worse than it would otherwise be, but also requires that it be depicted as even more tragic than it actually is.

The child of divorced parents probably runs no greater risk of a stepparent situation than does the bereaved child. But he does run a risk, as the latter does not, of falling into *two* such situations, because both parents may remarry and he may be shifted from one household to the other. Actually this does not happen in a large percentage of cases, but it happens often enough to give point to novels and plays about "part-time children." The parents may have moved far away from each other and remarried in different social circles. The child may thus have to divide his life between two radically different milieus, with a resulting confusion in his personality development. Because of bitterness between the estranged parents, he is apt to be under a taboo upon what he can say concerning events in the other household. Not only must he suppress part of his memories, but he must alter his personal habits and his family terminology each time that a shift is made. The situation is so new in our culture that no adequate terminology exists. What, for instance, is the new spouse of the divorced parent to be called by the child? "Stepmother" is hardly the correct term, because it implies that the child's real mother is dead. When the child talks to playmates about his father's wife, he accordingly has a hard time describing her, and outsiders frequently make mistakes that embarrass them and consequently him. Finally, he almost inevitably comes to prefer one household to the other, a fact taken by one parent as a breach of affection and an expression of a perverse devotion to the stepparent (perhaps the original corespondent) in the other household.

One thing that makes any stepchild situation difficult is the mystical importance our culture attaches to biological parenthood. A "real" son or daughter must be one's "own." When the stepchild is the offspring of a person still living, who once had and (even worse) may still have the primary affection of one's mate, then the difficulty of loving the child is increased.

In some ways, therefore, the child of divorced parents is less fortunate than the bereaved child, but the reason lies chiefly in the emotional and moral implications with which our culture surrounds divorce. If spouses would divorce amicably, without blame or recrimination; if the law would cease to search for the guilty party; if the public would accept divorce as a natural occurrence—if, in short, all the attitudes and sentiments which control the institution of the family were abandoned, then the position of the child after divorce would not be anomalous, and writers of fiction would not feel obligated to paint his lot in somber colors. But in such a free and easy society there would be hardly any necessity of marriage, and hence no such thing as divorce. Mating would be on an informal basis, and the children would be cared for by whoever felt inclined, if anybody.

As previously mentioned, our peculiar institutional structure places considerable reliance upon the immediate family. Since this unit has lost many of its functions it can be broken without disturbing many aspects of society. Such dissolution does, however, affect seriously the rearing of children, which is an extremely important function in any society. Therefore, if the current social system for rearing children is to be maintained, divorce cannot become a matter of absolute indifference. There is, however, good evidence to indicate that easy divorce does not necessarily imply the disintegration of society. Many societies having high divorce rates are every bit as stable as many having low divorce rates. Egypt, for example, has an extremely high divorce rate (much higher than the United States), yet its fertility, the stability of its institutions, and the contentment of its people are apparently as great as they are in India, which has a low rate. In nineteenth-century Japan the divorce rate was much higher than in China, yet Japanese social organization was, if anything, more efficient. There is no reason to believe, therefore, that a highly tolerant attitude toward divorce in the United States will mean the decline and fall of our civilization. In practice we seem to be moving in the direction of easier divorce anyway, and as this movement continues the position of the child of divorced parents should improve. The only necessity is that some sort of social machinery be worked out for rearing the child properly—a necessity hard to supply in our culture. Once this is accomplished the incidence of divorce is of little consequence to the stability of the larger society.

Six · A Therapeutic Approach to the Problem of Divorce

PAUL W. ALEXANDER
Judge, Court of Common Pleas
Toledo, Ohio

A judge who has handled some 25,000 divorce cases in his court during the past 13 years describes below * *some weaknesses in divorce laws and outlines some desirable reforms.*

SELDOM has any branch of our jurisprudence set such an example of ineffable ineptitude and brought upon itself such serious censure from such varied sources as has the law of divorce.

Let's listen a moment to the Supreme Court of Ohio, per Hitchcock, J., in *Harter* v. *Harter:*

* Reprinted from *Law Forum*, 1950, 36: 105–108, 168–172, by permission of the author and the University of Illinois.

> Perhaps there is no statute in Ohio more abused than the statute concerning "divorce and alimony." Perhaps there is no statute under which greater imposition is practiced upon the court and more injustice done to individuals. . . . The hearings are generally *ex parte*. Witnesses are examined, friendly to the applicant, and it is almost, if not utterly, impossible for the court in most instances to arrive at the real truths of the case. . . . But of the great multitude of cases which are before this court I am confident that by far the greater number are not [meritorious].

Please note the phrases "abused," "imposition on the court," "injustice to individuals," "real truths," "great multitude," "not meritorious." Do these have a familiar ring? Is this a fairly typical statement, in supreme courtish language, of the current criticism of our divorce law?

Well, the significant thing about this pronouncement, reported in 5 Ohio 319, is that it was uttered in 1832. No, that's not a misprint. It was not eighteen, but 118 years ago, when the divorce *rate* was well under one-tenth what it is now and the *volume* perhaps one-fiftieth!

PREVIOUS REFORM ATTEMPTS FOREDOOMED TO FAILURE

Does anyone care to stand forth and suggest that matters have improved any in the past century? If they haven't, it's not for lack of effort. In 1879 the American Bar Association recognized existing evils and moved toward a uniform law. In 1884 came the first of a long series of congressional moves toward a federal divorce law. In 1905 the American Bar Association had an "Act on Divorce Procedure," approved by an inter-church conference. A year later a national divorce congress, convened by the Governor of Pennsylvania, drafted a model act. The National Conference of Commissioners on Uniform State Laws has long had divorce law conspicuously on its agenda and has offered many distinct improvements.

As we look back now, it seems that these efforts were foredoomed to failure. For one thing, many appear to have been primarily concerned with achieving uniformity, reform being incidental. For another, they appear to have occupied themselves mainly with seeking an ideal set of "grounds" of divorce. Uniformity is desirable, of course, but who wants a uniform bad law? And how much good would mere uniformity do that 97 per cent of litigants who do not migrate but patronize home industry?

We suggest previous efforts may have failed because they were mainly attempts to graft good branches upon an ailing tree—to patch up a rotten structure on a sand foundation with a sound plank here and there. Clearly they were not basic or fundamental;

they did not go to the real roots of the evil. They appear to have accepted most if not all of the prevailing fallacies and misconceptions on the part of the law and the public.

A FLAGRANT MISCONCEPTION ABOUT RESULTS OF DIVORCE

The trouble starts with a flagrant misconception about what divorce really does. Almost everybody believes, and the law takes for granted, that divorce destroys marriage and breaks up the family. This simply is not true. Divorce is the end result of the marriage failure, the broken family, not the cause of it.

THE STRIKING AMBIVALENCE OF THE LAW

We intimated the law regards itself as divorcing spouses, thus destroying marriages and breaking homes. Consequently it looks with extreme disfavor upon divorce. It abhors divorce in general. On the other hand almost from the beginning of recorded history, the law has sanctioned some form of divorce. To meet the ever-growing popular demand for divorce within the past century or so, it has sanctioned divorce as we know it in every state. But it has done so grudgingly.

In its efforts to resist the evils of divorce, the law has unwittingly engendered new evils, to wit, most of the obstacles it has erected in the path of the divorce-seeker. It has merely made divorce something of a hurdle race, in which if you can't clear the hurdles you knock them down. Or they are something like Peer Gynt's Great Boyg: if you can't surmount it, you go around it.

DOMICILE ON EVIL BUT NOT A NECESSARY ONE

The first one we encounter is the requirement of *domicile*. Our statutes mostly say "residence" for a given period. Our courts tell us the statutes don't mean what they say, that they really mean "domicile." And thus they have opened a Pandora's box.

> Why should domicile of the plaintiff in the forum be important at all, apart from the requirement of local law? . . . It is conceivable that the requirement of domicile could be abandoned for nowhere is it mentioned in the Constitution. Constitutional doctrine might have been evolved to give finality to divorces obtained anywhere upon personal jurisdiction over the defendant. And if this had been done it may be doubted whether more collusion would exist than exists today in obtaining divorce. But it is too late now to urge this view.

Does it *have* to be too late to urge this view? Construing "residence" to mean "domicile" having failed of its intended purpose and having served to make bad matters worse, are we "stuck" with this idea forever? Factually it is the state where the parties actually live that is adversely affected by their marriage failure—not some distant state they may *think* is their home. And if they are living in different states, it is those states where the individuals have actually resided a reasonable length of time that are adversely affected (although certain states which prostitute their honor in order to fatten on marital misfortune could hardly be expected to subscribe to this view). Moreover, the real truth about the alleged marriage failure, the root of the trouble, can best be investigated and determined in those states where the parties have actually been residing.

GUILT IS THE ONLY CRITERION OF DIVORCE

When may a divorce be granted? Only when one party is guilty. That is the only criterion fixed by the law in every state. Guilt is made the cause of divorce. What form of guilt is specified by the "grounds," the overt acts or omissions which the law says shall be sufficient cause—things we used to call sin.

True, specific sinning is often the *proximate* cause, the last straw, but rarely, if ever, the ultimate cause. When mamma nags or is cold and drives papa to the corner "nite club" and a "drug-store blonde," the blonde is only a superficial, intervening cause (in more ways than one!). She is really effect, not cause, of the ostensible marriage failure. And it isn't necessarily a marriage failure—yet—both parties to the contrary notwithstanding. And divorce is not necessarily the right prescription, no matter how loudly either or both parties may proclaim it is.

LAW PERMITS PATIENT TO WRITE OWN PRESCRIPTION

Medical science doesn't allow the patient to write his own prescription; though pain drive him to demand amputation of his shattered leg, the surgeon won't amputate if the leg can be repaired. Must the law always permit the divorce litigant to write his own prescription, especially when it proclaims the state is a party to the action and professes to have a vital interest in the preservation of family life?

One of the saddest things confronting the fellow who hears divorce cases by the thousands is the utter lack of insight on the part of the divorce-seeker into the basic factors underlying what he believes to be an irreparable marriage failure. Maybe only one in ten may wonder, and vaguely at that, just where, when, how, and why the trouble started. Maybe only one in a hundred is endowed with sufficient mental capacity, intellectual honesty, and emotional objectivity to put his finger on the causative factors, to diagnose his own case. As for the remainder, their pride is too deeply wounded, they are too hurt, they are too angry to be able to think straight. They can only feel, and how! "He had the blonde, didn't he? Then give me my divorce." And that's that.

LAW'S ONLY INTEREST IS IN SUPERFICIAL FACTORS

But saddest of all is the law's own lack of insight into, or even interest in, sub-surface causative factors and proper remedial measures. It offers divorce as a supposed remedy—but what a tragically imperfect remedy, and how often the wrong one altogether! In prescribing divorce for every fracture of the marital vows, it is like a surgeon who knows only to prescribe amputation for every fracture of a limb. It deludes itself, and most of society, into believing that if the spouse is guilty of the prescribed surface-manifestation or outward symptom, the only cure is divorce.

Incidentally, one lesson impressed upon those who hear the multitude of divorce cases is that comparatively minor *legal* guilt can be and often is vastly more devastating to the parties and definitely more disruptive of family life than that guilt which the law, religion, and society regard as most offensive, to wit, adultery. Case histories by the hundred could be cited where the plaintiff has said: "I could put up with the blonde if only he wouldn't—" do this or that or the other thing which is generally regarded as trivial by comparison. And the plaintiff really means it.

And so it appears that the law by making guilt the index of marriage failure and by placing so much emphasis upon the grounds or forms of guilt has contributed to its own failure in its avowed purpose to preserve marriage and the family. It is not preventive; it is punitive. It does not conserve; it disserves.

ADVERSARY PROCEDURES OBSOLETE AND OBSTRUCTIVE

Further to impede divorce, the law forbids a decree by default. That would too patently be divorce by mutual consent. So although in some 90 per cent of cases the defendant stays carefully away, the plaintiff must, nevertheless, put on an exhibition of shadow-boxing and give the shadow a knockout to the satisfaction of the law. Whoever originated the forms and procedures for divorce litigation little realized that he was setting the stage for a sham battle against the little man who isn't there. Yet to this day all our forms and procedures remain those designed for adversary litigation.

Thus the law not only makes a mockery of itself and stultifies litigants, lawyers, and judges; it defeats its own end. Instead of doing all in its power to facilitate reconciliation of the parties so that there won't have to be a divorce, it forces them into a position of hostility and antagonism so that a divorce is almost inevitable. It arrays one against the other in battle formation and makes the plaintiff assault the enemy with all the venom at his command.

Probably in less than 1 per cent of the grand total of all cases is there a sincere contest over the single issue of divorce.

GUILT BEGETS RECRIMINATION, A PRIZE ANOMALY

As a sort of corollary, or perhaps a syndrome of the doctrine of guilt, the law has adopted the defense of recrimination. Although divorce is generally supposed to be an action *in rem,* neither *ex contractu, ex delicto,* criminal, nor wholly equitable in nature, our courts, having no other precedent to follow, have followed in the footsteps of the ecclesiastical courts and espoused the equitable defense of clean hands. And thereby the law has placed itself in the anomalous position of saying, to the amazement and amusement of laymen and lawyers alike, that if both spouses have grounds for divorce, neither has ground.

The main practical effects of recrimination appear to be three-fold. First, it reduces the trial to a mud-slinging, name-calling contest, the parties vying in vengefulness, vindictiveness, vituperation, and vilification. Each is driven to the greatest lengths to save face and deprive the other of victory. Trivia are blown up into monstrosities; fancies are fabricated as fact. Be the court lax or strict, it is altogether an experience harrowing to all concerned; damaging to the parties, their personalities, characters, reputations, and social position; often damaging to both financially by causing loss of jobs, business, public confidence, etc.; cruelly torturing the children, who are sometimes called upon to take sides, and often irreparably injuring them; and not at all helpful to the court.

Second, it makes it next to impossible for either spouse to obtain a decree. This is because, human nature being what it is, it is next to impossible to find all the guilt on one side, all the innocence on the other. Some may consider recrimination a good thing because it serves to prevent the granting of even a comparatively few divorces; some do not. If there can ever be social need for divorce when only one spouse is known to be guilty—and the law of every state says there is—it is hard to see why the social need is not greater when both are guilty. Plenty of case histories could be adduced indicating that the mere refusal of a divorce cures nothing; that the frustrations entailed thereby mainly drive the parties into sinning in the open, into taking on new types of sinning, into neuroticism, and sometimes into crimes of violence.

YET RECRIMINATION HAS A FAINT SILVER LINING

Third, the availability of the defense of recrimination is often used as a threat or lever by either or both parties in negotiating for a settlement of alimony and property claims (not so often child custody or support, for the parents are not wholly free to bargain in these respects, and the court will do what is best for the child regardless of the wishes of either or both parties). If the wife's demands appear exorbitant and the husband's offers niggardly, the well-grounded fear that a court battle will result in a draw and that each will leave the scene of battle exactly as he entered it (except for fresh wounds and salt for old ones) serves to bring into the arena a faint scent of sweet reasonableness so that a compromise is effected. There is some evidence that about five out of every six contested cases assigned for trial are thus settled at the eleventh hour, just as the parties are called to enter the ring. And since the settlement must be submitted to and approved by the court, there is very little danger that substantial justice will not be done.

Thus the availability—not the application—of the defense of recrimination appears to be something of a boon to counsel, clients and court, albeit an unwitting one.

COLLUSION, BASTARD CHILD OF GUILT AND RECRIMINATION

The doctrine of collusion looks like the bastard, incestuous off-spring of the doctrines of guilt and recrimination. The plaintiff must be free of statutory guilt. Nobody knows better than the defendant, generally speaking, whether the plaintiff is so free. If the defendant would only come into court and tell what he knows about the plaintiff, that would stop the performance. But nine times out of ten that isn't what the defendant wants, so he remains entirely off stage.

Now the defendant is under neither moral nor legal obligation to appear and defend; or if, as happens in one or two cases in ten, he has filed a defense or cross complaint, he is at liberty to think better of it and withdraw the same and stay away. But if, as commonly occurs, he talks things over with the plaintiff, or writes from outside the jurisdiction, and decides not to defend, and the court finds out about it, the court is supposed to find that he and the plaintiff have agreed to deceive the court by offering false evidence or suppressing material evidence.

And the court would usually be warranted in finding that there was an agreement of some sort, possibly express, or possibly a wholly unvoiced understanding. For without saying a word to each other, both understand—and agree—that if the defendant keeps still, the case will be prosecuted to final decree and both will get what they want.

DISAGREEING DISAGREEABLY IS ALL RIGHT; AGREEABLY IS ILLEGAL

Now no court can ever be expected to tolerate an actual con-spiracy to deceive which would involve *mens rea*. But it is not easy to see how the plaintiff by doing what he presumably has a legal right to do, or the defendant by not doing what he has neither moral nor legal obligation to do, is guilty of an attempt to deceive the court—is guilty of collusion.

In actual practice an overwhelming majority of cases are agreed-to cases. Everybody knows it, even judges. Yet the existence of the doctrine of collusion puts everybody, including the judge who is supposed to speak for the law, in the ignominious position of pretending not to know it in any given case, of conniving at the actual fact—certainly not a salutary situation.

On the whole it appears that the doctrine of collusion as construed and applied in actual practice is productive of considerably more harm than good. After all—legally—to disagree isn't necessarily evil in itself. If the parties feel they must disagree, isn't it better to have it done agreeably than antagonistically? And isn't a considerable amount of agreement inevitable? Yet the position of the law is tantamount to forbidding agreement. (Agreement must not be confused with divorce by mutual consent.)

DIVORCE LAW LESS CIVILIZED THAN CRIMINAL LAW

In criminal law the quality of mercy is not strained. It is blessed by the law itself as well as the recipient. In divorce law the quality of mercy is *verboten*. At no stage of the proceedings does the law authorize anything akin to it, and if the plaintiff extends mercy to the defendant, the law punishes him for it. By the doctrine of condonation, the law presumes to subvert the divine attribute of forgiveness. And thereby the law opens the door to trickery, perjury, duress; closes the door upon honest attempts at reconciliation! And thus the law of divorce appears to be even less civilized than the criminal law.

In practice condonation is less a defense than a nuisance. It is comparatively seldom pleaded by the defendant, and less often proved. Most often it comes to light inadvertently, especially in those courts which don't always accept all of the plaintiff's testimony at face value but make some effort to elicit a little real truth by questioning the plaintiff. Then to the consternation of counsel, the plaintiff lets the cat out of the bag, and all the court can do is to tell the plaintiff: "Sorry, you'll have to go home and wait until your spouse gives you new ground for divorce. That is the penalty the law imposes upon you for forgiving him and for your honesty in telling us about it."

Where the doctrine of condonation gets in some of its worst licks is in the lawyer's office when counsel in accord with ethical canon, advises the client of the legal consequences of her acts and admonishes: "Now if you really want your divorce, you mustn't have anything to do with your husband. If he wants to kiss and make up, better send him away because if you fall for his line and the judge finds out about it, he'll throw your case out of court." We hear people criticize the lawyer for not doing more to head off the divorce-seeker; yet we require him to advise against the one thing most likely to lead to withdrawal of the suit!

TIME FOR BASIC REFORM LONG UPON US

So much for the iniquitous ineptitude of our divorce philosophy and procedure. If they were in a bad way 118 or 70 years ago, it would seem the time has already been far too long upon us to do something about it—not something superficial, not something just to relieve symptoms here and there, not a crazy-quilt pattern of patch-work, but something basic, fundamental, radical, something going to the roots of the evil.

Threescore and ten years after its initial effort, the American Bar Association again proposes to do something about it, this time something plenty radical. It has a special committee on divorce and marriage laws and family courts, and this committee has tossed out a football for the legal profession, the clergy, the sociologists, and the laity to kick around. Instead of the ball being promptly punctured, it has been received with open arms by an amazing proportion of representatives of all these groups.

LAW SHOULD CONSERVE, NOT DISSERVE FAMILY LIFE

No blueprint has yet been drawn. An architect does not put pen to paper until he has a pretty clear idea of what the client wants. And if the client wants to tear down an old, evil-smelling structure infested by rats and termites, and in its place erect a brand new type of building with only a limited and comparatively unknown precedent to go on, he will be wise to consult every available source of experience, opinion, warning, criticism, and suggestion. And that is exactly what the American Bar Association committee is striving to do.

What all of us want is not to open the floodgates for more divorces; not to sanction divorce by mutual consent (which is what we now have in actual reality). What every right-thinking person wants is to see our philosophy so shaped, our law—substantive and adjective—so designed that it will tend to conserve not disserve family life; that it will be constructive, not destructive of marriage; that it will be preventive, not punitive toward marriage failure; that it will be helpful, not harmful to the individual spouses and their children.

TO CAST OUT OLD CONCEPTS, EMULATE JUVENILE COURT

To these ends the American Bar Association committee has offered some proposals—and that is all they are, proposals. Keeping ever in mind the postulates that divorce is effect, not cause, and that the true function of a divorce decree is only to terminate the legal fiction remaining after the spouses themselves have reduced their marriage to a factual fiction by destroying the emotional, physical, social, and material bonds which actually united them, the committee proposes that we repudiate those concepts, doctrines, and procedures with which the law has shackled itself and so ineptly defeated its own ends, including domicile, guilt and punishment, adversary litigation, recrimination, collusion, and condonation.

Wiping the slate clean and starting from scratch, the committee proposes to take a leaf from a movement characterized by Roscoe Pound as an outstanding example of American institutional inventiveness and as "the outstanding achievement in penal and correctional law and administration in the present century and indeed the most significant development in our criminal law since the reforms of the beginning of the nineteenth century." Unfortunately, through no fault of their own, this movement is really familiar to few lawyers and to fewer judges. The juvenile court is probably the least understood and most misunderstood of all our courts.

It would be unwise and unfair for one to try to evaluate the soundness of the committee's suggestion unless he were thoroughly acquainted with juvenile court philosophy and *modus operandi*. And space does not permit us to expound that here.

A FEW ELEMENTARY POINTS ABOUT PROPOSED PROTOTYPE

In a few words, the *standard* juvenile court substitutes diagnosis and therapy for guilt and punishment. It is more interested in ultimate than proximate cause. It doesn't hold trials to determine the child's guilt or innocence. Its skillful approach is friendly; its aim, to help the child; its criterion, what is best for the child.

It operates within the law but does not confine itself to the law. It invokes the aid of other sciences and disciplines, such as religion, medicine, psychology, psychiatry, sociology, and education. It operates under a judicial officer but does not confine itself to the judge. It employs trained technicians and skilled specialists. Even the judge must make himself into a specialist.

According to Dean Pound it has five characteristics of equity jurisdiction: "(1) It is relatively informal in its procedure. . . . (2) As with all equity jurisdiction it is remedial, not punitive. (3) It acts preventively in advance of commission of any specific wrongdoing. (4) It employs administrative rather than adversary methods. (5) It can adapt its action to the circumstances of individual cases and so achieve a high degree of individualization, which is demanded by justice, if not always by security."

At the same time the *standard* juvenile court appreciates "the importance of the ethics of judicial adjudication, of hearing both sides fully, of acting on evidence of logical probative force, and of not combining the function of accuser, prosecutor, advocate of the complaint, and judge; of a record from which it can be seen what has been done and how and on what basis; and of possibility of review before a bench of judges in order to save fundamental constitutional and legal rights. . . ."

Its energies and skills are mainly directed toward discovering and removing or rectifying the underlying, sub-surface causal factors which brought about the child's delinquency.

TO CONVERT THE MORGUE INTO A HOSPITAL

It happens that the court over which I preside handles both divorce and delinquency. Years ago I became aware that we were able to straighten out and do a good repair job upon an impressive majority of the delinquent children; while at the same time, in an appalling proportion of the divorce cases, little, if any, respectable effort was made or opportunity presented to do any kind of a repair job. The juvenile court was a hospital where the ailing behavior of the children was diagnosed and treated; the divorce court was a morgue where ailing marriages were merely pronounced dead upon superficial examination, and burial certificates were issued in the form of divorce decrees.

The American Bar Association committee proposes to transform the divorce court from a morgue into a hospital; to handle our ailing marriages and delinquent spouses much as we handle our delinquent children—for often their behavior is not unlike that of a delinquent child and for much the same reasons. Instead of looking only at the guilt of the defendant, it proposes to examine the whole marriage, endeavor to discover the basic causative factors, and seek to remove or rectify them, enlisting the aid of other sciences and disciplines and of all available community resources.

NEW CRITERION: WHAT IS BEST FOR THIS FAMILY?

The fresh approach, the new philosophy would be signified by the very titling of the case; instead of it being "*John Doe* v. *Mary Doe*," it would be titled "*In the Interest of the John Doe Family*." There would be no plaintiff, no defendant—only an applicant or joint applicants. The application would be not for divorce but for the remedial services of the state. Petition for divorce would be permitted only after complete investigation and report. The new plan would take over almost bodily the entire philosophy, procedure, and techniques of the juvenile court. As in the juvenile court the criterion (fixed by law as well as philosophy) is "What is best for this child?" so in the divorce court the criterion would be "What is best for this family?"

To do this sort of thing would obviously require a special kind of court which, for convenience, has been called the "Family Court." As Dean Pound points out in speaking of the juvenile court there are strong reasons for not making it a separate court but a branch of the court of general jurisdiction of first instance. It would seem necessary to endow it with the broadest possible equitable, civil, and even criminal jurisdiction. It should have the same dignity and status as the court of general jurisdiction; its quarters should be adequate in size, advantageously located, designed for functional efficiency, equipped, and decorated so as to command respect for the law which it will administer.

THE FAMILY COURT SURPASSES OTHERS IN IMPORTANCE

Among the reasons for this is that although the family court may deal in dimes while other branches of the court deal in dollars, nevertheless, because it is bound to have so many more clients than the ordinary civil and criminal courts and their problems strike home so intimately into their everyday life, the family court cannot fail to have a greater impact upon the sum total of human welfare and happiness than perhaps all other branches of the court combined.

Like the juvenile court, the family court would require an adequate staff of trained technicians and skilled specialists, such as the social caseworker, psychiatric caseworker, clinical psychologist, psychiatrist, marriage counsellor, and others, and, of course, a proper clerical force.

FAMILY COURT JUDGE MUST BECOME A SPECIALIST

Most important, the court would require a specialist judge or judges. No court can be expected to rise above its judge. No matter how able a lawyer he may be or how filled with the spirit of altruism, he will have to school himself in quite a number of fields of learning and disciplines for which his legal training and experiences have not prepared him. Among these are social casework, group work, counselling, diagnosis and therapy, several branches of psychology (especially so-called abnormal psychology), penology, criminology, the basic principles of psychiatry, medical casework, community organization, child and family welfare, and some others.

As Dean Pound puts it: "Just because the procedure is so flexible and the scope for personal discretion and individualization of treatment is so great, it is imperative that the judges who sit in [juvenile] courts be exceptionally qualified. Bad consequences have flowed in more than one locality from the unfortunate practice of rotation which prevails so generally in American judicial organization. . . . But it is still true in too many jurisdictions in courts of first instance with a number of co-ordinate judges, that they sit successively in turn in civil jury cases, equity cases, criminal cases, and divorce proceedings. Thus each has to learn what he may by a brief experience as to the art of handling special classes of judicial work only to pass to some other special class where he must learn in a short time a new art."

Obtaining the right kind of judges, the fitting of square pegs into square holes, poses something of a problem, but surely not an insurmountable one. The 1949 revision of the Standard Juvenile Court Act by the National Probation and Parole Association proposes a plan for the selection of the right type of juvenile court judge. This plan was adapted from the American Bar Association or "Missouri" plan, and something along this line should prove equally adaptable to the family court.

ONE INTEGRATED COURT FOR ALL JUSTICIABLE FAMILY PROBLEMS

In view of the approximate identity of philosophy, procedure, techniques, and type of staff of the juvenile court and the family court, and because most problems of juvenile delinquency are in essence family problems, it has been proposed that the new court handle *all* justiciable family problems from juvenile delinquency to divorce. This proposal is far from new. The National Probation and Parole Association (Roscoe Pound, chairman) has been advocating it since 1917. It has been tried and has long since passed the experimental stage. For a third of a century Cincinnati has had such a court. From the outset the soundness of the idea became more and more apparent, and soon other Ohio cities fell in line; for years the seven largest (next after Cleveland, which has an independent juvenile court) have had such integrated family courts. They have a cumulative experience of over 150 years of successful operation, during which no serious objection has been raised to this type of "domestic relations" court. It is a division of the court of general jurisdiction. The judge is elected to this particular division and must "stay with it." There is no rotation.

Most of the advantages of having all socio-legal family problems handled by one integrated court are obvious. There is an additional advantage not apparent to the uninitiated. As previously indicated, marriages fail because of the defects of the spouses. Spouses of this sort who have children are apt to have contact with the juvenile court. Then when they wind up in the divorce court, the judge has before him the complete family record. One year in one such court in as high as 40 per cent of the divorce cases, the family had previously had contact with the juvenile court. The information gleaned from these family records enabled the judge to get at the whole truth and to find the best solution for the family as a whole.

Conversely, as pointed out by Judge Edwin A. Robson of Chicago in a recent study of divorce in Illinois, many young wards of the divorce court are destined, because of the broken family, to become wards of the juvenile court; and like advantages could be expected from combining the two courts.

The principal disadvantage of this type of court is seldom mentioned. In counties with a population of a quarter million or more, the volume of cases, adult and juvenile, and the administrative problem of handling a staff of thirty or forty or more, with an annual budget well into six figures, combine to make the judge work under such relentless pressure that he cannot always give his very best to the clients—who are entitled to an unhurried hearing before an unharried judge. The job can be a man-killer for the judge; but the obvious simple solution would be to have two or more judges for the larger courts.

In the case of the smaller community which would not warrant the establishment of a full-time family court with a full-time specialist judge, it is proposed to take a leaf from the experience in Connecticut and Utah, where state juvenile courts are presided over by three judges who travel from county to county with an office and full-time worker in each county.

THE LAWYER AN INDISPENSABLE PART OF THE PICTURE

Where will the lawyer fit into the picture? In the view of the American Bar Association committee, the lawyer's services will be indispensable. No legitimate avenue of income will be closed to him. Provision should be made for his protection in this respect. His services when he helps salvage a broken family should be of greater value to both the parties and the state than when he merely procures the court to administer the *coup de grâce*.

However, instead of playing a purely destructive rôle as he is now called upon to do, he will play a constructive rôle. In the juvenile court more often than not, the lawyer is an effective ally of the court in "selling" the best plan to his client. Because the client had confidence enough in him to retain him, the lawyer is sometimes in a better position than the court worker to persuade the client to do what is best for the child. There is no reason apparent why he could not fulfill a corresponding function in the family court.

WE MUST NOT WAIT FOR PERFECTION OR UNANIMITY

In conclusion, I hope no one will get the idea that the foregoing proposals are even a remote attempt at a definite blueprint. On the contrary they should be construed as an invitation for criticisms and suggestions which the American Bar Association committee solicits and promises to consider.

Perfection is desirable. So is unanimity of opinion. We should strive for perfection and we should strive for unanimity, but we had best resign ourselves to the fact that we shall never achieve either. If we wait for either perfection or unanimity we shall wait forever, and that is unthinkable. I reiterate, the time for *fundamental* reform has already been *too* long upon us.

XIII · WHAT ROLE FOR WOMEN

One · Cultural Contradictions and Sex Roles

MIRRA KOMAROVSKY

Sociologist, Barnard College

The subject of the acceptable role or roles for women in our culture is a highly controversial one. Mirra Komarovsky says that certain problems set forth in her article, which follows,* will persist "until the adult sex roles of women are redefined in greater harmony with the socioeconomic and ideological character of modern society."

Is it possible to redefine women's roles? Are roles already being redefined to such an extent that we are well on the way through a transition period toward changed conceptions of what are properly the functions and expectations of each sex? Those questions cannot yet be answered. The Komarovsky reading deals with problems arising for a group of college women because of cultural contradictions regarding sex roles.

PROFOUND changes in the roles of women during the past century have been accompanied by innumerable contradictions and inconsistencies. With our rapidly changing and highly differentiated culture, with migrations and multiplied social contacts, the stage is set for myriads of combinations of incongruous elements. Cultural norms are often functionally unsuited to the social situations to which they apply. Thus they may deter an individual from a course of action which would serve his own, and society's, interests best. Or, if behavior contrary to the norm is engaged in, the individual may suffer from guilt over violating mores which no longer serve any socially useful end. Sometimes culturally defined roles are adhered to in the face of new conditions without a conscious realization of the discrepancies involved. The reciprocal actions dictated by the roles may be at variance with those demanded by the actual situation. This may result in an imbalance of privileges and obligations or in some frustration of basic interests.

Again, problems arise because changes in the mode of life have created new situations which have not as yet been defined by culture. Individuals left thus without social guidance tend to act in

* Reprinted from *The American Journal of Sociology*, 1946, 52: 184–189, by permission of the author and of the University of Chicago Press.

terms of egotistic or "short-run hedonistic" motives which at times defeat their own long-term interests or create conflict with others. The precise obligation of a gainfully employed wife toward the support of the family is one such undefined situation.

Finally, a third mode of discrepancy arises in the existence of incompatible cultural definitions of the same social situation, such as the clash of "old-fashioned" and "radical" mores, of religion and law, of norms of economic and familial institutions.

The problems raised by these discrepancies are social problems in the sense that they engender mental conflict or social conflict or otherwise frustrate some basic interest of large segments of the population.

This article sets forth in detail the nature of certain incompatible sex roles imposed by our society upon the college woman. It is based on data collected in 1942 and 1943. Members of an undergraduate course on the family were asked for two successive years to submit autobiographical documents focused on the topic; 73 were collected. In addition, 80 interviews, lasting about an hour each, were conducted with every member of a course in social psychology of the same institution—making a total of 153 documents ranging from a minimum of five to a maximum of thirty typewritten pages.

The generalization emerging from these documents is the existence of serious contradictions between two roles present in the social environment of the college woman. The goals set by each role are mutually exclusive, and the fundamental personality traits each evokes are at points diametrically opposed, so that what are assets for one become liabilities for the other, and the full realization of one role threatens defeat in the other.

One of these roles may be termed the "feminine" role. While there are a number of permissive variants of the feminine role for women of college age (the "good sport," the "glamour girl," the "young lady," the domestic "home girl," etc.), they have a common core of attributes defining the proper attitudes to men, family, work, love, etc., and a set of personality traits often described with reference to the male sex role as "not as dominant, or aggressive as men" or "more emotional, sympathetic."

The other and more recent role is, in a sense, no *sex* role at all, because it partly obliterates the differentiation in sex. It demands of the woman much the same virtues, patterns of behavior, and attitude that it does of the men of a corresponding age. We shall refer to this as the "modern" role.

Both roles are present in the social environment of these women throughout their lives, though, as the precise content of each sex role varies with age, so does the nature of their clashes change from one stage to another. In the period under discussion the conflict between the two roles apparently centers about academic work, social life, vocational plans, excellence in specific fields of endeavor, and a number of personality traits.

One manifestation of the problem is in the inconsistency of the goals set for the girl by her family.

Forty, or 26 per cent, of the respondents expressed some grievance against their families for failure to confront them with clear-cut and consistent goals. The majority, 74 per cent, denied having had such experiences. One student writes:

> How am I to pursue any course single-mindedly when some way along the line a person I respect is sure to say, "You are on the wrong track and are wasting your time." Uncle John telephones every Sunday morning. His first question is: "Did you go out last night?" He would think me a "grind" if I were to stay home Saturday night to finish a term paper. My father expects me to get an "A" in every subject and is disappointed by a "B." He says I have plenty of time for social life. Mother says, "That 'A' in Philosophy is very nice, dear. But please don't become so deep that no man will be good enough for you." And, finally, Aunt Mary's line is careers for women. "Prepare yourself for some profession. This is the only way to insure yourself independence and an interesting life. You have plenty of time to marry."

A Senior writes:

> I get a letter from my mother at least three times a week. One week her letters will say, "Remember that this is your last year at college. Subordinate everything to your studies. You must have a good record to secure a job." The next week her letters are full of wedding news. This friend of mine got married; that one is engaged; my young cousin's wedding is only a week off. When, my mother wonders, will I make up my mind? Surely, I wouldn't want to be the only unmarried one in my group. It is high time, she feels, that I give some thought to it.

A student reminisces:

> All through high school my family urged me to work hard because they wished me to enter a first-rate college. At the same time they were always raving about a girl schoolmate who lived next door to us. How pretty and sweet she was, how popular, and what taste in clothes! Couldn't I also pay more attention to my appearance and to social life? They were overlooking the fact that this carefree friend of mine had little time left for school work and had failed several subjects. It seemed that my family had expected me to become Eve Curie and Hedy Lamar wrapped up in one.

Another comments:

> My mother thinks that it is very nice to be smart in college
> but only if it doesn't take too much effort. She always tells me
> not to be too intellectual on dates, to be clever in a light sort
> of way. My father, on the other hand, wants me to study law.
> He thinks that if I applied myself I could make an excellent
> lawyer and keeps telling me that I am better fitted for this
> profession than my brother.

The students testified to a certain bewilderment and confusion
caused by the failure on the part of the family to smooth the passage from one role to another, especially when the roles involved
were contradictory. It seemed to some of them that they had awakened one morning to find their world upside down: what had
hitherto evoked praise and rewards from relatives, now suddenly
aroused censure. A student recollects:

> I could match my older brother in skating, sledding, riflery,
> ball, and many of the other games we played. He enjoyed
> teaching me and took great pride in my accomplishments.
> Then one day it all changed. He must have suddenly become
> conscious of the fact that girls ought to be feminine. I was
> walking with him, proud to be able to make long strides and
> keep up with his long-legged steps when he turned to me in
> annoyance, "Can't you walk like a lady?" I still remember feel-
> ing hurt and bewildered by his scorn, when I had been led to
> expect approval.

Once during her freshman year in college, after a delightful date,
a student wrote her brother with great elation:

> "What a wonderful evening at ————— fraternity house! You
> would be proud of me, Johnny! I won all ping-pong games but
> one!"
> "For heaven's sake," came the reply, "when will you grow up?
> Don't you know that a boy likes to think he is better than a
> girl? Give him a little competition, sure, but miss a few serves
> in the end. Should you join the Debate Club? By all means,
> but don't practice too much on the boys." Believe me I was
> stunned by this letter, but then I saw that he was right. To be
> a success in the dorms one must date, to date one must not
> win too many ping-pong games. At first I resented this bitterly.
> But now I am more or less used to it and live in hope of one
> day meeting a man who is my superior so that I may be my
> natural self.

It is the parents and not the older sibling who reversed their expectations in the following excerpt:

All through grammar school and high school my parents led me to feel that to do well in school was my chief responsibility. A good report card, an election to student office, these were the news Mother bragged about in telephone conversations with her friends. But recently they suddenly got worried about me: I don't pay enough attention to social life, a woman needs *some* education but not that much. They are disturbed by my determination to go to the School of Social Work. Why my ambitions should surprise them after they have exposed me for four years to some of the most inspired and stimulating social scientists in the country, I can't imagine. They have some mighty strong arguments on their side. What is the use, they say, of investing years in training for a profession, only to drop it in a few years? Chances of meeting men are slim in this profession. Besides, I may become so preoccupied with it as to sacrifice social life. The next few years are, after all, the proper time to find a mate. But the urge to apply what I have learned, and the challenge of this profession is so strong that I shall go on despite the family opposition.

The final excerpt illustrates both the sudden transition of roles and the ambiguity of standards:

I major in English composition. This is not a completely "approved" field for girls so I usually just say "English." An English Literature major is quite liked and approved by boys. Somehow it is lumped with all the other arts and even has a little glamour. But a composition major is a girl to beware of because she supposedly will notice all your grammar mistakes, look at your letters too critically, and consider your ordinary speech and conversation as too crude.

I also work for a big metropolitan daily as a correspondent in the city room. I am well liked there and may possibly stay as a reporter after graduation in February. I have had several spreads [stories running to more than eight or ten inches of space], and this is considered pretty good for a college correspondent. Naturally, I was elated and pleased at such breaks, and as far as the city room is concerned I'm off to a very good start on a career that is hard for a man to achieve and even harder for a woman. General reporting is still a man's work in the opinion of most people. I have a lot of acclaim but also criticism, and I find it confusing and difficult to be praised for being clever and working hard and then, when my efforts promise to be successful, to be condemned and criticized for being unfeminine and ambitious.

Here are a few of these reactions:

My father: "I don't like this newspaper set-up at all. The people you meet are making you less interested in marriage than ever. You're getting too educated and intellectual to be attractive to men."

My mother: "I don't like your attitude toward people. The

paper is making you too analytical and calculating. Above all, you shouldn't sacrifice your education and career for marriage."

A lieutenant with two years of college: "It pleased me greatly to hear about your news assignment—good girl."

A Navy pilot with one year of college: "Undoubtedly, I'm old-fashioned, but I could never expect or feel right about a girl giving up a very promising or interesting future to hang around waiting for me to finish college. Nevertheless, congratulations on your job on the paper. Where in the world do you get that wonderful energy? Anyway I know you were thrilled at getting it and feel very glad for you. I've an idea that it means the same to you as that letter saying 'report for active duty' meant to me."

A graduate metallurgist now a private in the Army: "It was good to hear that you got that break with the paper. I am sure that talent will prove itself and that you will go far. But not too far, as I don't think you should become a career woman. You'll get repressed and not be interested enough in having fun if you keep after that career."

A lieutenant with a year and a half of college: "All this career business is nonsense. A woman belongs in the home and absolutely no place else. My wife will have to stay home. That should keep her happy. Men are just superior in everything, and women have no right to expect to compete with them. They should do just what will keep their husbands happy."

A graduate engineer—my fiancé: "Go right ahead and get as far as you can in your field. I am glad you are ambitious and clever, and I'm as anxious to see you happily successful as I am myself. It is a shame to let all those brains go to waste over just dusting and washing dishes. I think the usual home life and children are small sacrifices to make if a career will keep you happy. But I'd rather see you in radio because I am a bit wary of the effect upon our marriage of the way of life you will have around the newspaper."

Sixty-one, or 40 per cent, of the students indicated that they have occasionally "played dumb" on dates, that is, concealed some academic honor, pretended ignorance of some subject, or allowed the man the last word in an intellectual discussion. Among these were women who "threw games" and in general played down certain skills in obedience to the unwritten law that men must possess these skills to a superior degree. At the same time, in other areas of life, social pressures were being exerted upon these women to "play to win," to compete to the utmost of their abilities for intellectual distinction and academic honors. One student writes:

I was glad to transfer to a women's college. The two years at the co-ed university produced a constant strain. I am a good student; my family expects me to get good marks. At the same time I am normal enough to want to be invited to the Saturday night dance. Well, everyone knew that on that campus a reputation of a "brain" killed a girl socially. I was always fearful lest I say too much in class or answer a question which the boys I dated couldn't answer.

Here are some significant remarks made from the interviews:

I am engaged to a southern boy who doesn't think too much of the woman's intellect. In spite of myself, I play up to his theories because the less one knows and does, the more he does for you and thinks you "cute" into the bargain. . . . I allow him to explain things to me in great detail and to treat me as a child in financial matters.

When my date said that he considers Ravel's *Bolero* the greatest piece of music ever written, I changed the subject because I knew I would talk down to him.

A boy advised me not to tell of my proficiency in math and not to talk of my plans to study medicine unless I knew my date well.

My fiancé didn't go to college. I intend to finish college and work hard at it, but in talking to him I make college appear a kind of a game.

Once I went sailing with a man who so obviously enjoyed the role of a protector that I told him I didn't know how to sail. As it turned out he didn't either. We got into a tough spot, and I was torn between a desire to get a hold of the boat and a fear to reveal that I had lied to him.

It embarrassed me that my "steady" in high school got worse marks than I. A boy should naturally do better in school. I would never tell him my marks and would often ask him to help me with my homework.

I am better in math than my fiancé. But while I let him explain politics to me, we never talk about math even though, being a math major, I could tell him some interesting things.

I was once at a work camp. The girls did the same work as the boys. If some girls worked better, the boys resented it fiercely. The director told one capable girl to slow down to keep peace in the group.

How to do the job and remain popular was a tough task. If you worked your best, the boys resented the competition; if you acted feminine, they complained that you were clumsy.

On dates I always go through the "I-don't-care-anything-you-want-to-do" routine. It gets monotonous but boys fear girls who make decisions. They think such girls would make nagging wives.

I am a natural leader and, when in the company of girls, usually take the lead. That is why I am so active in college activities. But I know that men fear bossy women, and I always have to watch myself on dates not to assume the "executive" role. Once a boy walking to the theater with me took the wrong street. I knew a short cut but kept quiet.

I let my fiancé make most of the decisions when we are out. It annoys me, but he prefers it.

I sometimes "play dumb" on dates, but it leaves a bad taste. The emotions are complicated. Part of me enjoys "putting something over" on the unsuspecting male. But this sense of superiority over him is mixed with feeling of guilt for my hypocrisy. Toward the "date" I feel some contempt because he is "taken in" by my technique, or if I like the boy, a kind of a maternal condescension. At times I resent him! Why isn't he my superior in all ways in which a man should excel so that I could be my natural self? What am I doing here with him, anyhow? Slumming?

And the funny part of it is that the man, I think, is not always so unsuspecting. He may sense the truth and become uneasy in the relation. "Where do I stand? Is she laughing up her sleeve or did she mean this praise? Was she really impressed with that little speech of mine or did she only pretend to know nothing about politics?" And once or twice I felt that the joke was on me: the boy saw through my wiles and felt contempt for me for stooping to such tricks.

Another aspect of the problem is the conflict between the psychogenetic personality of the girl and the cultural role foisted upon her by the milieu. At times it is the girl with "masculine" interests and personality traits who chafes under the pressure to conform to the "feminine" pattern. At other times it is the family and the college who thrusts upon the reluctant girl the "modern" role.

While, historically, the "modern" role is the most recent one, ontogenetically it is the one emphasized earlier in the education of the college girl, if these 153 documents are representative. Society confronts the girl with powerful challenges and strong pressure to excel in certain competitive lines of endeavor and to develop certain techniques of adaptations very similar to those expected of her brothers. But, then, quite suddenly as it appears to these girls, the very success in meeting these challenges begins to cause anxiety. It is precisely those most successful in the earlier role who are now penalized.

It is not only the passage from age to age but the moving to another region or type of campus which may create for the girl similar problems. The precise content of sex roles, or, to put it in another way, the degree of their differentiation, varies with regional class, nativity, and other subcultures.

Whenever individuals show differences in response to some social situation, as have our 153 respondents, the question naturally arises as to the causes. It will be remembered that 40 per cent admitted some difficulties in personal relations with men due to conflicting sex roles but that 60 per cent said that they had no such problems. Inconsistency of parental expectations troubled 26 per cent of the students.

To account for individual differences would require another study, involving a classification of personalities in relation to the peculiar social environments of each. Generally speaking, it would seem that it is the girl with a "middle-of-the-road personality" who is most happily adjusted to the present historical moment. She is not a perfect incarnation of either role but is flexible enough to play both. She is a girl who is intelligent enough to do well in school but not so brilliant as to "get all 'A' 's"; informed and alert but not consumed by an intellectual passion; capable but not talented in areas relatively new to women; able to stand on her own feet and to earn a living but not so good a living as to compete with men; capable of doing some job well (in case she does not marry or, otherwise, has to work) but not so identified with a profession as to need it for her happiness.

A search for less immediate causes of individual reactions would lead us further back to the study of genesis of the personality differences found relevant to the problem. One of the clues will certainly be provided by the relation of the child to the parent of the same and of the opposite sex. This relation affects the conception of self and the inclination for a particular sex role.

The problems set forth in this article will persist, in the opinion of the writer, until the adult sex roles of women are redefined in greater harmony with the socioeconomic and ideological character of modern society. Until then neither the formal education nor the unverbalized sex roles of the adolescent woman can be cleared of intrinsic contradictions.

Two · Cultural Contradictions
and Sex Roles: A Repeat Study

PAUL WALLIN
Sociologist, Stanford University

If some women find it necessary to pretend inferiority to the male in order to associate with men successfully, is the need for such pretense necessarily disturbing to the woman? Paul Wallin also investigated the subject of cultural contradictions and sex roles among college women, and reprinted here * is his summary, which raises some questions concerning Dr. Komarovsky's conclusions in the preceding reading.

THIS article reports an approximate replication of a study by Komarovsky in 1942–43 on incompatible sex roles in the social environment of the college girl.

THE REPEAT STUDY

A replication of Komarovsky's investigation seemed worthwhile for two reasons: (1) because the original sample consisted of seniors in a single institution who were taking a course in the family or social psychology, there was some question as to whether the findings were more generally applicable, and (2) since the subjects of Komarovsky's research did not participate anonymously, what they wrote or said conceivably might have been influenced by their conception of what would present them in the most favorable light to the investigator or the interviewer.

The repeat study was carried out in 1949 in a western coeducational university where the ratio of men to women is about 3 to 1. A ten per cent random sample of unmarried, undergraduate female students was drawn from the campus directory. The 163 women so selected were asked to fill out a brief anonymous questionnaire and were given a short interview.

INTERPRETATION OF THE FINDINGS OF THE TWO STUDIES

The findings of the questionnaire data of the repeat study are in essential agreement with those of the original study based on case materials. They agree (a) that a substantial proportion of college

---

* Reprinted from the *American Sociological Review*, 1950, 15: 288–293, by permission of the author and the *American Sociological Review*.

women feel called upon on occasion to pretend inferiority to men while conceiving of themselves as equal (or superior) to them, and (b) that many college women are exposed to inconsistent parental expectations or (in terms of the repeat study) have views contradictory to those of either or both their parents as to how they should be spending their time in college. This congruence of findings from studies employing different methods and using samples from two institutions in opposite regions of the country argues for the presumption that the condition to which the findings refer is rather widespread. However, the interview data of the repeat study dispose the writer to the tentative conclusion that the problem is less momentous for the college woman than is suggested by Komarovsky's report.

The impression derived from Komarovsky's analysis and some of the excerpts quoted from her personal documents is that the college woman faced with incompatible expectations tends to be considerably disturbed by the experience. The writer's viewpoint is that in the large majority of cases the incompatibility either is not taken seriously or is rather readily resolved.

This judgment is based on the fact that in all but a few cases the subjects of the repeat study when interviewed expressed no grievance or resentment against parents or other persons for confusing or creating a conflict in them about the course they were to pursue in college or afterwards. The relatively unemotional statements made by subjects in regard to differences between them and their parents suggest that as a rule the differences are not pressed by the latter and at most are regarded as an annoyance by the former.

There is likewise little indication in the interview data that most college women who sometimes simulate inferiority to the male are at all agitated by the contradiction between their behavior and their conception of themselves as equals of the male. The interview data point to some considerations which may account for this. There appears to be a selective process at work which leads women to whom this contradiction would be upsetting to favor the company of male companions with whom they feel simulation is not necessary. The women who simulate may not be unduly troubled because they tend to regard their occasional pretense of inferiority as part of a "line" which is appropriate to the dating situation in which it characteristically occurs. Because she is not deeply involved in the casual dating relationship, the college woman seems to be able to use the "line" without being perturbed by the thought that in doing so she is not "being herself," namely the equal of the male. But when her association with a particular male develops into a more meaningful companionship or love relationship, the dating role and its "line" are no longer called for and she *can* be herself. It is only in the probably infrequent instances when a woman temperamentally or otherwise strongly disposed to the modern role becomes emotionally involved with a male who requires the feminine role of her that great psychological stress might be anticipated.

There are a number of possible explanations of the difference between Komarovsky's evaluation and that proposed here of the psychological consequences for the college woman when she is exposed to conflicting role conceptions. The writer's interpretation may not be valid because of the inadequacies of the interview data on which it is based. Or Komarovsky's case history excerpts—from which her evaluation has, in part, been inferred by the writer— inadvertently may not be typical of her entire sample in regard to the particular issue at question. Finally the possibility must be considered that there are some critical differences between the women of the original and repeat studies. The women investigated in the latter research are almost unanimously oriented to marriage, a home and children, and unlike college women to be militantly attached to the modern role. If Komarovsky's group included an appreciable number of career women, their vested interest in the modern role would have weighted the sample with persons for whom a conflict between the modern and feminine roles would be a matter of greater consequence.

Three · *Inconsistency in Marriage Roles and Marriage Conflict*

CLIFFORD KIRKPATRICK
Sociologist, Indiana University

*In their role in life do women want privileges without obligations? Do men expect women to fulfill the obligations that go with certain roles, but resist conceding the privileges also? The following selection * explores some inconsistencies in the thinking of men and women concerning women's roles, and examines the effect of such inconsistencies upon marital adjustment.*

MUCH of our thinking in regard to family life is as inconsistent and garbled as would be a hurried stenographic report of a discussion between Pericles, Augustine, Peter Lombard, Archbishop Hayes, Dr. Anna Howard Shaw, Bertrand Russell, H. L. Mencken, and Karl Marx. It is no wonder that women in particular find themselves confused as to their place in the modern world.

* Reprinted from *The International Journal of Ethics*, 1936, XLVI: 444– 460, by permission of the author and the University of Chicago Press.

From cultural confusion has sprung diversity of function and an increase in the number of roles open to the married woman.

It is useful to analyze the adjustment problems of the modern married woman with reference to three marriage roles. A marriage role is a useful fiction, for few women may be classified unambiguously with reference to such a role. We may distinguish then between three roles that may be played by the married woman, each implying certain privileges and certain obligations.

(1) The *wife-and-mother* role is the traditional role of the married woman. It implies as privileges security, the right to support, alimony in the case of divorce, respect as a wife and mother, a certain amount of domestic authority, loyalty of the husband to one who has borne him children, and a more or less sentimental gratitude from husband and children. Corresponding obligations include bearing and rearing children, making a home, rendering domestic service, loyal subordination of self to the economic interests of the husband, an acceptance of a dependent social and economic status, and the acceptance of a limited range of interests and activity.

(2) The *companion* role is essentially a leisure-class phenomenon. The privileges pertaining to this role include sharing pleasures with the husband, receiving a more romantic emotional response, being the object of admiration, receiving funds adequate for dress and recreation, having leisure for social and educational activity, and the receiving of a certain amount of chivalrous attention. On the other hand, it implies as obligations the preservation of beauty under the penalty of marital insecurity, the rendering of ego and libido satisfaction to the husband, and the cultivation of social contacts advantageous to him, the maintenance of intellectual alertness, and the responsibility for exorcising the demon of boredom.

(3) Finally, there is the *partner* role, corresponding to a new definition of the cultural situation which is gradually emerging. This entails the privileges of economic independence, equal authority in regard to family finances, acceptance as an equal, exemption from one-sided personal or domestic service to the husband, equal voice in determining locale of residence, and equality in regard to social and moral liberty. The obligation side of the balance sheet would include renouncing alimony save in the case of dependent children, complete sharing of the legal responsibilities of the family, willingness to dispense with any appeal to chivalry, and equal responsibility to maintain the family status by success in a career.

Obviously there is much overlapping of these roles and hence much greater complexity and confusion and worry. . . . The multiplicity of roles now open to married women contributes to personality conflict in at least four ways.

(1) One form of personality conflict arises from the fact that women have difficulty in choosing between roles. Such indecision may be as productive of personality tensions and conflicts as frus-

tration. There is reason to think that human beings can stand almost any situation which is inevitable, unambiguous, and clearly defined. It may be that the unmitigated drudgery of the pioneer woman in a patriarchal social order was no more disastrous than the effort of a modern wife to decide which of the many branches of married life she is going to choose. . . .

(2) Another form of personality conflict based on confusion and multiplicity of roles is the frustration of the woman performing one role through duty or habit while longing for a different role.

(3) Again there may be personality conflict by virtue of misunderstanding between husband and wife in regard to the role each expects the married woman to play. A woman expecting to be a wife and mother may find that her husband expects her to be a partner.

(4) Finally, there is the possibility of ethical inconsistency in the sense of attitudes favoring an unfair distribution of obligations and privileges. Since a privilege to the wife involves a certain obligation on the part of the husband, any disposition on the part of the wife to claim the privileges of more than one role without accepting the corresponding obligations makes for unfairness in the marriage relationship. On the other hand, a woman who accepts the obligations of more than one role while being denied the corresponding privileges receives an unfair share of the satisfaction of marriage as compared with the husband.

There are women who want to be respected as mothers without bearing children, receive gratitude without earning it, have security as parasites rather than helpmates, be admired in spite of obesity and careless dress, be thought attractive in spite of ignorance and stupidity, and to receive half or more of the family income without any creation of goods or services. On the other hand, there are women who bear children, perform household drudgery, work as many hours outside the home as the husband, maintain personal charm, and demonstrate intellectual equality but who are without gratitude, security, affection, or recognition. Naturally, it is easy for husband and wife to regard the distribution of obligations and privileges from different points of view. There is reason to think that there is a disposition for women to desire the privileges of more than one role and for men to be ethically inconsistent in expecting the fulfillment of obligations in more than one role.

It is highly desirable that a hypothesis that men and women are inconsistent and at odds with each other in regard to the distribution of obligations and privileges be checked by quantitative empirical evidence. The specific hypothesis may be worded as follows: There is a tendency on the part of women to approve more strongly than men of privileges of more than one feminine marriage role. There is a corresponding tendency on the part of men compared with women to indorse the obligations of more than one marriage role. Putting the matter more briefly: Women want a double dose of privilege, and men want them to have a double dose of obligation. If this hypothesis is confirmed, much marital discord stands explained.

An instrument for measuring attitudes toward feminism was constructed. The scale contained eighty evaluational propositions bearing on the various issues concerned with the status of women. Forty propositions were classified by judges as being feministic and forty anti-feministic. It seemed desirable to classify as many as possible of these propositions into pairs, implying the indorsement of either the privileges of more than one marital role or the obligations of more than one marital role. Returns are available from 161 male and 241 female University of Minnesota students taking the test. These students were asked to have the scale for measuring attitudes toward feminism filled out by both parents. Complete parental returns could not be obtained from all students but blanks were filled out by 152 fathers and 165 mothers.

In Table 1 numbers of propositions are associated when the propositions, if both checked, imply indorsement of a double dose of privilege or of a double dose of obligations. For example, to hold that "women have the right to compete with men in every sphere of economic activity" and "alimony is an appropriate protection for women as members of the weaker sex" implies some slight tendency to indorse both the privileges of a partner and the privileges of a wife. Naturally there are circumstances in which this would be ethically appropriate. A considerable number of such somewhat inconsistent indorsements would, however, imply a confusion in regard to the marital roles for women and a tendency to indorse double doses of privileges.

It is apparent from the results that there is a decided tendency in both generations for females to indorse to a greater extent the privileges of both the wife-and-mother and partner roles. There is also some evidence that the younger generation, disregarding sex, is a little more inclined to check fewer pairs which are ethically inconsistent.

The sex differences in regard to indorsements are reversed when obligations are considered for the males in both generations tend to indorse the obligations of both the wife-and-mother and partner roles. Again, the sex differences between the two generations is about equal, being only slightly greater for the student group. The tendency to ethical inconsistency is again a trifle larger for the older generations, although in this case the males rather than females are most inconsistent.

Again a sex difference appears in regard to the indorsement of double doses of privileges. In both generations the females are especially inclined to indorse the privileges of both the partner and

TABLE 1. PROPOSITION PAIRS IMPLYING PRIVILEGES OF BOTH PARTNER AND WIFE-AND-MOTHER ROLES TOGETHER WITH PERCENTAGES OF SUBJECTS INDORSING BOTH MEMBERS OF THE PAIRS

Proposition Pairs	Percentage Male N-161	Percentage Female N-241	Percentage Fathers N-152	Percentage Mothers N-165
1–70 "Women have the right to compete with men in every sphere of economic activity" and "Alimony is an appropriate protection for women as members of the weaker sex"	16.8	20.7	21.1	27.3
11–70 "There should be a strict merit system of public appointment and promotion without regard to sex" and "Alimony is an appropriate protection for women as members of the weaker sex"	14.2	21.2	21.1	23.6
25–70 "Women should be given equal opportunities with men for vocational and professional training" and "Alimony is," etc.	19.8	24.5	23.0	32.1
33–70 "Regardless of sex, there should be equal pay for equal work" and "Alimony is," etc.	16.7	23.2	19.1	27.9
69–70 "It is foolish to question the intellectual equality of women with men" and "Alimony is," etc.	8.7	12.4	15.1	17.6
Average of Percentages	15.2	20.4	19.9	25.7

the companion roles. The sex difference is about the same in the two generations, but the student generations show a slightly greater tendency to ethical inconsistency.

The males of both generations are much more inclined than the females to indorse the obligations of both the companion and the partner roles for women. The sex difference is about equal in the two generations, and there is only a slight tendency for the older generation to show greater ethical inconsistency. Relatively few propositions on the scale reflected companion privileges as contrasted to wife privileges.

Evidence of a decided ambiguity of marital roles for women and of ethical inconsistency in regard to them is revealed in this study. The reader may disagree as to whether various propositions really imply the role privileges and role obligations to the degree assumed in this discussion. The mass effect seems to be clear, however, and lends statistical support to the hypothesis that there is a genuine ethical inconsistency on the part of both sexes.

With mathematical regularity the sex differences are reversed when obligations replace privileges. Women are inclined to cheer for a privilege of more than one marriage role. Men rise to cheer lustily when pairs of feminine obligations are paraded. Men want women not only to put their shoulder to the wheel but also to pull the wagon. If the samples can be regarded as in some degree representative, it would seem that the two halves of the population are engaged in a tug of war on either side of an abyss of misunderstanding.

Granted that substantial evidence of ethical inconsistency in regard to marriage roles has been presented, then light is thrown on the causation of modern marital discord. Given the tendency of women to want the privileges of more than one marriage role and the tendency of men to assign them obligations, it is no wonder that there is an argument about who gets cheated in marriage. From such arguments, born of cultural confusion and a multiplicity of possible roles, arise discord and divorce.

The difference of opinion between men and women here revealed and the unfair balance between privileges and obligations which doubtless results are due both to the fact that the various roles are not yet clearly defined in terms of obligations and privileges and to the fact that more than one role is now possible. While there is nothing inappropriate in an attempt by modern women to pursue more than one role, providing a fair balance of privileges and obligations is maintained, it should be noted that there was little ambiguity and inconsistency when to be a wife and mother was a married woman's only role. If social and economic trends should force the majority of married women into the partner role, a more generally recognized equilibrium of obligations and privileges would probably result.

There are at the present time certain obstacles which oppose a clarification of the situation by wider acceptance of the partner role. These conditions perpetuate the present unfairness in the relation between husband and wife in so far as this unfairness is based on confusion of roles. Furthermore, they create a discrepancy between the burden of one family group taken as a whole as compared with another. The most important condition having these effects is differential reproduction. The fact that some adults have children and others do not has upset an ancient ethical equilibrium. The woman who bears children may also stagger under the obligations of the companion and partner roles. She is handicapped as compared with other women working outside the home. Her family group enjoys only a single income in spite of increased expenses, and the wages of her husband as a provider are probably lowered by the competition of married women without children, whose homes are supported by double incomes in spite of freedom from expense of offspring. The only solution which would permit a general acceptance of the partner role and a new ethical integration of obligations and privileges is some form of endowment of motherhood by the state.

The future of family relations cannot be predicted, but meanwhile some knowledge of existing conditions and attitudes paves the way for better understanding in the family group and for sympathetic insight into the problems of the feminine half of the human race.

*Four · Problems
of the Modern Homemaker-Mother*

DELLA D. CYRUS
Professional Social Worker and Mother

Women disagree, just as psychologists and sociologists do, upon what are the real basic factors creating adjustment problems for modern women. The next selection,* with its somewhat pessimistic viewpoint, can serve as material for analysis and discussion.

LET us look at some specific ways in which the family fails to meet our needs as individuals. Because women usually work within the limits of the family, they suffer most from its failures. It isolates them especially from any vital relationship with the world outside the family, and under modern conditions they cannot find an adequate sense of calling or purpose within the family. Not only are they forced into unhealthy dependence on their husbands and children for most of the satisfactions of their lives, but the family does not even provide them with a physical or spiritual environment in which they can be successful wives and mothers.

Modern conveniences plus modern high standards, while freeing women from the back-breaking physical labor of the pioneer woman, have increased enormously her petty cleaning-up tasks. The number of things which modern women have to wash and polish and starch and iron and sterilize, and the number of times they have to do it, have multiplied until many housewives spend most of their time cleaning one thing or another, and cannot imagine how the pioneer woman found time to do all she did. If the pioneer woman had spent so much time on the luxury and boredom of cleanliness, she wouldn't have been paying her way, and the modern woman knows in her heart that she isn't paying hers either. She knows that

* Excerpts from "What's Wrong with the Family," *Atlantic Monthly,* 1946, 178: 67–73, and "Why Mothers Fail," *Atlantic Monthly,* 1947, 179: 57–60, by permission of the author and *The Atlantic Monthly.*

in a world dirty and bloody with wars, alive with hatred and starving children, it is criminal waste to devote a lifetime to the cleanliness of a single family.

The preparing of food has a little more status as important work and may have the virtue of saving some women from complete futility. But even this is very different from the role the pioneer woman played in providing a family with food. Then the preparing of a meal was an incidental task in the long process of growing, picking, processing, and storing in which she had taken an essential part. The modern woman, spending money earned by her husband to buy food already produced, canned, or tastelessly prepared by others, cannot have the same feeling of being an essential part of life.

Women who have servants to do their cooking and cleaning up for them are not average American women. In the best of times, the great majority of American homes are without domestic help of any kind, and the indications are that domestic help will be progressively more expensive and less available. Let the magazines call a woman Homemaker, Queen of the Kitchen, Princess of the Parlor— the woman herself knows that she is the unhired help doing the hack work of the world. Her multitude of petty cares leaves her feeling essentially futile, menial, and lonely, until her human nature, and only incidentally her woman nature, hits back with glaring failures as wife and mother.

But, we keep arguing, housekeeping and cooking are not the essential jobs of a woman. These jobs take time, of course, and involve a considerable amount of drudgery, but everyone has some drudgery—even business executives and college presidents. A woman's real job is the care and training of her children. No job is more important, more satisfying, more close to life, than the directing of young lives from infancy to maturity. A mother has a full-time job by definition. Any woman who can't be satisfied with a home and children should never get married. These are prevalent beliefs which amount to a national faith and sink so far into so many generations of feeling that many people are incapable of examining them at all.

Because modern families are small, children are often hungry for friends. Most children under five are thrown entirely on their mothers for a twelve hours a day, seven days a week companionship which is as much a starvation diet for them as it is for their mothers. Both are yearning for companionship with their contemporaries; both are wanting to do things in the world which can't be done within the four walls of a house. Modern psychology has succeeded in making everyone aware of the importance of the mother-child relationship, but it seems to have left almost everybody with the impression that all that is required is that there *be* a relationship. All that is necessary is that mothers "stay home with their children."

Actually the intense, mutually exhausting emotional and physical relationships which develop between mothers and preschool children in the typical urban family lead inevitably to that worst of all maternal sins, overmothering with undercurrents of hostility, and that most fatal of all child responses, overdependence with undercurrents of resentment. With no place for her children to play and no aunts or grandparents to watch them, the young mother is as bound to her home as if she were tied to it with a rope, and cannot even go to the corner drugstore without running the risk that the house will burn over her children's heads.

The crucial years in the life of the family are the years during which there are children under school age. They are the years when the important groundwork of the child's personality is being formed. They are the years which convince everybody that a woman should never try to be anything but a mother, and they account for the fact that most women linger pointlessly at home long after their job as a mother is done. They are the years which place the heaviest burdens on marriage. Divorces are not so frequent during these years as they are later, but this is the period when many marriages in fact get broken, whether or not they end in divorce.

Why are these years so difficult and so often fatal? Exactly what takes place in a family of two or three small children? The mother in this family, whether she has a fourth-grade education or a Ph.D. in philosophy, has less freedom and less leisure than anyone else in our society. Even if she has a washing machine, mangle, vacuum cleaner, and Mixmaster (sometimes she doesn't have any of these things), she works hours which have long been illegal for anyone in industry. When her children are well, she works twelve hours a day, seven days a week. When they are ill or when there is a new baby, she works from fourteen to twenty hours, often going for months without an adequate period of unbroken sleep. And never, even in her deepest sleep, is she entirely free from her responsibility. Consequently, a woman is almost always tired during these years, if not actually ill, and this alone makes her an unhappy and unfit companion for her husband and children.

The mother's working day is divided between caring for the house and caring for the children, which, under modern conditions, is a simple neurosis-producing situation. In the small shut-in urban dwelling, these two jobs are mutually conflicting, if not mutually exclusive. The mother and her children are constantly at cross purposes, because the children, if they are normal, are bent on noise, mess, dirt, and destruction, while she is struggling to create quiet, order, and cleanliness. Her children, because of their lack of equipment and companionship, and because of their very youngness, need her attention, her time, and her help, while she needs more time and energy than she has, to accomplish the essential jobs of washing, cooking, cleaning, and putting away. In this contest, either the house or the child is bound to lose; and whichever happens, the mother is left with a feeling of incompetence and failure. Nor is there any time or place, from her children's waking in the morning until their going to bed at night, and sometimes not even then, which the mother can count on as her own to rest or read, to collect her thoughts, to regain her perspective and her self-respect and begin over again.

As she drags hopelessly about the work of her house, her children bump into her, spill things, write on the walls, fall down, cry, whine, fight, and require a thousand attentions which she stops her work to give. She forgets what she was trying to do before she was interrupted. The telephone and doorbells ring. Something boils over on the stove, the puppy howls to go out and makes a puddle, and the man to read the meter pounds on the back door.

This is material for boisterous, low-comedy slapstick, full of the kind of frustration and anguish which depraved people laugh at. Every father has heard the story of this day repeated until he has become bored with its shameful and petty details, and it should never be repeated again if it were not for the fact that its very triviality blinds everyone to its true significance. These troubles of a young mother are not real troubles, but such days, following one after another, month after month, and year after year, corrode the spirits of women, wear away their minds and talents, eat into their self-respect, destroy their sense of direction, until they know hours and days of desperation and defeat so complete and final as to make it a matter of wonder that there are any good mothers at all, or that any mother is ever a successful person.

Most people recognize this period in a woman's life as a difficult but inevitable one. The typical remark made most often by older women is: "But it only lasts a few years and then you wish you had your children back again." This endlessly repeated bit of wisdom is, all unwittingly, the most devastating comment which could be made on the prevailing ideal for the mother. It amounts to smug acceptance of the fact that in those years the mother loses the value of her education and training for other work, loses touch with the large problems of a larger world, and loses confidence in herself as a mature citizen of the world who might have something of value to contribute to it. It is acceptance of the fact that women really have nothing to live for after their children are grown, and that if they do, by the grace of God, allow their children to grow up, they are faced with long empty years which they must fill somehow as best they can. And so they fill them with keeping their houses cleaner than ever, or by joining organizations which, though they may have social value, are too frittering and inefficient to give any strong and capable human being a clear sense of usefulness or integration in society.

"Only a few years" in the life of the child means the most crucial years of his development, during which he is cramped and lonely and pushed away and overwatched by a mother who is too tired and too busy and too unhappy to give him the kind of mothering he needs. Sometimes an honest older woman will recognize this fact by expressing deep regret over the lack of time she had for her children, and, above all, the lack of energy she had for just loving them and enjoying them when they were young.

Young mothers themselves are often the most timid about expressing dissatisfaction with their lives. Because it doesn't occur to them that anything could be wrong with the family, they suppose the fault lies in themselves. They want desperately to be good mothers, and when they get too much of it, they are ashamed of their unhappiness. Haven't they everything they want in the world? A home, a husband, children? Of course they have, and so to cover up their disappointment and confusion, they concentrate on all the small materialistic devices which are supposed to make a home beautiful and happy—flowered stencils for the kitchen cupboards, lace and satin for the bassinet.

Young mothers will discuss for hours the problems and irritations of home and children and will express with feeling their frustration at being tied down and their frank relief at getting their children in bed for the night, but such discussions are guiltily ended with, "Children are a lot of fun, though." This is their wistful way of saying that they know children are supposed to be a lot of fun, and could be a lot of fun, but somehow they are hardly any fun at all.

Meanwhile, what is happening to the marriage during these years? If the husband is a mature and sympathetic person who can throw himself into the spirit of the rough-and-tumble life of babies, diapers, chaotic meals, and sleepless nights; if he is vocationally adjusted, economically secure, hopeful for his future, not too overworked, and takes the attitude that things are temporarily a bit too tough for his wife, they can grit their teeth and pull through without irreparably damaging their relationship. When these favorable conditions prevail, they can, on occasion, laugh and have fun together. But obviously these are rare conditions.

Too many men in the modern city get too little satisfaction from their work, are worried about money, overworked, and apprehensive of the future. These are just the years when men are trying hardest to make a career or to make money. Far from being able to wade happily into the noisy discontent which is their homes, most men have far too little energy for their children and almost none for the problems of their wives. Instead, they need someone to sympathize with *them*, someone to allay their fears and listen to their plans. Above all, they need someone to play with, laugh with, and relax with.

So they come home to a physically exhausted, nervously taut, emotionally dissipated woman who still has several hours of work to do. Both are so aware of their own needs that even when they understand the needs of the other, there is little they can do about it. Both know that somewhere there should be help for this situation, that somewhere in the world there should be rest and laughter and love. Almost in spite of themselves, they hit out at each other, because it was in their marriage that both had expected to find these things.

Both are caught in a situation too painful and too difficult to understand, and the air rings with accusations, demands, resentment, or hysterics. Finally the marriage falls to pieces in fact, if not in court, or it settles down into the quietness of resignation and despair. Couples caught in this situation often feel that it could be saved if they could leave the home together and go somewhere to dance or drink or talk in a new atmosphere. But even this kind of shock treatment too often is unavailable, because it is too difficult and too expensive to get anybody to stay with the children.

Playing at home is more difficult still. If the children don't shatter the relationship between husband and wife—and very small children are capable of breaking into life's most poignant moments at any hour of the day or night—still the home is the wife's eternal workshop and she, at least, cannot experience there the sense of freedom and new experience which she and her husband both need. Because playing together is so hard to arrange, a frequent solution is for the husband to go off to bowl or to work overtime, or to make love to someone who is available and gay and will take him the way he is, while the wife stays home more lonely and resentful than ever.

Add to all of these difficulties of marriage and children the problems of emotionally warped individuals who demand an abnormal amount of love and consideration, the sexually repressed or maladjusted, the physically ill who cannot carry their share of the load, and it is hard to understand, not why so many families break up, but why so many still hang together.

Men are even less critical of the family than women because, superficially, they are less affected by its shortcomings. Men suffer because women suffer, and, suffering, cannot give them what they need and expect to find in the family. But although men are aware of the disappointing contrast between what they want and what they get, they are so blinded by the traditional promises of home, love, food, and fireside that when these things are cold and unappetizing they look everywhere but at the family itself for the trouble. If, night after night, the children are crying and the living room is a shambles and the dinner isn't ready and his wife snaps at him to stop reading his paper and lend a hand, the husband is likely to conclude that his wife is the nervous type, or women are funny, or life is hell, and let it go at that until he can get away.

That he might find what he wanted in a very different kind of family life rarely occurs to him, and he resists changing the family pattern long after his wife is willing to do so or in fact has changed it by going to work outside their home. His resistance is not difficult to understand, because young mothers who work at outside jobs can almost never make arrangements for home and children which are satisfactory for everybody.

If a good nursery school is available for the children and the family can get and pay for a first-rate housekeeper, the woman may work at an outside job she likes, to the greater satisfaction of everybody, including her husband. But desirable housekeepers and nursery schools are available to only a select few. Most mothers must resort to makeshift arrangements which are bad for the children and leave the mother with most of the work to do at home in addition to her other job. Under these circumstances, women may be more tired and demanding than when they stay at home all day, thus justifying their husbands' reinforced conviction that home is where their place is.

The family's failures have not ended when it has sent its last child off to school. The mother may have gained a few blessed hours which she can fill according to a plan of her own, but she is still bound to the same pattern of life and cannot, for several years, engage in any interest or work which requires more than two or three consecutive hours of her time. Because this is true, and because "there is always something to do around a house," and because most mothers by this time don't believe there is anything else they can do anyway, women continue to live an isolated, undernourished, haphazard life within the family, brightened now and then with meetings, bridge parties, and shopping tours.

The young child, if he is still reasonably normal, is so happy to be in school and among his contemporaries that he takes life in his stride for several years without causing anybody too much anxiety. But what about the older child and particularly the adolescent? What does the family do for him? It may have disintegrated altogether, leaving him without any real ties to anybody. Or the parents may be hanging together by threads of grim duty or resigned boredom waiting for him to get old enough so that they can stop pretending to be a family. Or the mother may have thrown all of her longing for life into plans for her adolescent child so that he is unable to have any life of his own. But even if none of these frequent conditions exist, the very best family cannot meet all the needs of an adolescent in the modern world.

The significant thing about women in America is that all of them are either rebelling against or trying to fit into a social pattern for women which was originally intended as a pattern for full-time mothers—the homemaker-mother pattern. The much talked about freedom of American women is not freedom in any real sense at all. It is simply freedom for some women to break away from the homemaker pattern if they have the personal courage and energy which breaking away from an established pattern requires. And neither the woman who conforms to the pattern nor the woman who breaks away can express her whole self as a woman and a person.

The homemaker way of life once applied to mothers who kept on having babies for the greater part of their lives, and to a time when most of the work of the world was done within the home. In present-day urban life, with almost all of the world's work being done outside the home, our mores and our mechanics of living still compel most women to be homemakers if they want to be mothers. Women may, and significantly do, renounce motherhood and refuse to be homemakers, but in spite of our toleration and even admiration for women who "do things" in the world, we have no ideal which permits us to *expect* any achievement from women beyond the achievement of homemaking. As long as women are forced to be homemakers in order to be mothers, we are compelled to hold fast to our one inadequate ideal for women—the homemaker-mother ideal.

Every modern mother feels—in some degree—a conflict between the kind of life she is trained in America to want and expect, and the kind of life she must in fact lead as a mother. More than that, it is a conflict between the kind of woman she hoped to become and the kind of woman our homemaker-mother ideal usually compels her to be.

This difference between what women are educated to be and what they must in fact become can be described almost entirely in terms of their relationship to men and to the world outside the family. Up to the point of marriage most women participate fully in the work, the recreation, and the aspirations of the males of their own age. From kindergarten to graduate school they read the same books, compete in many of the same contests, talk the same talk, follow the same daily routine, eat in the same drugstores and cafeterias, make the same plans for exploring or dazzling or remaking the world. For them there is no such thing as "woman's work" or a "man's world." There are only men and women and the world's work and the world's pleasure.

No one can estimate the shock which getting married and having a child gives to this American educated woman. From the exhilarating threshold of the world with all its problems and possibilities, from the daily companionship of men and other women, she is catapulted into a house—a house, furthermore, from which she has no escape. Her husband disappears into the outside world on business of his own, while for hours and days at a time she has no companion except her child, and the hands with which she had planned to remake the world are, incredibly enough, in the laundry tubs, the dishpan, and the scrub bucket. And so her first experience of what it means to be a mother, however much she may love her baby, is an experience full to overflowing with confusion, disappointment, humiliation, and above all, loneliness.

Usually the shock of becoming a homemaker-mother is more devastating to the college-educated woman than to the woman with less education, as our birth statistics significantly indicate. But almost no woman is free from some dissatisfaction with the isolation and bondage of motherhood. As long as we educate women, even partially, to be interested in and responsible for the needs and problems of their world, and then isolate them in houses as soon as they become mothers and load them with work which they spent their youth learning to regard as menial and unintelligent, we should stop being surprised if they emerge finally with no faith in themselves and no real interest in anybody or anything but their own narrowed and distorted desires.

Women who at best are lonely and disappointed, and who are separated from their husbands in so many important ways, are almost doomed to failure as mothers. It isn't only that they see too much of their children and too little of anybody else, or even that they particularly resent doing a certain amount of sordid and trivial work. Most of them carry, whether they know it or not, a burden of unused ability and frustrated purpose which falls resentfully on the child. To make the day-long occupations of washing, ironing, cooking, and scrubbing an inevitable condition of motherhood is obviously as wasteful of the miracle and variety of human talent as it would be to make gardening, street cleaning, and bookkeeping a necessary condition of fatherhood. It means that all mothers who have trained themselves to be violinists, teachers, actresses, business women, or just plain citizens of their world, are struggling under permanent vocational maladjustment.

The question is often asked, What would mothers do if freed from housework? Many women aren't capable of anything else. Wouldn't they be worse off in factories and stores? These questions condemn our whole society and all its values, or lack of them. They reflect our belief that people work only because they have to and only to earn money. No one would think to ask what women would do if we took it for granted that the right work for a woman is as important as the right husband—if we took it for granted that women from earliest childhood were training their minds and developing their abilities, not to fill in the time until marriage and motherhood, but in order to contribute their serious share to the enrichment of all life for as long as they live.

Many mothers do adjust to modern conditions of motherhood. They may have sought in marriage an escape from parents or from the boredom of an uncongenial job. They may have hoped to find in marriage an escape from inner emptiness and lack of personal direction. Bringing to marriage a great residue of childish needs, they may sink gratefully into the protection of a comfortable home.

Accepting as inevitable the separation of their husbands' interests from their own, they may resign themselves and finally adapt themselves to life in a child's world. While their children are young they give up, and then forget they ever had, a need for privacy in which to read or think. They make do with the limited and meager opportunities for adult relationships open to them and they sometimes manage, by stunting their own growth, to love their children without undue conflict or resentment.

One sometimes hears the "well-adjusted" mother express her self-abnegation in heroic terms. "After all," she says, "the children come first. They're all that really matters."

To such an attitude there is only one possible response. If the purpose of an adult human being is to rear a child or two so that those children can in turn rear children, ad infinitum, then life is unquestionably the absurd treadmill it sometimes seems and there is nothing to do but relax. How can the mother who believes she herself doesn't matter rear her children *for* anything? The only bearable theory is that we bring our children up to adulthood because we believe in adulthood—in its satisfactions and in the possibilities it offers for infinite growth and development.

The mother who adjusts to a life which forces her to be less than an adult is not only betraying herself and the purposes for which she was intended. She is not only, by example, belittling for her children the importance of full maturity. She is, worst of all, depriving them of a mother who has real wisdom about the world. And in this time, no other kind of mother will do. No other kind of mother can begin to prepare her children for the conflict of interests, the confusion of values, the groping for new forms of living, which make up the world in which those same children must some day try to be adults.

So we come to the ironic truth that the mothers who make the best adjustment to the conditions now implicit in our homemaker-mother ideal are by that very adjustment incapable of fulfilling their full obligations as mothers. In their immaturity and isolation they tend to teach their children that it is more important to keep their feet dry than it is to know and understand their world.

How can modern mothers serve at the same time their children, their men, themselves, and their world? Obviously only by becoming the vital and complete citizens of the world which they wanted and expected to be in the beginning.

That obstacle, of course, is the homemaker-mother pattern and, more significantly, the prevailing notion, embodied in the modern distortion of that pattern, that mothers must be the constant, hour by hour, day by day, nursemaids and supervisors of their own children.

Surely if one woman is to be in complete charge of a child twenty-four hours a day for the first five or six years of its life, then it should be a woman who in the depths of her mind and soul honestly has nothing else to do and nowhere else to go. Either we should deprive women of all their education and civilization and send them back to some primitive state of instinctual and timeless life so that they can be happy full-time mothers of small children (a well-known and valuable fascist technique), or we should find a satisfactory way to care for children away from their mothers part of the time so that mothers can be a fully developed, responsible part of the world their children will inherit.

The problem is inherent in the education of women, as many people knew and feared that it would be. It is intrinsic in the fact that the urban way of life has deprived mothers of significant work, separated them from their husbands, and created a physical environment incompatible with the raising of children. It is not a problem which mothers can solve for themselves. It is a social problem which must be solved by whole communities. It means some kind of community plan for the care of homes and children—and not for a few odd hours now and then, but for several absolutely dependable hours every day.

Only with practical, specific plans for making time available to mothers can we justify our claim that American women are emancipated, and create a new ideal for all women which demands the fullest use of their talent and power. When we have freed all women from the modern curse of the full-time homemaker-mother ideal, more intelligent women will have babies, more women will love and cherish the babies they have, and more women without babies will use their lives to some good end.

One · Sexual Behavior, What is Acceptable?

GEORGE P. MURDOCK
Anthropologist, Yale University

LUTHER E. WOODWARD
Mental Hygienist, New York Department
of Mental Health

FREDERICK BOLMAN
Philosopher, New York University

*Following are viewpoints on acceptable sexual be-
havior presented by an anthropologist, a mental hygienist, and a
professor of philosophy.* On some points they agree and on others
they hold conflicting views. As a part of Social Hygiene Day
observance of the American Social Hygiene Association in February,
1950, these authorities discussed the subject, "Sexual Behavior, How
Shall We Define and Motivate What is Acceptable?" The discussion
took the form of a debate, since the speakers had the opportunity
for rejoinders after the introductory discussion.*

*The remarks and the rejoinders here presented merit thoughtful
consideration by students of the American family.*

(*George P. Murdock*)

I know of only two criteria by which science can judge
the acceptability of sexual behavior, namely, biological adaptiveness and social utility. From the point of view of science, a particular code of sex behavior is acceptable to the extent, first, that it
accords with the biologically determined sexual propensities inherent in men and women, and, second, that it contributes to social
order and continuity. These two criteria are in some measure
antagonistic, since social order requires rather substantial regulation
of the biological impulse. For every society, therefore, the problem
is one of finding a satisfactory balance and reconciliation between
the two factors and of shifting this balance as underlying conditions
change.

BIOLOGICAL ADAPTABILITY OF THE SEX DRIVE

The sex drive in man is biologically imperative. If it were not, the
species would not have survived. Fortunately, however, it is also
flexible—much more so, for example, than the hunger drive. It can
therefore be readily deflected and redirected, and human cultures

* Excerpts from *Journal of Social Hygiene*, 1950, 36: 1–31, by permission
of the authors and the American Social Hygiene Association.

have done so in countless ways to achieve socially useful goals. It can also be inhibited to some extent, but it cannot be blocked entirely, for if too seriously interfered with it finds devious outlets in anti-social forms or in psychic disturbances. So long as a system of cultural checks and balances leaves open to adult men and women a socially sanctioned channel of gratifying sex expression, it cannot be pronounced biologically maladaptive.

History and anthropology reveal a few societies which do not meet this biological criterion of acceptability. Among them, one of the most patently defective was the sex code of medieval Europe. Not only did it deprive a considerable segment of society of any socially sanctioned channel of expression through the rule of ecclesiastical celibacy; it even invested normal marital sexuality with an oppressive aura of guilt and sin. Undoubtedly the greatest single step in modern history toward the achievement of an acceptable sexual code was the decision of the Protestant churches during the Reformation to permit their clergy to marry. This assured that the spiritual advisors of congregations would be personally familiar with culturally normative sexual behavior. It is difficult to conceive of a less reliable source of guidance on sexual matters than a celibate priest, since his vows practically compel him to choose between hypocrisy and perversion. Since the Middle Ages we have come a long way toward a biologically adaptive sex code, though remnants of excessive restrictiveness still survive here and there.

SOCIAL UTILITY OF SEX RESTRICTIONS

The criterion of biological adaptiveness relates to a system of sex regulation as a whole. The criterion of social utility, on the other hand, is applicable to each component part of such a system. Any particular sex taboo is scientifically validated if it can be demonstrated to contribute in some important respect to the stability and continuity of society. The most reliable evidence of whether it does or does not make such a contribution is the extent to which it approaches universality. Types of sex regulation that are found in all or most societies show by this very fact that they are socially necessary, that peoples all over the world and throughout history have been compelled by circumstances to accept and enforce them. The experience of post-revolutionary Russia with permissive abortion is an eloquent illustration of the mechanism by which societies come to reject maladaptive innovations in sexual practices and are brought back into conformity with the regulative controls that most peoples have learned to respect.

IMPORTANCE OF THE FAMILY AS BASIC SOCIAL UNIT

In nearly all cases where science can establish the social utility of a cultural restriction on sexual behavior, comparative and analytical research reveals that the restriction contributes to the integrity of the family. I wish I could convey to you an adequate conception of the tremendous importance of this social group. It is, for one thing, absolutely universal. There is no society known to history or anthropology which lacks the family. Indeed, there is not a society on record that does not have families of precisely the form known to ourselves, namely, the "nuclear family" consisting of one man, one woman, and their children. Though often compounded into larger familial aggregates unfamiliar to us, the nuclear family, is everywhere discernible and functionally important. Moreover, there is no society which does not recognize marriage as the legitimate way of founding a family. In view of the almost limitless diversity of human cultures in so many respects, this universality of the nuclear family and of marriage must be regarded as a genuinely extraordinary phenomenon.

There is no escape from the scientific conclusion that marriage and the family play so crucial a role in social life that no society has been able to survive without them. Let us look for a moment at the reasons for their importance. First of all, marriage is the original and most basic form of economic organization. In every known society husband and wife specialize in different economic activities, and share their products. Second, marriage always provides an approved outlet for sexual expression. Thirdly, children born to a married man and woman are always legitimate, and in most societies other children are illegitimate. In the fourth place, the family is always charged with the physical care and education of children. Though this duty is sometimes shared in part by other relatives such as grandparents, or by public institutions such as schools, the primary responsibility rests universally with the family.

In short, the family is the basic economic, reproductive, and educational unit in every known society. Without economic skills and cooperation, human life would cease. Without provision for reproduction and child care, any society would soon become extinct. Without education, culture and technical knowledge would disappear in a single generation. When we recognize that all these basic functions depend primarily upon the family, we begin to gain some comprehension of the immense utility of this social group, and to realize the importance of protecting and preserving it.

TABOOS THAT SAFEGUARD THE FAMILY

A sexual prohibition that demonstrably serves to bulwark the family must be regarded as scientifically acceptable, even though it is biologically quite restrictive. As a matter of fact, such prohibitions are nearly as universal as the family itself.

Foremost among them are primary incest taboos. It may surprise some of you to learn that there is not a single society among the thousands of which we have record—not even the most backward in culture—that does not impose upon its members a strong prohibition of both sexual intercourse and marriage between mother and son, father and daughter, and brother and sister. Individual instances of the violation of these taboos do occur in many if not most societies, but they merely reflect the strength of the sex drive, and a very few cultures exempt persons of exalted status, as among the Ptolemies of Egypt and the Incas of Peru, but nowhere can an average citizen commit incest without severe social condemnation. These prohibitions are commonly supported by quite irrational beliefs, such as our own that the offspring of near relatives are prone to hereditary defects, but the taboos themselves have a high social utility. They inhibit sexual rivalry and jealousy within the family, which might seriously interfere with the adequate performance of the latter's important social functions, and by compelling out-marriage they bind the families of the larger society to one another by ramifying kinship ties. Comparative anthropology warns us not to relax our incest taboos, and even suggests that we not object too strongly to the irrational beliefs that support them.

MARITAL FIDELITY A SOCIAL BULWARK

Nearly as universal are prohibitions of adultery. In my worldwide sample of 250 societies I found only five—or a mere two per cent of the total—in which adulterous relationships are socially condoned. This suggests that the ideal of marital fidelity, like the prohibition of incest, has a strong practical utility. Extramarital affairs are peculiarly likely to generate jealousy and discord between spouses which will interfere with their cooperative performance of the family's essential functions, so that most societies have found it necessary to forbid them. The experience of mankind thus warns us to resist the development of a permissive attitude toward adultery, such as is said to characterize certain so-called "emancipated circles" in our own society. Marital fidelity is far from being an outmoded superstition. On the contrary, it is one of the main buttresses of any social structure.

PREMARITAL CHASTITY AND SCIENTIFIC VALUES

Some sex taboos, like those against rape and the seduction of children, have a social utility derived from sources other than family stability, and they too are nearly universal. But there are others of restricted or sporadic distribution which either serve no socially useful purpose whatsoever or have a limited utility under very special social conditions. From the standpoint of science these are neither acceptable nor unacceptable but of neutral or indifferent value, unless they happen to violate one of the two aforementioned criteria, in which case they must be adjudged scientifically unacceptable.

Premarital sex relations deserve special attention in this connection. The comparative evidence is illuminating. Whereas only two per cent of the societies of my sample sanction adultery, 70 per cent permit sexual experimentation before marriage. In the thirty per cent minority that disapprove of premarital sexuality, moreover, the taboo usually applies only to females, and girls customarily marry shortly after puberty, so that the prohibition is really directed against prepubertal rather than against premarital intercourse. There is thus nothing in man's social experience to indicate that the ideal of premarital chastity has any scientific value. Most peoples have clearly found sexual permissiveness before marriage quite compatible with postmarital fidelity and with the stability and adequate functioning of the family institution.

I have recently done intensive personal field work in one society with a completely permissive attitude toward premarital sexuality, namely, among the natives of Truk, the former Japanese naval bastion in the mid-Pacific. My experience on Truk, corroborated by a wealth of sound anthropological data from societies in other parts of the world, shows that popular notions about premarital freedom are seriously distorted. Sex behavior among the unmarried in such societies is far from orgiastic. As a matter of fact, the actual frequency of intercourse among post-adolescents is apparently no greater than Kinsey and many sociologists have revealed for our own society in all but a relatively small middle-class minority. The main difference is that it is conducted in a more seemly manner and has been pressed into the service of society as a means of preparing for marriage.

PREMARITAL LAXITY AS A SOCIAL PROBLEM

The sexual laxity current among our own youth is admittedly an unlovely phenomenon from an esthetic point of view, and it is scientifically valueless or wasted since it is oriented primarily toward transitory sensual gratification rather than toward some useful social goal. In accordance with my promise, I refrain from characterizing it in ethical terms. I see no grounds, however, for regarding it as socially dangerous. It is probably here to stay, since the principal props of the older morality have disappeared with the advent of contraception and the scientific mastery of venereal infection.

In this situation three courses are possible. We can continue the hopeless effort to reinstate or preserve the old controls. We can let social evolution take its normal course, which I would expect to produce general social tolerance in about three generations. Or we can expedite the transition by converting a social evil into a positive social value by an act of social engineering.

EXPERIMENT OF OTHER SOCIETIES

The comparative evidence shows clearly the social uses to which other peoples have turned premarital sex freedom. Lifting the taboo lessens the burden of guilt accompanying such behavior, and thereby presumably reduces the incidence of psychoneuroses. A socially sanctioned channel for the physical expression of the sex drive is provided during the period of life when, according to Kinsey, its vigor is at the maximum and when economic or educational mores may make marriage impossible, thus satisfying our biological criterion of acceptability.

Thirdly, adolescents are enabled to establish the normal heterosexual habits that are adaptive in married life, instead of being driven through anxiety into less preferred patterns of sexual behavior. Perversions like bestiality and homosexuality, shown by the Kinsey report to be surprisingly prevalent in our own society, are unknown or exceedingly rare among more lenient peoples.

Fourthly, permissiveness educates the young to a realistic appreciation of the role of sex in personal life, and helps them to estimate more fully the importance of other factors that contribute to a satisfactory marital adjustment. In the history of mankind, most peoples seem to have discovered that relief from sexual frustration is a very inadequate motive for marriage.

(Luther E. Woodward)

Professor Murdock has given us some interesting observations from the vantage point of an anthropologist. I shall approach the same subject from the viewpoint of the mental hygienist. I shall be looking, I suppose, at a somewhat different set of facts than those presented by Professor Murdock. At least it appears to us in the clinical field that the anthropologist stands off and looks at man from the outside. When he studies the cultures of various peoples he records facts which have to do basically with their habits, their mode of relating person to person, and group to group, their customs, their conventions, their taboos, especially as expressed in group practice. When we view human beings from a mental hygiene focus, we are concerned primarily with the integration of the inner and the outer man, as it were. We are well aware that different types of family life, different community conditions, differing cultural beliefs and patterns of action make a difference in the inner responses of the individual. Vice versa, how a person thinks and feels determines most of his specific choices and his general behavior. I have elsewhere defined a mature and mentally healthy person as:

> *(1) One who first respects and has confidence in himself, and, because he knows his true worth, wastes no time proving it to himself and others; (2) one who accepts, works with and to a large extent enjoys other people; and (3) one who carries on his work, his play and his family and social life, with con-*

fidence and enthusiasm and with a minimum of fear and
hostility.

This may suffice to indicate the approach of the mental hygienist.

Coming to the specific subject at hand, I would say that sexual
behavior to be minimally acceptable, from the mental hygiene viewpoint, must satisfy both the demands of the biological organism for
release and pleasure, and the demands of the personality for meaning and worth. To be maximally acceptable, sexual behavior must
satisfy the demands of the partners' biological organisms for release
and pleasure and the demands of their personalities for a continuing, mutually satisfying, meaningful and enriching relationship.
Only so can the dual need of human beings for integration and for
fellowship be met through sexual activity. "They twain shall be
one flesh" suggests not only intellectual and spiritual fellowship
but actual integration of biological organisms. There is abundant
evidence that the achievement of such integration makes for family
stability.

If we can agree that sexual behavior is fully acceptable only if it
involves full-fledged respect for personality and the existence of a
loving and on-going relationship between two personalities, then, I
think we can motivate for such behavior.

The most basic and most certain way to motivate for such behavior is through parental love and guidance that fosters psychosexual maturing and builds up an effective and continuing
association in the child's mind of sexual behavior with love and the
best of family living.

It means, in the first place, that the child must live in an atmosphere of love and enjoyment; that his parents must help him to
have as full satisfactions as possible at each stage of growth; that
they consistently approve desirable forms of behavior by giving
positive recognition and that they disapprove unacceptable behavior with considerate and consistent firmness. This emphasis on
positive satisfactions and on being cherished provides the child with
a backlog of congenial, happy experience with the parents which
supplies the primary motivation for the child's own self-discipline.
This is the primary motivation for the child's learning to control his
appetites in accordance with the demands of the family group. It
is the means by which he learns to temper his desires and demands
with consideration for his parents and others. It supplies motivation for his efforts to keep his aggressive tendencies within the
bounds of social propriety and personal safety. By the same token
it supplies the most dynamic motivation for integrating his curiosity about life's origin, about sexual differences and about his own
sexual activities with the rest of his knowledge and with the people
he cares most about.

It is only the child whose training and home guidance have

fostered his integration as a personality who has full opportunity to integrate his sexual activities with the rest of his interests in life in a form that is acceptable to him and to others. Only so can the child accept sexual interest and activity as he does sight, hearing or speech—as normal, wholesome, God-given and to be used for the enrichment of life.

It may be noted, too, that several kinds of undesirable psychological behavior tend to accompany unacceptable sexual behavior: such patterns as marked feelings of dependency or inferiority, strong feelings of guilt and shame, arrested development at the narcissistic or anal erotic level, and relatively unrewarding efforts to compensate for such feelings of inadequacy, guilt or immaturity.

An amazing amount of sexual behavior as we find it today here in America is not primarily sexual in its motivation. Boys who pressure girls to allow them premature intimacies quite often do so to prove that they are he-men. Girls who yield to such pressure often do so on the ground that it is expected of them and that they may become unpopular if they don't. In both instances it is primarily an ego rather than a sexual drive. I could cite instances of adults whose sexual behavior has gotten them into all sorts of difficulties where the motivation likewise was a compensatory effort to make up for some other kind of felt lack. There is a good deal of clinical evidence, apparently not considered by Professor Murdock, to challenge the view that sex taboos are the chief cause of divorce and of some of our other socially undesirable outcomes. There is plenty in the press right now, much of it from Hollywood, where the divorce rate is exceptionally high, to suggest that narcissism looms larger in divorce than does sexual repression. It is a rather naïve assumption that divorce springs primarily from our sexual mores. Actually there is more ego immaturity in most divorces than there is sexual inhibition. In short, if we are going to motivate for acceptable sexual behavior, we shall have to motivate children for full-fledged emotional maturity. And, as I have already indicated, congenial family experiences in which self-confidence is developed and sexual behavior is wholeheartedly accepted as a healthy and worthwhile phase of life give the assurance that young people's patterns of thought and feeling will be constructive and make for integration.

EDUCATION FOR FAMILY LIVING

We can motivate for acceptable sexual behavior by education in the true sense in an atmosphere of confidence and esteem. Facts honestly presented and integrated with the experience of both learner and teacher become motivating forces. The appeal is to reality, not to fear; to individual dignity and to the normal desire for integration and a full life.

A most helpful point at which to provide true education for

family living is at the premarital level, working with young people in the age range of sixteen to twenty-five or older. There is much in favor of presenting informal out-of-school courses to this age group, using such existing groups as church organizations, Y's, service clubs, and others. Lists of questions that have been raised in various groups in my experience show a rather marked degree of uniformity and cover the entire range of family needs and problems, from working wives and budget needs to getting along with in-laws, the sexual side of marriage, and the planning of families and spacing of children.

Discussion is greatly stimulated by throwing the course open to questions and discussion immediately.

Leadership, of course, is essential. The leader must not only be well-informed regarding all phases of family life, but must have achieved a high degree of objectivity in dealing with problems and viewpoints that are charged with strong emotion. This means that the leader must be able to discuss the sex side of marriage freely and without even slight embarrassment. It may mean, too, that he will have to deal objectively yet considerately with patterns of hostility and guilt in the course of the discussions. The aim is to help the members of the group acquire fuller understanding of all that is involved in marriage and family living, correct their own perspective in so far as it has been false, and achieve confidence in themselves to manage wisely their premarital or marriage relationships. The mental attitude and emotional tone of the leader should be characterized by genuine interest, emotional warmth, real acceptance of the group as persons, and readiness to give fully of one's knowledge.

In my opinion, premarital education, when well done, is especially valuable in motivating acceptable sexual behavior.

MOTIVATION BY REORIENTATION

We can motivate acceptable sexual behavior by emotional and social reorientation. This becomes necessary for all those who have arrived at young adulthood with warped attitudes, with more than average psychological conflicts, or who anticipate adult sexual functioning with fear and anxiety. It is needed by all who have been badly conditioned by their past experiences and whose patterns are not conducive to health and social acceptance.

This is especially true of women who are psychologically frigid, and men who are sexually impotent, or fear that they may be. It is the only method available for those with strong homosexual tendencies who wish to achieve a heterosexual pattern. It is the only process by which we can reach those who have been spoiling their sexual experience because of the imposition of personality problems that get in the way. Psychotherapy, case work and counselling, however these may be defined, are essentially the processes which have to be used in this reorientation and re-education task. Those concerned to promote both social hygiene and mental hygiene do well to make clinical services available as an essential supplement to group educational efforts.

(Frederick deWolfe Bolman, Jr.)

Throughout my remarks I want to keep in mind one central point of view: *sexual behavior is not an isolated problem but is one aspect of interpersonal relations.* We all have a more or less common urge towards sexual outlet. Our biological structure and needs haven't changed in many a moon. But what happens to that urge, how we act, is different for every individual. Sexual behavior is one slice of our social life. Our approach to love, like our approach to politics, reveals the kind of persons we are. Each one of us has a basic set of attitudes towards others which guide his behavior, and I believe we must concentrate on these attitudes for clues to the meaning, over and beyond biological meaning, of sexual behavior.

For example, I know a business man who makes a lot of money but who has a completely unsatisfactory love life. He suffers from impotence, he has what he calls a Don Juan complex, and any marriage he gets into is fretfully unstable. He wants to know why. Well, for one thing, he lacks the ability to trust another person. For another, he fears failure. Finally, he needs to dominate other people. All of these attitudes lead him to success in business, but they ruin his chances for sex satisfaction.

SEX BEHAVIOR AS PERSONALITY INDEX

In our discussion we ought to guard against a false isolation of our sex behavior from our basic attitudes. There really is no sex behavior problem, but only the problem of how we approach other people. Many people have wondered why Freud considered sex development the key to the understanding of adjustment and maladjustment. The reason is that he thought that character could be defined in terms of sexual outlet. Today we know enough to turn this answer around: we say sexual behavior is important to know about because it is a sensitive weather vane showing a person's basic attitudes, how he feels about other people, his approach to life itself.

Ideally, *acceptable sexual behavior is whatever a person with satisfactory interpersonal relations does.* But until we understand the meaning of our terms, such a statement is not much help.

CAN PHILOSOPHY FURNISH A MEASURING STICK?

A most important problem to face is this: *what do we mean by satisfactory interpersonal relations? What shall our criteria be?* I would deny that the descriptive sciences, like Dr. Kinsey's research into male sexual behavior in America, or Professor Murdock's description of common practices around the world, can ever give us any criteria for satisfaction. Suppose that most people in America, or in the world, are not as adjusted or happy as they can be. Professor Murdock defends common practices because he says they are socially useful. That completely skips the point. Look for a moment at the field of medicine. Is everybody as healthy as he possibly can be? Or is the average health in America as good as we can make it? There may be all kinds of curious social and economic benefits arising from the fact that many people die of heart diseases, cancer, and tuberculosis. But I am willing to wager that nobody here wants to have a heart attack, or cancer, or TB! Any *real* science of control for our betterment must have aims or values beyond what it finds in the way of facts within its field. Let's look at the last page in Dr. Kinsey's book to see how he feels. He concludes:

> The social values of human activities must be measured by many scales other than those which are available to the scientist. Individual responsibilities towards others in the social organization, and the long-range outcome of behavior which represents the individual's response to the stimuli of the immediate moment, are things which persons other than scientists must evaluate.

Perhaps it is just at the point where the specialized empirical and experimental sciences leave off, that philosophy can help us by searching out the best criteria for evaluation. Philosophers have been saying for over two thousand years that the greatest good for man is happiness. Philosophy's special job right here and now is to analyze the ingredients, our capacities and potentialities, which make for happiness. My own brand of philosophy does not look for eternal truths. I am not persuaded that any exist. But I do believe that philosophy can begin with whatever science discovers, envisage ideal ends, and help evaluate hypotheses about such ends. Of course, every statement about the "good life," something better than we already have, must be revised as we come to know more. We need to start with facts as they are. We need to envisage something better than we have. And we need constantly to check our ideas about something better with the facts. The scientist and the philosopher can work together to separate the possible from the improbable.

FREEDOM STRIKES A BALANCE

Now let's get back to the business of criteria for judging our social life. I believe that satisfactory interpersonal relations come about when people are able to use all their capacities freely, and when they are able to care for someone else enough to want him to do the same. We know a lot more about maladjustment in social relations than we do about adjustment. Sadism and masochism are two out of many forms of failure to achieve satisfactory interpersonal relations. It is harder to pin down what we mean by adjustment. But I think we can spot it in the person who is able to develop and use three capacities—his rational, his emotional, and his sensuous resources—without any one of the three being crushed, or stifled, or made a slave to the others. Neglect any one of these capacities, and you get maladjustment.

Let's look at some typical instances of failure to achieve a balance. The Puritan type looks down on sense pleasures as sinful or "dirty." He loses touch with reality and leads a chilly life. The 1920's saw a revolt against the Puritan. But some people then forgot what other resources they had. The revolt ended for them in nausea.

Or again, take the man who doesn't trust his emotions or who is afraid that his emotions will make a slave of him. This person loses a sense of vitality and direction. No one is apt to find much warmth in him. Some popular psychological literature today is revolting against this attitude. It tries to make you "feel better" about yourself and about other people. This over-emphasis on "feeling better," however, seems to some of us as unbalanced as the attitude of the man who doesn't trust his emotions.

Finally, take the person who doesn't want to stop to think, who can't stand reasoning much about things because he feels that thinking much leads in circles. Well, maybe his thinking does run in circles, but why let a resource go to rot? If he doesn't work to discover how to use his reason, he ends by letting circumstances get the better of him, by becoming hysterical when he is thwarted, by destroying himself and anyone else he can.

Satisfactory relations with others depend on a balance, on the freest and fullest interplay of our reason, our emotion, and our sensuous capacities with respect to another person—and our positive enjoyment of the same freedom for that other person. If we really take care of ourselves, have genuine self-regard for our own balance, we are apt to appreciate it in others. When we have this kind of self-regard, we find that we need other people but don't want to exploit them.

SEXUAL BEHAVIOR SCORED ON A PHILOSOPHICAL BASIS

What does our notion of "balance" and "free use and appreciation of capacities in interpersonal relations" tell us about our sexual behavior? For one thing, we can say that, if Dr. Kinsey's reports are accurate, a large percentage of American males do not achieve the most satisfactory sexual relations possible for man. Remember now, we're trying to focus on a possible ideal—not just the facts as they are, and not something improbable. Furthermore, remember that we are proposing to judge sexual behavior in terms of the most that can be got out of interpersonal relations, the very highest form of intimate companionship we can envisage. Let's run through some of the forms of sex outlet as Dr. Kinsey classifies them. Auto-eroticism and animal contacts must appear quite low on our value scale. They are pretty lonely activities! If one, or both of these, are the supreme sensuous achievement of a person, we will just have to score his enjoyment as low.

Take one that's harder to score—homosexuality. Frankly, I don't think we know enough about homosexuality yet to make a sound judgment. If it is a pathological symptom, then it will rate low. Another big trouble here is that we have forgotten all about the role of a family and children—a dangerous omission, to which I want to return in a minute. A family is an amazingly fruitful context for the fullest use of a person's capacities. Homosexuality, then, might rate above auto-eroticism and animal contact, but not much.

Now let's take one with an entirely different caste—prostitution. This form of outlet may turn out to be somewhere in the range of homosexuality. Prostitution is generally exploitative. If it persists in a person, as a continuous form of outlet, we expect to find exploitative attitudes towards others in all of his social attitudes. I think we have enough evidence here to say that when one person exploits another or has exploitative tendencies, he is damaging some of his own capacities. Prostitution doesn't rate high on our scale.

Now what about heterosexual promiscuity—either before or after marriage? Promiscuity is usually defended on grounds of experimentation, as Professor Murdock defended it here today, or else on grounds of dissatisfaction with any one particular partner, which is a kind of perpetual experiment. The big problem here is: *what is a valid experiment in the area of sexual behavior?* Until we have compared promiscuity with monogamy, we may have some difficulty in evaluating promiscuous heterosexual relations as an outlet. What needs to be said here, however, is that most such sexual relations are too short-lived for the fullest sense of satisfaction.

MONOGAMY AS THE IDEAL

Let's consider monogamy next. This appears to offer the best chances for fulfilling our ideal, the best chances for all that a person can achieve with another. The development of the rational, emotional and sensuous capacities of one person with another takes time—all the time that our biological functions permit us. Men always boast about their abilities, but few if any of us can possibly achieve this ideal development with more than one woman! Those who find themselves unable to achieve monogamy are either poor judges of their prospective mates for one reason or another, or else they are incapable of mating in the fullest sense. Until we know that physical mismating is a widespread problem, some of the best grounds for picking a partner are those experiences which can be had quite apart from intercourse itself. Again, I'd like to remind us that sex is just one aspect of our attachment to another person. I grant that it is the triumph of mutual pleasure, but there are lots of other conditions for it to be a lasting pleasure. The danger of promiscuity is that so frequently it is symptomatic of an inability to achieve satisfactory intimacy with anyone. Finally, from this interpersonal standpoint, we have a strong urge for children. Relatively unlimited opportunities of exercising all our capacities in family life bring married love as close to the ideal as we can get.

Throughout I have been trying to evaluate forms of sexual outlet, not to judge people or condemn them for the phases or difficulties through which they may pass for one reason or another. As a form of sexual behavior, monogamy comes closest to our ideal. That we are shocked by its scarcity only indicates that we sometimes forget that this is not the best of all possible worlds, nor are we the happiest of all possible men.

REJOINDER (*Woodward*)

In my initial statement I tried to indicate what is perhaps a basic difference in viewpoints between the anthropologist and the mental hygienist—viewpoints which are more supplemental than contradictory. It seems to me that the anthropologist, unless he studies some individuals intensively, or supplements his finding with those of the clinicians—psychiatrists, psychologists and case-workers—is apt to miss some of the personal meanings which behavior has for the individuals. The outer behavior of two people may appear very similar yet have radically different motivation and meaning.

Specifically, with regard to sexual behavior, for instance, two men may each have five orgasms a week. One may do so to boost his insecure ego and convince himself that he is a regular man, prostituting his partner completely while he affords himself this psychological tonic. The orgasm of another may be achieved as the expression of a deep and abiding affection and as a part of a mutually enriching experience which gives him and his partner both a profound sense of belongingness and of shared purpose. If orgasms are the only measure, or if conformance to the hetero-sexual pattern is the only norm, the two men would appear alike. Yet their experiences are fundamentally different and have very differing kinds of value just as the sun and a tallow candle are very different and have widely different value though the light from each vibrates at the same rate.

We have to get at meanings. We cannot for instance transplant the habits of Okinawans or inhabitants of Truk into Judaic-Christian industrial America and get the same value and meanings. While neuroses are few among the first-named, efforts to transplant the habits of those people into our culture might make neuroses even more numerous than they are here in America. The fact that there is unanimity among cultures in forbidding incest and adultery, and lack of unanimity regarding premarital relations and premarital chastity, may mean only that a society can survive either way and that one way is better for some people and another way better for others, depending on the meaning they incorporate in their sexual experience. I raise this question: May it not be true that an ideal of premarital chastity has more significance in a society that insists that sexual intercourse be an experience of mutual and lasting affection and an ongoing social purpose, than in a society that places primary value on physiological reactions and elevates the orgasm to a position of supreme good? Whatever values or lacks of values may be associated with it, much sexual activity—especially in forms the acceptability of which is not fully established—is basically not sexual, and, when seen in true perspective, even ceases to be acceptable. I refer to efforts of the many who use sexual activity to compensate for an insecure ego, or who hope thereby to cure their loneliness and become cherished. The choice is not necessarily between unrestrained impulse and moral rigidities that are blindly enforced by taboo. With enlightenment through sound education, we have a chance both to achieve personal freedom and fulfillment and to stabilize the family.

If I may again refer to my own experience in premarital education, I have been permissive at least to this extent. Consistently, when young people ask whether premarital intercourse is permissible, I refuse to answer yes or no. I remind them that that is a decision which each one has to make for him or herself. I point out that most people like to associate love and sexual relations, that it has much more meaning when these are kept together. (This can be elaborated in an hour of discussion.) The typical response from the group is "Gee, you are liberal!" with sometimes the added phrase, "for a clergyman." I have substantial evidence that they are much less likely to divorce other values from sex when they see all that is involved. Some, perhaps a majority, may choose premarital chastity wholeheartedly and without either anxiety or guilt. I would not care to impose a so-called "liberal" view any more than I would appeal to the taboo. Young people ought still to be free to make their own choices of ethical values and to regulate their lives accordingly. In the 25 or more groups with whom I have carried on such discussions, there is considerable evidence that frank, full discussions, far from leading to looseness or indiscriminate behavior, have tended toward conservative sexual practices, but from much more adequate motivation. Their choices are made in the light of fuller knowledge and a proper perspective of all the values involved.

Professor Murdock implied that our whole repertory of social ills, including mental illness, is due to our sexually inhibiting mores.

That is an amazing assumption. From my acquaintance with thousands of mental patients I would predict that if he made studies of a cross section of population of mental hospitals he would find an even wider range of sexual activity (prior to actual illness) than is found in so-called normal groups.

May I suggest, too, that while conversion hysteria has a well-known sexual basis, this has almost disappeared from the scene as a clinical entity. Instead we have an abundance of character neuroses, which spring much more from inadequate ego structure than from sexual repressions, and more from hostility and hatreds and resentments that are turned against the self than from societal taboos regarding sex. In addition, recent studies of sexual offenders indicate that basically we are dealing with inadequate personality structure rather than with sexual aberrations *per se*. Softening or even removing our sexual taboos will, in my opinion, supply no panacea for mental health.

Admittedly our sexual taboos have been crude, and often cruel, but while crude and cruel they have none the less conserved a set of personal and social values which people living under our culture at least are reluctant to give up—the linking of personal affection with sexual experience, the goal of marriage for life, and the building of strong family ties. I agree with Professor Murdock in one regard that our taboos as such are outliving their usefulness, but the substitution of easy experimentation is not the answer. It is high time we replaced the taboo with something that is better. Personally I will settle only for true enlightenment and insight which can be brought about only through informed family living and an extensive program of family life education. In that way we can retain the positive values which the taboo has crudely protected and avoid the ills which it has unwittingly produced.

REJOINDER (*Murdock*)

I distinctly do not advocate premarital license as a guiding principle in individual conduct. Sexual restraint has undoubted value as an ethical ideal—a corollary, if you will, of the ideal of moderation in all things. Chastity before marriage, for those who will and can achieve it, is laudable. I find myself, in fact, appreciably less "liberal" than Dr. Woodward claims to be, and am profoundly shocked by his avowed policy that "when young people ask whether premarital intercourse is permissible, I refuse to answer yes or no." Premarital intercourse is most definitely not permissible in our society, and if I did not frankly admit this to a young person coming to me for advice, and point out clearly the social sanctions he or she might expect for violating the taboo, I should have serious trouble with my conscience.

I do not even approve the current laxity among our youth, which I specifically stigmatized in my paper as "unlovely." I have merely faced the fact, denied by no other speaker, that premarital laxity is rampant today and that there is no reasonable prospect that it will decline in the near future. Wide disparity between ethical ideals and actual practice is always socially dangerous—prohibition provides a recent case in point—and where it occurs the public-spirited citizen is under obligation to make remedial suggestions.

I have offered a suggestion based on professional knowledge of how hundreds of other societies have coped with the same problem. I have not addressed myself to our young people, advising that they imitate the Samoans or some other permissive society. I have addressed myself rather to the clergy and other responsible moral leaders suggesting, not that they condone promiscuity in individual behavior, but that they consider a modification in the ethical code itself whereby a distinction be drawn between selfish sensual indulgence and experimentation oriented toward forming a satisfactory and enduring marital relationship. Such a solution, could it be reached, would certainly have to be adjusted to the specific conditions prevailing in our own society, including our ethical standards, and would have to conform to Dr. Bolman's criterion of "satisfactory interpersonal relations." Until and unless such a change occurs, whether by normal evolutionary processes or by an act of social engineering, we have no alternative as sensible men but to accept the existing code and try to operate as intelligently as we can within it.

Two • *Sound Attitudes Toward Sex*

LESTER A. KIRKENDALL
Family Life
Oregon State College

American attitudes toward sex are frequently amazing to travelers from other countries. We are accused of being excessively inhibited or aggressively vocal on the subject, and certainly, we are in the midst of a change in attitudes about sex. The Kinsey report has brought sex into the open, and an accumulating mass of research is producing evidence that sex cannot be dissociated from the total personality. The following appraisal of sex attitudes* raises the question whether the present freedom of discussion of sex will be used constructively by parents and responsible educators.

* Reprinted from *Journal of Social Hygiene*, 1951, 37: 241–251, by permission of the author and the American Social Hygiene Association.

WITHOUT doubt, we need an improvement in our attitudes toward sex. After sex has been treated so unnaturally, and tabooed for so long, this is a hard task. With so little experience with what is natural and mature, it is difficult to judge what is unnatural and immature. We are so involved in our own attitudes that we are unable to appraise them.

For these reasons, I shall analyze here seven of our common attitudes toward sex, and suggest improvements in them.

1. We need to move from

$$\frac{\text{an attitude regarding sex}}{\text{as primarily physical}} \left.\right\} \text{to} \ \frac{\text{a concept of sex as an}}{\text{attribute of total personality}}$$

People will never comprehend the place of sex in life nor understand sex behavior so long as they regard it as primarily a physical experience. Yet this is a common view. Many people. assume that all sex behavior is motivated by the desire for sensory pleasure. They are unaware of the numerous factors which motivate it. They do not realize that sex behavior is an aspect of total personality adjustment, nor do they see the interaction between sex and other aspects of personality.

Many people are uncertain of the relation between sex and love.

SEX AND AFFECTION

Dr. O. Spurgeon English has contributed to our understanding on this point. He says that to think of expressions of affection as touch-pressure relationships helps us to see the relation of sex to affection. Whenever we feel affection for people, we want to be close to them. We want to touch, to embrace, to come close. We find pleasure in close physical intimacy.

An obvious example is when parents embrace and caress their children in infancy. Both parents and children enjoy this. The same expression is seen in animal life. A dog, or a horse, will press close against his master. The pet enjoys the close physical contact. The master, in turn, pats and caresses the animal. Much adolescent petting has the same origin. Carried to its logical conclusion, it involves love-stricken youth in sexual intercourse, for sexual intercourse is the most intimate and pleasurable of all touch-pressure relationships. The desire for it is a natural consequence of a growing feeling of love and affection, although, of course, sexual intercourse with a definite degree of physical pleasure may occur when there is no affectional attachment.

Two studies have demonstrated the relationship between sexual behavior and total personality adjustment. They were made in the San Francisco Psychiatric Clinic. The studies, with 365 women and

255 men as subjects, probed the motivation for promiscuity. Was it a desire for physical satisfaction, or something deeper?

This quotation was taken from the study on women:

> Contrary to popular belief, no evidence was revealed to indicate that this problem is produced by above-average sex drive. In fact, *the majority of habitually promiscuous patients used promiscuity in an attempt to meet other problems rather than in an attempt to secure sexual satisfaction.*

In discussing the motivation for habitual promiscuity in men, the investigators say:

> Promiscuity . . . was revealed to be a problem in inter-personal relationships . . . was engaged in in an attempt to solve other problems. In nearly all cases, this behavior appeared to be the result of conflicts, inadequacies or disorganization within the personality. Incapacity for sustained love relationships, or impairment of that capacity, was revealed by almost every patient. Active hostility toward women was present in varying degrees among some of the men. . . .
> . . . no evidence could be secured that promiscuity was the result of greater-than-average sex drive.

UNMARRIED MOTHERS

A study of unmarried mothers gives further evidence of the close relationship between personality development, home conditions, education and sex behavior. This study concludes:

> . . . the typical unmarried mother of this study tended to come from an unhappy home usually broken by either the death of one or both of the parents, in which case the mother generally worked out—or where the parents, or particularly the mother, was suffering from some form of ill health, and where the parents, although often affectionate toward their children, were not in the majority of cases considered real 'pals.' . . .
> The unmarried mother tended to be ignorant or partially ignorant of the facts of reproduction, having received what information she possessed, true or false, from friends and companions rather than from her school or home. . . .

When people understand that sexual behavior is an aspect of total adjustment, it will be neither possible nor desirable to ignore it. Those who indulge in harmful and exploitative sex behavior will still have to be controlled, but they will be regarded more as immature and unsocial personalities than as sinners.

Sex has three functions in life.

The first is the reproductive function, which is so well understood that it needs no further elaboration here.

The second is physical pleasure and satisfaction. This function is often disproportionately emphasized, especially by poorly informed persons. It is a legitimate aspect of sex, however, and should be so recognized.

The third function is the use of sex as a communicative, unifying factor. This function of sex is hard to explain to those who have always thought of sex in physical and sensual terms. Yet we communicate with each other through caresses, embraces and handclasps. In grief, or under strain, these methods of communication are sometimes even more meaningful than verbal expressions.

In stressing techniques and procedures of intercourse as the key to sexual satisfaction, many marriage manuals seem to overlook this function of sex. They equip couples with the mechanics of expression, but fail to realize that they may have nothing to express to begin with.

The communicative and unifying satisfactions of sex can be experienced only as psychological and personality values are associated with it. This carries one far beyond the merely physical aspects of sex.

2. We need to move from

irrational moralism
———————————
non-moral attitudes ⎬ to ___insightful morality___

SEX AND SIN

For centuries many people have clung to the idea that any expression of sex, especially during the premarital period, was sinful. Some went even further. Sex might be necessary for procreation in marriage, but it was not to be enjoyed. Sex was not to be discussed. The moral person subdued all thoughts, feelings and expressions of sex during the premarital period, and indulged in it after marriage in complete secrecy.

The consequences of this attitude toward sex are still seen in counseling. Counselors meet disturbed boys and girls who fight to repress and seek to disown their sexual nature. They think of their normal impulses and desires as base and unworthy, and deprecate themselves when they cannot subdue them.

Seeking to escape this unrealistic and harmful attitude, some few persons take the point of view that sexual considerations are nonmoral. Sex is regarded as a "natural" function and, because it is, it may be exercised whenever "normal" desires impel the person.

Extremely harmful exploitation, without doubt, may occur in the name of sexual satisfaction. Social problems and individual maladjustments may be created or increased by the way in which sex is used.

Dr. Kinsey has been criticized for taking a "non-moral" view of sex. Yet in his volume, so largely devoted to statistics, is this sentence: "Sexual histories often involve a record of things that have hurt, of frustrations, of pain, of unsatisfied longings, of disappointments, of desperately tragic situations, and of complete catastrophe." If this statement is true, as we know it is, we must reject the idea that sexual behavior is a strictly non-moral matter.

An insightful morality is needed. We should neither be afraid of sex nor laud it just because it is sex. Our problem is to recognize it as a normal phase of living and approach it in an understanding manner.

This attitude is particularly important in the education of young people. Youth seeks not to disregard morality, but to understand the reasons for it. I remember a boy who, questioning the prevailing standard of premarital chastity, began by saying, "I know religion is against sexual relations before marriage, but what is the 'real scoop'?"

The "real scoop" means understanding, in terms of life adjustments, the advantages, disadvantages, problems and recompenses of the different modes of sexual adjustment which youth see, hear discussed or read about.

MEETING QUESTIONS SQUARELY

"What is the harm of masturbation?" "If a couple love each other, and use contraceptive measures, isn't it all right for them to have intercourse?" "Why should we deny sex desire, when it is natural?" "Why is prostitution wrong?" These are questions which must be met squarely and without evasion. Platitudes and pious evasions will be rejected by youth. They want to understand why certain standards exist, and, if they are observed, what may be gained from following them.

This means that the average person must probe the relationship between sexual behavior and the total personal and social adjustment a great deal more thoroughly than he has ever done before. We have much rethinking and re-evaluating to do.

An example of a questionable evaluation which needs to be rethought is the opprobrium which still too often attaches to the unmarried mother, as compared to the person, who having been involved in adultery and having contributed to breaking up a home, is still received in polite society. One would think that the unmarried mother had broken all her vows and harmed society in a much greater degree than the person who has committed adultery. Or why should the unmarried mother attract more social disapproval than the unmarried father?

The scientific findings regarding masturbation, premarital intercourse, homosexuality, prostitution and other social practices need to be studied, related to human values and goals, and an insightful morality developed.

3. We need to move from a

hush-hush attitude
$\overline{}$
garrulous attitude } to $\dfrac{\text{an objective consideration of sex}}{}$

The first attitude is an obvious and common one. It is an ostrich-like denial that there is such a thing as sex.

People who react against the old hush-hush approach often express their emancipation by becoming garrulous about sex. Reacting against former taboos, they now discuss it at every opportunity, whether the occasion justifies it or not.

The sweeping away of taboos from a subject of vital interest always has this result. A tremendous reservoir of curiosity and suppressed interest is released and we are inundated with words, articles, books and talk. We are now in this stage. Dr. Kinsey's publications and the resulting comment have been especially influential in breaking through the barriers. His study has been hallowed and protected by the scientific approach. With its publication, it suddenly became more permissible to talk about sex. The result has been a garrulous outpouring of books and articles.

The issue, of course, is actually not quantity, but quality and purpose. We need an objective consideration of sex to help us understand the place of sex in life, and understand how to direct sex wisely.

If we can develop an attitude of objective, purposeful consideration toward sex, in the long run there will be less talk about it. This will be no virtue either, unless it signifies that at last people have gained long-needed insight and understanding.

POISED ACCEPTANCE

4. We need to move from a

grim, dour attitude
$\overline{}$
frivolous attitude } to $\dfrac{\text{poised acceptance}}{}$

I shall always remember an introduction I received to a class of boys in physical education. Their instructor had invited me to discuss some questions about sex which the boys had raised. As the instructor closed the introduction, he turned to the boys and, almost glaring at them, said, "I don't want any smiles from any of you fellows while Dr. Kirkendall is talking. Wipe 'em off."

As I stepped forward, I staged a hasty debate and decided that the joke I had thought of using was now necessary to relieve the tension which had been created. Not smile, indeed! Of course, I wasn't wanting frivolity, but neither did I want the boys sitting there tense and grim.

Our problem is to find a satisfactory middle ground. Like the tight-rope walker who has lost his balance, we swing first in one direction and then the other in our attempt to attain it. Our trouble is that, never having had a balanced attitude, we don't know when we have gained one.

An attitude of poised acceptance would surely grant that there are both serious and light-hearted things about sex . . . that it has its serious and its amusing sides. In fact, a sense of humor is often a saving grace. I'm encouraged to believe that we are moving in the direction of poised acceptance.

5. We need to move from an attitude of

fear and dread
——————————
shocking bluntness } to   straight-forward frankness
——————————————

Our present problems of handling sex grow, in a large measure, from fears associated with it. We *fear* sex. We fear our boys and girls will be involved in some form of sexual behavior. We fear the consequences if they are. We fear community reactions. We dread the day when we have to face questions of sex frankly with our children.

We sometimes make strenuous efforts to avoid direct involvement with sex. Some time ago I received a sex education pamphlet addressed to adolescents. The author seemed quite elated that the entire pamphlet did not once contain the word "sex." He used "physical need," "the creative urge," "the conjugal relationship," "the illicit union" and similar phrases. Personally, I feel that such an effort only strengthens our attitude of fear and dread.

This attitude is expressed in the many emotionally-toned words which we use in writing about or discussing sex. For example, masturbation is still called "self-abuse" by some. It is defined in the dictionary as "self-pollution." I recently read a theme on child development in which the writer, a mature graduate student, spoke of the common genital exploration of a child. She referred to this as "violating himself."

HOMOSEXUALITY

We call conduct which deviates too much from common, accepted practices a "perversion." Homosexuality is an example. Yet if we accept the psychiatric explanations of causation, we can hardly apply the dictionary definition of "perversion" to homosexuality. According to the dictionary, perversion means "obstinate in the wrong, willful." The synonym given is "cranky." This hardly describes the situation of a person whose emotional growth is thwarted by environmental circumstances so that he is blocked at the homosexual level.

A shocking, searing bluntness can, of course, damage efforts. to build good attitudes toward sex. This extreme should be avoided.

We do need an attitude and a vocabulary which will enable us to speak frankly and straight-forwardly about sex.

6. We need to move from an attitude of

$$\frac{\text{strictly individual concern}}{} \text{ to } \frac{\text{a recognition of social}}{\text{implications of sex}}$$

Sex has been considered for so long a strictly private matter that the average person finds it hard to think of sex in social terms. Ask an individual or a group if the sex life of an individual, or of partners in a sexual experience, is any business of people in general. The usual reaction is that it is not. What the person or couple do in their sexual relationship is their concern alone. Let society mind its own business!

Yet a little thought very shortly indicates that a strictly *laissez-faire* attitude is unacceptable. We need to consider the relationship of sexual behavior to social welfare, and to support an attitude which predisposes individuals to think in terms of group welfare.

7. We need to move from an attitude of

rigid masculine dominance, and female subordination / regarding the sexes as alike in all respects } to a flexible, equalitarian regard for individual personality and an acceptance of the unique values of sex membership

The inclusion of this attitude represents the growing concern for making all aspects of male-female relations a part of the consideration of sex education. There is much to be said on this topic, and books have been written on it.

The last century has seen women gaining much greater freedom. A wider range of activities has been opened to them. New occupations, voting privileges and political influence have accrued to women. Yet in many of our attitudes we have failed to accept these changes in the status of women. The American philosophy, someone has said, is that "men and women are equal, only men are more equal than women."

Early feminist leaders reacted to the rigid patterns of masculine dominance—feminine subordination which are part of the paternalistic family system with a counter-argument. Men and women, they said, are exactly alike and should be treated alike in all respects. The leaders of the early "equal rights for women" movement were especially vigorous in espousing this idea.

UNIQUE CONTRIBUTION OF EACH SEX

Liberal thinkers have pretty largely emerged from that stage today, however. They now believe that men and women need to accept each other as individuals with different capacities and potentialities. The more traditional, self-conscious awareness that each belongs to the "opposite sex" is a hampering attitude. They realize that each sex has an important and unique contribution to make to family and social life. This is an important element in a more satisfactory attitude. It enables both men and women to gain their personal satisfaction and prestige from their own contributions, rather than at the expense of members of the other sex.

The area of masculine-feminine understanding is one of our frontiers in developing improved relations between the sexes.

Three • *Penicillin is Not Enough*

RICHARD A. KOCH, M.D.
San Francisco, California

*The chief of the Venereal Disease Division of a department of public health describes sexual promiscuity as a personality problem growing out of an unsatisfactory home and family background.**

VENEREAL disease prevention is by no means a medical problem alone. Health workers charged with the responsibility of the control of syphilis and gonorrhea realize today more than ever before that VD is just one of the casualties resulting from anti-social or irresponsible social behavior.

THE SAN FRANCISCO PROGRAM

San Francisco has developed a series of community-wide programs directed toward the solution of the social problems related to venereal disease control. These programs have been formulated with the cooperation and guidance of all agencies whose efforts are directed at meeting problems of anti-social or irresponsible social behavior, including the San Francisco Social Hygiene Association, the local Mental Health Society, the Congress of Parents and Teachers, the League of Women Voters, community chest agencies and the city school system.

* Excepts from *Journal of Social Hygiene*, 1950, 36: 3–6, by permission of the author and the American Social Hygiene Association.

A Psychiatric Approach to Sexual Promiscuity. The realization of
community needs developed following the establishment of a psychiatric service at the city venereal disease clinic. This service was
established through the personal efforts of members of the local
social hygiene association and the state and local departments of
public health, with funds from the U. S. Public Health Service. It
was designed to apply the skills of psychiatric knowledge to venereal disease control. The objective was to determine the factors
motivating promiscuity and to determine to what extent psychiatry
and case work treatment might be effective in assisting the promiscuous and potentially promiscuous in making satisfactory adjustments, and especially to assist them in reducing their promiscuity,
thus reducing the incidence of venereal disease.

We found that patients varied from one another in their attitudes
when they were first interviewed by the psychiatric social workers.
Some were actively concerned regarding their infections, others
were distrustful and fearful of the intention of the interviewer. The
patient had to convince himself of the sincerity of the service in
helping him with his problems rather than imposing the help upon
him. In the initial interview the worker discussed such matters as
the patient's reaction to the venereal disease or the possibility of
venereal disease, worries and misgivings, special problems, familial
and marital conflicts, vocational plans, and sexual adjustment. Some
patients in the course of establishing their behavior had so rationalized it that they appeared at first to be entirely accepting it as
satisfactory. In the process of exploring the patients' attitudes some
expressed doubts about their purported satisfaction with themselves and some of them sought advice and guidance in developing
healthier attitudes.

Our study revealed that the patients were typically both socially
and emotionally immature, although their physical development
was normal. The patients attempted to find and assume self-direc-
tion before they were ready for it.

It was found that in adolescence many patients were separated
from their families by physical removal rather than emotional
emancipation. They tended to act impulsively without considering
the consequences of their behavior. Many patients had unrealistic
goals. They were lax in assuming responsibilities for their behavior.
Men were characteristically passive. Few patients were sensual or
sensuous. Sixty per cent came from broken homes. In a large percentage of the patients the homes were broken before adolescence.
In the homes which were not broken, marital difficulties were almost universally present. A division of loyalties between the parents
was commonly reported.

Generally difficulties reported by patients in emotional concepts
within the family centered around insufficient love or understanding
on the part of the parents for the child. Some patients were overly

resentful toward one or both parents. In numerous instances there was an absence of loyalty to the family group and absence of affectional ties to other members of the family.

It appears that the more the family pattern was disrupted, the more patients were inclined to express strong preferences for one parent or the other during childhood. Most patients who showed promiscuous behavior, appeared to show it as a result of conflicts, inadequacies, or disorientation within the personality. The intimate connection between the unfavorable childhood experiences and later sexual maladjustment was graphically portrayed by the patients' complaints of traumatic childhood experiences and frustration as they were being asked questions about their sexual history.

Although current environmental factors, such as unsatisfactory living conditions, the absence of community ties, and the making of casual friendships, were often found to have contributed to the promiscuous sexual behavior of our patients, these *per se* could not be considered to be the primary cause of the patients' habitual sexual promiscuity.

Our psychiatric study thus indicated that much of the sexual behavior of promiscuous men and women represents an effort to substitute sexual activity for more appropriate responses as a solution to emotional problems not related directly to sex needs or sex expression. Sexual promiscuity appeared to be a response to emotional and environmental problems. Thus we reached the conclusion that sexual promiscuity is a psychiatric problem.

As venereal diseases are spread by promiscuity, an aspect of venereal disease control, then, is psychiatric service for patients. The doctor must work on the theorem that one must treat the patient as well as the disease. Thus one cannot be content to treat the infection alone, but one must consider the overall patient and his problem. We believe that the psychiatric treatment of the promiscuous patient is an effective preventive measure to reduce the spread of venereal disease, and that mental hygiene becomes an important measure in reducing sexual promiscuity even before venereal diseases enter into the social picture as a problem.

The psychiatric treatment of patients has been productive of surprisingly promising results in that fifty per cent of the patients who received intensive treatment ceased their sexual promiscuity and ninety per cent either ceased or definitely reduced their promiscuity.

XV · AGED FAMILY MEMBERS

One · Age is Meant for Living

ESTHER McGINNIS
Director, Merrill-Palmer School, Detroit

As a result of the great increase in life expectancy during the past fifty years, the age structure of the family has changed. There are now more old people among living family members. The following reading * *summarizes briefly the findings of research concerning what makes for happiness and contentment in old age.*

SINCE old age makes the person more like what he already is, preparation for later years begins in youth. Psychologists believe that living each stage of development completely and satisfyingly enables the individual to move on easily to the next stage and to accept it fully, enjoying its satisfactions and meeting its difficulties. Life then becomes a challenge, and each stage is looked forward to and met in the spirit of adventure.

The needs of human beings, basically the same in each stage of life's journey, have been summed up as: "To love and be loved and use one's powers." Old people who have been loved deeply and unconditionally in each stage of life are better able to call forth love from their children, their friends, and their contemporaries. Even the next generation's affection, appreciation, and enjoyment may be theirs.

More important, perhaps, than being loved is the ability to feel love for others and to communicate that love to them. This is something that cannot be learned in old age but must grow through the years, with its beginnings in infancy. Amy Holway has indicated that children who are so treated in infancy that they are not fearful, angry at the world, or hurt are able to relate to people more easily and express their feelings more readily and realistically to people and the world around them. Old people have more difficulty than young ones in feeling loved and expressing their love for others, some because they lack experience in earlier life, others because they doubt their attractiveness to others and so tend to withdraw, waiting for expressions of love and affection and feeling hurt when these are not forthcoming.

* Reprinted from *Journal of Home Economics,* 1950, 42: 9–12, by permission of the author and the American Home Economics Association.

Any older person can acquire the physical attractiveness that comes from the scrubbed and tidy look which makes a good impression at any age. Well-cut clothes of good design but not too youthful, and as lovely as can be afforded, enhance one's self-confidence and attractiveness to others. If one has little money, and this is often the case, it pays to have a few good things and keep them in first-rate condition. Color is important. There is no reason for retiring to unbecoming blacks and browns. Soft colors harmonize better with the changes in skin and hair tones, and contrasts in color bring out special assets. Something about an old person's estimate of himself can be told from his appearance, and others tend to judge us by our appraisals of ourselves.

KEEPING ACTIVE PAYS DIVIDENDS

To grow old gracefully, one should keep physically active. When people begin to take on excess weight and slow down in middle age, it is time to take stock of the situation. Walking, gardening, dancing, housework of all kinds including outdoor tasks, golfing, fishing, hunting, and other sports are all ways of keeping active. Some of these skills are best acquired in earlier life. If these activities are carried on at a comfortable pace—not in that spirit of meeting deadlines of time and amounts of work which so many of us impose on ourselves, thus inducing tensions and anxieties—they will pay dividends in the later years. Accepting the frustrations of a body that will no longer do exactly what we want it to do and breaking up work or play into shorter periods rather than giving it up entirely help in making the necessary changes of pace.

Men who find satisfaction in caring for their yards and doing "a man's work" about the house can share the housework too when they no longer have jobs outside the home. Women often find it less difficult than men to adjust to old age, and one reason is that they continue to be useful in the home. Cooking, sewing, handwork, and caring for children must go on; and the older woman's help with them is often accepted gratefully by younger people. However, allowing oneself to become a drudge and doormat for the younger people is wrong and shows a lack of self-respect. Young people should bear their own burdens and shoulder their own responsibilities. It is good for them to do so, and they should not be deprived of the experience.

VARIETY OF INTERESTS ATTRACTS FRIENDS

One way to avoid being imposed upon is to keep so busy that one does not depend on others for time and attention. The older person whose days are full of activity and interest is usually the one whose ideas and activities others are eager to share and who is invited to visit, dine, and make trips with them. Preparation for such a life begins years earlier when skills and interests are developed which can be continued into old age, such as sewing and handwork of all kinds, painting, group singing, playing with amateur musical groups, acting, sports, and writing. Thorndike has shown, however, that it is never too late to learn something new. The author knows of a couple who learned to dance at 60; of a man who began composing verse at 50 and who wrote some charming poetry for children when past 70; of a woman past 80 who paints lovely water colors and oils.

Old people, like children, enjoy routine in their daily schedules —a rhythmic pattern of activity and rest, with an occasional high spot to which they may look forward. A quiet game of cards before bedtime, a telephone call from a daughter at noon, a friend who drops in for a cup of tea in the afternoon, games that are continued from day to day or week to week—all are cherished and enhance daily living.

To retire *to* something is important, particularly for professional people. Some choose to continue in one phase of their work in which the experience and competence they have achieved are an asset. Others should plan to enter a different kind of work which is not so demanding but will yield some income and make a contribution. These are individual choices, but they should be planned in advance if the transition is to take place smoothly. Retirement to idleness and uselessness is fatal, both physically and psychologically.

Since the proportion of old people in our population is increasing so rapidly, society is beginning to modify its requirements and employers to provide opportunities for older people to continue their work. When retirement becomes necessary, volunteer activities for young friends or work in an agency where one's help is welcomed can provide the feeling of usefulness which a job formerly gave. All over the country, old people are now planning or joining in group activities and recreation.

Older people are important to children in the family. Grandparents, uncles, and aunts have a role to play in the lives of children, even though they do not live with them. They have a special feeling for children which the children sense. Sometimes they understand a child better than his parents do. They may coddle and "spoil" where parents have to "bring up" and "teach." They have time to listen and explain and to do the special things for each child which may be crucial in helping him to accept himself and his family. To help children accept older people is to lay by insurance for one's own old age.

A CONSTRUCTIVE SPIRIT BRINGS JOY

Even more important than all these considerations is the spirit with which one faces life. A worrier finds more to worry about as

friends become incapacitated, as his children or other young relatives meet disaster, and as the world changes and "isn't as it used
to be." Self-pity finds food for growth in thoughts of one's own
failing powers, of one's increased loneliness as contemporaries die
or move away and none are left who knew one's youth and call one
by one's first name. Learning to enjoy being alone should begin in
childhood and should be cultivated throughout life. In the midst of
all our group living, with nursery schools, clubs, dormitories, com-
mittees, and organizations, many people miss the experience of
becoming acquainted with and liking themselves. They fail to build
within themselves the resources which make being alone a source
of serenity and joy. Meditation is foreign to them and makes them
feel uncomfortable and queer. They are afraid to be alone. Since
in old age one is increasingly alone, to enjoy solitude and use it
constructively is a real asset. Finding ways of being alone in
crowded family living and in a busy professional life is difficult,
but it brings its reward at the time; and cultivation of the arts of
meditation and thinking, of enjoying peace and quiet, makes for
happiness in old age.

It is dangerously easy for old people to become engrossed in
what used to be and to live in the past. To do so is boring to others
and deadening to one's own growth. Old people who are still curious about what is coming and who anticipate the next ten years of
their lives retain a youthful zest and spirit. To cultivate a sense. of
curiosity and enjoy the fun of satisfying it is to prepare in some
measure for an interesting time in one's later years.

Good health helps to maintain the joy of living, but even handicapped and helpless people have been able to keep youthful in
spirit and to enjoy some of the everyday sources of satisfaction
available to all—nature, color, beauty in any form, people, babies
and children, books, and using one's hands.

LIVING ARRANGEMENTS ARE IMPORTANT

One of the most difficult problems of old age is that of where and
how to live. To share another person's home, particularly a son's or
daughter's or grandchild's, when the arrangement is the result of a
sense of obligation rather than a genuine desire for one's company,
may lead to tension and conflict. Under such conditions, sharing the
same house may become almost intolerable for both young and old.
Differences in habits of sleep, rates of moving about, use of the
radio, attitudes toward drinking, card playing, churchgoing, recreation, and ways of bringing up children can become sources of acute
disagreement and hurt feelings. To the extent that there can be
separate quarters and resources of activity and interest for the old
people, these sources of difficulty may be minimized. By the same
token, to the extent that the older person is living his life through
that of the younger one, it becomes unhealthy and intolerable.

In general, it is probably wiser to provide some degree of separateness in living for the older and younger generations and for the older person to stay in his own home and community as long as possible. To go to a strange community and leave the place "where I am somebody," as one person who is a part-time librarian at 81 puts it, is fatal for most old people. Children sometimes feel that to leave old people alone in an apartment or room or house, or alone in a different community, can be interpreted as neglect. They are more afraid of what neighbors or friends may say than of what may happen to the spirit and happiness of the old people. The older person who has the responsibility of maintaining and caring for his own home is able to keep physically active, has the satisfaction of living among his own possessions, and feels useful.

The ability to accept separation and death, with the heart-breaking changes they bring, is a test of one's maturity. To feel that all that one has had and been is not lost but goes on through the lives of others brings a creative acceptance of sorrow and grief and a feeling of hope for the future.

Time moves swiftly in old age. Time perspectives change, but as Anne Morrow Lindbergh writes:

> That is only when one looks on life in the wrong time-sense. The events of a life are not notches in a perpendicular bar, one above the other. They are not imbedded in one spot in time. They are more like horizontal threads in a tapestry. That red thread that appears only at one point in your life, the red center of a flower—has it not been there all the time, hidden underneath, on the back side of the tapestry, waiting till it should find its place in the pattern, disappearing again once it has fulfilled its role; but there underneath all the time, forming part of the whole firm, intricate, varied, structure of the woof?

NOW WE SEE AGE IN A DIFFERENT LIGHT

In his introduction to Cowdry's pioneering book on the problems of aging, John Dewey, whose own ninetieth birthday was celebrated in October 1949, wrote that he had once been asked by a well-known person for the titles of books on the psychology and sociology of old age and was obliged to answer that he knew of none. In the past few years, America has awakened to the implications of the change in the age composition of its population; and there are now many books, both professional and popular, on all phases of "Living and Aging," as one university extension course is titled. Social measures, such as pensions and other provisions for security in old age, do much to free older people from the fear of being dependent upon and a handicap to those they love. Advances in medicine have not only prolonged life but have also made old age a more vital and comfortable period. In many ways, the last of life is thus becoming actually what the poets and philosophers have long said it was ideally—a time of serenity and fulfillment, and sometimes of genuine achievement as well.

Two · *The Age Problem in Workers*

N. W. SHOCK
Gerontologist, U. S. Public Health
Service

What is physiological aging, or, in other words, when is an individual old? Is chronological age a sound standard for establishing the time at which industrial or professional retirement is required?

A gerontologist attempts to define aging,* and calls attention to how little yet is known about the processes and changes which are called aging, and the rates at which these processes take place.

AGING is a problem common to all of us. It is a process that begins with conception and continues throughout life. In the past most people have regarded aging as something like the weather—something to be talked about but about which nothing much could be done. There have also been a great many recommendations about appropriate formulas for increasing longevity. As early as 1780, Luigi Cornaro published a book on how to live to be 100. Since that time many others have added prescriptions—or restrictions—that they believe will lengthen life. Some have recommended eating nothing but raw meat or raw vegetables. Others have suggested goat milk, yogurt, etc. At the present time there are those who believe that after the age of 40 one should avoid milk and eggs in the diet. Similarly, the ill-effects of many pleasures, including smoking and drinking, have been held up as factors limiting longevity. However, none of these recommendations has been subjected to rigorous scientific tests.

The problem for discussion—"What is physiological aging, and how does it influence research productivity?"—poses a double-barreled difficulty. In the first place, we need to consider the question of how physiological characteristics influence mental performance in general and, second, how these may change with increasing age. Although we are convinced that the brain is an essential part of the

* Reprinted from *The Science Monthly*, 1951, 62: 353–355, by permission of the author and the American Association for the Advancement of Science.

body and that creative activities are dependent upon a well-functioning brain, the precise manner in which physiological conditions within the brain influence behavior and productivity has not been worked out in any detail. We may, however, depend on the validity of the common-sense assumption that intellectual productivity is in some way dependent upon bodily vigor. How, then, does bodily vigor change with age, and what are the conditions that maintain it?

What, then, is aging? Since all animals, including unicellular ones, age and die, we make the general assumption that the aging process is fundamentally one of cellular biology. However, very little is known about the characteristics of aging cells. In fact, most of the studies of cellular activities in old animals fail to show anything strikingly different from similar functions observed in young ones. With the development of new techniques and greater knowledge of enzymes and the chemical processes going on within cells, we may look to substantial advances in this area in the future. On the other hand, when we examine aggregations of cells that are put together into tissues and organs for specific functional purposes, we do find definite differences between old and young tissues. The most striking difference is that in the old tissues there is an accumulation of extracellular materials filling up the spaces where functioning cells have disappeared. Studies of the functioning of separate organ systems have shown that the organs of older animals in general tend to perform less well than those of young animals. It should be pointed out that the primary difference observed is often a reduction in reserve capacity in the old animals; that is, they are able to meet the day-to-day needs in an adequate fashion but, when called upon to perform under conditions of stress or extra load, they are unable to meet the demands as well as young animals.

This is not the place to indulge in a detailed review of research on the physiological aspects of aging. Review of this work, as well as our own studies, leads us to three general conclusions that I believe are of importance: Aging is a gradual, continuous process, the rates of aging of different organ systems may vary widely within the same individual, and there are marked individual differences in the rate of aging in humans.

Aging is a gradual, continuous process insofar as we now know it. Unfortunately this conclusion must be based on measurements made on different people at different ages. These observations all show a gradual loss of efficiency or performance, oftentimes beginning at relatively early ages and continuing to the highest age levels. For example, the maximum elasticity of blood vessels is reached at the age of 14 or 15 years and diminishes gradually thereafter. Although the rates of change with age differ markedly for different functions, the average changes are all gradual. In some functions there is a long plateau throughout middle life when little change appears, but in no instance is there a precipitous drop beyond a certain age. These observations do not exclude the possibility that within an individual age changes may occur rapidly. This question can be answered only when we have observations made serially on the same individual as he grows older. Opportunities for this kind of research require the cooperation of active middle-aged people who will serve as experimental subjects over their life span.

The different organ systems in the same person do not all age at the same rate. In our studies in Baltimore, evaluations of the functional capacity of different organ systems have been carried out in older people. We have not been able to demonstrate any close relationship between rates of aging in the kidney, the heart, and blood vessels, metabolism, nerves and muscles, perceptual capacities, and mental performance. Our most extreme deviate is a man who claims to be 91 years old. He has a kidney function equal to the average 60-year-old man, a nerve conduction time of the average 30-year-old man, perceptual capacity of the average 80-year-old man, but the metabolism of the average 90-year-old group. This person represents an extreme complexity of the aging process, but most individuals show some discrepancies.

There are wide individual differences in the rate of aging in different people. All our studies have shown that with increasing age individuals become less similar. For instance, the range in values for kidney blood flow in 30-year-old adults is roughly 900–1,200 ml per minute, whereas in the 80-to-89-year-old group, the range is approximately 200–800 ml per minute. We have also observed some men in their eighties whose effective renal blood flow is as great as the average of the 40-year-old group. Similar individual differences have been shown in tests of mental performance as well as of physiological factors.

What are the implications from these findings? First of all, it is clear that there can be no answer to the general question "When is a man old?" If this question is to have any significance, we must always say, "Old—with respect to what performance?" Since many performances are highly specific, it may well be necessary to resort to an overall evaluation, subjective though it may be, to answer this question for a particular individual. This conclusion also has important implications for determining appropriate ages for retirement. It is obvious that dependence upon strict chronological age can have no real meaning. All that can recommend chronological age is the administrative convenience in its application. However, with increasing numbers of elderly people, and the need for maximum productivity to maintain our economy, it is highly questionable whether we can afford the waste involved in discarding effective employees simply because they have obtained a given chronological age. Our most important problem is to devise ways and means of maintaining the effectiveness of older people so they can be retained in their positions. Research productivity in itself has never been closely correlated with physiological states. We can, however, regard the maintenance of physiological vigor and health as an aid to full productivity and mental alertness. This is primarily a problem of personal hygiene, with perhaps the added advantage of periodic health examinations to detect early stages of disease and pathology that are more easily remedied then than later. The most productive research workers are notorious in disregarding fundamentals of hygiene. Long hours and work under pressure may or may not result in the development of gastric ulcer, coronary artery disease, etc. Nevertheless, certain broad principles of hygiene are undoubtedly of value in maintaining health and vigor. Research workers should be given opportunity and encouraged to follow these principles as we now know them.

A problem of identifying and describing age changes in human beings is one that should receive the attention of industrial research in the future. From its early beginnings, where industrial research was concerned primarily with specific practical problems, there has been a gradual shift to emphasis on fundamental research. Experience has shown that the building up of a backlog of fundamental research is of great value to industry in developing new and better products. There is need now for industrial research to turn its attention to the producer as well as to the product. Many important problems relating to the productivity of older workers can be solved only within the framework of industry. Important questions about the changes of attitudes toward work with advancing age, as well as the effect of programs designed to train people for retirement, should also be considered. Nor should the physiological aspects of aging be neglected. With increasing stability of workers within plants and industries, serial examinations on the same individual as he ages should be made by industry itself or in collaboration with university scientists. The questions of middle age and later maturity can be answered only with the active assistance of industry where large groups of people are actively working and producing, just as our knowledge about growth and development of children resulted from cooperative studies with schools and universities. As our population ages there will be greater need for this fundamental information. It offers a real challenge to research.

XVI · FAMILY LIFE—EDUCATION, COUNSELING, RESEARCH

One · The Contemporary Status of Marriage Counseling *

EMILY HARTSHORNE MUDD
Counselor, Marriage Council
of Philadelphia

MALCOLM G. PRESTON
Psychologist, University of Pennsylvania

MARRIAGE counseling in some form is as old as human life. As a potential social and scientific discipline, its beginnings date within the last three decades: first in the German-speaking sections of the European Continent, then in the Scandinavian countries and England, and later in the United States, beginning about 1930. The emergence of the German dictatorship resulted in the closing of the type of counseling service reported earlier in German-speaking countries. In the United States, the chronological development of marriage counseling on a formal basis has been along the following general lines: (1) as a by-product of the early practice of professionally trained individuals; (2) as an adjunct of religious, educational, welfare, legal, and other community services; (3) as independent service; and (4) as a profession.

The purpose of marriage counseling in the broad sense is the promotion of adequate preparation for and adjustment in marriage. It has been nurtured through the following approaches: (1) courses on marriage and the family in schools, colleges, and community groups; (2) the informal counseling of ministers, teachers, lawyers, and other professional persons as a by-product of their daily work; (3) the compilation of sound source and reference material; (4) the organization of marriage counseling services; and (5) the intensified interest, promotion, and participation in research.

PROFESSIONAL MARRIAGE COUNSELING SERVICES

Marriage counseling is practiced formally only through services staffed by professional personnel with specialized experience and training. Services meeting such a criterion vary greatly in their objectives. Among such groups, for example, there are the "Family

---

* Reprinted from *The Annals*, 1950, 272: 102–109, by permission of the authors and The Annals of the American Academy of Political and Social Science.

Societies" that meet the membership requirements of the Family Service Association of America. These agencies for the most part do not *announce* marriage counseling as a special service. In some, a considerable proportion of their work with family members is in marital adjustment problems; in others, the proportion is small. In most of these services there is very little if any work in premarital preparation.

Then, there is a smaller group of services, probably not more than thirty or forty, which focus on marriage counseling work both nominally and functionally. These agencies offer service both before and after marriage. They are organized differently in different communities. Some are under the auspices of welfare, educational, or legal organizations; some are under religious leadership; some are an integral part of university campus activities; and some are independent services under the leadership of professional and lay persons of recognized status in their communities. Such specialized services are all in urban communities and, although few in number, have wide geographic distribution.

TYPES OF CLIENTS AND WHERE THEY COME FROM

Quite naturally the type of person who applies to these services for marriage counseling varies in accordance with the purposes of the agency to which he applies, the auspices under which it functions, the methods of intake employed, and the local community served. For instance, a service open without charge to students on a university campus would be expected to have more young unmarried and engaged clients with problems of parental weaning, mate selection, and premarital adjustment than the office of a family society located in an industrial area. However, as services become more widely known in a local community or nationally, and as they are made more available to the general population, intake becomes less specific.

Surveys made by six selected agencies indicate that about onehalf to two-thirds of their clients are women; 0 to 66 per cent are unmarried; ages range between 18 and 50 with a definite majority between 20 and 35; about one-third to one-half or more are Protestant, and the remainder are Jews, Catholics, and persons who report themselves as unaffiliated. A small proportion of reporting services indicate a larger proportion of Catholic than of Jewish clients. The majority of clients have had a high school education at the least.

Clients are referred from professional persons, such as doctors, ministers, teachers, lawyers, and social workers; from community and government agencies; from educational institutions; from lay persons, friends and former clients; and from books, periodicals, radio, and the press.

PROBLEMS BROUGHT FOR COUNSELING
AND LENGTH OF CONTACT

The reasons which prompt people to come for marriage counseling are often more complex than those which are given at the time of application for service or during the first interview. The given reasons are usually vague or oversimplified. At later interviews clients indicate additional problems, and often the focus of the case changes. The counselor also often feels that he is cognizant of problems in the client's situation of which the client is not at first, or perhaps ever, aware.

Reasons for seeking marriage counseling include the following: general preparation for marriage; whether to have medical examination; parental ties and parental attitudes toward client's marriage; doubts and questions about marriage in general or about a specific partner; whether or not to have children and when; adjustment to partner, including personality, friction, and lack of communication; problem of postponing marriage or breaking engagement; illegitimate pregnancy; a whole gamut of questions pertaining to sexual adjustment, such as unfocused fears about sex or past sexual behavior of self and/or partner; contemporaneous sex adjustment to partner; lack of sex desire and homosexuality; and situational and environmental reasons, including reasons related specifically to illness and difficulties of the partner or the self. In addition, many applicants come with requests for information which may require specialized help and referral, and also requests for information relating to community resources, household management, and employment.

Insight into the relative proportions of the premarital and marital groups is gained from figures from the six agencies already cited. In a study of 2,566 consecutive cases at Marriage Council of Philadelphia, the percentages of total intake recorded, broken down under reasons for coming given by the client at the first interview, were: 23 per cent general preparation for marriage; 16 per cent specific premarital problems, such as parent relations (2 per cent), considering engagement (6 per cent), illegitimate pregnancy (1 per cent), advice in connection with others (1 per cent), and others (6 per cent); 61 per cent problems of married persons, such as sexual difficulties (15 per cent), general adjustment (21 per cent), specific problems (15 per cent), and considering separation or divorce (10 per cent).

COUNSELING METHODS

Methods utilized in marriage counseling vary considerably, depending largely upon the background training of the director of the service and of the staff members. In the member agencies of the Family Service Association of America, marriage counseling is carried out on the basis of social case-work methods. According to Florence Hollis, an authority in this field, these consist of environmental modification, psychological support, and insight development. Some of the independent marriage counseling services, where graduate case workers are in charge, employ methods essentially similar to those of social case work, although these may be supplemented by additional techniques specific to marriage counseling. The following activities are reported from one service active in this field for seventeen years, as most characteristic for the counselor.

> Discussion of agency function and structuring client's feeling and behavior; exploration of situation or problem, providing a sympathetic listener, reassurance and approval; offering of information and education; interpretation; offering suggestions, advice and proposal of activity; persuasion and use of authoritative firmness; use of disapproval, disagreement or criticism; discussion of referral; environmental modification exclusive of referral.

Through use of these activities the counselor, broadly speaking, hopes to give to the client, in Florence Hollis' terms, "psychological support and clarification aiding in the development of insight."

Certain psychologists undertaking marriage counseling report that they employ personality ratings, profiles, prediction tests, and other technical tools as important implements in the counseling interview. Other psychologists, led by Carl Rogers, have pioneered in the evolution of the "inactive or passive" counselor's role, or, as it has been more recently termed, client-centered therapy. Sociologists and educators often emphasize patterns of behavior, partner roles, and environmental conditioning and modification, with active participation on the part of the counselor. Important research contributions also have been made by this group in connection with analyzing factors which contribute to marital harmony or disharmony.

COUNSELING PROCEDURES AND PHILOSOPHY

Methods of marriage counseling are thought by many students to differ from methods in psychiatric or psychoanalytic treatment in that interviewing is face to face (a time lapse of at least several days and usually a week occurs between interviews), and that explanations are limited to conscious and near-conscious material. The counselor refrains from interpretations of highly symbolic material; insistence on free association is absent, and comments on dream material are not made except where the meaning is obvious from the manifest rather than the latent content. In general, the counseling is designed to keep the treatment from entering the realm of the deep unconscious. The chief distinction between psychiatric treatment or analysis and marriage counseling is one of depth—depth of the transference, of the worker's comments, and of the material reviewed by the client.

Marriage counselors in general agree that a philosophy of marriage counseling is well represented by the definition of a happy family as "one which manages to solve its problems, not one which has no problems at all." The goal of the marriage counselor is to help persons who seek aid, over the spots that seem rough to them in their marriages and to assist them to come to grips with their own problems so that they can work them out themselves. This philosophy and goal must be realized through the attitudes of the counselor. For this reason, personal as well as professional qualifications are important. A counselor should show interest, warmth, and kindness towards people, understanding and acceptance of many types of behavior, and at the same time the ability to remain objective and emotionally unentangled in another person's situation.

EVALUATION OF MARRIAGE COUNSELING

Marriage counseling may be evaluated by the use of criteria applied either to the marriage or to the personal adjustment of the partners in the marriage. These two groups of criteria are undoubtedly interrelated, the personal adjustment of the partners being known to affect the quality of the marital relationship in many cases. But, they are also, at the least, logically independent, since always remaining as questions of fact are: (1) whether personal maladjustment is or is not affecting the quality of a marriage, and (2) whether the marriage is or is not a factor in a given case of personal maladjustment. For this reason, judgment cannot be based on either marriage or personal adjustment to the exclusion of the other.

The practical application of the various criteria for evaluating marriage and personal adjustment in marriage is affected by all the difficulties which have come to be recognized in recent years by students of the problem of evaluating the results of therapy. What is meant by an "improvement in personal adjustment"? What are its criteria? What is meant by an "improvement in the quality" of a marriage? What are its criteria? To what extent can such criteria be formulated in a way which will render them suitable to the application of quantitative methods, so that the powerful techniques of modern statistical analysis, particularly that branch of statistics which has to do with the evaluation of the reliability of results, may be applied to them?

These questions are in the process of being answered by research being conducted in a variety of fields which are linked together by their common use of the psychotherapies, particularly psychiatry, social work, and clinical psychology. In such studies the following lines of evidence play a role in supporting conclusions as to the results of a psychotherapeutic experience: (1) statements of the counselor or therapist as to his opinion of the results of counseling or therapy; (2) statements of the person under counseling or therapy as to his opinion of the results of the counseling or therapy; (3) evidences of changes in the behavior of the individual undergoing counseling, such as reduction in frequency and intensity of hostilities, increased communication with partner, increased ability to make decisions, appearance of ability or increased ability to use information constructively, and decrease in emotional upset and tension during counseling; (4) evidences of permanence in changes of the foregoing nature.

Divorce rates poor criterion. Students of the social sciences are probably more interested in marriage counseling as it affects the quality of the marriage relationship than as it contributes to personal adjustment. On this account some special treatment of this aspect of the problem of evaluation is warranted here. That the problem is not simple is indicated by a number of obvious considerations. There is first the fact that comparison of the divorce rates among people who have been counseled (which rates in fact are not known at the present time) with those of uncounseled people throws little light upon the effectiveness of counseling, since the assumption that *all* existing marriages should be saved if possible is unwarranted. The interests of society at large and of persons directly concerned in the marriage, particularly children, are at times best served by the separation of the marriage partners. If counseling contributes to separation under such conditions, it is not to be credited with a failure but rather with a success.

A second obvious consideration which must be borne in mind in evaluating counseling from the point of view of family stability is the fact that the function of the counseling differs depending on whether it is offered prior to marriage or subsequent to marriage in connection with an existing problem. As to postmarital counseling, no study of divorce rates can possibly touch the question of its consequences, since in many if not most instances, no question of divorce is raised or indeed appears to be present even in tacit form. In such instances the effects of the counseling must be evaluated, from the point of view of the marriage relationship, on the basis of increase in communication between the partners, increase in the number of common goals (goals shared by both partners), increase in acceptance of the other partner for what he or she really is, and increase in the effectiveness of the marriage as an institution in the lives of the partners and their children. As to premarital counseling also, it is evident that the real test of the usefulness of the experience lies not in the comparison of divorce rates but rather in the evaluation of the positive qualities of the marriage as an institution.

Positive measures of evaluation needed. All of this leads to the conclusion that extensive criterion research (research designed to reveal specific aspects of marriage which can be used as a basis for evaluating its quality) is needed to add to what is known about the properties of *successful* marriages. Up to the present, research has been directed in great measure toward a variety of aspects of the *unsuccessful* marriage, and understandably so; but the needs of the marriage counselor, like the needs of psychotherapists in general, are ill served by any viewpoint which supposes that successful living is merely the negative of unsuccessful living. Such criterion research is a necessary preliminary not only to the evaluation of the general effectiveness of marriage counseling, but also to the evaluation of all helping services.

Life is full of pain, uncertainty, and frustration, and in our immediate times threatened with unpredictable dangers. Even with such a fate, men and women within all types of political systems possess an inherent capacity for relationship. Relationships can engender beauty and warmth and can promote living which permits others, no matter how different, also to live. Clinical experience in marriage counseling provides the hypothesis that this type of relationship, at least in the American culture, is based on the ability of marriage partners to share and to communicate, to accept differences, to take responsibility, and to have the capacity for change and the strength for growth. Systematic research should provide at least partial answers to the many significant questions raised by this hypothesis.

Two · The Present Status and Future Orientation of Research on the Family

LEONARD S. COTTRELL, JR.
Sociologist, Cornell University

Students of human behavior are devoting more and more effort to understanding the family. This concluding selection * *offers an appraisal of family research and considers the direction family research should take.*

PRESENT STATE OF KNOWLEDGE

WE are very fortunate that in our present undertaking of review and appraisal we can draw heavily upon an excellent

* Reprinted from the *American Sociological Review*, 1948, 13: 123–229, by permission of the author and the publisher.

article recently published by Ernest W. Burgess in which he discusses our present state of knowledge and points to some important gaps which require new research. The availability of this statement by Burgess enables us to devote a minimum of space in this paper to reviewing the present state of our knowledge and makes it possible for us to devote most of our discussion to the problem of a productive orientation for future research.

The following is a brief summary of Burgess' main findings:

1. Our most adequate and accurate knowledge of the family is with respect to the trends which can be indicated statistically; size of the family, rates of marriage and divorce, urbanization, economic base, loss of certain historic institutional functions, etc. There are certain trends for which statistical indices are not readily available but which are indicated by other types of evidence clearly enough to warrant the confident assertion that the changes are taking place. These trends are in the changing concepts of the family, e.g., from authority to equalitarian control; from institutional relations to companionship relations; from familism to individualism; from integration based on roles defined in the mores to that which is based on much more individualized patterns of relationship. Some of the implications of these trends for family stability, adjustment in the family, and personality development are already evident; but an adequate understanding of their full impact waits upon more research.

In connection with his discussion of trends, Burgess points to the need for more data on the family which could be obtained by the inclusion of more detail on marriage licenses and divorce petitions and in census enumeration forms. He also points to the fruitful possibilities of accumulating attitude and opinion material on marriage and the family through public opinion research operations.

2. There is a large body of knowledge accumulated for the most part by psychiatrists and child psychologists, on the dynamics of inter-personal relations and personality developments in the family. Sociologists have not contributed nearly as much as might be expected to theory and methods in this research. A review of work in this area shows clearly that it would benefit greatly by the introduction of a better integration of the concepts of culture with personality theory and a more adequate theory of social interaction. It is in these directions that sociologists with special interest in social psychology could contribute an extremely valuable frame of reference and methodology.

In this connection it should be pointed out that we need to extend the work already done in the description of structures and dynamics of family relations in the different segments of our own society. We need comparative descriptive studies of family patterns in the different urban, rural, class and ethnic settings, together with analyses of the personality structures which emerge from these different family patterns. So far there is no work of this type which compares with the study of the Negro family in the United States by E. Franklin Frazier.

3. We have made a reasonably good beginning in research on family crises which seem to threaten the family stability, the factors affecting the ability of the family to resolve the crisis situation, and the processes by which adjustments are made. In these studies the concept of the role has proved to be of great importance.

4. During the past fifteen years the greatest advance in our knowledge of the family has been in the field of mate selection and marital adjustment. Substantial progress has been made in defining and measuring adjustment in courtship and marriage; in demonstrating significant statistical relationships between a variety of premarital background characteristics and adjustment in courtship and marriage relations; and in demonstrating that a fair degree of accuracy is possible in the classification of couples according to probabilities for good adjustment.

In addition to the statistical analyses and prediction, important advances have been made in the analysis of personality patterns which persons bring to courtship and marriage and in demonstrating how these patterns operate in determining the nature of the marriage relations. Studies of the dynamics of marital interaction and the factors affecting marital adjustment continue to be a focus of great interest and activity. However, workers in this area will be the first to admit that we are just beginning to scratch the surface.

5. The sociology and social psychology of sex have hardly been touched. The result of extensive studies conducted by Alfred C. Kinsey as well as clinical findings of more intensive analyses has contributed much to our knowledge in this area, but there is a definite need to place behavior described in studies such as that by Kinsey and in clinical findings in their proper social interactional contexts if we are adequately to understand sexual behavior.

6. No summary would be complete without reference to research in what might be called homemaking or family management. Studies of standards of living, economics of the home, child care, family nutrition and health, housing, and similar matters have resulted in an imposing body of facts which are of great practical importance. However much of this work is of a scattered and piecemeal variety and requires a much more adequate systematization than now obtains.

7. The sense of need for understanding the problem of the family has not only served to motivate research, but has also given rise to efforts to apply knowledge in education for family life and family counselling. There appears now to be a growing opinion that research is needed to evaluate the effects of family life education and of family counselling. There are obviously great difficulties in such evaluative studies, but they certainly offer opportunities for re-

search which would have great importance not only from a practical point of view but theoretically and methodologically as well.

Neither an outline such as the foregoing or an article such as the one by Burgess could possibly do justice to the task of summarizing the present state of our knowledge about the family. They serve merely to point out the main foci of recent research interest and to give some indication of the nature of the knowledge which is resulting from such research. In my opinion there is a real need now, even with our incomplete knowledge, for a detailed systematic work on the subject, "What We Know About the Family." I am reasonably confident that we ourselves would be as surprised at how much we know as at how much we do not know.

ORIENTATION FOR FURTHER RESEARCH

With this brief review as a background we can now turn to the question of what should be the directions and foci of future research on the family. The answers to this question will, of course, be as varied as the different ways investigators perceive the family and structure its problems. It is my opinion, however, that research could be more highly productive in the next decade, say, if we could achieve enough of a consensus in our definition of the situation to enable us to make a concerted attack on what could be agreed upon as the more important problems, and in so doing use a common frame of reference for our analyses and interpretations. If this were done by a substantial proportion of investigators, the results of the efforts would be more likely to "add up to something" than if each of us selects our problems and hypotheses more or less haphazardly. I am not by any means suggesting that we attempt to limit any of the freedoms, but simply that we are at a point where some intensive efforts at developing some common perspectives and pooling our efforts to achieve some common objectives will greatly facilitate more rapid progress toward significant and useful results.

The research proposals which I shall suggest here are offered in the hope that they will provoke other opinions. In discussing contrasting views, we may arrive at some common orientations which may lead to collaborative effort among ourselves and investigators in other relevant scientific disciplines.

To consider the orientations I wish to suggest, we need to view the family as a functional mechanism. Various investigators have pointed out that through changes in the character of our social structure the family has progressively lost many of the social functions for which it formerly was primarily responsible. From the evidence it seems that the greatest losses in function have been in areas of activity classified as economic, educational, recreational, protective, and religious.

Let us assume this to be the case. (Although it should be noted parenthetically that some very important economic, educational, etc., functions do remain even in highly urbanized families and, further, that research on these particular functional aspects has probably been too much neglected.) Notwithstanding the loss of many of its social functions there remain several very important ones for which the family is and will probably continue to be the most important social machinery. Most of us would agree that probably the most important of these remaining functions are: reproduction; the satisfaction of the intimate affectional response needs; and socialization and personality patterning. I strongly suspect that great advances will be made in family research if a considerable number of investigators would make these functions the foci of concerted attack and would coordinate their efforts in developing a series of basic hypotheses with respect to each and direct this research toward testing such hypotheses. In the interest of stimulating some discussion of the desirability of the kind of focus and coordination suggested, I offer the following observations on each of the functional areas suggested above.

1. *Reproduction.* I shall not elaborate on the possibilities in this functional area because I wish to use the available time on the other two areas which, I think, are in greater need of structuring for systematic research. This neglect does not indicate any tendency on my part to give a low priority to problems centering around the reproductive functions of the family. The intensive work on the social and psychological factors affecting fertility being conducted by Kiser and Whelpton will undoubtedly produce significant results and serve as a model and stimulus for a continued and broadened collaborative research in this area.

2. *The Satisfaction of the Affectional Response Needs.* Those who have studied human relations in the family have reported a wide variety of patterns in which the affectional responses have been cast. There are some people who seem to require an affectional relation in which they are always on the receiving end of pampering behavior. Others can love only in a situation where the object of their affections is a weak, dependent person. Still others establish what we vaguely refer to as a mature affectional relation. There are complicated patterns in which the object of affection is also the object of hostile destructive behavior. There are people who literally do not know how to be loved and some of them never learn. There are some who never learn how to give love to another person.

We not only find a wide variety of affectional patterns in a given population but we also know that in the course of development of the individual he passes through a series of different patterns of affectional interaction. Now the Freudian psychoanalysts have, of course, developed an imposing theory and body of clinical observation on the patterning of the libidinal drives, and there can be no question of the tremendous amount of insight and understanding they have developed. There is certainly no need to deny the value of their theoretical formulations or their empirical findings. But it seems to me we are now at a point where we need a fresh look at the problem in the interest of a more comprehensive formulation of theory in terms of interpersonal dynamics.

There is definite need to take theory and findings in psychoanalysis, psychosomatics, interpersonal dynamics, and cultural anthropology and build a more comprehensive theory of affectional patterning. This is no easy task and it certainly calls for intensive collaboration among a number of investigators who are trained in the different fields and who also (and this is very important) are the kinds of personalities who can share and communicate and integrate new points of view into their own thinking and orientation.

With a more comprehensive theoretical formulation we should then seek to:

(a) Describe the variety of patterns of affectional relations;
(b) Trace the processes through which they develop and change;
(c) Determine which of these patterns make for the most stable and affectionally satisfying marriage and parent-child relations; and
(d) Describe the kind of treatment and training of children and adolescents in the family, as well as in the schools and character building agencies which promote and hinder the development of these preferred patterns.

3. *Socialization and Personality Patterning.* Students of the family are constantly pointing out that the family is the matrix of social experience in which the basic socialization of the organism takes place and in which the most persistent and pervasive personality patterns are formed. If this be the case then it would appear highly desirable that we focus a substantial amount of intensive collaborative effort in theoretical formulation and in planning and conducting research to test relevant hypotheses regarding the factors and processes in socialization.

Socialization is a term which is rather loosely used in the literature. In some contexts it has a normative valuational connotation; in others it is a term of general reference to learning of the habits and attitudes characteristic of a social group. It seems to me that whatever else the term may imply it refers to a process whereby social interactive systems become incorporated into the response system of the individual. This means that a basic process involved in social relations is what we can call the empathic responses. That is to say those reactions whereby the individual takes the role of the others. It is my opinion that in all social integration, all social interaction, communication and understanding, and even in thought itself, the empathic responses are of central importance.

It is therefore surprising that so little attention has been given to research on this fundamental factor in social relations. And it is for this reason that I would urge that a great deal of research in the family be oriented to an exhaustive study of empathic reactions and abilities. We need to know how to measure empathic ability. We need to know the range and distribution of the ability under various life conditions. We need to analyze the kinds of interactive experiences in infancy, childhood and adolescence which promote and hinder the development of this ability. Can the ability be modified by training? Are persons characterized by high empathic ability in a given situation better adjusted, more insightful, and better able to handle conflicts than those who rate low in this ability? These and many other questions point to serious gaps in our knowledge of a critical factor in socialization. Family research workers should be in a particularly good position to contribute greatly to the development of theory and methods for studying empathic responses and their roots in the context of family interaction.

Empathic ability and its development, manifestations and implications are not the only aspect of personality development in the family which should concern students in this field. (I have, of course, already referred to the patterning of affectional responses as another important focus of research effort.) There are many other important personality characteristics which are developed primarily in the family context about which investigators have already accumulated a great deal of knowledge. However, much of this work has been done with a focus and orientation appropriate to the clinician's preoccupation with the individual and his special characteristics and problems of personal adjustment. It is probably attributable to our basic cultural orientation to the values of individualism that we have not raised serious research questions about the implications of individual personality patterning in the family for our social system. What the family does to the individual person is important not only because it largely determines his individual patterns of social relations and adjustment but also because it determines the extent to which his attitudes and behavior are consistent with and supportive of the social system of which he is a part. In view of this latter point I should like to propose another orientation for family research. In brief this research would be directed to the question of what kind of personality characteristics and skills are required for adequate functioning in democratic relations and what kind of family interaction develops those traits and skills. In outlining this orientation I shall merely quote from a memorandum I recently prepared on this subject.

1. Every society is confronted by the task of molding its constituent personalities in such a way that their personality organizations are supportive of that society and can function

in the social system with a reasonable amount of consistency and adjustment. Some societies accomplish this more or less informally and unsystematically; others are more deliberate, systematic, and self-conscious in accomplishing this end.

2. It is assumed by many students of the family, with considerable justification, that the family is a major institutional device for the transmission of the basic value systems and personality characteristics required by a given society for its continuation. This is not to say, of course, that other institutional components of a society, such as school, church, et cetera, do not also contribute heavily to the patterning process, but for the moment our attention is focused on the family.

3. It is assumed here for purposes of this discussion that the weight of opinion in the United States is in favor of maintaining and extending a system of values and correlative patterns of human relations which may be described as democratic. This assumption will, of course, have to be carefully examined at the appropriate time.

4. Paragraphs 1, 2, and 3 lead to the following questions:

a. In certain critical areas of human relations in our society how should people behave, what attitudes should they have, and what skills in dealing with situations should they possess, if they are to react in a manner consistent with democratic values and supportive of a democratic system?

b. What basic personality characteristics must they have if they are to react in such a manner with the minimum of anxiety and frustration, or in other words if they are to be well adapted to function in democratic human relations?

c. What kinds of treatment and training of children and adolescents in the family are conducive to the production of the basic personality characteristics and social skills called for in a and b?

d. Similarly what kinds of treatment and training encourage the development of those characteristics and skills antithetical to democratic human relations?

5. In the opinion of the writer, the adoption of an explicit orientation suggested in the foregoing assumptions and questions would give much more pointed relevance to family research than it now has, both from a practical and a theoretical standpoint. Such an orientation should not only be productive of new and highly relevant hypotheses regarding personality formation in the family and the relation between the structure in the family and that of the larger society, but would also serve as a means of organizing and focusing existing hypotheses that are relevant to this field. Studies of change in family patterns should take on new significance when cast in this context. Comparative studies of the families in different cultures would have a much more explicit theoretical as well as practical relevance and significance than such studies now have. Child development studies obviously could be given more point and direction in some such frame of reference as is suggested above. An important by-product of such an effort would be further

clarification in behavioral terms of our conception of what are democratic human relations and a focusing of attention on the possible contribution of social science to achieving these relations.

6. Notes and observations:

a. Research with the proposed orientation could be done with a view to relating personality products of the family to democratic and non-democratic behavior in the wider range of community life generally, or it could be done with the more limited target of relating personality resultants of family life to democratic and non-democratic behavior in marriage and parent-child relations.

b. The proposed orientation calls for much more explicit definitions of what constitutes democratic human relations than we now have. Question *a* under Paragraph *4* is an extremely difficult one to answer, but if social scientists are to bring their research to bear explicitly on the problem of a democratic society, this question has to be answered in unambiguous terms.

c. It is obvious that this orientation could be used for research on other social institutions as well, particularly those institutions which assume responsibility for transmitting the culture and developing the character and skills needed by the society, *e.g.*, the school, the church, character building agencies, recreational agencies, and the like.

CONCLUSION

I have emphasized what appear to me to be important orientations for research on the family. These orientations derive from regarding the family as the major social device for the performance of the function of reproduction; satisfying needs for intimate affectional response; and the function of basic socialization and personality patterning. In offering these proposals I wish to make it quite clear that I am not urging that they supplant present research emphases on family trends, marital adjustment, descriptive study of family group patterns in various segments of our society, comparative studies of the family in various cultures, and other significant lines of attack. Moreover, the suggestions are all within areas of interest which are familiar to students of the family. The merit of the proposals lies chiefly in calling attention to certain critical problems around which a great deal of individual and collaborative research could profitably be organized.

INDEX